The Body and the Screen

The Body and the Screen

Theories of Internet Spectatorship

Michele White

The MIT Press
Cambridge, Massachusetts
London, England

MIT Press books may be purchased at special quantity discounts for business or sales promotional use. For information, please email special_sales@mitpress.mit.edu or write to Special Sales Department, The MIT Press, 55 Hayward Street, Cambridge, MA 02142.

This book was set in Stone Sans and Stone Serif by The MIT Press.

Printed and bound in the United States of America.

Library of Congress Cataloging-in-Publication Data

White, Michele.
The body and the screen : theories of Internet spectatorship / Michele White.
  p. cm.
Includes bibliographical references and index.
ISBN 0-262-23249-9 (alk. paper)
1. Internet—Philosophy. 2. Cyberfeminism. 3. Art and technology. 4. Human-computer interaction. I. Title.

TK5105.875.I57W5275   2006
004.67'8—dc22

2006042005

10 9 8 7 6 5 4 3 2 1

Contents

Illustrations

The Body, the Screen, and Representations: An Introduction to Theories of Internet Spectatorship

Individuals do more than use the Internet and computer; they are instructed to personalize things and follow rules. They are also encouraged to interact, find community, and identify with representations that "live" within Internet "space." For instance, an instant messenger client offers the "ICQ Universe," Cheap Tickets directs the viewer to "just click, you're there," and a webcam site is "just my little space on the web which houses me."[1] Through these devices, Internet sites and computer interfaces address the individual, depict the kinds of bodies that are expected to engage, and render and regulate the spectator. Spectatorship affects how settings and interfaces are understood and helps to shape larger conceptions of self and society. The significance of such positions should encourage academics to further incorporate spectatorship into Internet and new media studies. Academics, journalists, programmers, and users might also consider these forms of spectatorship because hardware, software, and Internet settings increasingly facilitate communication and analysis. Nevertheless, few extended critical considerations exist in this area. This book introduces Internet and computer spectatorship and provides theoretical models that readers can employ when considering other settings. Internet and computer spectatorship is conceptualized through apparatus and feminist psychoanalytic film theories, art history, gender studies, queer theory, race and postcolonial studies, and other theories of cultural production. I provide general comments and detailed case studies of how spectatorship is constructed in synchronous MOO settings, women's webcams, net art web sites, the Virtual Places graphical "chat" setting, digital imaging, and sites that describe programmers' bodies.

The bodies of Internet and computer spectators are rendered through a variety of visual and textual strategies. An active and empowered Internet "user," who is in control of the interface, situated within the screen, and moves actively through Internet "space," is suggested by AOL's striding yellow figure and the interface hand, which appears when manipulating software and hypertext links. "Welcome" messages and links that are labeled "enter" indicate that there is a way for the spectator to get into the setting. For instance, the American Association for the Advancement of Science's report on the "Ethical and Legal Aspects of Human Subjects in Cyberspace" uses an image of Leonardo da Vinci's *Vitruvian Man*, which employs geometry to indicate that all aspects of the body are rational and knowable, and directly maps him onto the computer screen (figure I.1).[2] The image supports the report's claim that there are subjects "in" or within Internet "space," suggests that the gender of this subject is male, depicts his arms and legs encompassing the whole screen, and indicates that he controls the technology. Gateway's depiction of a young male student, who is standing in front of a chalkboard, drawing a laptop, and preparing to materialize his every technological desire, evokes Harold's creation of a world in *Harold and the Purple Crayon* and also suggests a male control of the technology.[3]

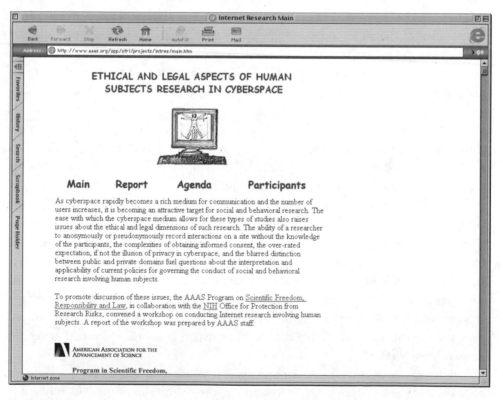

Figure I.1
American Association for the Advancement of Science, "Ethical and Legal Aspects of Human Subjects in Cyberspace," 1999, 15 Sept. 2004, <http://www.aaas.org/spp/dspp/sfrl/projects/intres/main.htm>.

Web sites that market computer technologies address particular kinds of Internet and computer spectators by suggesting what they look like. For instance, the IBM site features an overhead image of a white man working with his laptop and a depiction of a white man standing confidently in the doorway, while some undifferentiated figures sit in the background.[4] The images and texts on the IBM site suggest that it is offering "Resources" for "Business," "Government," "Education," "Investors," and "Journalists" and "Jobs at IBM" to white men. In a similar manner, Logitech presents a businessman who is standing, suited, slipping a mouse into his briefcase, and on the move (figure I.2).[5] When images of women appear in these advertisements, they are often lounging and reclining, ignoring the technology, engaged socially rather than in business transactions, and available for the visual contemplation of the spectator. Standing or squarely sitting male figures suggest authority, coherence, control, and engagement while reclining females, who are often positioned on a diagonal, provide

Figure I.2
Logitech, "Logitech—Leading Web Camera, Wireless Keyboard," 15 Aug. 2004, <http://www
.logitech.com/index.cfm?countryid=19&languageid=1>.

a way for the viewer to look upon the women, visually enter the picture plane, and suggest her immobility, laziness, and reduced control. For instance, below Logitech's image of the male businessman is an advertisement for webcams and video dating that features a woman sitting near the computer, her head tipped to the side and her mouth open in laughter, performing for the camera and a prospective date, and not working with mouse, keyboard, and screen. The Dell computer web site also represents a white woman lounging in the grass and looking-up expectantly, with her laptop almost cut out of the picture.[6] Her similarly tilted head and welcoming smile suggest that she is greeting the spectator and welcoming "his" view of her.

Representations of these available women situate white heterosexual men in a familiar spectatorial position. Other individuals may find it more difficult to engage. Risks exist in identifying what race and ethnicity look like, but it is important to note that there are few images of people of color working with computers or standing in an authoritative way on web sites marketing computer technologies.[7] Women and people of color are more likely to be depicted lounging together in social and leisure settings and using such technologies as stereo systems, headphones, and boom boxes. These images threaten to perpetuate stereotypes about unruly urban behavior because the groups depicted with stereo equipment are often comprised of people from the African diaspora, Asians, Latinos/as and other people of color. Microsoft does depict a white woman, a white man, and a black man arranged on a diagonal, which directs the spectator's attention to the question: "Are you ready for the new school year?" (figure I.3).[8] The white woman in the foreground is half cropped out by three edges of the image, so close that her face becomes blurry, and she is looking down rather that meeting the spectator's view. The black male is pushed to the background, slumped, mostly blocked by the middle figure's shoulder, and also looking down. Only the white male figure addresses the spectator and is sitting erect and "ready."

Depictions of eager white male heterosexual computer users, which appear in *Wired*, other media sources, and Internet forums, are not surprising since the web sites for computer graphics designers, gamers, and programmers implicitly address these individuals and often include renderings of sexualized female bodies for their pleasure. Computer-generated depictions of nearly naked women with large breasts, narrow waists, and puckered lips regularly appear on web sites for computer graphics software and related hardware. For instance, ATI Technologies presents a computer rendering of "Ruby" looking down provocatively and inviting the spectator to look at her.[9] Ruby's large breasts, narrow waist, and expanses of pale skin are still partially mapped with the kind of grid used in rendering her. This suggests that she is forever adjustable to the desires of male viewers. The otherwise naked body of another light-skinned,

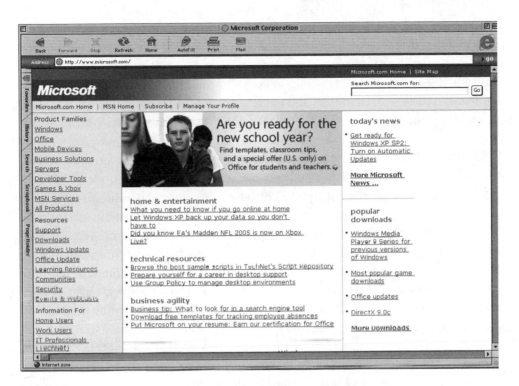

Figure I.3
Microsoft, "Microsoft Corporation," 14 Aug. 2004, <http://www.microsoft.com/>.

computer-generated woman is only partially concealed by NewTek's spiraling LightWave 3D logo, which hovers in front of her breasts and directs the spectator's attention to her cleavage.[10] Web sites, software boxes, and other forms of advertising present fairies, swimming mermaids, and other scantily clad fantastical female figures as appropriate output.[11] These renderings indicate the kind of images and spectatorial positions that should be produced by Internet and computer technologies.[12]

Employing the term "spectator," when considering these Internet and computer settings, indicates how individuals are looking at representations, are acknowledged or displaced by visual and textual addresses, and gain an understanding of the setting and their experiences through narratives and renderings. This approach is significantly different from engaging with Internet and computer technologies as unbiased tools, which are directed by individuals and always under their control. My use of the term is intended to suggest how Internet spectators continue to be rendered and regulated by technologies and representations and to reference apparatus and feminist psycho-analytic film theory, feminist art history, and visual culture studies. As it is currently employed in film theory, spectator indicates "an artificial construct" that is produced and animated by the apparatus and cultural beliefs.[13] Spectatorial positions do not exactly describe the experience of any individual, but all viewers are addressed and shaped by media forms. Spectatorship indicates the processes of watching and listening, identification with characters and images, the various values with which viewing is invested, and how these ideas continue even after the spectator has stopped viewing.[14]

My use of the phrase "Internet and computer spectator" and the term "spectatorship" also indicates a commitment to employing theory in order to understand texts and an interest in developing hybrid critical models that can assist in analyzing specific Internet and computer settings. Theories by such film scholars as Mary Ann Doane, Christian Metz, and Laura Mulvey are an important part of this book.[15] Their work has emerged from or even articulated apparatus and feminist psychoanalytic film theory, a set of methodologies that sometimes overlap and at other times are resistant to the other discourse, and their theories continue to inform research about spectatorship. These approaches were first articulated in the 1970s, influenced by the work of Sigmund Freud and Jacques Lacan, and their limitations have generated lively debates and other forms of media history, criticism, and theory.[16] Theories of film spectatorship are paralleled, informed, and influenced by philosophers' inquiries about the rendering of the subject and literary critics' concern with the production of the reader.[17] This introduction addresses the significance of such literature and suggests its productive redeployment for Internet studies. However, my intent is to provide the reader with critical revisions of these and other methodologies, which are suited to specific Internet settings, rather than an account of apparatus and feminist psychoanalytic film theory and the debates that continue in the field. Critical works by Judith Mayne; Robert Stam, Robert Burgoyne, and Sandy Flitterman-Lewis; Kaja Silverman; and a variety of other scholars successfully outline and critique psychoanalytic models of film theory.[18]

Film theorists indicated, in the 1970s, that Hollywood cinema represented the desires and beliefs of modern Western industrial countries.[19] While psychoanalysis can be problematic and reproduce these underlying myths, it also provides ways to understand and reveal the invisible ideology of cinema, society, and aspects of sexual difference, including the cultural construction of femininity and masculinity.[20] These myths that society lives by and assumes to be part of a natural and unproblematic reality also tend to provide the spectator with mastery and stability.[21] Nevertheless, the spectator is subjected to the power of another vision and assumes positions with significant cultural ramifications when viewing the cinema and Internet sites, reading, and listening. Most film theorists differentiate between the subject, or the position that is assigned to the film viewer by the varied aspects of the cinema, and the viewer, or the person who watches a film, but the differences in these positions have never been fully resolved. Doane distinguishes between the subject and the individual, and she relates the cinematic subject to the psychoanalytic investigation of the spectator, but this book is more aligned with Mayne's indication that the term "spectator" indicates some level of distrust in fully separating the subject from people.[22] In Internet and computer viewing, the forms of spectatorship articulated by the technologies and representations are constantly acted out by using the system.

Apparatus theorists like Jean-Louis Baudry and Christian Metz describe a centered spectator who is "within" and in front of the screen and the power that is derived from such a position.[23] While these film theorists tend to suggest that viewing provides cohesion and mastery, the psychoanalytic models they employ indicate that wholeness is an illusion. Despite contradictions in their work, the theories of Baudry and Metz help explain and critique how Internet images render coherent and empowered spectators. Mulvey's apparatus-based approach, Doane's theory of masquerade, and more recent feminist scholarship provide important methods for considering the production of male Internet spectators and the forms of identity and embodiment that are not acknowledged.[24] Mulvey attributes the production of sexual difference, or the articulation of inscribed male and female positions, to the structures of pleasure and identification that occur in classical cinema. She indicates that the subject of the gaze is male, and his empowered position is supported by the camera's viewpoint, while its object is female, and she exists in order to be viewed.[25] A version of such positions is articulated by web sites marketing computer technologies, computer-generated images of women that are rendered in order to be erotically enjoyed, and depictions of bodies in textual and graphical communication settings. Doane's theory of a female gaze and women's indication that they also operate webcams and other Internet technologies can help rethink these culturally produced positions.[26]

Theories of spectatorship and the gaze are also employed in considering other cultural forms.[27] Formalist examinations by Michael Fried and Clement Greenberg, which are concerned with the internal terms and questions of art, conceive of the spectator as a disembodied eye that sees and surveys everything.[28] John Berger's account, which is distinctly different from their formalist investigations, indicates that paintings and other static visual images produce particular ways of seeing. He critiques the ways the spectator is gendered as male and suggests that spectatorship is based on a binary opposition between men who "act" and women who "appear."[29] Griselda Pollock and other feminist art historians provide more detailed analysis of gendered forms of looking, apply psychoanalytic film theory to static visual images, and consider the relationship between constructed spectators and historical viewers.[30] Pollock resists formalist analysis, which is based on "eyesight alone," because it does not address the embodied positions and identities of spectators.[31] Her indication that traditional renderings of space establish gendered spheres and forms of spectatorship suggests that there are also problems with depictions of Internet space.

Apparatus theory can be complicit with its object of analysis and produce limited conceptions of women.[32] Feminist psychoanalytic film theory challenges this absence of viable positions for women and indicates that the female spectator articulated completely by her sex does not exist, as Doane argues, except as "an effect of discourse" and the "focal point of an address."[33] Feminist theorists are also concerned that psychoanalytic models of spectatorship do not consider physical people, simplify and misunderstand psychoanalysis, ignore the historical specificity of viewers and film production, rely solely on the camera obscura as the model of vision, do not consider how some genres address women, leave no possible positions for women's spectatorial resistance, and fail to consider issues of class, ethnicity, race, sexuality and other forms of difference.[34] Apparatus and feminist psychoanalytic film theory have limitations, which need to be questioned, but they also offer the most comprehensive critical approaches to film as well as significant methods, especially when adjusted to acknowledge problems, to address Internet and computer spectatorship.[35] Academics, critics, and spectators should always question theoretical choices but exceptions to critical models do not indicate that they are always unproductive. E. Ann Kaplan argues that psychoanalytic theory explains the myths that society lives by at a particular time and can be employed critically without accepting that the narratives of sexual difference are real and necessary.[36] In this book, apparatus and feminist psychoanalytic film theory are combined with other critical models to interrogate the forms of spectatorship that are promised by Internet settings and to indicate when these positions are not delivered.

The term "spectator" is rarely employed in Internet settings and in academic and popular literature about these sites, perhaps because it emphasizes the processes of reading and viewing. I intend for the term "spectator" to evoke the concept of the Internet user but disagree with Anne Friedberg's notion that computer "'users' are not spectators, not viewers."[37] Looking is a significant aspect of Internet and computer use. Yet Internet viewing is sometimes referred to as lurking, which indicates that when spectators are looking, reading, and thinking, they benefit from the shared ideas without contributing.[38] References to Internet and computer spectatorship should highlight how individuals spend time reading and viewing as well as writing and interacting. A discussion of spectatorship and the structuring of the individual can foreground the passive aspects of engagement and the mediation of the screen. These elements are downplayed because they do not support the concept of an active and animate Internet. However, it is also the case that no spectator is a completely unmoving and passive receiver of ideology. In her work on spectatorship, Mayne encourages theories that complicate such dualistic thinking as "critical" and "complacent" spectatorship.[39] I hope to offer similarly complicated theories of Internet and computer spectatorship, which focus on the ways spectators are constructed by the technologies and cultural narratives, and to indicate that resistance is difficult but possible. While it is tempting to write an account that is completely about the possibility of "oppositional gazes" and alternative spectatorial positions, this does not provide the critical strategies needed to consider the ways Internet spectators are constructed.

Using terms like "spectator" and "spectatorship" can produce an uneasy experience or even a sense that the wrong term is being employed because of how we have been trained to understand Internet and computer settings. However, this rupture can also provide opportunities to examine Internet representations. My use of this and other critical vocabularies is not meant to be an overarching dismissal of the ways meaning and value are produced for setting participants. Instead, my descriptions should indicate my own attractions to Internet and computer technologies and my resistance to some of what results. I have also employed the term "user" in other research, in my everyday speech, and to a more limited extent in this book. However, the term presents problems when performing close textual analysis and critique because it is so embedded in the language that renders particular notions of the Internet and computer. The concept of the user and Internet use, which suggests that something is put into service and employed, is also problematic because it makes these settings and technologies appear to be completely under the spectator's control.[40]

Academics like Espen Aarseth employ "user" because it indicates all the "textual practices that can be observed or imagined," is "ambivalent," and suggests "active participation and dependency."[41] Aarseth's description of the user as an employer and dependant is promising. However, the construction and regulation of the Internet and computer spectator remain largely unnoted. George P. Landow indicates that technology "empowers those who possess it, those who make use of it, and those who have access to it."[42] Friedberg suggests that the "'user' interacts directly with the framed image on a small flat screen . . . to manipulate what is contained within" it.[43] Narratives about interactivity produce spectators and replace visual contemplation with a discourse about agency and participation. Such Internet forms as instant messaging (IM), "chat" settings, and "bulletin boards" are constantly contextualized with descriptions of talking, participating, entering a spatial environment, and being connected with "real" people. These visual and textual representations of Internet activity and empowerment displace the more static processes of Internet looking and reading, the significant ways interactions are scripted, limitations on what can be manipulated, and how some individuals are disempowered.

Considerations of spectatorship indicate that media forms are "culturally significant events" and have an effect on viewers even after they disengage from a particular representation.[44] Diane Carr notes the intense correlation between spectator and manipulated computer representation and observes that viewers often respond to gaming by "flinching when their avatar bangs their head" and moving when the avatar changes position.[45] Her indication that avatars are "our emissaries and, at least to a degree, our doubles," which is repeated in dictionary definitions and synchronous communication setting descriptions, suggests how identification continues after leaving the screen. The ways spectators are structured to engage and society's ideas about the medium determine the questions that can be asked and whether the representational aspects of stereotypes can be perceived and critiqued. All of this suggests that there are significant ramifications of how Internet and computer representations downplay the computer screen, processor, and constructed viewing positions. Internet and computer spectatorship has an even more consequential effect on identification than do film and other media because the spectator spends significant amounts of time engaging with computers; computers and networks also appear in film, television, and print advertising; dream or trance-like experiences are often part of the engagement; the connection with characters and other representations can be intense; and there is an idea that the spectator is part of the setting, people are alive, and bodies are accessible through the Internet.

Highlighting the processes that render spectatorship indicates how Internet and computer settings function and provides ways to oppose dominant narratives about viewing that would otherwise shape individual experiences. These strategies of resistance include emphasizing the limits and failures of the technology, examining how Internet and computer positions do not meet the promised cultural ideals, and depicting producers who are a different age, gender, race, and sexuality than those proscribed by cultural norms. Focusing on spectatorship also provides a broader understanding of the function of Internet and computer representations, the constructed aspects of Internet settings, and the ways that texts and images become spatial environments, material objects, and embodied human subjects. I quote a variety of sources, which are commonly available to Internet spectators, to support the arguments in this book and provide references for the information. I try to be sensitive to the ways spectators produce and use Internet and computer settings and critical of the problems and stereotypes that are instituted. Guidelines exist for ethical Internet research, which all Internet researchers should note.[46] However, the tendency in these documents to conclude that all Internet research is human subject research does not address the deeply produced aspects of Internet settings and the humanities methods that apply when writing about such representations.[47]

The guidelines of the Association of Internet Researchers (AoIR), which I contributed to in a small way, encourage academics to consider whether "participants" are "best understood as 'subjects' (in the senses common in human subjects research in medicine and the social sciences)—or as authors whose texts/artifacts are intended as public."[48] The AoIR document poses important questions about different types of research, disciplinary approaches, existent guidelines, and the ethical research models already established in particular countries. However, it does not address how Internet settings convey cultural forms rather than physical authors. This book considers the texts of cultural producers and highlights how Internet depictions of artists, authors, designers, programmers, and spectators are rendered as real. A different set of critical models is employed in each chapter because there is no theory that fully explains the ways Internet and computer interfaces produce spectatorial positions. These critical approaches include apparatus and feminist psychoanalytic film theory, gender and queer theory, conceptions of technological failure, ideas about reader response and authorship, fan and hypertext studies, postcolonial theory, issues of photographic reproduction, and discourses about morphing and the fold. In some cases, these models are used in different configurations in other chapters to suggest how academics, journalists, programmers, and viewers can continually restructure theories to address particular Internet and computer settings.

Chapter 1 describes how spectators are produced by Internet settings, provides an introduction to the academic and popular discourse about Internet engagement, and presents methods that can explain how sites function. Internet and computer settings are often represented as a space that the spectator can enter, a place where real objects and bodies exist, and as living things. These depictions of materiality, renderings of the empowered user, addresses that appear to acknowledge the individual, sign-up forms that render binary gender, and conventions of the monitor and computer design are important to note because they structure the spectator's experience. For instance, a brief analysis of web-based sign-up forms, where the spectator must indicate a binary gender and "male" is usually listed above or before "female" on the form, indicates how traditional genders and desires are reproduced. Males, who are often presumed to be the employer of many of these interfaces, are promised a right to technology through such devices. However, when the flaws in the technology and representations are highlighted, they present some problems with understanding Internet spectatorship as inherently empowered and the spectator's position as coherent. A close analysis suggests that despite the cohesive position that the spectator is promised, fragmentation and confusion are a constant aspect of Internet spectatorship.

Chapter 2 indicates how spectatorship in Lambda and other MOOs (multi-user object-oriented settings) is produced through writing and system-generated texts. The textual processes of looking and gazing, which seem to allow the spectator to view real bodies, can be understood through feminist theories of the gaze by Mary Ann Doane, Judith Mayne, Laura Mulvey, and Renata Salecl and Slavoj Žižek.[49] The "gaze" and the "look" are privileged terms in these settings because of the programming decision to associate information inquiries with the typed command to "look <character or object name>." The constructed nature of the MOO character, which is literally produced by text, is partially concealed by the insistence that the metaphorical sight of the look is the equivalent of truth. The virtual look of certain characters, which seem able to penetrate into any "space" in order to examine other characters and determine their gender, renders an empowered spectatorial gaze. The mastering gaze of spectators and characters and the voyeuristic terminology of MOO commands, which include @watch, @peruse, @kgb, @fbi, @scope, glance, @peep, and @gawk, perpetuate a series of limiting identity constructs. Understanding how the look functions and developing critical methods to consider Internet identity processes can also inform studies of other Internet and computer settings.

Ideas about looking also play a significant part in women's webcams. I reflect on the functions of women's webcams in chapter 3 and argue that the webcam spectator cannot fully achieve the empowered looks and erotic engagement with bodies that are promised. Instead, the presence of the camera, delivery failures, and webcam operators who refuse to meet the spectator's demands are common aspects of this form. Feminist considerations of spectatorship and the gaze, which are established as important methodologies for Internet study in chapter 2, and critical considerations of closeness and voyeurism, by Noël Burch, Mary Ann Doane, and Christian Metz, offer techniques for considering the position of the webcam spectator and operator.[50] Being intimately close to the screen, which is a basic aspect of computer spectatorship and is highlighted by the functions of the webcam form, is related to the confined cinema viewing positions that are associated with women and culturally coded as undesirable. The webcam spectator may have less control than expected, but women operators exert authority and achieve agency through their visibility. While spectatorship is being culturally and technologically reconceptualized, the webcam form and its failures, which are produced by the technologies and operators, offer some unique opportunities to intervene in the ways certain versions of gender and sexual difference are produced through spectatorship.

The spectator also engages with intentional failures in many net artworks. Chapter 4 describes how net artists like Jodi, Peter Luining, and Michaël Samyn reflexively quote the technological failures of Internet technologies. Jodi's *%20Wrong*, Luining's *D-TOY 2.502.338*, and Samyn's *The Fire from the Sea* have been described as formalist, but they do more than consider the medium because they employ misquotation, misdirection, and interface breakdown in order to question the Internet's ordinary effects and critically comment on its vernacular.[51] Theories of failure and repetition, by such authors as Judith Butler, Jonathan Crary, and Stuart Moulthrop, provide ways to critically consider the political effects of these artworks.[52] Net art may encourage the spectator to address the medium or allow the initiated spectator to engage while others are prevented from understanding. An aesthetic of failure can invite the spectator to critically look at technology, reproduce power discrepancies, or become no more than a style.

The Virtual Places (VP) graphical "chat" setting also provides opportunities to consider how spectators engage with Internet art forms. Chapter 5 suggests how the setting-specific reading and meaning-making practices of VP help the spectator understand avatar images as both bodies and original artworks. VP painters make avatars from previously produced material—mostly from music, movies, and erotic magazines and web sites—and offer them to other participants in web-based paint shops. VP presents some uncommon concepts of authorship, cultural works, and the ways that previously produced materials should be identified and treated. Painters tend to conceptualize the avatar images that they "cut" from popular sources, using software commands as originals while preventing the reuse of avatar images on other VP sites. Fan, hypertext, and other theories of authorship by Roland Barthes, Jay David Bolter, Rosemary J. Coombe, Henry Jenkins, and George P. Landow offer vital ways to understand how such texts are read.[53] However, academic claims for the liberating potential of subcultural practices are not mindful of the tendencies in VP and other Internet settings to reinstitute hierarchical structures and traditional conceptions of the body. Combining these theories with feminist, postcolonial, and queer theories of authorship, including works by Nancy Hartsock, Trinh T. Minh-ha, Edward Said, and Eve Kosofsky Sedgwick, provides models that are more attentive to gender, race, and sexuality issues and can indicate how power is reinscribed.[54]

Chapter 6 indicates how Carol Selter, Susan Silton, and Ken Gonzales-Day foreground their digital image production processes and the resultant viewing positions.[55] The popular tendency to refer to digital images as "photographic representations," "digital photography," or "post-photography" connects computer imaging to photography, encourages the spectator to understand these representations as records of real things, and limits the critical interventions that can be performed because the mediated and produced aspects of the image are elided. The work of Roland Barthes and other photography and apparatus theorists provides ways to address digital engagements and cultural conceptions of photography.[56] Theories of folding and morphing by Gilles Deleuze and Vivian Sobchack offer further methods for articulating the occurrence of fragmented and disempowered Internet and computer viewing.[57]

When Internet and computer spectators indicate that their bodies are fat, folded in chairs, painful, and unruly, they also contradict the narratives about empowered users. The afterword considers the many self-identified male programmers who write in Internet forums about their soft flesh, "extra" weight, and long periods of time slumped in computer chairs. These programmers represent male flesh in ways that are quite uncommon in physical settings, and their descriptions deserve more attention since women have long been identified with the body in Western society. The connection between men and mind is continued in early cyberpunk fiction and in Ray Kurzweil's and Hans Moravec's artificial intelligence narratives, which indicate how men will leave the "meat" behind. Depictions of seated and folded viewers and the writings of Susan Bordo, Luce Irigaray, and Klaus Theweleit offer a different way to theorize the body of the Internet and computer spectator, resist some of the narratives about users, and consider how other forms of spectatorship may be less vertical than expected.[58]

These chapters indicate that there are reasons to simultaneously address Internet and computer settings, academic and popular descriptions, and the construction of the spectator. For instance, the most common image of the spectator is the rendering of white and white-gloved hands that are part of the interface.[59] The computer's arrow-shaped cursor, or pointer, turns into a pointing and clicking hand when "mousing" over web links and a grasping hand when programs or images can be changed. These hands move when the user manipulates the mouse, emphasize the relationship between physical hand and representation, and indicate "where" the spectator is in the setting. The different images of the hand render an empowered user who can point, move, grasp, and touch. The depictions of hands stand in for the whole body, suggest that the individual can enter the setting, and provide complicated messages about race. Spectators become attached to these hands because they chronicle actions and options within the setting. However, these hands do not equally represent all individuals. They tend to be white, light pink, or white and gloved, and they provide spectators with constant messages about what individuals who use Internet and computer settings look like.

The indication that Internet spectators are white continues with the images that appear on web sites. For instance, the representations that accompany the Ask Jeeves search engine site depict the computer interface as a Caucasian butler.[60] His hands are positioned in order to evoke the pointing, clicking, and mousing hand of the interface.[61] Whether white or a pale pink, the hands of the Ask Jeeves butler, hand-pointer of the interface, references to hands in IM emoticons, and the evaluative thumbs-up hands of web sites race the interface. The white hand-pointer acts as a kind of avatar, supports other renderings of the body, and becomes "attached" to depictions of Caucasians in advertisements, graphical communication settings, and web greeting cards. It may seem that the white color of the hand is a design convention and is needed to make the interface hand visible against varied screen backgrounds, but the arrow and cursor are often black, outlined in white, and quite visible. Instead, the white hand-pointer suggests a racial "inside" and "outside" in Internet and computer settings.[62] Visual analysis, critical race studies, and postcolonial theory offer methods to further address the implications of this device. Without such possible interventions, the representation of the Caucasian individual's hand, which seems to float over various landscapes, promises that some spectators can possess all situations and terrain.

This book provides theoretical models for rethinking aspects of the interface, including the hand-pointer, and critically using Internet sites and computer software. Each case study indicates a strategy and critical concept, which include gazing, closeness, failure, reading and meaning making, morphing, and folding that can be used to engage with and question Internet and computer representations. I suggest instances in which Internet and computer settings provide new techniques of control and theorize strategies of resistance. However, it is unwise to presume that such interventions are available to all spectators or that they will prove powerful enough to always disable dominant modes of representation. This book is meant to model another language for thinking about, writing, and viewing the Internet. It is my hope that this analysis and language encourage a reconceptualization of the Internet and computer.

| **Making Computer and Internet Spectators**

Introduction

The continued appearance of the computer hand-pointer, when engaging with software programs and web sites, suggests how overarching conventions continue even when the spectator is focused on one site or type of operation. The parameters of Internet and computer engagement are produced by software and operating system design, visible screen icons and screen savers, the monitor and computer processor, and previously conveyed conceptions of the Internet and computer. For instance, some of the icons that are used for various programs—and that are often saved to the visible setting of the computer, or the "desktop"—encourage the spectator to conflate material bodies and objects with Internet and computer representations. Email software is indicated with icons of addressed paper envelopes and mailboxes so that the asynchronous communication, which these programs manage, is conceptualized as mail. The use of the envelope icon in cell phone voice message indicators and on-screen digital cable provider updates also connects email to forms that are materially and conceptually different from envelopes and letters. After an unsuccessful attempt to get a malfunctioning hotel voice message system to work, I confusedly referred to it as a "mailbox" because of the envelope icon on the phone. As these representational systems and my related mistake suggest, spectatorship is shaped by metaphors, depictions of materiality, renderings of the empowered user, direct forms of address, questionnaires that enforce traditional identity categories, and the downplaying of the interface.

A variety of devices in Internet and computer settings make representations seem like an extension of the spectator's lived space. Referring to the computer screen image even metaphorically as the "desktop" encourages the spectator to understand the accompanying images as a continuation of the desk, home office, or workplace.[1] Friedberg indicates that the rendering of "familiar objects in space," which is a part of interface design, is in response to the increasingly digital aspects of images.[2] Ken Hillis describes the ways space is employed in virtual reality technologies and suggests that the effects of such representations need to be more carefully considered.[3] The problem with these spatial metaphors and analogies is that they elide computer representations and processes, make images seem like material things, and suggest that the spectator can enter the interface. Garnet Hertz's icons for Elmer's glue, fried rice, milk, red tape, and a myriad of other things playfully suggest how physical objects are reproduced through computer operations (figure 1.1).[4] However, his representations, as well as other icons, include renderings of white and light-skinned hands that reach out as if the spectator can manipulate a material object and have direct contact with the screen.

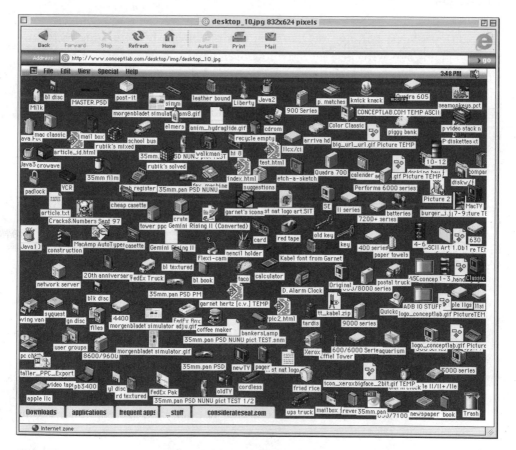

Figure 1.1
Garnet Hertz, "Desktop_10jpg. 832x264 Pixels," 21 Nov. 2003, <http://www.conceptlab.com/desktop/img/desktop_10.jpg>.

Hertz's hands reference the interface hands and, as I have already suggested, become "our" hands if we can mesh with these depictions. The accompanying indication that certain spectators have license to touch, view, and acquire is particularly disturbing when using the pointing and grasping hand to engage with images of women and people of color. These representations articulate Internet and computer spectators by producing a setting that discourages others from engaging.[5] Anna Everett is concerned with the computer start-up message and its "Pri Master Disk, Pri. Slave Disk, Sec. Master, Sec. Slave," which indicates that some programmers choose to base Internet and computer culture on a "digitally configured 'master/slave' relationship."[6] Programmers also employ varied visual representations and erotic terms to facilitate their desires and fantasies. For example, the "finger" utility can be used to gain information about those logged into a system and has resulted in phrases like "I fingered her."[7] Such computer narratives make Everett and others at least temporarily hold back from engaging. At the same time, white male spectators are encouraged to believe that they possess an extended power and have entered the screen.

Rendering Liveness, Materiality, and Space

Spectators are encouraged to accept Internet conventions because the setting is depicted as animate, physical, and unmediated. Academic and popular writing indicate that the Internet is populated.[8] For example, Esther Dyson suggests that "the Net includes all the people, cultures, and communities that live in it."[9] Luciano Paccagnella describes the Internet as a "dense bazaar inhabited by all kinds of people."[10] Alan J. Munro, Kristina Höök, and David Benyon indicate a computer-facilitated "area" where people engage with each other.[11] The Internet appears to provide a nutritive environment in which physical bodies exist because graphical-"chat"-setting avatars are described as "your presence in the virtual communities growing inside two and three dimensional virtual worlds."[12] However, Jennifer Gonzalez indicates that spectators should resist the idea that people are situated inside the screen.[13] Descriptions of populated Internet "environments" tend to erase the produced and stereotyped aspects of Internet settings.

Sherry Turkle encouraged the idea that things are alive and people have entered the Internet and computer by titling her book *Life on the Screen*.[14] Norman K. Denzin alludes to Turkle when he refers to "Life on the Net" and "Internet Life."[15] Yahoo! and Ziff-Davis uphold this animate vision of the Internet and the idea that people are inside the system by calling their magazine *Yahoo! Internet Life*. The Internet is rendered as if it were a living thing when Paccagnella describes "logs and messages taken from the actual life of a virtual community."[16] According to the character Fritz, in *Buffy the Vampire Slayer*, "information isn't bound up anymore; it is alive."[17] Of course, Internet "information," "logs," and "communities" are facilitated through writing and visually depicting. Fritz's high valuation of the Internet and his insistence that "if you are not jacked-in, you are not alive" evoke the narratives of mainstream cyberpunk science fiction literature.[18] The cyberpunk genre, which has modeled some of the ways programmers and other people understand Internet technologies and continues to affect how we talk about the Internet, has also provided accounts of nonhumans being alive.[19] Such novels as *Dreamships*, *Neuromancer*, and *Synners* depict artificial intelligence roaming the net.[20] Characters like Dixie Flatline, in William Gibson's *Neuromancer*, were dead but somehow still present within the computer system through software facilitation.

Computers are often spoken about as if they were animate. Phrases like "it told me" are used to describe system error notices and other software-generated texts. The idea of a corporeal screen and processor is supported by web-based greeting cards that express concern about computer "bugs" and "viruses," mourn the "death" of a favored system, and provide "congratulations on your new arrival," with a depiction of a stork delivering an iMac "baby" to a celebrating couple.[21] The technological and screen-based qualities of computers are often elided when they are depicted as a form of body. These renderings include images of the computer with a face that projects out beyond the screen surface and Microsoft Office's reinterpretation of the help system as a lively computer that appears to sulk when ignored. These depictions collapse the distance between spectator and screen and justify the spectator's conversation with the box.

The first sentence of Gibson's *Neuromancer* indicates that physical settings and screens will combine. In his dystopian narrative about the future, "the sky above the port was the color of television, tuned to a dead channel."[22] Gibson begins *Neuromancer* with a gray screen, but he ends it with live programs, cyber "space," and populated interfaces. He further supports the notion of embodied and navigable networks by stating that everyone he knows "who works with computers seems to develop an intuitive faith that there's some kind of actual space behind the screen."[23] Gretchen Barbatsis, Michael Fegan, and Kenneth Hansen suggest that "it is childlike to think that the people and places are somehow actually behind the screen, in that box," but "we nonetheless engage the computer screen as a gateway to another place."[24] Jan Fernback indicates that the metaphors used to describe the Internet and computer are "'*place centered*'" and then insists that "there is a there there."[25] Fernback reaches a different conclusion than does Jonathan G. S. Koppell in "No 'There' There: Why Cyberspace Isn't Anyplace."[26] Koppell has argued that the use of spatial and navigational terms depicts the Internet as a tangible place, but that this is not the case.[27] The spatial vernacular that accompanies Internet and computer settings makes it seem as though spectators can enter the Internet, be synonymous with characters and other depictions, and directly engage with other people.

Henry Jenkins indicates that people are invested in Internet and computer representations, children sway with the game character's movement on the screen, and we "speak not just of controlling the characters but of 'owning' the space of the game."[28] The notion of Internet space is produced through a variety of devices. There are described progressions and architectural settings, the labeling of certain sites as "home," maps that make it seem as though the user can move between rooms, and renderings of the computer screen and box as spatial. Webcam operators encourage the spectator to "enter the life of a college student."[29] Aerial images of cities, like the one on the Art Institute of Chicago's site, make it seem as though the spectator can enter a physical space.[30] The edges of the aerial view are blurred so that the "outside" cannot be articulated, but the rendering promises a way of moving in on a tangible view. AOL's instant messenger depiction of a figure standing inside an open doorway, which "buddies" see when the spectator is starting to use the program, also suggests movement and a shared "Internet space."

Browser icons and the animated logos, which are in the upper right corner of the frame and technically just signal when data is being downloaded, refigure the spectator's experience so that it seems like movement through physical locations. For instance, some of Microsoft Internet Explorer's animated download logos depict an "e" with a transparent globe and planetary ring that passes across it. This rendering of an available world, which appears to move at the spectator's command, suggests that browser-based viewing is global contact and travel. Browser names transform the spectator into an "explorer" and "navigator" who is guided with Netscape's animated lighthouse logo, star strewn sky, and ship's wheel. NetLingo defines "navigate" as the "act of moving around the Web" where "you move from one computer to another and from one server to another."[31] Lev Manovich renders a similar spatial progression when he notes that "following hyperlinks, the user 'teleports' from one server to another from one physical location to the next."[32] The spectator seems to be positioned in the setting because the reading experiences and textual aspects of hypertexts are displaced. Frank Odasz goes so far as to describe "networking" as "the highway to commute to work."[33] Despite these ongoing narratives about Internet-facilitated movement, Tarek and other programmers indicate that they spend "eight or more hours of sitting and slouching" per day.[34] The Internet and computer spectator is situated in front of the screen. However, the concept of Internet travel displaces the chair and sitting. Seated positions, which are considered in more detail in the afterword, are perceived as lazy, an aspect of "goofing off," and are not culturally respected in the West.[35]

Internet "movement" makes it seem as though the spectator has a high level of agency when engaging with Internet settings. Microsoft's Internet Explorer offers the "go" menu, and its advertising campaign appears to directly address the spectator when asking, "Where do you want to go today?" Andrew L. Shapiro suggests that Microsoft's "motto places the individual at the center of the action. It asks you where you will go, what you will do, with whom you will interact" and tries to convince spectators that they are in control while depriving them of options.[36] As Shapiro's comments suggest, computer interactivity often means adopting pre-scripted narratives and buying things. Nevertheless, the browser's "click-able" arrows, which are labeled "back" and forward" in some versions of Explorer, turn site viewing into spatial and directional engagements and suggest that spectators can go anywhere they desire. There always seems to be the possibility of "returning" because a house or directional arrow indicates that spectators can regain their original location. I sometimes think or even speak terms like "back," "forward," and "home" when using browsers and other software because it is difficult to develop another vocabulary. However, browsers provide temporal engagements that take up lived time; there is no return to a pre-existing state.

Notions of the Empowered User

There is an often-held belief, which is encouraged by the renderings of software manufacturers and Internet sites, that users with increased capacities produce, change, and control settings and selves. For instance, Alain J-J. Cohen argues that the spectator has been replaced by the "hyper-spectator" who can choose an infinite number of positions. According to Cohen, "He/she/it is both plastic and modular, sexually polymorphous and transnational, switching sex, class and anthropology at a click of prostheses—the mouse or the remote control."[37] He indicates that spectators are reconfigured by new technologies. However, people are already articulated within an age, class, ethnicity, gender, race, and sex system and think of themselves through these terms.[38] New technologies, which Cohen indicates will afford an escape from normative identity, already provide distinct messages about ideal spectatorial positions and appropriate forms of engagement. For instance, narratives about Internet engagement are gendered and raced. Being from the African diaspora, Asian, Latino/a, or from an indigenous culture is often noted in character and profile descriptions, while being Caucasian is presumed to be the default and is ordinarily not mentioned.

Such concepts as "surfing" seem to suggest a relaxed way of engaging with the Internet that has nothing to do with articulating normative identity. However, surfing also renders spectatorial power and control because it is understood as "the ease with which an expert user can use the waves of information flowing around the Internet to get where he wants."[39] This use of male pronouns, which is presumed to be a way of representing everyone, has an even more insidious effect when describing Internet and computer settings because computer programmers and other empowered users are often believed to be men. Justine Cassell and Henry Jenkins indicate that boys use computers more frequently than girls and that even kindergarten children believe that video games are more appropriate for boys.[40] Some recent studies indicate that women are using the Internet more than men but their engagement is still associated with web-based shopping and IM and men continue to be aligned with the technology.[41] While the relationship between men and technology is reinforced by ongoing indications that the typical Internet user "is a fat middle-aged man," such narratives may also undermine men's right to power with dismissive references to weight and age.[42]

There are numerous narratives about the power of Internet and computer spectatorship, but there are also representations of spectatorial failure. The parodying of error messages by net artists, fears about Y2K problems, renderings of failed Microsoft products, and depictions of frustrated individuals suggest that there is often an unbalanced distribution of power between the spectator and technology producer. These renderings can call into question cultural narratives about the user's right to power and control of the computer apparatus. For instance, web-based greeting cards depict the disastrous arrival of Windows or one of the three "catastrophes" of all times that literally cracks the monitor case and leaves it smoking, the Windows 98 logo holding the computer and presumably the spectator hostage at gunpoint, and the inexplicable disasters that result from simple computer operations.[43] Of course, such representations also articulate a power and knowledge difference between spectators and programmers. Women's and abjectly figured men's lack of control is often contrasted with programmers' skills. The articulated differences in informed users and "clueless newbies," such as the urban myth about the person mistaking the CD-ROM drive for a cup holder, allow for the continuation of hierarchy.

Addressing the Spectator

The problems with spectatorial authority are at least partially displaced by ongoing indications that individuals choose and shape texts. The Internet spectator is targeted with pronouns like "you" in order to make it seem as if the text is produced specifically for the individual. This direct address, which is also used in such television genres as home improvement shows, home shopping programs, MTV, news, sporting events, and talk shows, encourages the viewer to have a more personal engagement.[44] Direct address appears to acknowledge personal interests while allowing the media producer to render an even more detailed version of the spectator's desires, viewing behaviors, and buying habits. The Internet is like commercial television in that it "constantly addresses, appeals, implores, demands, wheedles, urges, and attempts to seduce the viewer."[45] MOOs, web sites, and other Internet interfaces use direct address to support the idea that the Internet is "many to many"—individuals are "communicating" with individuals—and that spectators can actively achieve their particular desires. Of course, the intent of direct address is to produce longer engagements with sites and better buying habits. Direct address renders an I/you relationship and an implied face-to-face communication in order to inform spectators about the appropriate ways to engage. There are constant instructional greetings to "sign in" and "enter." Web sites use cookies so that they can target the spectator by name or alias and make it seem as if they have a personal interest. After signing in or being "recognized," the named spectator is greeted with Yahoo!'s "Welcome!," Travelocity's "Welcome back" and "Hi," the "Welcome to Cheap Tickets!," and a variety of other greetings.[46]

The Amazon bookseller site uses direct address and a variety of other devices in order to make it seem as if its web site "store" is designed according to the individual's desires. Personalization begins on Amazon's first page, with a "hello" to the returning consumer, a promise that "we have recommendations for you," and a rendered series of options that include "your favorite stores," "your recommendations," "new for you," and "your bargains."[47] A sort of "home page" called "about you" can be completed with a photo and description of interests as well as the opportunity to write and review reviews, create book lists, post a "wish list," and make a favorite people list. Many of these options are organized around the purchase of books and other objects. Internet sites, even more than television programs, remind the spectator that "*you* are the 'you' it wishes to speak to."[48] Amazon's and other companies' direct addresses, reminders of the opportunities that they provide, and instructions are designed to convince spectators to accept their scripted role and reply by buying.

Amazon's personalization options seem to allow spectators, who are depicted as active users, to write into the system and program it according to their desires. Lev Grossman indicates that Amazon's "Customer Reviews" system and the Internet are "narrowing and blurring" the "rift between professional writers and their readers by giving the readers a chance to talk back."[49] Fan fiction and hypertext critics use similar arguments and indicate that the Internet breaks down the hierarchy between readers and writers. Nevertheless, the Amazon "conversation" that Grossman describes is accompanied by a mandate to "order," "explore," and "rate items." Many Internet cultural producers, as suggested in chapter 5, use Internet settings to establish their own authorial and artistic worth. Despite the indications of Grossman, web sites, and other Internet settings, spectatorship is not always so active. For instance, the Amazon "page *you* made, by you, for you, in real time" is a site "based on your recent clicks" rather than designed by you.[50] Amazon and other web sites indicate that they offer lived experience and a personally selected engagement, but many of the features are preproduced and coded by the setting.

Stabilizing Identity

Some spectators use the Internet with the idea that personal information cannot be verified and, as Steiner's cartoon asserts, the idea that "on the Internet, nobody knows you're a dog."[51] Steiner's portrayal of Internet anonymity is repeated in the numerous web-based greeting cards that depict animals employing computers.[52] In Virginia Shea's often-quoted "netiquette" guidelines, she indicates that spectators are not judged according to their age, body size, class, and race because of Internet anonymity.[53] The Jargon File attributes hackers' "gender- and color-blindness" to their engagement with text-based communication, but as the afterword indicates, many instances of intolerance exist.[54] Celebrations of anonymity persist in academic and popular writing and in Internet settings, but there are also increasing attempts to make Internet sites more reliable and the identity of spectators more verifiable.

Web "portals" like Google, Microsoft Network, and Yahoo! seem to resolve confusing views, information that is disconnected from authors and other sources, and problems with verifying vendors because they provide a clearly named and visually constant setting through logos and other design devices. They offer a variety of services, which include "chat" rooms, classified services, email, film and television schedules, games, maps and travel information, music, shopping, searching, news articles, stock quotes, and weather reports, so that there is no need to view other sites.[55] Even Amazon tries to mime the portal by consolidating varied stores and selling strategies under the Amazon logo, diversifying content, and offering a "messages" link, which is another preproduced mandate to buy.[56] Portals seem to offer reliability, safety, and stability because of their architectural narratives, consolidation of services, and recognizable status.[57] Yahoo! describes its "wallet" feature, which allows spectators to store their credit card information, as "Safe, Simple, Secure."[58] However, "security" produces traditional notions of body and identity because of the kinds of information that these sites require in order to get an account.[59]

The spectator is instructed to "sign up to personalize Yahoo!"[60] This personalization results in a loss of privacy because Yahoo! and other similar sites require the spectator to submit revealing information in order to get an ID and password. The Yahoo! form has sections for "First Name," "Last Name," and "Zip/Postal Code," and pulldown options for "Language & Content," "Gender," "Industry," "Title," and "Speciali-zation."[61] Spectators have to submit to being gender coded in order to get an account.[62] The only gender choices that Yahoo! offers on the form are "male" and "female." Once the profile is edited, and notification is provided that the information will be visible, the gender and identity listed on the form circulate among participants because "default" and active profiles are viewable in a number of ways.[63] It is encour-aging to note that the gender on the default profile is listed as "No Answer" rather than the binary gender that the spectator selected during the sign-up process.[64] However, spectators can search Yahoo! profiles by gender.[65] The initial form and inter-face indicate that there is no place outside of binary gender, the spectator begins with a clearly articulated gender identity, and the only possible option other than "male" and "female" is to choose not to answer. Some spectators notice the enforced kinds of identity that the form produces and that the site is making them. Other spectators just develop a more fixed Internet identity.

The legal notices on these sites are designed to regulate the gender and other pro-file information that spectators provide. Web-based email accounts and other services require the spectator to consent to the terms of service and privacy policy agreements. For instance, Yahoo! asks spectators to agree to "provide true, accurate, current and complete information about [themselves] as prompted by the Service's registration form."[66] Yahoo! clearly indicates that refusing to identify within the proscribed codes can result in account termination and denial of future services. Losing an email account and Internet "identities" can be significant because people rely on these accounts for work, to correspond with friends and family, and to participate in a vari-ety of forums. Even spectators who knowingly provide different information on the form are affected because the system articulates acceptable categories. The notices interpret the empty parts of the form and creative responses as a withholding of infor-mation and fictitious answers, both of which can result in legal action. Through the notices and other effects, these sites underscore traditional forms of identity and indi-cate that there are risks and limits to anonymity for their spectators.

The forms of spectatorial identity that are produced by Yahoo! are also instituted in other Internet settings. Such sites as Excite, GeoPortals, Go, and Netscape also have "male" and "female" options that must be designated in order to get an account. The spectator who chooses not to select a gender will be prompted to provide this information and cannot complete the registration process without submitting to this categorization. The Microsoft Network options are "Male," "Female," and "Prefer not to disclose."[67] On Lycos, there is no gender menu but the "Title" category forces the spectator to choose between "Mrs., Ms., and Mr."[68] Such gender-neutral but class-conscious addresses as "Dr." and "Esq." are not available. These sites inform spectators that even with the Internet, as Geo notes, "gender must be specified."[69] Power is also frequently reinscribed along with gender differences. They often list the male option above or before female on the form, which suggests that males are more likely to use these Internet settings or that they are better than females.

In settings with fewer reasons for verification, Internet spectators should be able to produce identities in a variety of ways. However, IM systems and other forms of Internet communication are also increasingly requiring the name, age, gender, and email address of spectators before providing accounts. This is a notable change since these settings were celebrated for the opportunity to choose different genders. The Delphi Forums bulletin board has "Male" and "Female" options.[70] The ICQ instant messenger client registration form has sections for "Your First Name," "Your Last Name," and "Your Age," as well as a pulldown form for "Your Gender."[71] By employing the pronoun "your" in the registration form, ICQ directs the questions to the spectator's physical state and indicates that questions should not be answered about an alternate or constructed identity.

Spectators could represent themselves in different ways but systems like Yahoo! make binary gender an implicit and explicitly visible aspect of Internet identity formation. Yahoo!'s sign-up form explains that "this information will help us personalize various areas of Yahoo! with content that is relevant to you" and, more recently, that "Yahoo! will try to provide more relevant content and advertising based on the information collected on this page and on the Yahoo! products and services you use."[72] ICQ also provides different spectatorial experiences once gender is selected because collected information is used to "fit offerings to you as an individual."[73] Commercial sites use the information from registration forms in order to attract advertisers interested in reaching particular populations. They also sell it to aggregators who use the data to understand Internet trends and continue to resell this information for profit. However, artists and other noncommercial sites also employ gender questions on their forms. For instance, Ken Goldberg's *Ouija 2000* artwork includes "Male" and "Female" options and requires registration in order to "play."[74] There is no essential body type or set of desires that women share.[75] However, the ways spectators are addressed and explanations of how demographic information is used indicate that Internet sites produce differences. For instance, Yahoo! enforces desire along with binary gender. The spectator who is not signed in is encouraged to "give fate a nudge. Find your match, post a free ad."[76] However, the female identified spectator is additionally coaxed to "go on, he's waiting."[77] Yahoo! displaces the possibility of bisexuality, lesbian desire, and relationships that are not motivated by binary gender positions with such narratives about heterosexuality.

The sites that are directed at children also produce gendered forms of spectatorship. For example, toy manufacturer and store web sites use gender-coded color schemes and links to direct customers. Their use of color, as a way of differentiating between girls' and boys' products, echoes the traditional use of color in children's clothing, which informs people how to gender bodies, as well as the color schemes in toy stores, which direct purchasers to gendered sections.[78] The Trendmaster's web site offers "Girls' Toys" and "Boys' Toys" as well as "Games" links.[79] The control "buttons" turn pink when the girls' page is accessed. The manufacturer Playmates presents links for "Dolls," "TM Ninja Turtles," and "Action Figures/Vehicles." However, Playmates discourages the possibility of relating these toy categories to divergent gender positions through color and labeling. The dolls section of this site is gendered with a hot pink menu, "Girls' Toys" title, and reference to girls in the URL.[80]

As web sites become more complex, spectators can look at images of toys in different ways. For instance, the Toys "R" Us site presents links for various age categories, but the conception of gender-specific toys has already been established by the "Gifts for Boys" and "Gifts for Girls" links.[81] Right Start also has a variety of linking structures, but the "Gift Store Departments" prominently features links "For Boys" and "For Girls."[82] Such color-coded and labeled "maps" indicate the toys that parents and other adults should buy for a particular child and direct children into gender-segregated settings. For instance, Playmates notes, "OK, girls, here's your section!" on the "Girls' Toys" part of the site.[83] These demarcations encourage girls to occupy a different setting and subject position from boys and render binary gender as a necessary component of mediated settings.

The employment of these gender categories supports or even produces limited conceptions of identity and the body. Teresa de Lauretis indicates that when "M" or "F" is marked on a form, it results in "M" and "F" categorizing, ordering, and shaping the individual.[84] After marking the form, individuals identify with and self-represent as that gender. Through the processes of Internet sites, such social representations as gender and desire may be, as de Lauretis indicates, "accepted and absorbed by an individual as her (or his) own representation, and so becomes, for that individual, real, even though it is in fact imaginary."[85] Unfortunately, these imaginary categories are maintained through extreme forms of social regulation. For instance, women are encouraged to be soft and domestic in many physical and Internet settings while men are instructed to be rugged and business-focused. Society indicates the punishments for not participating in traditional gender categories, which include comments, harassment, beatings, even the rape and murder of individuals like Brandon Teena for "passing."

Erasing the Interface

Gender representations appear to be real and an essential part of the engagement because the mediated aspects of the Internet and computer are downplayed. For example, Yahoo! advertises its messenger program with a depiction of two young women standing in the same space.[86] One woman whispers into the other's ear while talk emoticons, which hover overhead, indicate that their news is a secret. The representation equates synchronous communication with gossiping, suggests that this is a woman's activity, and downplays women's employment of Internet and computer technologies. The representation helps make synchronous Internet communications, or "chat," into speech.[87] Synchronous text-based and graphical communication is often described as "talking" and derives from the talk program, which allowed participants to initiate a session where text appeared in real time on a split screen.[88] iVillage states that "chat is a great way to take a break and talk with others."[89] William Mitchell indicates that there are "some characters hanging out, ready to talk" in graphical communication settings.[90] The Computers, Telephony, and Electronics Glossary also turns reading and typing into a spatial experience by equating synchronous communication to "chatting at a party."[91]

These representations suggest that "chat" settings facilitate physical connections between individuals and allow them to "meet."[92] The names of services, the imaging and configuration of sites, and the narratives about "chat" rooms render space and a place-oriented experience. For instance, varied message forums and synchronous settings employ names like The Chat House, ChatSpot, ChaTTown, Habbo Hotel, iVillage, Link Room, and @ourplace.com in an attempt to make the Internet into a space.[93] Club Gabbay's tagline is a "place to chat" and the site features an icon of a welcoming tent with a glowing yellow door that invites the spectator to enter.[94] The Gathering Chat! login link is labeled "Let Me In!" and the site presents an image of an open castle with a wooden bridge that appears to connect the spectator's space to one within the setting.[95]

Synchronous communication settings and instant messenger clients, which repeat some of the browser conventions, depict an extremely mobile user. AOL Internet

Messenger (AIM) depicts a striding yellow figure rather than a seated spectator. The LinguaMOO synchronous communication setting has an animated logo of two spectators with hands connected and bodies gyrating.[96] This rendering of spectators, who are making contact through the Internet, is supported by Lingua and other MOO depictions of spaces. The ICQ messenger client also depicts participants holding hands and dancing around a globe.[97] ICQ suggests that it is a global phenomenon by depicting flags from varied nations, promising that individuals can "download ICQ in your language," and describing the "global community" as "Online Happiness."[98] These visual and textual representations downplay the strife over global issues and the questionable behaviors that occur with IM. It remains unclear how people communicate in their own languages and understand each other, but ICQ also depicts them in the same room. ICQ downplays the technology and collapses distance by indicating that it is a "small program" and "as straightforward as calling across a room" and provides an image of two individuals talking together.[99]

Telepresence art projects, which employ virtual reality and web technologies to create the "sensation of being elsewhere," also render views of living things in order to animate the Internet and downplay the technological aspects of the engagement.[100] In Eduardo Kac's *Teleporting an Unknown State* (1994/1996, 1998, and 2001), a plant depended on "online participants to send light from eight areas of the world" so that it could "grow in a completely dark room."[101] Kac renders the "Internet as a life-supporting system" and suggests that there is "birth, growth, and death on the Internet."[102] In Ken Goldberg and Joseph Santarromana's *Telegarden* (1995), Internet participants "plant, water, and monitor the progress of seedlings via the tender movements of an industrial robot arm"[103] By describing the technology as caring, Goldberg and Santarromana make it more corporeal. They also make it seem as if spectators can enter the screen by depicting people already present in a bountiful growing space. The concept of a populated Internet setting and visible web viewer appear to be facilitated by "the member tracker overlay."[104] The spectator is assured that "one can not only see who but where other members are within the garden."[105] Of course, this promise to visualize and situate the individual within the material space of the garden is misleading. In *The Robot in the Garden* anthology, Goldberg notes that sites can be deceptive and real-time images are not always delivered. Nevertheless, he continues to conceptualize telepresence as an extension of the spectator's "reach" and means to "visit."[106]

Goldberg and Santarromana use a variety of visual devices in *Telegarden* to suggest that the spectator can see into or even through the Internet. The two rendered circles of the interface, which represent the robotic mechanism and the view of the garden on various screens, equate graphic with optical representations and suggest a porthole into another world. In a similar manner, Manovich indicates that a "computer monitor connected to a network becomes a window through which we can enter places thousands of miles away."[107] Windows are used to render Internet space because they usually provide views "onto" other terrain and articulate an inside and outside. Thomas J. Campanella suggests that webcams are the "Web's windows on the world" and "knit the Net to the physical spaces we inhabit."[108] The accompanying illustration by Jack Desrocher supports this conception by depicting the monitor as a curtained window, incorporating it into the home setting, and indicating that it provides a view out onto another place (figure 1.2). However, the woman who is situated in front of the computer is not looking at the screen or engaged in reading; a book rests on her lap and a newspaper has fallen unnoticed to the floor. This rendering of the computer window turns the woman's manipulation of advanced technologies into passive viewing and disinterested reading. Representations of women webcam operators,

Figure 1.2
Jack Desrocher, "Salon | 21st: Be There Now," Salon, 7 Aug. 1997, 27 Sept. 2004, <http://www .salon.com/aug97/21st/cam970807.html>.

which are considered in chapter 3, also risk displacing women's technological skills when they suggest that webcams provide an unmediated entrance into domestic space.

Conclusion: Active Users by Design

Recent developments in flat-panel and flat-screen designs also make the monitor less visible. A DuPont advertisement for flat-screen televisions and monitors depicts a glassless screen.[109] It seems as if the spectator could go through the frame or "enter" another world if he—and gender is a notable aspect of this rendering—so desired. iMacs further knit the "space back there" to physical space by encouraging the spectator to look into and through the computer. The design of Apple's flat screen displaces the glasslike shine from the viewing surface and onto the frame. However, the base also begins to disappear because the spectator can see through the transparent legs and edging. All of this suggests that the window onto another world, which narratives about the computer promise, is becoming increasingly easy to breach. For instance, Apple's advertisement for its Cinema HD Display with its angled entrance implies that monitors provide access to the city environment (figure 1.3). The computer cards and other hardware are not so much displaced as grafted onto the cityscape. This conception of an architectural computer space had already been instituted in a variety of cyberpunk novels.

The collapse of material space and computer-mediated representations is also suggested by one of Microsoft's and Expedia's "Where do you want to go today" advertisements, which have been critiqued for their colonial vision of access. In this depiction, the thin frame of the browser and neutral advertising banner are all that separates the computer screen image from the "real" tropical ocean location. The two-page advertising spread, with its central seam, encourages readers to ignore boundaries and to repair the split between different pages and registers. The continuity between the "real" space and Internet setting is rendered by the angle of the dock that leads the viewer's eyes "into" the location and suggests that material bodies can enter into the computer. Another advertisement also transforms the monitor into a detailed world when it suggests that the "closer you look, the more you'll see" (figure 1.4).[110] However, everything around the monitor except for the text is whited-out so that the rendered view and the marketing promises become the reality and truth. It may be a "flat screen," but the spectator is promised materiality through "fat sound." In this and other advertisements for computer screens, the technology and computer box are displaced so that the spectator can become immersed in the depicted natural environ-

Figure 1.3
Apple, "Apple," 23 Mar. 2002, <http://www.apple.com>.

ment of fields, mountains, seacoast, flowers, or other plants. The insistent use of diagonals directs the spectator's gaze into the view and suggests that the environment is waiting to be populated. These depictions, as well as telepresence art, indicate that living plants and other things can be accessed and experienced through the Internet and computer.

The employment of spatial narratives, including the suggestion that computer screens provide an entrance into an untouched landscape, is repeated in the indications that the Internet is the last open space, "electronic frontier," and "new frontier of civilization."[111] Such writers as Guillermo Gomez-Peña indicate that these descriptions of the utopian possibilities of the Internet also evoke "a sanitized version of the pioneer and frontier mentalities of the Old West" where space was believed to be unmarked, unoccupied, and available for the taking.[112] Internet technologies are

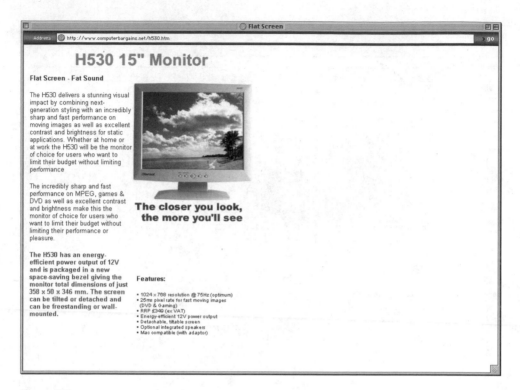

Figure 1.4
Computer Bargains, "Flat Screen," 16 Jan. 2003, <http://www.computerbargains.net/h530.htm>.

produced and employed by a variety of people and communities and can be "owned" in ways that are distinct from material environments. However, a debilitating discourse is enabled when Internet "spaces" displace the qualities of the computer screen. Critical theory and close visual and textual analysis, which are employed throughout this book, can begin to render a vocabulary for describing and conceptualizing these representations. James T. Costigan argues that writing about the Internet has consequences. Writing, which includes visual renderings and the work of hardware and software designers, determines what the Internet can become, what it is, and how settings and technologies are evaluated.[113] The chapters in this book suggest other languages for writing, designing, and visually rendering the Internet and computers since these acts produce settings. Without such strategies, metaphors will continue to produce an Internet that can be conveniently critiqued and politically resisted through words.

2 Visual Pleasure through Textual Passages: Gazing in Multi-user Object-oriented Settings (MOOs)

Introduction

Studying multi-user object-oriented settings, or MOOs, suggests some of the ways that writing produces the Internet and empowered spectatorial positions. Texts are used in these synchronous communication settings to describe what sites look like, explain their function, exchange messages, and program. However, information generated by the system and typed commands also make textual MOO processes seem like the empowered visual examination of people and objects. This occurs because the "look" and other gazing-oriented commands are consistently employed. For instance, a typed command to "look <character name>" is likely to result in a detailed description of eye color, hair color, and clothing. There is also a notice, which appears on the other spectator's screen, that "<character name> is looking at you." All texts have visual aspects, but MOO programming and narratives suggest that a visual environment has supplanted typographic design. These texts render MOOs and the Internet as "living environments" where people seem to look at each other, enter the interface, and congregate.[1]

Feminist theories about the gaze help to explain how MOOs construct virtual sight and corporeal spectators. There is a wealth of feminist and gender scholarship that considers how the gaze, which can be defined as a form of power-laden staring, renders and enforces gendered spectatorial positions but the gaze of Internet spectators remains largely unconsidered. Gazing must be radically rethought in Internet settings because the traditional understanding of subject and object, which explains how viewers look at things, does not easily apply to these settings. In MOOs, there is no physical space and the self is represented by numerous depictions. The MOO spectator sits in front of the computer screen, but most interfaces and academic and popular writing do not articulate this position. The character and its programmed attributes are maintained by the host computer and directed by the spectator's typed commands.[2]

However, the spectator who looks at varied computer representations and the character that seems able to walk and move inside the setting are often conflated. For instance, Webopedia describes MUDs and MOOs as spaces of embodied interchange where spectators "interact with one another," and Wikipedia indicates that "players control a character."[3] Narratives of spectatorial "control" and indications that texts are visual objects make it easier to believe that the spectator is performing all the actions and is inside the screen.

Feminist theories of spectatorship, which analyze how power and incapacity are rendered through looking, offer important methods for considering MOO settings and their articulation of gendered positions. The discourse about looking, which is prevalent in MOO systems, is one way empowered spectators are produced and their behaviors validated. The concept of interactivity, with its indication that users can manipulate, control, and change all computer and Internet material, also promises versions of the empowered spectator in other Internet settings. For instance, the producers of graphical communication and Internet fan culture settings, which are considered in chapter 5, indicate that their remanipulation of media texts is an artistic practice. However, artists use the elite status gained in these settings to prevent others from reworking their cultural production. These differences in how spectators can engage indicate that not all viewers achieve the promised forms of interactivity and control.

A close reading of the text-based LambdaMOO setting and consideration of the essential scholarship on the gaze indicate how looking and gazing establish gendered positions, regulate virtual characters, and produce a version of the material body. A brief examination of the graphics and texts that are rendered in the LinguaMOO setting suggests that these outcomes continue and even increase in MOOs with graphical interfaces. A theory of MOO looking can also offer methods for analyzing how other text-based communication settings, including MUCKs, MUDs, and MUSHes, employ the look.[4] Feminist literature on the gaze can be further revised, as illustrated by my consideration of webcams in chapter 3, to indicate how gazing functions in other Internet settings. Image archives, meta-lists, museum sites, search engines, and webcams also offer but do not necessarily provide unlimited views, material things, and empowered forms of spectatorship.

MOOs

MOOs are a form of MUD, which have been defined as multi-user dungeons, domains, or dimensions. The employment of the term "user" in the MUD acronym suggests the interactive agency of spectators. It also downplays the ways individuals engage by viewing, reading, typing, and sitting. MUDs are a "class of multi-player interactive game, accessible via the Internet."[5] They provide social experiences, which are supported by a computer program and server, and often involve some kind of theme, which include vast castle structures with many rooms, periods in history, and references to fantasy and science fiction. LambdaMOO's "theme" is a mansion and its "core," which includes textual renderings of the kitchen, living room, bedrooms, and bathrooms, is based on a previous home of Pavel Curtis.[6] He is often described as LambdaMOO's "archwizard," or the designer of the system, even though such projects are always collaborative.

In his writing, Curtis acknowledges finding and radically revising Stephen White's MOO program and the efforts of other individuals in designing and supporting the system.[7] LambdaMOO, the oldest existing MOO, has been available through the Internet since October 1990 and maintains the largest number of characters.[8] Xerox PARC originally helped support LambdaMOO as part of a research project to design Internet settings in which scientists could communicate, then Stanford University and Placeware Incorporated assisted in supporting it.[9] Research and interest in MOOs persist, and a large number of scholars have considered various aspects of these settings.[10] Pavel Curtis, Roger Crew, and many other people now maintain LambdaMOO without specific institutional support.

LambdaMOO facilitates multiple simultaneous connections so spectators can participate in the synchronous setting. Spectators "login" or start a session with the host's computer and see an initial "Welcome" text, which provides information about the system and advice on how to engage. The text informs the spectator that LambdaMOO is "a new kind of society, where thousands of people voluntarily come together from all over the world."[11] The setting is equated with an "international city" where spectators engage with corporeal people. This suggests that viewers become empowered spectators, enter into the setting, and occupy the Internet as a space. The spectator "connects" as a named character, which the spectator has previously constructed, or as a guest. Named characters have a more stable identity within the system, but all characters have a unique name and number. LambdaMOO's programming and narratives indicate that spectators have a unique embodiment within the setting. However, the character is not a physical or visual entity, and there is no specific material space in which Internet interactions take place. All LambdaMOO communications are accomplished through descriptions that appear on the screen, and the setting is completely text-based.

The object-oriented programming of MOOs, which is similar to the C++ and Java computer languages, allows spectators to change some aspects of the system. Object-oriented programming, or OOP, "is a software design methodology and programming paradigm that defines programs in terms of 'classes of objects.'"[12] Objects are also described as "the fundamental building blocks" of LambdaMOO.[13] Information about LambdaMOO's programming language is available through the elaborate "help" system, which provides documentation for many of its common aspects. Detailed information about objects and their programming can also be acquired by using such MOO "commands" as "@show," "@list," "@verbs," and "@examine." The ability to read aspects of the programming and the elaborate help system make LambdaMOO a particularly useful site in which to interrogate looking, gazing, empowered spectatorship, and how writing produces the Internet. However, the seeming transparency of the system and the discourse about commands also suggests that the spectator controls and even becomes a character.

Help texts underscore the expectations and regulatory systems that are part of these settings. The login text warns that what "people say or do may not always be to your liking" and that "it is wise to be careful who you associate with and what you say."[14] LambdaMOO's rules are outlined in a "help manners" document. New characters and guests must consent to the rules by typing "yes" if they want to continue. The newting, or long-term exclusion from the system, of the characters Mao and WriTinG produced a vociferous debate about appropriate behavior and perpetuated the idea that rule breakers and troublemakers, including characters that persistently provoked the wizards that run the MOO, would be punished. The look and gaze are important aspects of this societal regulation. They suggest that a larger cultural force is at work in these settings and that there are LambdaMOO people, bodies, and spaces that need to be protected.

The Look and the Gaze

An initial consideration of MOOs, with their textual base, may make a consideration of spectatorship, looking relations, and theories of the gaze seem like an unlikely project. However, spectators virtually look in order to operate their characters because of the programming decision to associate information inquiries with the "look" verb, or typed commands to look at other textual characters, rooms, and things. So, the spectator initiates a command to look, and the viewer and character become consolidated as an empowered spectator, who seems to see, because of system-generated descriptions. In MOOs, the experience of reading text is supplanted by a doctrine of visual looking and seeing. It is perhaps not surprising when considering the vernacular of these systems that participants often comment that they have not read anything lately.[15]

The primacy of vision is an underlying ideology of MOO systems. The MOO's optical and visual vernaculars encourage spectators to think of characters as natural material bodies. To look is, after all, "to ascertain by the use of one's eyes,"[16] It is associated with the gaze because to look is also "to exercise the power of vision upon" someone or something.[17] Martin Jay simultaneously performs and critiques the ways optical metaphors have permeated our linguistic practices and suggests that such terms impede inquiry.[18] On MOOs, the look is intended to evoke visual processes and downplay the textual aspects of the system even when it is not explicitly about seeing. Jay's writing suggests that an examination of how vision is privileged in MOOs can also help disable its limiting aspects. For instance, the visual and optical vernacular of MOOs recreates parts of the physical world in order to structure a particular kind of reality. The virtual look, because it seems to provide access to physical bodies, is often employed as part of a conservative tendency to resist such gender transgressions as cross-dressing, defying gender characteristics, and discrepancies between the character's set gender and typed pronouns. The constructed aspects of the body, which are produced by texts, are partially concealed by the insistence that the metaphorical sight of the look is the equivalent of truth.

MOO processes of gazing are also employed to verify and control. A common dictionary definition of the gaze is "to fix the eyes in a steady intent look."[19] According to Salecl and Žižek, the gaze produces power and incapacity. This may occur when a spectator fixes another's eyes or actions by staring. Salecl and Žižek indicate that the gaze is "the medium of control (in the guise of the inspecting gaze) as well as of the fascination that entices the other into submission."[20] The "look" and "gaze" are described in similar ways in dictionary definitions, academic scholarship, and MOOs. There is a direct relationship between virtually looking and gazing, but not all MOO looks are equally related to the feminist psychoanalytical criticism that has produced some of the most significant contemporary theories of the gaze. Mulvey describes a deeply gendered process of looking and being looked at in "Visual Pleasure and Narrative Cinema."[21] Her article presented a groundbreaking analysis of the classical narrative cinema.[22]

Mulvey argues that the male cinema spectator gains a sense of agency by identifying with the active male protagonist. She attributes the production of binary gender to the forms of pleasure and identification that occur in the classical cinema. The subject of the gaze is male, assisted by an implicit association with the camera's viewpoint, while its object is female: "In a world ordered by sexual imbalance, pleasure in looking has been split between an active/male and passive/female. The determining male gaze projects its fantasy onto the female figure, which is styled accordingly. In their traditional exhibitionist role women are simultaneously looked at and displayed, with their appearance coded for strong visual and erotic impact so that they can be said to connote *to-be-looked-at-ness*."[23] Mulvey associates identification, voyeurism, and fetishism with the gaze. The concept of an empowered male gaze, which is theorized by Mulvey, Metz, and others, is a reconceptualization of Lacan's theory in which the gaze is not associated with a unified subject or desire.[24] Doane indicates that feminist film theorists made the gaze more subjective because Lacan's theory does not address the unequal positions of mastery and subjection and is thus not useful in considering sexual difference, or the ways femininity, masculinity, and sexuality are constructed.[25] In Lacan's model, everyone is subjected to an outside gaze that cannot be possessed. A number of scholars, including Mulvey, have reconsidered the early feminist film theory that described the gaze as a totalizing and purely patriarchal structure.[26] Doane's theory of a female gaze, which employs masquerade as a way of flaunting femininity and thus holding it at a distance, may provide an alternative model for discussing the ways that some MOO characters and spectators look.[27]

Doane proposed this critical model as a way to empower female spectators. However, she also notes the limits of her theory of masquerade.[28] Mayne encourages continued theoretical considerations of spectatorship and suggests that feminist critics need to rethink the binary positions or "sexual difference" that such theoretical work may support.[29] On MOOs, the rethinking of such binary oppositions as male and female must include the availability of about ten genders (neuter, male, female, splat, Spivak, royal, plural, 2nd, either, and egotistical), gender transgressions, and masquerades.[30] Current understandings of heterosexuality are also called into question by this gender system. Despite such challenges to traditional binaries and the appearance of new theoretical work on spectatorship and the gaze, Mulvey's thesis does help explain the deeply gendered and voyeuristic virtual looking that happens on MOOs. It also helps to clarify some of the forms of looking that happen in other settings.

MOO settings produce empowered spectators because of the ways textual looking is made into a culture where everything seems to be visually available. Apparatus theory suggests that the spectator is constructed through the text's point of view and identification with the technology.[31] The technology of MOO settings is quite different than that of the cinema. However, MOO accounts and narrative films both tend to elide the technology. Reflexive acknowledgments of the technology, which include MOO narratives about computers and film depictions of camera operators, acknowledge and then displace the apparatus, bring the spectator back into the story, and diffuse concerns about accepting imaginary worlds.[32] Through such devices, MOOs and narrative film render a coherence that encourages the spectator to believe in the existence of the depicted space.[33]

The mostly staid MOO spectator, with a body that remains in front of the computer screen, gains a striking mobility and agency by identifying and adopting the MOO character's point of view and "moving" through varied virtual terrain. Looking produces a more coherent space because MUDs and MOOs appear to offer "different locations to explore."[34] The object-oriented programming, which renders programmed textual elements as objects, continues this articulation of environment by indicating that the spectator can control any object in this space.[35] Of course, there are some problems with this depiction of Internet worlds. An examination of how the spectator cannot be properly sutured or bound into the setting, which is considered in greater depth in chapters 3 and 6, presents opportunities to consider how settings work and conceptualize Internet spectatorship and its processes of viewing in different ways.

The concept of the gaze is used in feminist film theory to describe looking relationships in which voyeurism, an empowered scopophilic stare, and erotic perusals are sometimes employed. The gaze is also utilized in other considerations of power relationships. For instance, Michel Foucault indicates that looking and gazing are part of a system of social regulation.[36] In his discussion of the panopticon, which was designed by Jeremy Bentham, the architectural layout of the prison or other building allows guards, officials, or citizens to surreptitiously watch. Prisoners know that they can be watched but they do not know when this observation occurs, who is looking at them, or when punishment might happen. Because of this effect, individuals subjected to the panopticon's field of visibility, or its gaze, learn to regulate their own behavior.

Foucault's theory of surveillance and self-regulation has been applied to Internet settings even though the physical architecture, which he indicates is an aspect of this system, is not present.[37] In Foucauldian considerations of Internet surveillance, the visibility of individual bodies within the panoptic structure is replaced by the consolidation of the individual's records into a "data image," search services that provide addresses and arrest details, aerial depictions that pinpoint home locations, "googling" to obtain personal facts, and cookies that record web usage. These Internet methods provide a vast amount of information, render an eerie feeling of being watched, suggest that the individual is ever seeable, and encourage people to regulate their behavior.[38] However, these methods of information retrieval do not place the body under visual surveillance even though they are associated with looking. MOOs also provide a great deal of information about characters, when the look and looking-oriented commands are employed, but information about spectators is more difficult to determine.

Character Creation and Attributes in MOOs

Abraxas
A slim 5′9 fellow who enjoys biking, golf and Windows programming. So go ahead and ask: "What do you do for fun?" (hmm) I enjoy watching Dave, and try not to get mugged when waiting for tickets. :)
He is awake, but has been staring off into space for 4 minutes.[39]

Olive_Guest
A hazel-eyed girl with white-blonde hair, a tight crop top and short shorts. She fills this outfit nicely, the low round neckline showing the upper slopes of her breasts, and carries a little beaded bag in one hand. Her feet are bare, her hair tousled as if she just got up from sleep.
She is awake and looks alert.[40]

Brown_Guest
Mark is 17 years old. He's got his mother's emerald green eyes, and his dad's dark brown, curly hair, cut very short on the sides, and a little longer on the top. He is 5′11, 180 lbs, and is wearing his favorite, almost worn out, blue jeans, and a tight, dark purple golf shirt.
He is awake, but has been staring off into space for 2 minutes.[41]

The first thing that the MOO spectator renders is a character. The attributes of a character, including the character's description, gender, the objects it carries, and the messages that appear when a character engages with the setting can be adjusted and readjusted at will. The text that provides a context for the character is known as the character's "description" and is set by typing "@describe me as <description>."[42] Guests can and often do use @describe as a way of personalizing their more temporary representations. Character descriptions often include such physical traits as age, height, weight, body type, eye color, hair color, and type of clothes.[43] The practice of rendering characters with physiognomic attributes is encouraged by the help text example for @describe, which states that "Munchkin types this: @describe me as 'A very fine fellow, if a bit on the short side.'"[44] The @describe help text suggests that community conventions require character descriptions that articulate physical attributes. It also invites capitalization that makes the character alias into a proper name. These commands and system instructions encourage MOO spectators to render virtual bodies and read other characters as the equivalent of physical individuals even though there is the possibility of rewriting character descriptions and having more than one description through a process called "morphing."[45]

The differences between spectator and character, which can often be quite extreme, are hidden by what appears to be the "truth" of lists of physical traits in character descriptions. Direct address confirms this consolidation so that "you" and the character both seem to be acknowledged in system-generated texts. The necessity of referring to the self when using such customization commands as "@gender me" also encourages the spectator to think of the MOO character as a version of the individual, or "i'm steve," as a guest description notes.[46] The MOO character is further articulated as a body because the "@messages me" command for some characters includes messages about arms, chest, hands, head, and groin. Beige_Guest's description assures spectators that characters are "in the flesh."[47] Jorge R. Barrios and Deanna Wilkes-Gibbs continue this connection between spectator and character when they indicate, "You can describe yourself."[48] As shown by the analysis in chapter 1, direct address and programming commands produce a specific action, person, and empowered spectator who has stepped into the setting and been recognized by the system. These methods continue the direct address methods that television advertising and talk shows use and connect the spectator to the depiction.[49] LambdaMOO policy maintains the direct correspondence between spectator and character because it generally expects "only one character per person."[50] However, the relationship between subjects and objects in physical environments and even feminist critiques of the gaze, which indicate that empowered male subjects look upon female objects of the gaze, may be problematized because characters are referred to as "objects" in MOO settings.

While MOOing, there is a cinematic-like segregation of space between spectator and character. However, the continued collapse of a spectator into an active character is different from descriptions of cinematic spectatorship as a passive form of identification with the apparatus and the actors on the screen. It is often difficult to differentiate between spectator and character, to describe the self that has the agency and undergoes the experiences, when talking about the MOO setting. These forms of identification are also related to the participatory structures that fan cultures produce. Fans and characters can speak or type the parts from their favorite books, comics, movies, and television shows.[51] However, the MOO spectator can never literally become the character even though there is a higher level of control over the performance than fans have with their favorite media texts. MOO characters have a relationship with MOO objects that spectators cannot attain because they exist outside the setting and are held back by the screen. For instance, characters can be programmed to virtually pick up objects, touch other characters, and record or even participate in events when the spectator is not engaged with the host computer. It is difficult to describe characters as subjects, even though the character "acts" while outside the spectator's control, because of the continued conflation of spectator and character.

The employment of gender also assists in the collapse of spectator and character because it supports the illusion that character descriptions depict "real" bodies. Most MOO spectators choose to depict themselves as either male or female despite the other gender choices.[52] All characters must have a gender, which is usually selected by the spectator, but such features as age, class, and race do not have to be chosen or indicated in the character's description.[53] The system provides information on gender when commands are employed to obtain the character's description. Gender is also highlighted when one character pages another because a preprogrammed message appears and is followed by the statement "she (he, it . . .) pages, <message>." When asked why the system constructs gendered characters by employing pronouns, many programmers argue that system-generated texts, such as the one just quoted, "require" pronouns to facilitate natural language parsing. This contention seems to be supported by the high occurrence of pronouns, which match the set gender of the character, in the system messages that describe character actions. But obviously, with some textual awkwardness, the character's name could be substituted for all pronominal markers.

The construction of gendered positions, physiognomic attributes, and detailed settings, all of which are available even when the spectator who programmed them is not logged on, support a detailed architecture of belief or uniform community outlook. Most spectators believe that quoting familiar architectural types is necessary because it makes the fractured aspects of MOOs legible. For example, "help theme" describes the textually rendered mansion as a "bit of a mongrel," but descriptions of themes and topologies also encourage spectators to follow spatial conventions when "building."[54] Rooms are supposed to reproduce traditional architectural and spatial rules, and a character that "goes" east through a door should also be able to reverse direction and go west.[55] The convention of describing separate settings as "rooms" encourages the spectator to conceive of the MOO as an ordered series of relational spaces. MOOs, as well as web sites, provide no ability to form a cohesive map of the structure without such contextual markers.

MOOs also support spatial coherency by rendering the character's "movement" through "rooms." The character can "walk" when the spectator types such compass directions as "north" and "teleport" with the command "@go <room number>." The textual reproduction of doors, sofas, and other architectural features works as a marker for the material body and suggests that an empowered spectator can traverse the setting. Of course, there is no physical movement of the character involved when retrieving programmed texts from the system. The typed commands of the spectator, who is usually positioned in front of the keyboard, do not align with descriptions of the character's engagement. Spatial devices and diagrammatic ASCII maps, which depict an architectural structure in which most walls meet at right angles, depict the MOO as a visual space and suggest that the spectator can enter.

The Look and the Gaze in MOOs

The look is a privileged term in MOO systems even though spectators communicate and comprehend the MOO setting by reading and writing texts. Characters need to virtually look in order to engage with the setting because of the programming decision to associate typed information inquiries with the look command.[56] The most common way to get information about MOO objects, which includes characters, is by typing "look <character or object name>." The importance of the look command is indicated by its inclusion in the introductory help text for LambdaMOO as one of "the first five kinds of commands you'll want to know."[57] The look provides a consistent set of information. When characters virtually look at a room setting, they receive the room's name, description, and contents (a list of objects and characters in that room). Characters that virtually look at another character receive the character's name, description, login status (the character is described as "awake" or "sleeping"), and level of activity if the character is logged-in (the character is described as "alert" or idle for a certain amount of time). This information retrieval command works in the same virtual room with "look <character name>" and works from any MOO setting with "look ~<character name>."

This inquiry is further associated with looking by the "look_detect" option that provides notice that "<character name> looks you over." Gender is always reinscribed when virtually looking at another character because the message notes that "she (he, it . . .) is awake and looks alert." The look command, look_detect feature, and accompanying system terminology work together to form a setting in which characters seem to gaze at gendered bodies. For instance, the look_detect notification is called the "@watched message." There is also an "@owatched me" message that can be set to notify everyone in the room when a character is being virtually looked at. Such public evidence sometimes leads to long bouts of virtual looking at particular characters. The weight of such MOO looks and their transformation into an empowered gaze is indicated by the distressed ways in which certain characters respond to being observed. For instance, a guest is "headless. Somebody bit it off. Ahh, the blood, the blood!! They oughtta put a warning on the look command, nobody told me it was socially unacceptable to use it."[58] These comments indicate the power of the look as well as the manner in which guests are dismissed and socially regulated.

The system provides a number of complex tools to patrol specific characters despite the aversion that some characters have to being virtually watched. For instance, spectators can surveil a particular character with the @watch command, which provides notification when the character stops idling. Spectators can also be immediately informed when characters on their "interesting list" become available. Viewers support the surveillant effects and design of the system and become empowered spectators when they employ such commands as @peruse, @kgb, @fbi, @scope, glance, @peep, @gawk, see, @dossier, @report, @whois, and @examine.[59] These forms of information inquiry are commonly thought of as a form of looking even though some of them do not trigger the character's @watch message and provide notice of the virtual look. The names of these messages clearly link information inquiries with the more disturbing system message that "you" are being looked over.

Everything is clocked, dated, and catalogued. For instance, typing "@spy <character name>" provides the character's status (the character is awake or asleep), object number, present room and room description, a list of objects and characters in that room, and a map of the surrounding rooms. The system usually supplies information that the spectator does not require. However, by using these commands and gaining a great deal of information, the spectator supports a system that is similar to the disciplinary mechanism that Foucault describes where the individual is "observed at every point," "all events are recorded," and an "uninterrupted work of writing links the centre and the periphery."[60] Writing renders all aspects of MOO systems, including the ways characters look and watch, but the body of the spectator is never seen. In other Internet and computer settings, the recording of keystrokes, which are used to determine productivity and sexual activity, and employers' consultation of listserv posts, before making hiring decisions, also seem to provide detailed chronicles of individuals. While there have been considerations of how Internet writing practices, databases, and surveillance interrelate, these "depictions" indicate a continued need for theories that examine both surveillance and the textual rendering of bodies.[61]

Some MOO commands more clearly indicate that the setting is implemented and engaged with by reading and writing texts. For instance, @examine provides information, including the different commands for an object, that look does not offer. Barrios and Wilkes-Gibbs conceptualize @examine as a way to engage with something other than descriptions or to "look beneath the surface," which of course still suggests some kind of spatial arrangement, and as a means to "step outside the virtual reality."[62] The cascading scroll of information that occurs with @examine can remind spectators of the textual aspects of MOOs. However, the @examine command still triggers the message that a character is "looking at you" and continues the visual discourse of MOOs. The look command is also more convenient to use than @examine, research indicates that look is employed more frequently, and some of the more visually oriented commands provide desirable information that is not available with @examine.[63]

The read and @read commands also connect the MOO setting to textual narratives. However, they are only employed when specific MOO documents are meant to stand in for written texts. According to "help read," the "read <note>" command "prints the text written on the named object, usually a note or letter."[64] The @read command allows characters to read listserv-like MOO mailing lists and to examine their personal MOO mail, which is the MOO's version of email. The read and @read commands complement the visual and object-oriented nature of the system by suggesting that there are multiple levels to the environment, which include tangible objects that can be read. Some of these objects are visual and dimensional, yet somehow produced through text, and others are meant to be purely textual. The general understanding of MOO objects as material things is produced by the community's understanding of the term "reading," the overwhelming use of descriptions, and MOO programming that requires characters to virtually pick up and conceptually touch and hold many MOO objects.

The comments about @kgb and @fbi also suggest that virtually looking provides characters with scopic power. Rusty indicates, "Life on the cutting edge! What does it all boil down to? WHO'S GOT INFO AND WHO DOESN'T! Those who @add-feature this baby are smugly in the former category."[65] Rusty's @kgb command provides one of the most detailed sets of information about a character.[66] Commands like @kgb, @fbi, @scope, and @report seem to be textual because they provide detailed tabulations but continue to reinscribe the MOO's visual discourse through a variety of means. For example, @kgb refers to descriptions as the character's "appearance." The user of the @report command receives the character's description and is then informed, "This is from eye-witness reports. <Character name> may be wearing different clothes at this time." The @report text indicates that MOO commands facilitate visual seeing and descriptions render clothed and embodied individuals. These descriptions highlight the ways individual characters can be documented and analyzed. For instance, the help text for @report states that it "calls up an X-File about anyone in the MOO."[67] Even the names of many of these commands, which clearly are meant to evoke voyeurism, link textual visual pleasure to power by making the MOO system into a scopic regime.

Gendered Gazing in MOOs

Yes I'm a guy, but hey this is cyberspace, right. You can be whatever you want, I'm CINDY. I love pantyhose, nylons and especially the hot lace body stocking I probably have on right now.[68]

Guest

He accidently turned himself into a female, while tampering with magic. She has long, blonde hair that reaches past her shoulders. She is wearing a short sundress, with spaghetti straps. The dark, peony pink dress is made from a thin cotton material that pinches in her small waist. The dress brushes the middle of her thighs. On her feet, she is wearing pink sandals with a two inch heel.[69]

Teal_Guest
A pretty little cumslut, on her knees, dress tugged up over the lace of her stockings. She looks up at you and you can see that her face, dress & hair are streaked & spattered with cum.[70]

Red_Guest
eyes downcast, blushing faintly. [71]

Mulvey argues that "cinematic codes create a gaze, a world and an object, thereby producing an illusion cut to the measure of desire."[72] According to her, such structures as the cinema create an architecture of belief in which a particular kind of desire is fulfilled. MOOs create a similar set of seemingly real illusions through the construction of an architecture of belief that includes erotic and sexually explicit character descriptions. It is perhaps not surprising that this series of illusions provide a number of fantasy structures for spectators. Within this fantasy context, male guests are often provided with such attributes as "tall," "tall and muscular," and the "strong, silent type."[73] Female guests, including guests that are facilitated by a male-identified spectator, are rendered as "little" and "petite" with "huge breasts," narrow waists, and a "short skirt."[74] The construction of this limited set of bodies where men are strong and women connote *"to-be-looked-at-ness,"* like Teal_Guest looking up in order to be looked at by an empowered male spectator, seems to support Mulvey's split of the gaze into active/male and passive/female.[75] The production of such stereotyped bodies may be in reaction to the ways this formula of looking is sometimes disrupted.

All characters connote *"to-be-looked-at-ness"* because spectators write descriptions so that other characters will look at them.[76] In this sense, all characters are the object of the gaze. The generic guest description states that by "definition, guests appear nondescript."[77] However, Ebony_Guest notes that "by definition, guests concoct alluring descriptions to enthrall and titillate potential partners."[78] Every character's position as the object of the virtual look is an important and as yet unexplored aspect of MOO culture. According to Silverman, feminists should also consider how men perform as objects of the gaze. In MOO settings, such actions include the ways self-identified male spectators write overly sexual female character descriptions to attract the gaze of others. Silverman questions the idea that simply "'giving' woman the gaze" can change the "scopic regime" of the dominant cinema.[79] She notes that it is more politically productive to indicate that no one can possess the gaze or escape being looked at. Male-identified MOO characters also experience the virtual looks that provide characters with detailed information.

Erotic male descriptions, which are more common among guests, may disturb the presumed naturalness of match-ups between male and female characters and attract the erotic gaze of other male characters. Male guests are often described as "hard and horny" with a "10-and-1/2-inch cock [that] stands fully erect."[80] The almost complete absence of explicitly sexual male (non-guest) character descriptions, which sometimes include height and eye color but almost never genital attributes, suggests that these descriptions do not represent an appropriate masculinity, offer an identity that spectators are willing to sustain with less anonymity, or attract a desired gaze.[81] Erotic representations of men are also resisted in such graphical communication settings as Virtual Places, which is considered in chapter 5, and homophobic exchanges are unfortunately common.

Characters sometimes become the object of the virtual look and the gaze for reasons other than their chosen and programmed gender. Characters are virtually looked at because they have a name that other characters find interesting, communicate with a character that does not recognize them, express an interesting or provocative statement while in the same room as other characters, gain notoriety from their posts to public MOO mail lists or dispute with other characters, or have their private sexual communication posted again to a MOO mail list. This suggests that the look can be part of a shared communication between characters or be turned into a more regulatory gaze when characters engage in some behavior that the community finds suspect. These forms of virtual looking have the potential to become invasive. Consistent and inexplicable bouts of being virtually looked at suggest that character attributes are being tabulated and patrolled by empowered spectators and the larger community.

The virtual look of certain characters, which seems to be penetrating into any space in order to examine other characters, renders surveillant forms of gazing. This suggests that there is a difference between the position that all characters have as the object of the look and the position that female characters are consistently culturally scripted into as the object of the gaze. It is possible to gain an equally detailed amount of information by virtually looking back. However, a returned virtual look is sometimes understood as an acceptance of an implicit request for erotic communication. Characters use "long-distance" virtual looking as a way to find appropriate net-sex partners. For instance, the character Renfair's feature object includes a gaze verb that "discreetly tells another [player] that you find them especially interesting."[82] This optical search for "appropriate" partners is supported by the emphasis on guests' eyes and descriptions of their desired partner. For instance, Silver_Guest has "green eyes" and is "looking for an interesting woman."[83] The character Create critiques the repetitive use of such devices when he ironically considers having "a description that is really cool and mysterious . . . maybe I should wear a dark cloak and have some stupid fucking twinkle in my eyes. now that would be original."[84] As Create's comments indicate, the look may sometimes be dismissed.

No one escapes specularity in MOOs, but a version of the classic cinematic looking relationship is still perpetuated. Virtually looking and gazing are too often the terrain of male-identified characters. It is not surprising that a guest that is "looking hard" is gendered as male since the optical power of the look and the phallus are associated with men in MOO settings.[85] Male characters "own" a disproportionately high number of the feature objects that make the different looking commands available. Female characters, because of their gender setting, are more likely to be the object of the virtual look. Frequent @owatched messages from female characters that are being virtually looked at, and discussions about this topic in rooms and MOO mailing lists, make the community aware of the different ways that male and female characters are viewed. Ironic descriptions, such as "I have gigantic breasts. Please hit on me relentlessly," also demonstrate how male and female characters are treated differently.[86] Some women have chosen to identify themselves as another gender in order to remove themselves from this dynamic. However, intergender characters also experience a disproportionate number of looks from male characters and are often presumed to be female.[87]

Female characters and female spectators could proactively employ virtual gazing in order to destabilize the male look. Of course, the relationship between female characters and spectators would remain largely unverified. Female-identified spectators indicate that subverting the gaze by virtually looking back is not easily accomplished. While this supports Silverman's arguments, the different ways male and female characters are virtually looked at also indicates that not all people experience specularity in the same way. Women are too often scripted as the object of the gaze in other settings. Spectators with female-identified MOO characters also quickly learn that gazing back at male characters generates such responses as "Do you like what you see?" These responses underscore the deeply ingrained visual vernacular of MOOs and indicate that virtual looking is employed to find appropriate net-sex partners. Looking back means something different from the initial process of gazing and is understood as a less powerful gesture.

In her consideration of the cinema, Doane indicates that female viewers cannot gain power by appropriating the gaze. The "male striptease" and "gigolo" represent the mechanism of reversal, are constituted as aberrations, and reinforce traditional conceptions of gender roles.[88] In MOOs, the female spectator's appropriation of the gaze reinscribes the male position by acknowledging it as the dominant model. As

Doane suggests, representations of passive male characters indicate the continued scopic power of male spectators in normative situations. Representations of male striptease have become a common Internet phenomenon. It unfortunately appears that such "men," if we presume that they are identified as such outside Internet settings, can choose to be submissive in MOOs and still assume their right to power in other environments.

Plaid_Guest
A really submissive guy, and he's really fun. . :) Please page him if you want to.[89]

Khaki_Guest
a shy but very willing submissive hoping to be discovered by a dominant female.[90]

Reading these characters as women might suggest some quite different possibilities, which would be based on performative drag masquerades, but little evidence exists for such a supposition. However, there is a great deal of lore and documentation to support the idea that men often perform as women in Internet settings. Some characters may even use narratives about magic and enforced womanhood to explain such transformations.

Mulvey's description of gendered gazing does not fully explain MOO looking. The objectifying look and gaze of male characters at available females should be disturbed by the acknowledgment, which is represented by Cindy's and other characters' descriptions, that men often construct the highly sexualized and available female characters. The binary relationship between active male and passive female should also be disordered by LambdaMOO's ten "standard" genders. However, cross-identified characters do not always describe themselves as intergender. A guest character description that reads "some fat white guy claiming to be a woman" is gendered as female.[91] Participants often believe that binary gender labels should be attached to alternative genders. For instance, Periwinkle_Guest asked an intergender character, "So, r u a male it, or a female it?"[92] The Spivak FAQ, which provided answers to frequently asked questions about intergender identification, is ironically subtitled "R U M OR F?"[93] Spectators also examine morph names and aliases in order to find clues that will indicate the spectator's "real" gender.

Requests, hysterical demands, and harassment often accompany gazes at intergender characters. Sometimes excessive methods are employed to try to determine a spectator's gender.

You sense that Infrared_Guest is looking for you in The Coat Closet.
It pages, "you are a girl, your name uis too feminine."
page infrared feminine like bobby and tony?

Your message has been sent.
You sense that Infrared_Guest is looking for you in The Coat Closet.
It pages, "Will you reveal your sex to me?"
page infrared I'm spivak
You sense that Infrared_Guest is looking for you in The Coat Closet.
It pages, "Would ypuou say hello or Hi?"
page infrared i don't know. would you?
You sense that Infrared_Guest is looking for you in The Coat Closet.
It pages, "It is obvious to me now that you are male, I am studying Psdychology."[94]

As this discussion indicates, there is a desire among some spectators to re-establish sci-entific methods, reason, and facts in Internet settings. Ideological disagreements over gender representations have resulted in the character Ibid being harassed by Downtime for having an intergender identity and in spectators having their physical whereabouts and attributes identified. These gender "problems" allow the binary of male and female to become the before and after of what becomes fictional Internet genders. Some spectators yearn for the material body when the MOO's multiple and not always clear gender positions are foregrounded. For example, the virtual bodies and objects of deceased users have been preserved. Virtual kitchens and bathrooms provide a setting for corporeal functions. However, there are no bodily requirements or wastes in Internet settings.

Mirrors and mirroring gazes also suggest that there are material bodies and spaces in MOO settings. For example, when you virtually look at "a useless mirror hung in the middle of the curve of the west wall," you see the virtual reflection of the corri-dor.[95] This suggests that lists of characters actually have a particular position and point of view within the "landscape" of the MOO. The mirroring gazes of characters produce similar spatial effects. Characters that look at Bewitch receive her description and the message that "Bewitch eyes you suspiciously." Characters seem to have a spatial rela-tionship to Bewitch when they see their own description reflected "in Bewitch's eyes."[96] These mirrors consolidate character descriptions into bodies by "reflecting" the MOO's spatial narratives and suggesting complex arrangements of objects.

The use of mirrors and the relationship between spectator and character could be interpreted as a re-invocation of Lacan's mirror stage.[97] In this stage, the child first acquires a sense of self and notices the agency of its body through a series of imagi-nary identifications and discovery of difference. Metz's employment of the mirror stage, as a way of analyzing the cinema viewer's identification with the ideal image on the screen, can also be applied to the spectator's identification with the character. However, Metz's privileging of the relationship between spectator and camera, which is further considered in chapter 6, does not have a corollary in MOO settings. In her consideration of the cinema, Doane questions the assurances that identification with the screen offers because it provides "a guarantee of the untroubled centrality and unity of the subject."[98] The use of the look and the gaze in MOOs offers the spectator a similar rendering of the empowered position and replaces the differences between spectator and character with a unified subject.

Graphical MOOs

Educational MOOs with graphical aspects, which include Diversity University and the many enCoreXpress MOOs, tend to present even more coherent spectatorial positions and settings.[99] They offer an opportunity to consider how textually rendered visual pleasure functions when there are images as well as texts. Jan Rune Holmevik and Cynthia Haynes, among others, reworked the code and concept of LambdaMOO in order to facilitate the enCoreXpress graphical user interface.[100] Their LinguaMOO project, which began in 1995 and encouraged the development of a number of educational MOOs, is used for classes, discussions about electronic writing, and other educational needs.[101] LinguaMOO's enCoreXpress server-supported graphical client provides a multisection interface and components that equate characters with individuals. Characters appear to be a form of material body because the default LinguaMOO character is represented with a fleshy pink head and torso. The connection between characters and spectators is intensified by requiring the viewer's real name and other identifying information during character registration and then making this data available through various MOO commands.[102]

The inclusion of the look command under "basic commands" in the "LinguaMOO Beginner's Guide to MOOing" and its availability as a menu "button" along the top of the browser indicate its continued importance.[103] The guide notes that to "see how the room (MOOspace) you're in looks like, just type 'look'" or "click on the LOOK button."[104] The user's guide for AlaMOO, which is another enCoreXpress MOO, explains that "looking at objects and people allows you to focus on them."[105] There are indications that "you're in" a particular space, that the "object (or person) is in the same room as you," and the programmed aspects of looking situate the individual in the setting and articulate a spatial relationship between spectators and rendered objects.[106] The placement of the body within the LinguaMOO representation and promise that textual commands and descriptions facilitate visual scenes is heightened in instances where "look room" generates visual depictions.

The link between looking and visual scenes begins immediately after connecting to LinguaMOO. The spectator is informed that "you view the Courtyard" in LinguaMOO and that "you view" things in other enCoreXpres MOOs.[107] Many of these settings repeat the LambdaMOO convention of indicating that "you see" things throughout the MOO setting. The MOO discourse about viewing and seeing and the related visual representations support the idea that texts allow spectators to look upon a physical world. For instance, the text about viewing the courtyard is accompanied by François Schuiten's visual rendering of a figure that looks out onto a spatial landscape. This figural stand-in for the spectator, which performs a function that is similar to AOL's striding body, appears in a number of LinguaMOO's visual images.[108] The LinguaMOO figure marks a place where the spectator can enter the setting, repeats the shape of the standard fleshy pink representation of the character, and connects the spectator to the character. Perspective lines direct the spectator to gaze into the rendered distance and also articulate a place for the spectator inside the screen. These renderings of entrance use some of the same conventions as academic and popular narratives about entering the Internet, depictions of doorways in varied Internet settings, and the diagonals in monitor advertisements.

LinguaMOO's login screen and the accompanying image also render an entrance.[109] An arc of trees and glowing aurora articulate a space and an unknown place, which seems about to be further illuminated, while a string of horizontal glyphs evoke code and flatness. The LinguaMOO "Welcome" indicates that there is an oscillation between materiality and words or "a new archi/TEXTural community where language and people are woven together."[110] Nevertheless, LinguaMOO and other enCoreXpress MOOs do not provide a consistent consideration of how texts and people interrelate. The current ways MOOs are conceptualized and programmed make it difficult to conceptualize a language that takes both their textual aspects and intense engagements into consideration. However, such a language could also facilitate considerations of how the Internet is written, other methods for producing settings, critiques of spectatorship, and questions about the identification and desires of viewers. As LinguaMOO indicates, this project is worth pursuing.

Conclusion: Between Multiple and Coherent Identity

It is certainly possible to focus on both body and text. MOOs already provide multiple points of identification with the morphing feature, which allows spectators to store different character descriptions, and the tendency to have characters in different settings. However, a number of the textual and graphical features of MOOs, which include the look and the gaze, encourage spectators to make their character into an ideal and cohesive image. In addition, many of the MOO's fragmenting tendencies also provide unifying possibilities. For instance, characters often use the same name on different MOO systems as a way of maintaining coherent identity, and morphs are always contained under the character's singular object number. Not only does MOO programming offer spectators, particularly those who employ a male character, the ability to form their virtual body into an ideal image, but there are also some elements and system rituals that prevent the design of these depictions from highlighting fragmentation and inadequacy.

LambdaMOO and other related text-based Internet settings seem like visual terrain because of the ability to "look" at character descriptions that have detailed physiognomic attributes. The prevalence of these renderings suggests that the bodies of spectators exist inside the setting. There are other types of character representations, but the use of the virtual look as a verifying tendency persists despite these anomalies. Female guest descriptions, which are clearly linked to male spectators, still include depictions that connote "*to-be-looked-at-ness*."[111] These descriptions perpetuate the dominant cinema's scripting of male subjects that control and look upon female objects. A troubling aspect of the MOO system is that female characters often "reply" to empowered gazes with "sleep in [their] eyes," "an innocent look," or downcast eyes.[112] This suggests that the mastering gaze also produces a corresponding passive female model. Salecl and Žižek suggest that the fascination with the "spectacle of power," and with being visual rather than having visual pleasure, is that it can entice "the other into submission."[113] These lures enable the mastering gaze of certain characters and the voyeuristic terminology of MOO commands to perpetuate a series of limiting identity constructs.

3 | Too Close to See, Too Intimate a Screen: Men, Women, and Webcams

Introduction

Internet settings often reproduce stereotyped ideas about bodies and support gendered ways of looking. Noticing and trying to rethink these Internet representations is imperative. It is also useful to consider how the gaze is sometimes disrupted in Internet settings, even if all spectators do not notice this, and the different understandings of the body that are achieved. This chapter considers how traditional ideas about body and identity are conveyed, the disempowered spectatorial positions that are produced by women's webcams, and the ways that being visual, looking, and gazing are restructured by webcam operator's practices. Women's webcams are free or low-cost representations that can be viewed when operators link a camera to a computer, employ software to deliver images, and construct web sites to frame and contextualize their representations. Despite this series of production processes, spectators often correlate the webcam to the referential or reality producing aspects of photography and other media. By suggesting an architectural entrance into women's lived spaces, webcam sites support the kinds of representations that occur in MOOs and other Internet settings and appear to deliver "real" bodies and unmediated environments. However, the promised reality of webcams is also disturbed by the overt camera processes, varied web site elements, blurred or static-infused views, and webcam operators who refuse to meet the spectator's demands.

Women's webcams do not provide spectators with an empowered gaze or access to private domains despite visual and textual promises. The refusal of women operators to furnish specific images on demand makes webcams different from "pornographic" sites that sell shows and other depictions of nude and partially clad bodies. Women webcam operators maintain control of their representations and develop a form of power by the ways that they become visible. Feminist considerations of looking and the gaze, which are also employed in chapter 2, and other theories of viewing, including the spectator's relationship to the screen, offer important methods for analyzing the positions of webcam operators and spectators. Internet and webcam spectators are close to the computer screen or even too near to see the desired images. This intimate position has been associated with women—who are believed to be in conversation with their own image—and is culturally coded as undesirable. Webcams compound this intimacy and nearness to the screen, by depicting individuals working at their computer, and propel spectators to see the way they must seem in front of the screen. This suggests that the spectator is involved or even intricately bound up with images of the self. The privileging of a distant male subject position, which is figured in such media as traditional Hollywood film, is becoming less viable as computers and close viewing experiences are increasingly incorporated into varied situations. At this point in time, the diverse valuation and functionality of the computer leaves the spectator uneasily shifting between privileged seeing and an abject near-blindness.

This unstable position provides a unique opportunity to intervene in the ways certain versions of age, class, gender, race, and sexuality are produced through spectatorship. Radical interventions into webcams and other technologies can have an effect on this developing medium and prevent new forms of empowered male spectatorship that are facilitated through closeness. It is important to note how spectatorial positions are constructed and theorize some strategies of resistance. These modes of opposition might include highlighting technological failures and observing the ways that women webcam operators maintain control of the apparatus, looking at things that the spectator cannot view, and occasionally deciding to be visibly not available. The mediated appearances of women webcam operators and the construction of selves, which occur with weblogs, "home" pages, and photo archives, suggest that sentiments about visibility are shifting. Critically studying these developments can explain how power is mediated through empowered looking, submission, and even controlled visibility.

A more detailed understanding of women's webcams is facilitated by considering the literature on webcams, their "history," women's role in running the technology and designing sites, the regulation of the spectator, the malfunctioning of viewing and voyeurism, depictions of operators looking back, and the relationship to men's webcam sites. The analysis of women's statements, web sites, and the associated literature suggest how women webcam operators intend their sites to be perceived and how being visual, looking, and gazing function in webcams. The advent of such Internet technologies and the accompanying practices of women webcam operators encourage a rethinking of how the spectator is structured to look as well as what the spectator sees. Despite the obvious import of such concepts, the spectator's distance from the screen and the incapacitated gaze remain largely unconsidered in Internet studies and computer-mediated communication literature. I hope to rectify this and encourage further writing in the field by providing information on how webcam spectatorship functions, suggesting the ways that the literature has misrepresented webcam practices, and indicating some theoretical models that can further explain computer and Internet spectatorship.

Feminism and Spectatorship

Feminist considerations of spectatorship, looking, and the gaze can suggest how women webcams operators use computer technologies to make themselves visible in controlled ways. The feminist literature employed in this chapter does not specifically address the Internet and computer but it does provide an important set of theoretical concepts for discussing spectatorship and the ways that webcam operators can gaze back. There is a wealth of feminist and gender scholarship that considers how the gaze, which can be defined as power-imbued staring, produces and enforces gendered positions. Some of this literature has already been employed in chapter 2, in order to show how looking is rendered through textual MOO narratives and how traditional forms of gazing are reproduced in Internet settings. Webcams have the potential to reinforce gender norms and provide erotic views. However, they also offer women a heightened control over their representations.

Feminist film theory suggests how the spectator's nearness to the computer screen prevents an ideal view as well as the means by which women webcam operators disable and restructure the empowered gaze. I intend for this consideration to be different from the kind of analysis that presumes visual media technologies have to be part of an objectifying process, which permits viewers to look upon and possess women's bodies. Such arguments sometimes derive from a simplistic reading of Mulvey's work on Hollywood film.[1] Mulvey has argued that the male subject looks and the object of the gaze is female. She relates this troubling binary relationship, which empowers the male viewer, to how technology and society script the male spectator into a voyeuristic position. Webcams offer a possible site of resistance to this dualistic structure of looking because the spectator is too close to the screen and the image is too fragmented for voyeurism to operate properly. Spectators and operators can begin to resist the binary logic of classical cinema and the objectifying gaze of other media by acknowledging the camera-based aspects of image production, the ways spectators look "through" technologies, and the fact that unmediated bodies and spaces are not delivered. Ignoring the constructed aspects of these representations makes it easier to institute webcam and other stereotyped representations as real.

The depictions of women webcam operators viewing the screen indicate that women look and are seen. Mulvey and a number of other scholars have rethought the connection between the gaze and patriarchal structures and tried to develop strategies to empower female spectators.[2] For instance, Doane uses instances where women look and even gaze back to envision forms of empowered female spectatorship.[3] Salecl and Žižek present a more gender-neutral conception of the gaze, describing it as a means of control and captivation with power that lures the other into submission.[4] They indicate that compliance and power can be the products as well as the instigators of the gaze. Nevertheless, certain kinds of heterosexual white men still tend to expect privileged forms of looking. The rendering of the computer as an empowering device, and its association with straight, white, and Western subjects, is troubling because it seems to provide access onto physical environments and bodies. In this chapter, I suggest how computer representations are constructed, instances of visible women viewers, and the ways incapacity also circulates in the webcam medium. Studying how spectatorial failure occurs in women's webcams can help to disable the entitled position of male users and programmers that has already been weakened by reporting of the bankruptcy and dissolution of dot com companies.

Critical and Journalistic Considerations of Webcams

A great deal of the literature about webcams focuses on the voyeuristic aspects of the medium and the "unbecoming" ways women become visible. For instance, Jesse Berst refers to webcam viewing as "virtual voyeurism."[5] John Dvorak describes the operator as an "exhibitionist who positions a cam on herself to titillate young boys."[6] In Howard A. Landman's "Sonnets to JenniCam," the potentially submissive aspects of being looked at are underscored by the mention of the "gaze" and the ways that the operator "offers up unto the world golden apples for our eyes."[7] Such comments suggest that women webcam operators too willingly relent to the sexual passions of men, enable traditional forms of spectatorship, and offer themselves up to the male gaze. Dvorak's assessment that there is "something creepy about having a camera pointing at you" is understandable because academic and popular descriptions suggest that webcams extend the spectator's body and sight into the operator's domain.[8] For example, Campanella argues that webcams "are a set of wired eyes" and a "digital extension of the human faculty of vision."[9] He briefly acknowledges the possibility that images are faked or prerecorded, but continues to support the idea that webcams allow us to "watch the real thing."[10] Simon Firth also describes these representations as a direct recording or even as an unmediated physicality when he suggests that women's webcams share "a fidelity to the moment."[11] Even if there "isn't that much to see," Steven Shaviro and others indicate that the ability to look is a key aspect of webcams.[12]

Academic and popular accounts indicate that webcams facilitate otherwise unattainable views and provide an entrance into private domains. Campanella rhapsodizes that he has "never set foot in Jerusalem, yet on most days I see the faithful gather at its Western Wall."[13] Sandra Blessum, who watches an African game reserve site, argues, "I may never get to SA (although I wish I could) but I go there EVERY day."[14] Their comments suggest that webcam sites do more than deliver pictures; they bring the spectator near otherwise distant terrain and bodies. Webcam movement, which is facilitated by the cycling of the screen, loading of images, and ongoing motion of figures, encourages Blessum to distinguish between going and being somewhere. The webcam interface renders a relationship to another place, but it never permanently places the spectator in the material environment or fully indicates that the spectator is the depicted operator. This makes the association between webcam spectator and operator different from the relationship between spectator and MOO character. Webcam spectatorship is rendered as intimate, but there are also acknowledgments of its limitations. Katharine Mieszkowski suggests that webams "offer a strange mixture of distance and intimacy," and Shaviro notes that they are "intimate, but not revealing."[15] Unfortunately, this intimacy is never related to the spectator's closeness to the computer screen.

Kristine Blair and Pamela Takayoshi briefly suggest that Jennifer Ringley may have some control over men's views of her webcam. However, they conclude that the "addressed and invoked audience for Jennifer's site is male, a creation of an image by a woman for a man."[16] My study of webcams, which considers the ways women control the technologies, act as viewers and fans, and refuse to respond to spectators' demands, suggests that Blair and Takayoshi's analysis of webcam spectatorship is incorrect. Their reading also risks damaging feminist politics, visibility, and empowerment. Feminist interventions into Internet representations should note the many women Internet spectators and producers. Treating the work of women webcam operators and other Internet producers as significant forms of cultural production acknowledges their interests and values. Suggesting that this medium is produced, directed, or employed only by men prevents a broader understanding of how interfaces function and can also prevent women from intervening in the more troubling aspects of Internet images and ideas; it also makes women distressingly invisible.

This chapter presents a different account than most of the webcam literature. I suggest that there are positive political aspects of women's webcams, which include the operators' defiant modes of address and resistance to fully producing images for the male gaze. In this study, I want to avoid replicating the concepts of Victor Burgin, Katharine Mieszkowski, and other writers who suggest that girls and young women are the only ones who portray themselves with webcams and thereby reduce their production strategies to childish practices, a transitional stage, and "rights of passage."[17] A productive cultural analysis should acknowledge the different people who use such Internet technologies as webcams at the same time as it attempts to theorize how these systems function. Only a study that addresses both personal statements and larger genre-wide trends can indicate the significant ways that looking and being looked at empower and subdue the individual.

Webcams

Webcams are sometimes called cams, livecams, homecams, or netcams. They periodically make images available to other Internet spectators through a web page.[18] The loading of new webcam images may occur as frequently as every few seconds or as infrequently as every few hours. There are also many instances when the webcam interface does not deliver any image, or at least any representation of something that is currently happening in front of the camera. A higher bandwidth can facilitate "streaming video," which may be described as "moving images," but it still provides the spectator with a staccato view or a sequence of stills.[19] Despite these delivery problems, various Internet dictionaries and webcam sites suggest that one of the key aspects of webcams is "liveness" and the way it delivers, or at least seems to deliver, "real-time" images.

Narratives about real time are an important aspect of the Internet, make settings seem real, and promise the spectator particular kinds of experiences. Real-time events occur at roughly the same speed that they would in "real life" so the highly simulated aspects of computer technologies are easier to displace.[20] Real time is understood as "sufficiently immediate."[21] Computers and other technologies produce real time but this facilitation is displaced. Margaret Morse indicates that computers simulate duration in ways that elide their extensive information processing and what occurs inside the computer.[22] The differences between the viewer and Internet representations can be partially displaced by relating the lived time of the individual to the real time of computers and webcams. This makes images seem like a physical setting that can be entered by the spectator.

The spectator is also encouraged to engage with webcam images as an unmediated reality because of the references to photography. The webcam is described as a "camera designed to take digital photographs."[23] Such statements invite spectators to ignore the constructed aspects of webcam images and the different media available on web-cam sites. The spectator's investment in photographs and webcams is based on the assumption that the camera has recorded the trace of an object that was in front of it, which Barthes refers to as *"that-has-been,"* and that viewing the image is like looking at the object and being in the moment.[24] Photographs are, according to Rosalind Krauss, "a kind of deposit of the real itself" because of the ways that light renders images and the visual similarities between the reproduction and what it depicts.[25] Webcams are also believed to deliver images that are the same as the depicted scene, although image breakdown, resolution problems, and their two-dimensionality make the images distinctly different from the operator's home space.[26] The mechanical and automatic qualities of the photography and webcam apparatus are thought to guaran-tee the unbiased rendering of a particular scene. Society has associated photography, webcams, and other digital images with the real because of these effects.

Early webcam views of fish tanks and coffeemakers seemed to deliver real and unmediated objects because of the simplicity of the visual shapes. In 1991, Quentin Stafford-Fraser and Paul Jardetzky, who were Cambridge University computer scien-tists, wrote some programs in order to present images of their coffeepot over a local network before the advent of the web.[27] Such "histories" suggest that webcams were employed as a way of providing a voyeuristic position with views of a changing spatial environment, since the fish's position and the level of coffee changed, but at the same time resisted total infiltration into operators' lives and intimate environ-ments. It is also likely that the low resolution of early webcam images and the length of time that it took for images to load determined the genre's conventions. These early chronicles indicate spectators' investment in the documentary aspects of webcams, the level of engagement operators had with their computers (since they were unwill-ing to disengage if there was no coffee), and the ways they employed the computer as a tool to map their local environment.

Some webcams still display coffee pots and fish tanks but there are also representa-tions of other animals, buildings, erotica, live events, people in their homes and offices, traffic, outdoor scenery, and weather. There has also been a significant increase in the number of webcams available as operators explore the possibilities of the medi-um. Worldwide Webcam Sites offered links to over 10,000 webcam-related sites in May 1999; 26,000 in December 2000; and 42,000 in September 2004.[28] This increase is based on the availability of cheaper webcams and Internet service providers, faster Internet downloads, more "user-friendly" webcam installations, heightened press cov-erage, and the growing public acceptance of this medium. Individual operators prob-ably encouraged the acceptability of webcams by quoting already established popular practices.

The webcam vernacular borrows from documentary and autobiographical genres. The contemporary fascination with packaging people's lives into documentary kinds of entertainment and the desire to surreptitiously watch people's most intimate moments is figured in recent films like *The Truman Show* (Peter Weir, 1998). Such artists as Laurie Anderson, Joseph Beuys, Karen Finley, Holly Hughes, Adrian Piper, and Carollee Schneeman produce works that seem to "share" their lives with the audience. Other artists, including Ana Voog and Julia Scher, have employed webcams in their work. The indication that people are presenting their home spaces and personal lives through webcams is related to such documentary explorations as PBS's *An American Family*, which represented the private lives of the Loud family on public television in 1973. Webcams are also related to the reality television genre, including such shows as *American Idol*, *Big Brother*, *Cops*, *Court TV*, *The Real World*, *Room Raiders*, and *Survivor*. Reality television provides viewers with lifestyle reassurances, since the interactions can be banal, and the voyeuristic thrill of watching "real" people going about their daily lives.

These media practices can provide a background for webcams, but there are also distinct production and spectatorial differences. For instance, reality television shows are usually taped rather than broadcast live. This allows these shows to be both "real" and highly edited in order to produce a more interesting story through the privileging of particular narrative plot developments. Such conventions as hearing participants' private conversations and testimonials about each other are as contextually important as seeing what people are doing. Webcams present individuals in unedited—at least in the sense this term is used in television—but still highly mediated real time. Interactions often remain incomprehensible because most webcam images are not accompanied by any diegetic sound. This means that viewers are reliant on visual cues in order to determine the action. However, "action" may be the improper word to describe images that often feature a webcam operator in front of a computer. JennyLee comments on this problem of inactivity in webcam views by titling her pop-up window "They're alive!!"[29] She states that "gamers are known to not move for a few hours at a time." This suggests that the position of the depicted subjects can be so static that the spectator may not be sure if the webcam is delivering new images or a steady stream of the same depiction.

In some more complex web sites, the presence of multiple webcams as well as the addition of diaries, chat forums, and other chronicles allows the spectator to weave a narrative and provide some kind of action. More important, these materials contextualize the webcam's otherwise unstable images and act as meaning producing mechanisms. Sometimes visual and material experiences are conveyed through written texts.

These devices suggest that the spectator has a privileged position and can gaze onto a compliant object, since there are multiple "entrances" into the webcam operator's personal life. For instance, Christopher R. Smit argues that "because these women, the Other, are available as images, they are seen as objects."[30] Even the shape of many webcams, a white orb with a smaller inset lens, is designed to indicate that the webcam facilitates a geographically unbounded human eye and empowered sight. This design implies that the spectator's body, or at least eye, has been incorporated into some larger seeing and surveying mechanism. However, impermanent and often illegible webcam images, as well as women webcam operators' control over sites, suggest a much more ambivalent relationship between the viewing "subject" and the "object" of contemplation.

Women and Webcams

Numerous women and men present their images on webcam sites. Ringley, who ran JenniCam from April 1996 through December 2003, is often credited with starting the "lifecam" trend (figure 3.1).[31] However, Teresa Senft has stated that Danni Ashe began her webcam site, which is designed for a "pornographic" market, two years earlier.[32] It seems that Ringley's combination of innocence and erotic possibility offered the media a more palatable vision of the webcam genre. Women's "lifecams" or "homecams" are slightly different from Ashe's site because the material is mainly representations of the woman in her home environment rather than eroticized performances designed for the camera. Of course, Ringley and a variety of operators have also offered shows and other scheduled events. Ringley has received her share of negative press. Her site was "the target of Roman Catholic wrath" as part of an attempt to promote Internet "morality."[33] There was a public outcry among JenniCam fans when Ringley became involved with a friend's boyfriend and documented the whole process on her web site. Her Paypal account, which allowed spectators to pay for site memberships, was canceled because of the availability of nude images.[34]

The continued importance of Ringley's project within the growing webcam subculture is suggested by the inclusion of JenniCam in webcam definitions and the many news stories about her terminating the site.[35] The What Is dictionary site notes that some "cams are in people's offices or homes. Probably the most famous is the Jennicam, which is in the home of a 'tall redhead.'"[36] If there is a history of webcams, then academic, popular, and webcam communities have all credited Ringley, rather than a hardware designer, with playing a key part or even "inventing" this practice. Ringley's own version of the "historical" narrative focuses on the move from whimsical

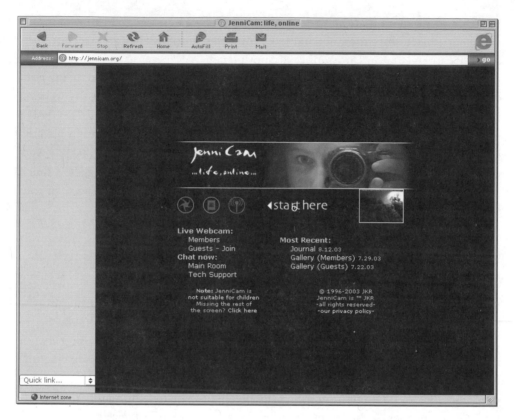

Figure 3.1
Jennifer Ringley, "JenniCam: Life, Online," 21 Nov. 2003, <http://www.jennicam.com/>.

exploration to the medium's more weighty implications: "JenniCam was started in April of 1996, when I was a junior in college. It was intended to be a fun way my mom or friends could keep tabs on me, and an interesting use for the digital camera I bought on a whim in the bookstore. I never really contemplated the ramifications of it."[37] Ringley's story of flighty discovery, which downplays the skills of the operator, is not that different from accounts by and about much earlier women photographers, such as Julia Margaret Cameron, Imogen Cunningham, and Eudora Welty, whose works continue to play a significant part in the photographic medium.

The comments of Ringley and other women webcam operators suggest that there are notable "ramifications" to running a webcam site. I am using the term "webcam operator" in an attempt to emphasize the significant work that women do in technologically, visually, and conceptually sustaining this practice. The more advanced sites, which run twenty-four hours a day, offer multiple webcam views, chat forums, and other features, and require a monetary investment and a great deal of technical upkeep. However, women webcam operators' commitment to the technology and continued development of their sites is too often downplayed in the critical and popular literature. Women webcam operators' complex skills are denigrated by the convention of describing them as "cam girls" and the suggestion that they pander to spectators in order to receive gifts and other favors.

The webcam operator's age and the content of the site have no effect on the tendency among spectators to use the cam girl label. Instead, this term has unfortunately encouraged spectators to simultaneously infantilize and eroticize women webcam operators. Even some operators are intolerant of certain webcam practices. Alicia Grace tells her spectators, "Don't call me a cam girl! I have a website and it happens to have a cam. I'm not one of those pathetic 14 year olds that runs around naked to impress some old geezer that will buy her cdnow gift certificates."[38] In "Candy from Strangers," Mieszkowski supports this description and describes webcams as an "online beg-fest" where teenagers "as young as 15 are getting into the act of asking for handouts."[39] The cam girl label suggests to spectators that women will respond to monetary rewards with personal favors, always be visibly available on the webcam, able to "chat" and respond to email on demand, recognize individuals by waving or holding up their name to the camera, smile and look happy while they are depicted, offer nude pictures or other salacious material in their archives, and flash their breasts or reveal other body parts on the webcam. These expectations have caused problems and even contestations within the webcam medium.

Regulating the Spectator

Detailed requests or even demands for women webcam operators to reveal themselves are quite common. Aimee parodies the conventions of the medium, conceptions of cam girls, and the expectations of spectators. She reacted to a directive that she appear naked by facetiously "offering" to "get out my sequined thong and dance around for you, just like in those strip bars that I secretly work in when I'm not out being a prostitute or making porn movies (you know that all women with web cameras do at least one of these things)."[40] Aimee's visible efforts to change the behavior of spectators through humiliation and critical commentary are representative of a larger trend among women webcam operators to regulate the spectator and maintain control over representations. For instance, Messy offers information so that spectators can instant message her, but she also advises, "But for fuck's sake, if she's busy, PISS OFF!"[41] Julie bans spectators from viewing her domain if they are disruptive.[42] Through these strategies, women webcam operators force the webcam technology and a set of presumed promises about the sexual availability and submissiveness of women to fail.

Comments by webcam operators in their rules, FAQs (frequently asked questions), and other postings establish a set of strikingly similar legislated behaviors that spectators must follow if they want to watch and perhaps synchronously communicate with the webcam operator through site-specific software. Justice informs her viewers, "You won't see me naked" and "You won't see me taking requests to smile, wave, blow kisses."[43] Cindy reminds her viewers, "I am not your virtual puppet. . . . I will not smile for you."[44] Kathy states, "I don't do requests and I don't do nudity. So don't ask."[45] Even webcam operators like Elektric who offer more explicit content such as "walking around nude" warn spectators that demanding things is rude and that she "will do what I want to do when I want to do it."[46] Such comments suggest the ways women webcam operators establish their power in interactions with spectators.

Power is structured in unique ways because women run, control, and depict themselves on their webcams. Assertions by women that they control the apparatus are an essential part of the webcam genre. For instance, Aimee suggests that webcams are "almost like being on your own TV show except that you own the network and make all the decisions. I can broadcast when I like and what I like."[47] Saski argues, "Nobody can tell you what to do or what not to do. It is a very creative and controllable form of expression."[48] Andi and Julie indicate that they can be in control and do what they want because they do not charge membership fees to spectators.[49] However, women webcam operators who charge membership fees to view their sites also put limits on their availability. It is always clear that the webcam is contained within the woman webcam operator's terrain and that the view may be terminated at any time. Even in cases where the technical maintenance or the economics of pay sites are managed by a boyfriend, girlfriend, partner, or some other person, the woman operator still largely determines how she addresses the webcam from moment to moment.

Women assert control over when they are available and what can be seen even though they may design sites in which their bodies are represented as erotic objects and allow spectators—both male and female—to look. Women webcam operators' narratives of control, which include doing what they want and changing the site, indicate that there are active as well as passive objects of contemplation. If the spectator is fixed in front of the screen, and waiting for the operator to provide a desired view, then it may be the operator rather than the spectator who is active and empowered. It is possible to dismiss these instances of control, which are achieved through the particular dynamics of webcam settings and may not work in other situations. However, men also gain control through the body, as suggested in the afterword, even when this power is achieved by denying fleshy forms of embodiment.

Operators like Messy make it clear that women's control of their webcams include the possibility of being visibly not visible. She warns her viewers that they should not expect her to be available at certain times and that she "turns off this cam when DOING IT."[50] Resistance and a kind of violence to the spectator's vision are important parts of women webcam operators' practices. Messy and Aimee address their spectators as "dumbass," "fuggin' twit," and "freak," and they "giggle at the intensity of the ignorance" that is so unbelievable that at least Messy wants "to poison the water supply."[51] Their obstruction of the spectator's demands and "right of way" are in conflict with indications that the Internet offers "direct access" to information and communication.[52] Women webcam operators' comments about control, as well as the problems that arise when women webcam operators assert authority over their representations, suggest the deeply contested stakes in webcam spectatorship as well as other processes of gazing.

Women Webcam Operators and Authority

The many documented cases of harassment, which appear on women's webcam sites, perpetuate conversations about operators' erotic limits and suggest that spectators can get attention through abusive tactics.[53] The posting of these cases suggests that operators' assertions that they "don't really care what anyone else thinks" may be self-protective and deceptive, an attempt to work through the comments about their bodies and a form of bravado. It would be simplistic and unproductive to suggest that women webcam operators are the passive "victims" of harassment. In some cases, bold personal statements and attempts to humiliate certain spectators have encouraged further unpleasant engagements. For instance, Aimee has a "Freak of the Week" section and "Freak Archive" in which she presents "insulting emails" that she makes fun of and critiques.[54] Operators like Aimee put themselves in a precarious position because they have an extremely difficult time extricating themselves from unpleasant and unproductive conversations. These confrontations are about the ability of women to control their own image and the views that spectators want to receive. Webcam sites are a hybrid structure in which internal fights for power between operators and spectators shape the genre. It is these confrontations rather than links or URLs that seem to structure the spectator's engagement.[55]

Cindy's animated opening sequence suggests the ways bodily visibility is articulated in this medium and the contradictions that still occur.[56] Cindy's site is designed in shades of bubblegum pink and purple. In the animation, a spinning cartoon flower attracts a bee. The spectator (bee) is drawn into a voyeuristic relationship and promised that she is "sexy, smart, alluring." This descriptive text seems to link this webcam to sites where the spectator pays for live shows, still images of naked women, and other services. However, the spectator is also advised that she is "never naked." The "but never naked" limits that Cindy places on her visibility can offer an erotic agency and high level of control to women webcam operators. However, it also explains the unruly behavior of many spectators. Many women webcam operators' statements about nudity become confusing. For example, Amy states that "anything goes" on her webcam but then notes that there is "no nudity."[57] It remains unclear what "anything goes" might mean since Amy has clear limits about what she wants to depict on her webcam. Aimee's and Cindy Roberts's notices that their sites are not pornographic are posted next to directions to "click here" for erotica.[58] The generic "here" in such directions implies that the spectator can, perhaps with some persistence, access nude images of the operator. Writers like Simon Firth even indicate that the rarity of the "glimpse" makes it all the more desirable.[59]

Barthes' work also suggests that webcams engage the spectator through an erotic of unexpected and fragmentary unveilings. He indicates that it is the "intermittence of skin flashing between two articles of clothing (trousers and sweater) between two edges (the open-necked shirt, the glove, and the sleeve); it is this flash itself which seduces, or rather: the staging of an appearance-as-disappearance."[60] Women webcam operators are seductive because of their brief depictions of skin. In other cases, the shivering movement of the webcam image downloading and unfolding entices and mesmerizes. The postponed and misdirected desires of webcam spectators, who never get to control what happens on the screen and see the body for any length of time, and the possible pleasurable masochism of spectatorship, which Leo Bersani theorizes, perpetuate a frustrated engagement.[61] Delays in receiving the expected information are also an important aspect of emailing, gaming, and "synchronous" communications. Internet spectators may stay engaged because of these aspects of waiting and possible futures rather than the promised immediacy and present.

Spectators react to this yearning and engage with operators in different ways. The About site's profiles of webcam operators, which include brief answers to a set of questions, indicate the strikingly different ways that viewers treat women and men operators. Many of the women answered the question "Is there an incident that has annoyed you so much you considered shutting off the cam for good?" by stating that they had considered quitting, had taken a break, or were bothered because of harassment.[62] Most of the men declared that they had not experienced any problems.[63]

Roberts wonders "why internet 'viewers' feel it's okay to criticize, slander, and down-right harass webcam women on the internet?"[64] The many webcam operators who have decided to stop having a site are as striking as the enormous number of people participating in this type of heightened visibility. However, women find a variety of ways to use webcams for their benefit despite the negative aspects of the medium.

Visibility and Webcams

Women's narratives about the ways they employ the technology discredit the pre-sumption that women become visible in order to meet the desires of spectators and to submit to a controlling gaze. A study of FAQs and About profiles indicates that many women webcam operators started using webcams in order to communicate with friends and family.[65] Women are interested in learning about the technology and "working through" some of their problems as well as being visible.[66] For instance, Ringley has described her early engagement with webcams as a way to learn about the technology and allow family to keep in contact.[67] Aimee also notes that she "just wanted to see if I could do it and it's a nifty way to let my friends and family check up on me every now and then."[68] Many women webcam operators produce sites in order to develop and advertise their computer skills. Amy indicates that the webcam site is an opportunity to "work on my html skills," and Mandy reports that it is an "outlet for me to showcase my creativity and some of my computer skills."[69] Ali also enjoys "designing the site and coming up with more features more than I do having the cam. The cam is just a way to get people to come to the site."[70] As these comments indicate, webcams provide women with a way to attract spectators to their web sites, and some women are more engaged with the Internet technologies than with being visible on the webcam.

Webcam spectators also fulfill the needs of operators by contributing money to sup-port the site, making fan art of the operator for the archives, and functioning as a kind of "surveillance system" or "security cam."[71] Many women webcam operators indicate that spectators protect their belongings and make sure that nothing happens to them. For instance, Roberts posted hate mail that she had received as well as the sender's address and "he got mail bombed" by her "regular viewers."[72] Films and other media texts may suggest that being available to the gaze can be dangerous, but a number of women feel safe and even comfortable while they are being watched:

I am very comfortable with people watching me. If I wasn't, I wouldn't be doing this. I am a rather shy person by nature, and being in front of the camera is very therapeutic for me. It allows me to "come out of my shell," but still maintain some distance. I feel very safe knowing that peo-ple are out there watching amy cam at all times of the day/night.[73]

It can be very comforting knowing there are people on the other side of the cameras, just checking in to see what's going on. . . . I've always been pretty shy with people, especially when we first meet. I've been able to open up a lot more through my website and cameras.[74]

Comments by Amy, Izzi, and other women webcam operators suggest that they accept being visually represented, the surveillant effect of technologies, and the social regulation that can result from being watched because being invisible is even more unappealing. Genres such as the slasher and stalker film have focused on the terrifying possibilities of being in the dark and out of the watchful and protective gaze of society. These films have indicated that there are ways of being properly visible and protected and ways of being endangered through obsessive and invisible surveillance. People also have similar concerns about webcams. For instance, Aimee reports that her family has worried "constantly if anyone will be able to stalk me, find me, kill me, etc etc. I remind them that could happen without the whole webcam thing."[75] But Roberts warns prospective webcam operators to avoid providing personal information and indicates that stalking does occur.[76]

The "Digital Babylon" episode of the science fiction television series *Level 9* (2000) goes even further than Roberts in suggesting the degree to which women are endangered when they employ webcams. It depicts the stalking and killing of women who do live webcam sex shows. In the television episode, the "live" material from the murders is then offered to a fascinated and horrified Internet audience. The reactions of most of the case investigators and spectators indicate that women webcam operators are too sexually available and improperly visible. The characters in the television program suggest that these women are taking unnecessary risks, even though they are only selling representations. News programs, talk shows, and other media encourage women to submit to being visible for their own safety and suggest that they remain on populated paths, in well-lighted corridors, and within the safe purview of surveillance cameras. The *Level 9* episode and these other media may seem to present conflicting "advice" on visibility. However, they all discourage women from being sexually and erotically engaged with their own image.

Being visible and allowing others to look is believed to disempower women. Foucault indicates that individuals who are knowingly "subjected to a field of visibility" learn to regulate their behavior because of potential physical and social reprisals.[77] Women webcam operators place themselves in a field of visibility. Some of them set up their own version of surveillant protection with webcams. However, their comments indicate that the controlled forms of visibility, which they choose, provide a much more empowering position than submitting to traditional forms of the gaze. Women webcam operators have more control over when and how they are visible than spectators have over the availability of their MOO characters. Carol Clover suggests that women who curb their sexuality and adopt an androgynous persona survive in slasher films.[78] However, some women webcam operators indicate that they gain a protective visibility and form of empowerment through their sexuality rather than at its expense. Their position resists traditional media narratives, which indicate that women will be punished for being sexual. Operators like Elektric enjoy "living out" their "exhibitionist tendencies."[79] Personal expressions of comfort and potentially pleasurable women's activities occur in webcam practices even though the media provides women operators with contrary messages.

Making Texts Real

Women webcam operators constitute a significant part of the viewing audience. They highlight their interest in particular women webcam operators and construction of a type of community by participating in synchronous webcam communication forums, contributing to fan sites, and posting to other operators' Internet weblogs and LiveJournals. During a contest to nominate the best female webcam operator, women enthusiastically reviewed sites and credited Voog and others with bringing them to the genre.[80] On the About site, women webcam operators like Ali, Charity, and Lilith also credited Voog and Ringley for their interest in webcams.[81] In such forums, women webcam operators have been much more likely to credit other women than men for inspiring them to start their own webcam site. Women's engagement with spectators and other operators allows them to produce a communal setting.

Unfortunately, such options also encourage operators and spectators to understand Internet representations as physical people. Women webcam operators use a variety of effects in order to make images and texts seem like a physical world. These strategies are part of the larger tendency to render Internet settings as material, spatial, and alive. For instance, the slogan for Jennifer Ringley's webcam site is "life, online" (figure 3.1).[82] The spectator is "welcomed" and encouraged to "enter" into the personal environment of the webcam operator. Gwen's advertisement encourages the spectator to "enter the life of a college student," while Mandy's invites the spectator to "look into [her] life."[83] Amy offers a "Welcome to AMYCAM, also known as The World I Know" on her opening page.[84] Such greetings suggest that the spectator has entered into a private domain and will gain intimate views of personal happenings. As I have already suggested, textual and visual representations of entering support claims of realness and authenticity. They suggest that physicality and presence are possible through the Internet. Such terms as "life," "live," and "real" are used within the webcam genre as well as in other Internet settings in an attempt to make Internet representations into a kind of physical and material reality.

Women operators make over sequential webcam representations so that they seem to provide spectators with the woman's body. There are also depictions of operators exiting the screen and presumably being physically present in the spectator's lived space. For instance, Aimee's flash-animated sequence depicts the spectator trying to program the computer to download her site as the site is actually loading (figure 3.2).[85] The depiction of Aimee breaches the monitor's glass and case and "walks" into the spectator's space with an erotic swing of her hips. Voog's flash sequence also represents her dogs leaving the computer monitor.[86] These animations render the computer as a porous window that provides access to a physical reality rather than a processor that renders representations.

Spectators support narratives about Internet access when they equate webcam viewing with having a physical relationship with the operator. For instance, Marius writes about being with Ringley and spending "countless hours together on your couch and in your bed."[87] Shaviro describes viewing as a physical invasion where Ringley has "allowed me, a stranger, into her bedroom" and this "body, this image, could be anyone's for the taking."[88] Shaviro points to one of the problems with webcam viewing and an inherent problem with the way photography is often perceived without fully critiquing it. In his descriptions, the availability of representations is conflated with the availability of bodies and spaces. Webcam sites rely on our willingness to connect digital images with photographs and to believe that we are receiving unmediated traces of the real or a virtual body that is still made of flesh. Shaviro suggests that the webcam spectator is allowed an intimate view and even to possess people's bodies but still does not have access to their thoughts and motivations; oddly, it is the virtual that still eludes the spectator.

Some Problems with Webcam Viewing

A number of aspects of the webcam technology prevent the spectator from achieving a seamless engagement with exposed and vulnerable bodies. These elements include the incremental appearance of the image, scrambled surfaces or "noise," the loss of image at the edge, the visibility of the pixels, and the omnipresence of the square format (figure 3.3). Webcam images of women, as well as other subjects, do not facilitate contemplation by remaining still or moving in a fluid way. The "edges" appear to be constantly in motion because images are downloaded incrementally. The full view

Figure 3.2
Aimee, "A Cam Girl Dot Com, a Free Live Web Cam Site," 21 Nov. 2003, <http://www
.acamgirl.com/>.

rarely remains accessible for any length of time. This means that the spectator is not
fully able to recognize things before they are replaced by another image. The computer interface promises both interactivity and a kind of manipulable content. However,
the rates at which webcam images flicker, appear, and disappear as well as the behavior of women operators remain out of the spectator's control. Banner advertisements
and other moving features magnify the effect of these flickering images. This constant
movement displaces any possibility of a contemplative viewing experience. Barthes'
work suggests that this flickering is an erotic aspect of the medium. However, the flickering also offers a place in which to resist claims that webcams deliver "real" views of
bodies and environments. It indicates that there are a variety of representations rather
than a unified perspective.

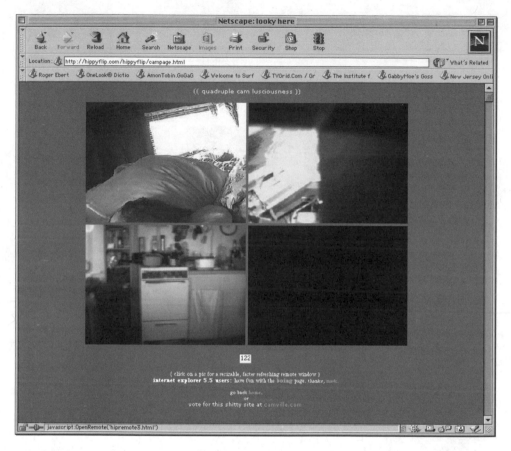

Figure 3.3
Hippyflip, "Looky Here," 20 Dec. 2000, <http://www.hippyflip.com/hippyflip/campage.html>.

Even the flickering is not always delivered. Many webcam sites promise consistent and unlimited access. For instance, Izzi notes that her webcam is "24/7/365 (wait, I will spell that out . . . twentyfourhoursaday slash sevendaysaweek slash threehundredandsixtyfivedaysayear) look into my life."[89] Despite the promises of Izzi and other operators, the webcam provides both liveness and rupture. Webcams are often unavailable because of technological reasons, or because the webcam operator has decided to take some time off or has changed site hosting. It is difficult to follow any particular webcam, research specific webcam sites, and update quotes because of the constant changes, disappearances, and reappearances of webcams. The exactness of time and date stamps also makes it clear that the spectator is only receiving sections of the view. There are lapses in time or missing parts of the visual narrative because of the ways images are delivered. This makes webcams appear to be more ruptured and partial than MOO texts. Webcam representations of women are neither moving nor still. They are part of an unfinished sequence that never achieves completion.

The unfinished and incomplete aspects of webcam viewing suggest that the spectator is too close to see the desired images of women. The spectator often obtains partial views because the woman webcam operator is near the camera lens. Instead of a fetishistic array of breasts, buttocks, and legs that are presented by the Hollywood cinema, promised in the webcam advertisements, and critiqued by Mulvey and others, the brief and often unidentifiable glimpses of women webcam operators prevent the spectator from gazing upon the desired body and gaining control.[90] The impression of an almost claustrophobic closeness, in which the spectator seems to be pushed up against the screen, is supported by the grainy and otherwise illegible images that webcams deliver. When the spectator's image is reflected on the screen and both spectator and operator are working at the computer, then they seem to be conjoined. Rather than the singular and empowered spectator indicated by apparatus theory and promised by Internet sites, this morphed position may be closer to the fragmented and unstable forms of identification proposed by Lacan, other psychoanalysts, and feminist film theorists. Vivian Sobchack relates such morphed experiences to computers.[91] These aspects of webcam spectatorship, and the qualities of digital imaging that are analyzed later in this book, indicate that Internet sites render bodily morphing and synthesis even though there are continued narratives about individual and empowered users.

Internet and computer spectators are already much too close to the screen in order to enact a classic film viewing position. Metz suggests that a clear distinction between subject and object and distance are necessary aspects of voyeurism—a process where individuals derive pleasure from secretly watching. He relates the voyeur's care in maintaining an "empty space" between the viewer and object to the ways cinema spectators avoid being too near or far from the screen.[92] Burch also indicates that it is necessary to see the whole visual field in order to have a comprehensive understanding.[93] According to their apparatus-based theories, male cinema viewers achieve an ideal spectatorial position because of their physical distance and intellectual detachment from the screen. However, female spectators are conceived as being inextricably bound to their bodily processes, tied to a version of their image within the screen, and thus unable to completely comprehend the text.[94]

Many photography and visual image critics are also invested in spectatorial distance. For instance, Susan Sontag indicates that there has to be "a distance" and "some detachment" between photographer and object.[95] Bolter notes that intellectual and emotional "distancing" is always an important aspect of reading and viewing.[96] The Internet spectator, like the photographer, reader, and cinema viewer, is expected to attain a complete, well-focused, and critical view when at a distance. However, Internet and computer viewing are intimate activities, and the spectator becomes wrapped up in the image rather than being able to grasp the whole representation. MOO and other spectators identify with the characters "built" in various Internet settings and seek out social and erotic interactions through these representations. Computers and software programs are seen as an extension of the individual when information is retrieved with the aid of the browser's hand-pointer. In this sense, all Internet spectators become collapsed with the computer and may fail to distinguish where subject ends and object begins.

Apparatus theory and the work of Metz indicate that the closeness of Internet and computer spectatorship is troubling because to "fill in this distance would threaten to overwhelm the subject, to lead him to consume the object (the object which is now too close so that he cannot see it anymore)."[97] So the spectator engages with the Internet and computer and is too close to see the desired view of the webcam operator. Or rather, Internet and computer spectators may see in ways that are more partial than cinema spectators and more enmeshed with the screen. The spectator, who is both subject and image, is situated in a position of intimate connection with the screen that has been associated with women and perceived to be undesirable. This suggests a certain feminization of the computer spectator, which may be connected to the portrayal of obsessive male computer users as abnormal and not "appropriately" masculine.

These aspects prevent the webcam spectator from achieving a voyeuristic position and attaining sexual gratification from seeing.[98] Nevertheless, webcam sites highlight the potentially voyeuristic aspects of the medium with such representations as Messy's binoculars, Gwen's fishbowls, and someone peeping.[99] Campanella describes webcam spectators as "armchair voyeurs" and Mike Musgrove characterizes JenniCam as a "voyeur Web site."[100] Wikked evokes *The Truman Show* and cultural narratives about surveillance by calling her page "Live: The Wikked Show" and "The View Out Of My Monitor (20 second updates) Brought to You by Big Brother."[101] However, webcam sites also suggest some of the problems with the voyeuristic aspects of the medium. For instance, the Camgirls' web ring logo depicts an eye pressed up against the keyhole so that the spectator is on the "wrong" side of the door and the view is blocked (figure 3.4).[102] Messy's refusal to respond to her fans and the almost illegible image inside Gwen's fishbowl also prevent viewing. For voyeurism to function, the view must seem under the spectator's control and to fulfill his or her desires.[103] Yet in the webcam medium, the FAQs and other declarations, representations, and images resist the spectator's desires and demands.

The instability of the webcam spectator's control over the image is also rendered by descriptions of such brief views as a "peek into the life" and a "peep into the room" rather than portrayals of a steady gaze.[104] Women webcam operators only ambivalently connote Mulvey's *"to-be-looked-at-ness"*—that which is to be looked at—because they are not readily available.[105] Certainly, there are plenty of still images where women are leaning back passively in chairs, being "caught" half dressed, reclining on beds or on the floor, sleepily relaxing in bathtubs, and bending over so that their cleavage or buttocks are revealed. Angled webcams, which render a view "into" the webcam operator's cleavage, are a common advertising convention on women's ranking pages. However, Roger Ebert contends that spectators serve the desires of the woman webcam operator and that he would be uncomfortable participating in "Jenni's game" because it would make him "a prop in her sex life."[106]

Ebert's description also indicates that women webcam operators resist classic spectatorial positions. Cultural narratives and critical theories of spectatorship suggest spectators usually read the person that they are viewing as an object. However, the webcam spectator cannot have the usual identification with the apparatus because the woman, who would be scripted as the object of the gaze by the classical cinema, notes

Figure 3.4
CamGirls Ring, 21 Nov. 2003, <http://www.camgirlsring.com>.

her control of the apparatus with phrases like "my webcam." The self-depictions of women webcam operators, which appear on many sites, also underscore the idea that women command and see through the medium. For instance, Ringley depicts the top portion of her face in a title banner (figure 3.1).[107] She holds a camera up so that the mechanism supplants one of her eyes and emphasizes her control of the technology. Her gesture echoes the self-portraits of many photographers. More interesting, a fuzzy depiction, which is reflected on her camera lens, appears to be the body of the spectator. The image suggests that Ringley can see her spectators and control them by employing her surveillant lens and empowered gaze.

Women's empowered sight is also underscored by depictions of eyes that are featured on other sites. Sometimes, like in the instance of the eye peeping through the keyhole, these images are meant to evoke male voyeurism but instead support the woman webcam operator's alliance with the camera and enabled sight. Classic voyeurism and the "male gaze" are destabilized by webcam practices because many of these depictions represent women's eyes. For instance, Aimee includes a graphic depiction of elaborately made-up eyes perched on top of the webcam frame so that the spectator is unblinkingly surveyed while watching the screen.[108] In a flash sequence, Voog depicts her eyes surveying the space like searchlights.[109] Alicia and Fabiana's site features a grainy black and white image of two eyes.[110] An eye from each of the webcam operators brackets their welcome text. The ability to combine these eyes into a unified body or point of view is disturbed by the physiognomic differences in these representations and the body reversal, which places a right eye on the left side of the image and a left eye on the right side. Such shifted points of view suggest the power reversal between operator and spectator.

Other types of lenses also play a part in the figuring of sight. Doane indicates that in films, wearing glasses provides women with a certain form of release from the ever present intimacy of her own image and position as the object of the gaze.[111] This is because glasses suggest that women can see as well as be seen. The agency that glasses facilitate, by accentuating women's ability to gaze, also makes them undesirable. Culture abounds with aphorisms like "no one makes passes at girls that wear glasses." Not only do glasses stress women's ability to look back, but they also impose a mediating frame, a kind of screen, between self and other. In this sense, glasses could suggest the ways that femininity is mediated and constructed. Glasses play a significant and mostly unnoticed part in webcam representations. When webcam operators wear glasses, an image of the computer screen is often reflected in the operator's lenses. Glasses indicate that women webcam operators look while they are being looked at.

When glasses literally reflect the computer screen, they reinsert the computer frame and mediation back into the webcam process. Glasses can screen the computer operator's eyes from the viewer while also allowing her to see. The webcam operator can view, edit, and comment upon images of herself but the spectator usually cannot see what she sees on the screen. Spectators are also reminded of their own physical relationship to the computer screen when they see the screen reflected back in the operator's lenses. Less detailed reflections may even suggest that the spectator is being watched and mirrored in the operator's glasses.

Pat Cadigan explores the possibility of being watched while watching webcams in her story "Icy You . . . Juicy Me" (I See You . . . You See Me).[112] Not surprisingly, the main character resists evidence that "people caught in the webcam's gaze" knew who was watching them. However, the title of Cadigan's story suggests that despite the ostensible empowerment of spectators gazing on compliant objects, there is always a mirroring aspect to watching even if it, like her title, initially remains difficult to understand. At the end of Cadigan's story, the main character can no longer deny that the person she is observing has also been invisibly watching her. A similar theme is rendered on a number of webcam sites. For instance, the design of MandyCam suggests that webcams also allow for the surveillance of spectators.[113] The background of each MandyCam page evokes the view through a video camera—complete with an almost full battery icon and flashing red indicator that lets the spectator know that footage is being recorded. Upon discovering that the lens is directed out toward them, webcam spectators may be increasingly more uncomfortable.

Obviously, there is no invisible webcam trained on the average spectator. However, these renderings remind Internet spectators that they are also observed. Internet-facilitated forms of surveillance include MOO commands that provide details about characters, the tracing of email and Internet protocol (IP) addresses to specific spectators, hacking into systems to gain personal information, and the use of search engines and other databases to connect information to an individual's name and physical location. This information seems visual because it provides such detailed accounts and is often referred to as a "data image."[114] Like the rendering of webcam operators through site texts and the transformation of text-based MOOs into a kind of seeing, the textual aspects of this "image" may not be noticed. The news reports about Internet surveillance, ways that Internet sites seem to provide direct access to corporeal individuals, and Cadigan's and Mandy's work place the spectator in an uneasy position. When spectators are reminded that they can also be watched, or that personal information about them can be retrieved, the power dichotomy between spectatorial mastery and the submission of the observed is disabled.

Just a Guy

Men webcam operators also displace the binary structure of viewing, where men look and women are available to be gazed at, by diminishing their position and making themselves available to the gaze. No matter how advanced their programming skills and style of self-representation, men webcam operators expect to be overshadowed by women operators. For instance, Bagu argues that men do not generate the same interest and web site "hits" and fail to be featured in general lifecam listings.[115] Men indicate that there may be limited interest in their depictions by describing their sites as "just a teen on cam" and "just a guy with a webcam."[116] Some male webcam operators apologize for their sites, indicating that spectators may be "totally bored to tears" and providing warnings that they will see a "boring looking bloke, looking bored, in a boring room, on a boring website."[117] These narratives help protect men webcam operators from external criticism, indicate that it may be difficult to find an audience—although many "chat" modules are filled with admiring comments, and suggest that there are limited models to help men determine how to be visually appealing.

Women webcam operators tend to address male viewers and envision them as the most unruly spectators.[118] This appeal to the male viewer, and promise that he can gaze upon available bodies, continues in men's webcam sites. Men webcam operators advertise with images of nude torsos, muscled chests, bulging briefs, and in some cases fully visible penises and asses, which repeat some of the advertising conventions of gay male erotica. The tendency among men webcam operators to visually address the gay male viewer is related to the many Internet sites designed particularly for gay male consumers and spectators and the more limited conceptions of how women erotically look at bodies and what they want to see. There are also ongoing stereotyped claims that women are less stimulated by the visual. Of course, images of lithe, exercised, and young male bodies can also appeal to women.

Personal statements from men webcam operators about their homosexuality appear in top 100 advertisements, FAQs, and other web site features. However, these identifications are less common than the visual addresses would suggest. There are many sites where the webcam operator simultaneously notes his heterosexuality and acknowledges that his spectators are gay men. For instance, Kenny's FAQ includes a question about his sexuality and indicates the common desiring position of his viewers when he answers, "Sorry guys, but I love the women."[119] Chad notes that he gets "quite a few Gay visitors for some reason and that is surprising because I am not gay."[120] Chris provocatively asks, "Want me in YOUR pants?"[121] However, the link leads to merchandise, where the spectator can buy new T-shirts with Chris's logo and then tuck the shirt into his or her pants, rather than providing the expected series of erotic images. Chris may address male desire, but he also indicates his heterosexuality and unavailability by providing images and statements about his "hottie" wife.[122] Through these tactics, men webcam operators attract gay male spectators while keeping some distance from homosexual desires. Their renderings suggest the complicated relationship among pleasurably self-presenting for the male gaze, personal sexuality, and the desired gender of partners. Such pleasures and desires are associated with queer identity, which acknowledges shifting sexual desires, opposes binary identity positions, and politically resists normative society, but this term rarely appears on men's webcam sites.

Women webcam operators frustrate male desire and gain power by making the ostensible views into their homes fail. The visual promises of men's webcams also fail when operators offer webcam views, private shows, videos, and items of worn clothing to male spectators but refuse to fully associate sexually, socially, or politically as queer or gay. Because they are more likely to require payments and memberships in order to see anything, men's webcam sites curtail viewing even more than women's sites. Spectatorial desires are also denied since promises of live webcams increasingly lead to advertisements with no relationship to webcams, sites without webcams, and instances where the webcam image has been pushed to the limits of the viewable screen. In many instances, weblogs and other forms of writing have supplanted webcams and continue to promise unlimited views into individuals' lives. These blogs are like text-based MOOs in that they promise visual pleasure through textual means.

Conclusion: The Politics of Being Seen

Webcam images of people at their computers disorder a fully empowered gaze onto distant objects because they provide such a familiar view. The comments of webcam operators and the reflective surfaces of the computer screen and eyeglasses suggest that the spectator is engaged with versions of his or her own image. For instance, Voog argues that "what u see at my site and your reactions to it say everything about YOU. anacam is just a mirror."[123] Christine Humphreys also indicates that webcams encourage spectators to reflect on their own visibility and feelings about being observed: "When alone, do you dance around your living room like Tom Cruise in Business? Do you read hefty novels while wearing a mud mask? Do you pick your nose, adjust your underwear or drink milk straight from the container? Would you do these things if you knew someone was watching?"[124] Humphreys's description evokes a surveillant society in which the possibility of being seen encourages individuals to self-regulate

Aesthetics is an aspect of all spectatorial positions, including the point-of-view that is scripted by individual net artworks, but this does not necessarily provide the spectator with an ideal or cohesive sight. The net art spectator is orchestrated into having certain responses, which include confusion about the function and purpose of the site and panic at perceived computer viruses and crashes, because there is inadequate information about the site design and programming. Some spectators also have trouble distinguishing between net art and other Internet failures. Devices that provide a context for the representational strategies of net artists are unusual. The Internet and computer spectator's position and ability to gaze upon the whole site are disturbed by the ways net art cannot be interacted with or controlled. Net art's disruption of spectatorial mastery, and its production of a distinctly different spectator than the one promised by such concepts as computer "interactivity," encourages the spectator to read Internet technologies differently.

The net art aesthetic also suggests that there are problems with maintaining unique Internet "objects" and authorship. Museums and other web sites, which seek to preserve the aura of objects, struggle with the lack of materiality, the copied and quoted aspects of net art, and the issues introduced in Walter Benjamin's "The Work of Art in the Age of Mechanical Reproduction."[2] Benjamin, whose work has influenced a group of theorists, cultural producers, and many net artists, argued that the value of art objects dissipates with mechanical reproduction. Varied aspects of Internet and computer settings contribute to this destabilization of singular and specific works. Different computers, monitors, browsers and connection speeds produce contrary views. Such problems encourage an interrogation of traditional reading and viewing positions. They also suggest that technologies, as well as cultural producers, play a part in the spectator's experience with Internet- and computer-facilitated representations.

Spectators are structured to look, and a version of artists can still be seen through such failures as misdirection, misquotation, and crashes. There is a possibility that net art authorship will remain elevated and intact because spectators are scripted to fail. While the failures of webcam spectatorship provide a form of power to women operators, who would otherwise be rendered as the object of the gaze, net artworks may continue to empower artists whose works of art and position tend to be canonized in other situations. Examining the relationship between aesthetics and net art, the different ways that the term "net art" is employed, critical and popular uses of failure, and the employment of failure in Jodi's, Luining's, and Samyn's net art can explain the positions of the net art spectator and artist. The failures represented by net artists can have a political effect on Internet spectatorship and be employed as critical strategies in researching and designing Internet sites. However, the net art tactic of questioning the familiar functions of the Internet by scripting some spectators to misunderstand, and rendering an ostracized other or "clueless newbie," indicates that the net art aesthetic of failure cannot work as an inclusive critical strategy without some revisions.

Aesthetics and Net Art

The spectator's engagement with net art aesthetics is informed by contemporary conceptions of art and new media. The *Oxford English Dictionary* indicates that aesthetics is "the philosophy or theory of taste."[3] Aesthetics has been understood as a coherent set of standards for judging art, which is based on morals, social, or visual criteria, or some combination of these.[4] However, some more recent arguments insist that the "social," in the form of cultural values and beliefs, always inform aesthetics. For instance, feminist aesthetics has encouraged spectators to acknowledge the cultural and ideological aspects of reading and viewing. According to Mary Devereaux, the development of feminist aesthetics, which occurred in the 1980s, helped to emphasize the many cultural, historical, and political variables that affect conceptions of artistic genius, aesthetic value, skill, and taste.[5] Sarah Worth indicates that feminist aesthetics "examines and questions aesthetic theory" rather than providing methods for judging art.[6] Hal Foster's "anti-aesthetic" is similar to feminist aesthetics and resists ongoing beliefs, which are often associated with Immanuel Kant, that aesthetic judgment, or deliberations about what is beautiful and pleasurable, are universal.[7] These related political projects continue to have an influence on such contemporary art practices as net art.

My consideration of net art is politically aligned with feminist aesthetics and a version of Foster's anti-aesthetics. The cultural aspects of aesthetics as well as such "taste"-oriented issues as color and composition are considered. Aesthetic engagement is always an aspect of spectatorship since objects are understood through particular embodied positions, cultural values, beliefs, and points of view. People are also understood through aesthetic criteria. For instance, power is delivered to certain individuals through seemingly universal codes of beauty, which include particular body shapes and skin colors. Contemporary artists may seem to resist aesthetics by downplaying bodily representations, beauty, and skillfully produced works in favor of a more theoretical project or an anti-aesthetic. However, artists like Sarah Charlesworth, Sherrie Levine, and Richard Prince still employ a set of aesthetic conventions through copying, and Mike Kelly, Karen Kilimnik, and Paul McCarthy through depictions of the low. Net artists like Jodi, Luining, and Samyn also employ an anti-aesthetic by critiquing art aesthetics and relating their sites to other forms of web production.

Net Art

Net art is sometimes described as "net.art" or even "art on the net." It has been widely discussed on listservs and other email communication forums, which include 7-11, Rhizome, The Thing, Museum-L, nettime, and the World Wide Web Artist's Consortium.[8] The term "net art" usually includes email projects and text-based performances, but web sites are probably the most common net art form.[9] The use of a singular term suggests that there is a consistent set of aesthetic guidelines for producing and evaluating these cultural works. Varied producers and critics have also tried to establish a vocabulary and set of expectations through discussions and production practices. Some of the recurring attributes of net art, which have been mentioned in these discussions, are collaboration, interactivity, formalism, and reflexivity. The works of Jodi, Luining, Samyn, and many other net artists share a loose set of aesthetic properties, but there are also Internet and net art practices with different criteria. Describing a completely unified net aesthetic is stymied because many of the artists resist delineated categories and stable terms. The net art aesthetic would seem to include a fluidity, which is represented by such strategies as challenging artistic identity, shifting the relationship between a title and the content of a work, and using display and organizational strategies to make "new" works. This variability makes it difficult for spectators to identify and engage with net art.

Net art is associated with a number of essential aspects of the web. For instance, Brett Stalbaum indicates that net art is a formalist strategy, as Greenberg articulated this concept, and that the work investigates "HTTP protocol, HTML, and browser specific features as a unique medium."[10] Stalbaum and other critics relate net art to formalism's privileging of form—in this case, the particular aspects of the Internet and computer—over content. A great deal of net art does visualize the web's language, a code that often remains hidden from the spectator, and re-represents the elements of the web in countless reflexive configurations. However, net artists pastiche and critique the ways that the Internet and computer work as well as directing the spectator to its structural elements. Steve Dietz argues that viewers and critics should not try to "assimilate" net art into traditional art-historical discourse, and this would include the connection to formalism, because these works could "problematize many of the very assumptions we take to be normal, if not natural."[11] In this case, net art could disturb the familiar position of the spectator and aesthetic criteria, which are structured by the gallery and museum. However, a variety of artistic movements have challenged art conventions and then been incorporated into the canon. Other Internet settings have also been lauded for their ability to radically alter cultural understandings of identity and production, but this has also not occurred.

Spectators familiar with contemporary art and cultural debates have an advantage in engaging with net art. Art remains a part of the net art discourse and is embedded in the movement's name, even though many net producers and critics have been ambivalent about calling these works "art." This is a familiar strategy. Jay David Bolter and Richard Grusin argue that "popular culture often wants to deny traditional high art a claim to superior status, but still to appropriate its cachet and vocabulary, as it does, for example, with the terms *digital art* or *computer art*."[12] Net artists use the strategies of denial and quotation to elide their relationship to such high art "problems" as class privilege, hierarchical evaluation, claims of mastery, and the exclusion of other voices while still directing the spectator to the importance and cultural worth of their work. Net art also has a history of exclusivity because net art sites like hell.com were once only available by invitation.

Resisting the art label makes net art incomprehensible to some spectators because these works are difficult to understand and culturally locate. Spectators more easily recognize art when museums, galleries, and other contextual devices demarcate it. These architectural brackets and labels can assist spectators in encountering new kinds of art and aesthetic strategies. They also limit the ways this art can function. In 1996, Alexei Shulgin and the Moscow WWW Art Centre commented on the function of art and aesthetics in Internet contexts and founded an award for web pages that provided an "art feeling" rather than sites that had intentionally been produced as works of art.[13] Their accompanying manifesto indicates that the "internet is an open space where the difference between 'art' and 'not art' has become blurred as never before in XX century. That's why there are so few 'artists' in this space."[14] It also may be why some spectators have difficulties identifying and viewing net art. The manifesto suggests that an artist's identity is reliant on institutional affiliations, but with the Internet there is the "possibility of misinterpretation and loss of 'artistic' identity" and there "are no familiar art institutions and infrastructures." However, familiar institutions and infrastructures are increasingly appearing as part of the Internet.

Net artists have presented their works in different ways and have different relationships to art structures. Early Internet organizations like äda'web, which released its first project in 1995, offered the spectator works by Heath Bunting, Jodi, Jenny Holzer, Michaël Samyn, Julia Scher, Alexei Shulgin, and Lawrence Weiner, but the term "art" was never mentioned.[15] Of course, the names of these artists immediately marked this as an art site for some spectators. A more obvious connection to art institutions was established when these net works were incorporated into the Walker Art Center's web site after äda'web lost its funding.[16] Other sites employ the term "art" more overtly. For instance, Jodi also appears on the Rhizome site where the term art is frequently employed. Rhizome is a nonprofit organization that funds net art, supports a number of listservs, presents information about new media-related issues, and offers a web-based "artbase." This artbase features "art objects" and an alphabetically organized database of documented works.[17] Rhizome and a growing number of other net art organizations counteract the indeterminacy of Internet identification by calling the varied representations that they offer art and by providing spectators with label-like details.[18]

The use of the term "rhizome" and other aspects of the web site reference the non-hierarchical networks and root-like structures theorized by Gilles Deleuze and Félix Guattari.[19] However, Rhizome instituted a membership fee, which was required for spectators to view the site, to resolve escalating costs and decreased funding opportunities in 2003.[20] During active conversations about instituting the fee, many Rhizome members noted their support but also expressed concerns that it would prevent spectators from viewing the artbase and locating artists' web sites—concerns that continue to intensify.[21] The response on nettime, other email lists, and Vladimir Kovacevic's "After Rhizome" web site were more hostile, suggested that the organization was elitist and American-centric, and indicated that it did not render rhizome-like "distributed systems."[22] The Rhizome proposal and implementation of a membership fee unintentionally generated other rhizome "shoots" or nodes in the network.[23] For instance, Luining announced that Net.Art Connexion was making a free "copy" of the artbase "as a sort of protest."[24] This copy intentionally indicates that net art and its accompanying structure of links are replicable and resistant to the kinds of original and valuable objects instituted within traditional museums.

Luining notes that net art is reproducible, but Rhizome continues to connect to museum structures, including an "affiliation" with the New Museum of Contemporary Art that also began in 2003.[25] The Rhizome membership has not been pleased with these institutional connections or the consequences of the membership fee, which resulted in fewer references to the site. For instance, t.whid indicates that Rhizome is gone because to "exist on the network you need to be linked."[26] There were calls to "FREE RHIZOME NOW" and indications that the concept of the rhizome was no longer applicable, since the site and email lists were "walled off."[27] The decision to establish a membership fee allowed Rhizome to continue, further established its "artbase" as art, and disconnected it from other sites and texts.

Even though Rhizome and many other sites use the term "art," there are still problems in conceptualizing net art's relationship to traditional art forms. The medium is unfamiliar, and space and display, which usually help spectators to understand how to relate to individual works, do not apply. For instance, the "edge" between works of net art and their surroundings are almost impossible to conceptualize without physicality. Web-based net art could include the browser frame, email interface, surrounding sites, computer screen, and computer processor. The mutability of net art and Luining's duplication of aspects of Rhizome indicate that even the traditional museum and other structures for displaying and selling art cannot fully transform digital reproductions into original and aura-imbued works. The museum and web sites, which seek to maintain the aura of objects, still struggle with the issues introduced in such articles as Benjamin's "The Work of Art in the Age of Mechanical Reproduction." Benjamin suggested that the authority of objects dissipate when they can be mechanically reproduced: "One might generalize by saying: the technique of reproduction detaches the reproduced object from the domain of tradition. By making many reproductions it substitutes a plurality of copies for a unique existence. And in permitting the reproduction to meet the beholder or listener in his own particular situation, it reactivates the object reproduced. These two processes lead to a tremendous shattering of tradition."[28] The shattering of tradition that Benjamin describes is only intensified in Internet settings where the material basis of the museum and its possession of objects are continually challenged.

Nevertheless, directors and curators of a number of leading museums believe that museums should play a significant part in the development of net art. The Guggenheim Museum, San Francisco Museum of Modern Art, Walker Art Center, and Whitney Museum of American Art make net art available through their web sites and in museum exhibitions.[29] When David Ross was director of the San Francisco Museum of Modern Art, he worked to link net art to more canonical forms of art production. He was interested in developing "standards and a critical evaluation framework" for net art that would be based on conceptions of art.[30] Yet his goals appeared to be different from those of some net critics and artists who wanted to challenge the art system through Internet production practices. Luther Blissett maintains that net art is "everyone with his own site, everyone with his own domain, everyone with his own gallery, they are throwing themselves into the trammels of traditional art."[31] SFMOMA certainly played a part in authorizing this form and situating it within art conventions by establishing a Webby prize for "Excellence in Online Art."[32] Its Webby symposium panel on "The Artwork in the Age of Online Communication" acknowledged "The Work of Art in the Age of Mechanical Reproduction." However, the panel also tried to displace Internet challenges to aura-imbued works with a new aura in the form of human interaction and visceral Internet presence—a tactic that relates to the ways that real time is employed in webcams and other settings.[33] Of course, Internet communication is often delivered textually. It is copied when portions of emails are reposted and people save their synchronous communication logs.

Other constituencies have also been interested in publicizing and commodifying net art. Art.Teleportacia and its "gallerist" Olia Lialina, who describes the site as "The First Real Net.Art Gallery" and more recently as the "first and the only real net art gallery," have worked to define the worth and originality of this form.[34] Art.Teleportacia and Lialina's insistent use of the terms "first" and "real" in referring to the site and Artcart's claim to be "the first net.art_shop" indicate that there are problems maintaining Internet aura.[35] Douglas Crimp suggests that the "withering away of the aura," which is an integral aspect of contemporary society, is accompanied by efforts to recuperate aura and pretend that the original is beneficial and welcome.[36] Art.Teleportacia and Lialina try to recuperate aura by developing ways for collectors and institutions to own "original" net art, and Artcart offers the "original print" along with screen-based works.[37] There are problems with these strategies because, as Bill Nichols indicates, the one element mechanical reproduction cannot reproduce is authenticity.[38] The multiple and reproducible aspects of net art, which can be understood as its distinct lack of uniqueness and originality, have also been part of its character. In this sense, the concept of uniqueness has not fully dissipated.

Attempts to authenticate and market net art have instead highlighted such "problems" as the lack of clearly official Internet agencies, the easy downloading and transferring of simple HTML projects to other web sites, and the inability to fully archive net art in other settings. Internet works can be transferred to more stable and clearly defined formats, like CD-ROMs and DVDs, but this transfer irrevocably alters the work and web site links are usually lost.[39] This destroys net art's relationship to the larger structures that many of these works are commenting on and quoting. To some extent, net art is only viable within the particular network in which it is situated. In other words, net art requires some supporting Internet structure to facilitate its full functioning.

While it is difficult to transfer net art to different media, the easy transference of HTML and some programming to other web sites is a problem for constituencies that want to make net art into a commodity. Art.Teleportacia and Lialina have tried to counteract this reproducibility by indicating that original net art works can be identified by the "location bar" or URL address.[40] Of course, there are certain instances where the URL can be faked. Art.Teleportacia and Lialina's argument suggests that the originality of net art is based on the uniqueness of its supporting address, which would presumably allow for the authentication of net art within virtual galleries or other institutional structures, rather than any unique attributes of the work. Location based originality and the existence of authorizing URLs would allow Internet galleries and museums a heightened control over net art works. Not surprisingly, a variety of artists argue that the connection between net art and the "address," which this argument presents as a kind of physical location, is ill conceived. Samyn indicates that "location" is not very important and that the "network has become a place on its own"[41] It might be more accurate to say that the network is a non-space that has no exact or fixed locations. The identity of specific supporting servers is supplanted by connections that are made through hypertextual links, search engine listings, listserv discussions, and spectator viewing.

Art.Teleportacia and Lialina proposed that unique URLs substantiate "original" net art works after their Miniatures of the Heroic Period web "show," which included a number of web pieces for sale, was manipulated and reposted to another site by 0100101110101101.org.[42] This collaborative continues to resist the institutionalization and commercialization of net art. Its manifesto evokes the political aspects of Benjamin's argument about mechanical reproduction and indicates that an aesthetic, which stresses the problems with original works of art, is necessary. They argue that all works of art can be copied but that net art reproductions are identical to the original, and it is therefore a "non-sense" to employ the concepts of authorship and authenticity in relationship to net art.[43] They believe that net art "requests new production, preservation, and fruition criteria that often conflict with the old rules of the art system, like the necessity of critics and museums." Net artists like 0100101110101101.org have chosen to sabotage other sites and make them "fail" in order to encourage spectators to critically consider what technology delivers. They negate the originality of net art by making copies. However, the varied claims for the critical work that copies can perform, and the celebration of other reproduction mediums, can also establish a kind of unique status for them. It is possible that reproductions hold their own type of aura for academics, artists, intellectuals, and Marxists. The dismissal of authenticity, rejection of traditional forms of aura-imbued art, and acknowledgment of indistinguishable copies may increase net art's worth in art markets where postmodern appropriation is institutionalized.

Some net artists promote the copy, which according to Benjamin can politically reconfigure art and culture by allowing the masses access into a system of exchange and power that previously excluded them. However, these critical uses of reproduction do not necessarily make net art comprehensible. Spectators are often unsure what will occur when they engage with particular links in hypertext and web-based works. This suggests that narratives about active spectators who knowingly engage with the web and other Internet interfaces do not describe the range of viewing experiences. Surfing provides one understanding of the Internet and suggests that skilled users employ Internet information to "get" to particular sites.[44] However, HTML and

Internet interfaces also produce unintended connections and mistaken trajectories. A more appropriate term for the spectator's encounter with net art and other Internet sites may be "blundering." This term suggests that spectators have difficulty recognizing net art and sites that do not fit into familiar genres, and settings are open to various interpretations. In some cases, artists and programmers actively produce this spectatorial confusion.

An Aesthetic of Failure

A number of hypertext critics indicate that linked computer documents produce newly empowered readers or even that these settings make readers into authors. Landow, a hypertext critic and practitioner, focuses on the productive aspects of computer and Internet settings, but he also suggests that breakdowns, coding errors, and the disorientation of spectators are important aspects of the medium.[45] He traces this cultural interest in confusion to modernist and postmodernist tendencies in the arts and literature. According to Landow, "Joyce's *Ulysses*, T. S. Eliot's *Waste Land*, and William Faulkner's *The Sound and the Fury*—to cite three classics of literary modernism—all make disorientation a central aesthetic experience."[46] Such aesthetics of disorientation have been incorporated into Internet and computer settings in order to encourage the spectator to perceive differently. However, if spectators notice the connections between hypertext and these cultural "classics," then disorientation and other kinds of spectatorial failure may also re-engage the spectator in elite forms of cultural activity.

Feminist aesthetics and anti-aesthetics invite alternative engagements because they consider the social structures that determine how spectators see objects. In a similar way, the intermingled formal and political aesthetic of net art encourages the spectator to address the ways that technology is understood. According to Crary, acknowledgments of failure and the simultaneous existence of streamlined technology and urban decay make spectators aware of aesthetics and the underlying presumptions that accompany technology. He indicates that society will increasingly engage with such conflicting technology-facilitated terrain as the world of "absolute speed," which Paul Virilio critiques, and "the decaying, digressive, terrain of the automobile-based city."[47] For Crary, "any sense of breakdown, of faulty circuits, of systemic malfunction" can begin to disrupt the production of a "fully delusional world." Crary's call to highlight and even produce failure, which he identifies with such cultural producers as Philip K. Dick and David Cronenberg, is also achieved by the actions of some net artists.[48]

The incompatible contemporary settings that Crary describes also appear in many literary and critical writings about technology. William Gibson, Bruce Sterling, Neal Stephenson, and other cyberpunk authors depict men who must correlate the almost omnipotent power that they can gain by "jacking in" to the machine with the limits of their physical environments and corporeal bodies.[49] Kim Cascone indicates that "post-digital" music engages with such failures as "glitches, bugs, application errors, system crashes, clipping, aliasing, distortion, quantization noise, and even the noise floor of computer sound cards."[50] Video artists, who may have been influenced by the work of electronic musicians, also render digital stutter and failure.[51] The artist Lee Bul tries to correlate the increasing belief in new technologies and "things constantly breaking down."[52] According to Bul, Korea is a "place of casual catastrophes: bridges and department stores collapse, subterranean gas mains explode, and the jumbo jets of Korean Air, the national carrier, routinely go down." Of course, an examination of international events indicates that the reliance on certain kinds of technologies and the failures of both human and machine readings are "global" issues. Bul's list of breakdowns has no national borders.[53]

Popular entertainment has also provided a fascinated and terrified audience with innumerable representations of technological failures. These include airplane disaster films like *Alive* (Frank Marshall, 1993), *Airport* (George Seaton, 1970), *Airport 1975* (Jack Smight, 1975), *Airport '77* (Jerry Jameson, 1977), and *The Concorde: Airport '79* (David Lowell Rich, 1979); other transportation failures such as *The Poseidon Adventure* (Ronald Neame, 1972) and *Runaway Train* (Andrei Konchalovsky, 1985); architectural horrors like the *Towering Inferno* (Irwin Allen and John Guillermin, 1974); and such computer-oriented failures as *2001: A Space Odyssey* (Stanley Kubrick, 1968), *The Net* (Irwin Winkler, 1995), and *War Games* (John Badham, 1983). In many of these films, instances of sabotage or other improper human interventions reveal poor construction practices and other technological insufficiencies. These films may confirm the spectator's concerns about technology or encourage the viewer to see the technological infrastructure in new and uneasy ways.

The familiarity if not outright fascination that contemporary culture has with such narratives of technological failings suggests why contemporary artists are interested in fallibility, boundaries, and rupture.[54] The net artists, who are engaged with failure, use strategies similar to those employed in disaster films. They shock the spectator with breakdowns, technological confusion, and illegibility in order to warn the spectator not to believe that technology is highly functional. Terry Winograd and Fernando Flores argue that breakdowns are incredibly important because they make individuals aware of their practices and equipment, which otherwise would not be addressed.[55]

Their discussion of the important function of breakdowns suggests that net artists perform important critical and cultural work when they render accidents. The highlighted and simulated failures, which net artists like Jodi, Luining, and Samyn produce, encourage the spectator to attend more carefully to the functional and aesthetic properties of the Internet. However, another group of spectators never engages with this political aesthetic because its codes remain incomprehensible or invisible. Critical considerations of failure need to be reworked to consider these different positions.

Jodi

Jodi, which is the collaborative project of Joan Heemskerk and Dirk Paesmans, produces an aesthetic of failure that encourages some spectators to attend to the properties of the Internet and prevents others from understanding. Jodi quotes such common web site blunders as improperly written HTML, broken forms, and malfunctioning Java (figures 4.1-4.2). The work is particularly challenging because spectators have to visually confront a version of web programming. Jodi renders "collages" of Internet and computer things that "go wrong" and believes that the "natural environment of us, of Jodi, is the net and you can find a certain condensed form of the net in Jodi."[56] Heemskerk and Paesmans disassociate Jodi from an art context when they describe the Internet as their "environment." When it first appeared on the web, this work produced a number of productive conversations on listservs about the parameters of net art. However, the solo exhibition of Jodi's work in the physical space of the Eyebeam gallery in 2003 indicates that net artists are continually being incorporated into traditional contexts.[57] *INSTALL.EXE: The First Time You Start Your Computer* consisted of "a collection of screen recordings" projected on the wall of the gallery.[58] In this work, Jodi depicts spectators failing to "properly" use computers.

In the Internet-based works, Jodi disrupts the familiar aspects of the web by overwriting it with all sorts of incomprehensible texts. Part of this disruption is the supporting code for web pages that has now been revealed to the spectator. On the web, this code is masked yet available through the use of the browser's "Page Source" menu option, which allows the spectator to see the HTML for any given page, or through error messages and other malfunctions, which make the programming of sites visible. Jodi's work suggests that the structure of the web is somehow turned around. This can produce a form of panic or trauma in spectators, because they mistranslate these texts and believe that the computer has crashed. When engaging with links after the Jodi site, the spectator is likely to misidentify coding errors and other glitches as part of Jodi's project. Through this process, the spectator is encouraged to read all web material in a different way after viewing Jodi's net art.

Jodi rejects a literal reading of HTML and print media in favor of a more visual presentation of text. Blocks and shaped units of words and other aspects of the web are offered up for the spectator's aesthetic contemplation. The revealed snippets of HTML, which are on various Jodi sites, suggest that documents are transparent. However, spectators who are not familiar with HTML, or who cannot imagine why a web page would intentionally be written "wrong," will fail in their contemplation because the supporting content layers are only accessible when spectators know how to view them. Peter Lunenfeld notes that Jodi's net art is not as "blank as it seems" when the spectator uses the browser menu to look at the "Document Source."[59] What is then "revealed is that there is a whole layer of pictorial ASCII text art 'below' the surface of *jodi.org*." Of course, his comments also indicate that not all spectators know how to or think to use these methods.

These remarks suggest that Jodi's net art is as much about blindness as it is about visibility. Jodi operates by shifting the spectator between confusion and comprehension. According to Jodi, the site generated a large number of emailed corrections and complaints: "People were seriously thinking that we made mistakes. So they wanted to teach us. They sent us emails saying: You have to put this tag in front of this code. Or: I am sorry to tell you that you forgot this or that command on your page."[60] Jodi's description indicates that some spectators are unwilling to give up certain forms of programming logic and control. However, it is Jodi's work that encourages these spectators to perform such "spectatorial limitations." Spectators may be alienated by Jodi's work or eventually be inculcated into the codes of net art and read the web differently. In either case, satisfaction in viewing Jodi's site is unfortunately based on the knowledge that other spectators fail to comprehend. Jodi and some other net artists, perhaps unintentionally, operate by creating an Internet "inside" and "outside." This is similar to the ways that such categories as "newbie" and "guest" consolidate power in MOOs and Virtual Places by labeling spectators who are not fully a part of the system.

Readings of Jodi's site as confusing or error riddled code are encouraged by the 404 message on the first screen of *%20Wrong* (figure 4.1). It evokes the common "404 Error-File Not Found" web message, which occurs when a spectator tries to view a file that is not available. The 404 message usually marks the termination of the user's engagement with a series of sites and links. However, in Jodi's work the 404 message marks the beginning. The spectator who detects the link can view the site, despite the error message, but has been warned that proper files, clearly marked links, and exact meaning are not available. Jodi's engagement with the 404 is part of a cultural trend. There are a number of sites that explore the history, examine the aesthetic, and even

Figure 4.1
Jodi, *%20Wrong*, 27 Sept. 2004, <http://404.jodi.org/>.

"collect" unusual versions of 404 messages.[61] The codes of the web have become so established that most of these sites refer to certain 404 messages as "classic." This suggests that 404s are an integral part of the web and, as Stuart Moulthrop indicates, say something "profound" about the web and represent "its shifting multiplicity."[62] These 404 messages act as a stand-in for the larger structure of the web where addresses and styles are temporary. For instance, Sarah Papesh's 404 message advises, "Oops! You didn't find the file you were looking for, but LOOK, here's all of those socks you lost in the clothes dryer!"[63] She implies that 404s provide a substitute for the expected while they remind us about what has been lost.

The error messages rendered by Jodi, Papesh, and other designers evoke loss or a missing gap in the web. They highlight the ways that the system functions and malfunctions. Speaking about hypertext, Terry Harpold argues that engaging with links and paths "presumes displacement, separation and loss, departures and farewells."[64] The missing gaps that Jodi foregrounds and the potentially melancholic sense of absence that they evoke are a crucial part of the Internet. Hypertexts and other Internet sites contain and intensify absences by making it more difficult to locate authorship or even articulate the physical location of the text.[65] However, the sense that something is missing or transient does not necessarily produce a completely negative experience. The 404 error messages and other kinds of disappearances may also offer an erotic of the medium.

Barthes indicates that brief moments of exposure or *"where the garment gapes"* is erotic.[66] The spectator finds pleasure and agitation in what is hidden, the mystery of missing elements, and brief moments of disclosure, such as those rendered by webcams. Barthes compares the momentary appearances of the body to the rhythms and desires of reading, which include absorption, skipping, looking up, and dipping in again.[67] The 404 error messages also render intermittence and, because something is missing, processes such as searching, skimming, and becoming immersed again. The downloading of web sites, the delivery of sequential webcam images, the flashing of banners, the staccato of Flash images, and the cycling of the screen also encourage versions of this intermittence. These aspects of Internet spectatorship may keep spectators engaged and waiting for more.

N. Katherine Hayles indicates that Internet and computer intermittence result in *"flickering signifiers"* with unexpected transformations.[68] This is a result of the "constantly refreshed image rather than a durable inscription," which makes meaning less stable.[69] These liminal moments and mutations occur with word processing, programming, and other aspects of the Internet. However, absence and shifting elements can also be stabilized and become a form of Internet materiality. For instance, Jodi and 404 fan sites change disappearances into appearances when they highlight error messages. They reconfigure the non-site of incorrectly typed addresses and missing information into desired "destinations."[70] With this restructuring of the 404, spectators see something that is meant to inform them that there is nothing there. This produces a significant rift between the intended conventions of the web and the ways these representations are read by some spectators.

Many of Jodi's net artworks encourage alternative readings. Jodi also makes different renditions of projects that invite disparate interpretations. For instance, the version of *%20Wrong* on the Rhizome site offers a completely different opening screen (figure 4.2).[71] In Rhizome's *%20Wrong*, Jodi evokes the processes of failure and breakdown, with the flickering background that abruptly shifts from black to gray, the "Transfer interrupted!" message, the visibility rather than functionality of HTML code, the "accessDeniedPage" warning, the malfunctioning forms, and the "%Disconnecting%Host%20wrong.htm" notice. Failure, or the spectator's inability to identify Jodi's

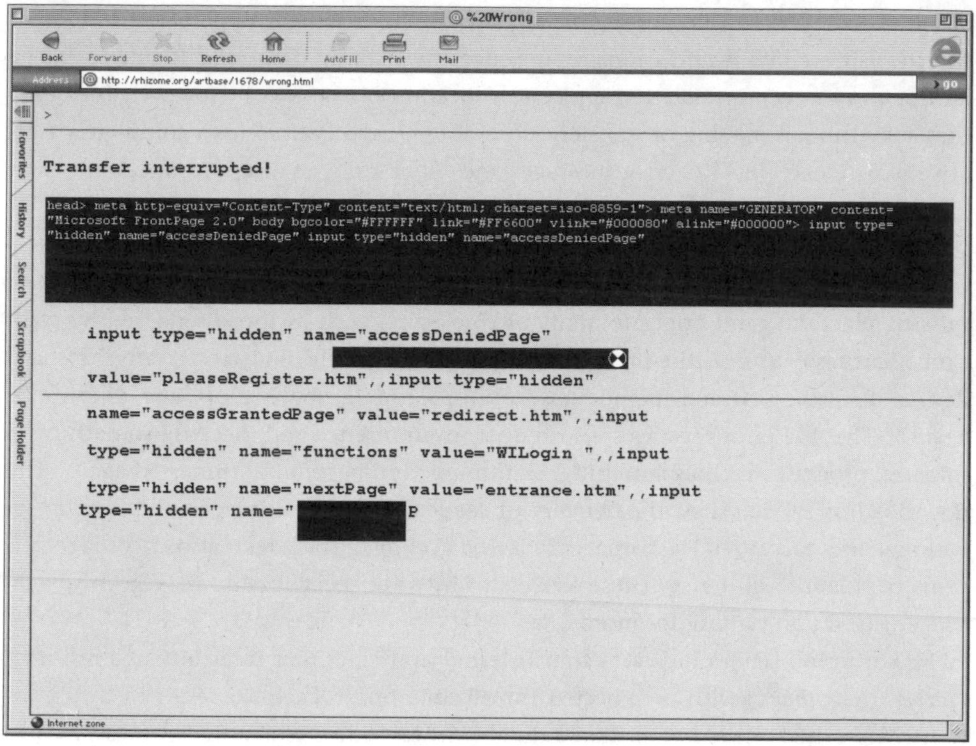

Figure 4.2
Jodi, *%20Wrong*, Rhizome, 1 Jan. 1996, 27 Sept. 2004, <http://rhizome.org/artbase/1678/wrong.html>.

work, also occurs because its position as a unique and sited work of fine art is repressed. As Heemskerk and Paesmans argue, there is "no 'art'-label on it."[72] Spectators who are not familiar with net art will have problems finding, viewing, and understanding this work while net art provides a politics for initiated spectators.

Jodi's and other net artists' rendering of disorientation, ideological failure, and a rupturing of the "law" are related to recent feminist theories. Butler argues that repetition and a failure to master certain identity categories offer the "other" a unique form of agency:

My recommendation is not to solve this crisis of identity politics, but to proliferate and intensify this crisis. This failure to master the foundational identity categories of feminism or gay politics is a political necessity, a failure to be safeguarded for political reasons. The task is not to resolve or restrain the tension, the crisis, the phantasmatic excess induced by the term, but to affirm identity categories as a site of inevitable rifting, in which the phantasmatic fails to preempt the linguistic prerogative of the real.[73]

Butler calls for the rifting of categories as a way of reconceptualizing identity politics.[74] She continually repeats or rehearses aspects of certain arguments until they fail. Net artists also use exacting repetition of technologies, sites, and styles and the failure to master craft as a way of reworking traditional ideas about artistic identity and spectatorship. Butler's proposal and the work of net artists like Jodi suggest a postmodern celebration of fragmented identities. Butler resists the idea that feminism is being destroyed through fragmentation and that this disintegration can be resolved through a coherent vision.[75] Her theories and the work of some net artists are antithetical to attempts to reintegrate or consolidate the divided self. For instance, Jodi employs failure for its political and disrupting effects. There is no interest in achieving a more readable and coherent work.

However, Jodi and other net artists disrupted their own politics by constantly employing and repeating ruptures, breakdowns, and confusion so that they are a formal aesthetic. So many net artists now work in this manner that it has become a conventional web strategy.[76] In discussions about net art, which appear on the Rhizome and nettime listservs and in other settings, Jodi is often used to provide a context for other net artworks. There has also been a tendency to collapse Jodi's work with other rupture-oriented net art. For instance, Eryk Salvaggio's Absolut Net.Art project, which includes a Jodi simulation, has often been mistaken for Jodi's work. His favorite response to the project was when a spectator noted, "I don't care who made it, its still JODI."[77] Such comments and forms of cultural production underscore the problems with establishing Internet authorship and specific categories, but they also suggest that artistic originality has been transmuted into a style rather than overturned.

Jodi's processes of confusion, which resist such things as legibility, linear reading, conventional culture, "high" art, and authorial mastery, are related to avant-garde art practices like dada and surrealism. However, like these other practices, Jodi's constant association with net art has institutionalized and legitimized the work.[78] The Rhizome site describes %20Wrong as "a nice tidbit from the kids who invented net.art."[79] There are also indications that Jodi "pioneered the use of the internet as an artistic medium" and that "jodi became net.art."[80] Jodi is incorporated into a series of art discourses, net art's lineage is articulated, and net art's worth is validated when Jodi is described as an "inventor." Jodi's work may become an origin story and a beginning point, and originality may be recreated, but some spectators still conceive of the Internet as a setting where mechanical and digital reproduction destabilizes the very possibility of originality.[81] Spectators accepted the "rightness" of an aesthetic that was once wrong and relied on the strange. The aesthetic of failure continues to falter with the incorporation of this material into the art canon.

Peter Luining

Peter Luining produces an equally troubled aesthetic of failure by juxtaposing and misquoting computer games and postpainterly abstraction in *D-TOY 2.502.338* (figure 4.3).[82] This work, which is part of a series of D-TOYs, presents the spectator with representations of brightly colored squares that move inside a larger square grid.[83] The gridlike arrangement and hard-edged quality of the colored units evoke postpainterly abstraction, but these formalist aspects are disturbed because the underlying "material" is code rather than paint. A white "background," which obviously is not any further away from the spectator than the other parts of the image, renders flatness. Yet this suggestion of flatness and computer immateriality is contradicted by the pulsating sounds that seem to accompany the shape's progression through the composition. In one part of the sequence, each shift of the units within the mazelike structure produces a reverberating sound as if the moving square is hitting against hollow walls. In

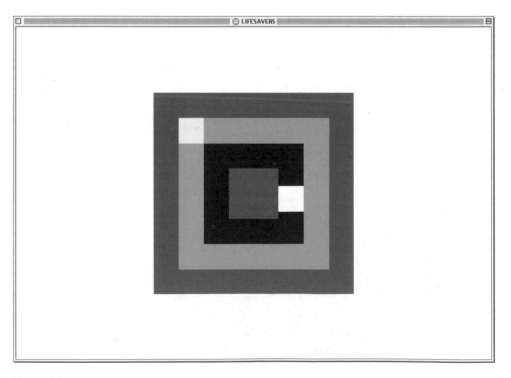

Figure 4.3
Peter Luining, *D-TOY 2.502.338*, Lifesavers, 9 Mar. 1999, 21 Nov. 2003, <http://www.vpro.nl/data/lifesavers/10/index.shtml>.

another sequence, a staticlike sound suggests that the moving square is scraping along an uneven channel that remains invisible to the eye. When the computer spectator "catches" and "clicks" on the moving elements, the color, composition, and accompanying sound change.

It may be difficult for the spectator to establish a relationship to these works or to read them "properly" because of the conflicting messages about form and content. In many of his works, Luining contradicts the spectator's visual and auditory perceptions. He dismantles the spectator's ability to determine things by allowing a high level of engagement or "interactivity." This contradicts various theories, from Barthes' work on the writerly text to Landow's arguments for hypertext, which imagine that readers have a greater agency when they can change the text. Instead, Luining's net art renders a bodily disorientation because things can be operated but signals—such as the relationship between sound and surface—are not reliable and the spectator cannot determine the outcome. The frenetic sound and speed of *D-TOY 2.502.338* seem to duplicate the intense fascination with and immersion into computer games. Luining emphasizes this association by titling these pieces "toys." Their design, which lets spectators manipulate simple abstract representations as if they were objects, may initially seem to reference games like Pong. However, in Pong the user identifies the white "blips" as paddles and ball, and Luining does not make any such stable references.

The limited instructions provided on the *D-TOY 2.502.338* site are called a "manual," which suggests that this is a game with rules and parameters, but there is no detailed explanation of the gameplay:

manual: click on the moving blocks
for maximum effect: put monitor brightness 50% & contrast 50%
soundvolume 20%

The aesthetic of these instructions, with terse commands and numerical adjustments, remove Luining's works from the realm of art. Yet, his "toys" fail to deliver a clear set of rules or a standard form of game play. There is no apparent success achieved through interaction, clear directions about the ways to engage, obvious ending, or means to win. Instead, each of his quotations acts as a false clue or misdirection. The shifting functions of the work, in which the spectator is alternately directed to read it as a form of art and as a computer game, suggest the computer technique of morphing, or the "transformation of one image into another by computer."[84] Luining's net art morphing, which is based on confusion, is quite different than LambdaMOO's character morphs.

The hosting site for *D-TOY 2.502.338* also purposefully keeps it in an unfixed state. Both Luining's *D-TOY 2.502.338* and Samyn's *The Fire from the Sea* are part of the Lifesavers project, which is sponsored by the Dutch television station VPRO. They are described as "small interactive programs" made for the Internet that were designed to "occupy the user for approximately five minutes" and operate "in the hazy area between media, art, and subcultures."[85] VPRO's interest in brief engagements connects net art, or art like the Lifesavers projects, with the intermittence and brief attention that is often designed into the television format. VPRO also suggests that these programs, like Jodi's works, are not fully identifiable. However, Lifesavers appear in other settings. They are represented by an image, which is designed by the producer of the interactive program, and appears in the VPRO television guide when the Lifesaver first appears on the web site.

In Luining's television guide depiction, an abstracted female figure contemplates a straight-edged work, which resembles the *D-TOY 2.502.338* composition (figure 4.4).[86] The spectator sees the art in a position that is slightly behind the female figure so that only her back is revealed. There are a number of contradictions in this depiction of aesthetic and transcendent contemplation, with the spectator waiting for her revelation in front of the art. Luining's image references a female figure from Oskar Schlemmer's *Bauhaus Stairway*, which was produced in about 1932. Luining's quotation disturbs the originality of *D-TOY 2.502.338* and the possibility of Internet authenticity. In Schlemmer's work, the female figure shifts her body in space as she navigates new architectural and educational environments. However, Luining's figure is pushed to the periphery of the composition so that the depicted figure, and thus the spectator viewing the design, is collapsed with the "art" and seems mired rather than liberated by engaging. These varied depictions and strategies suggest that Luining is ambivalent about presenting *D-TOY 2.502.338* as art. Instead, his rendering suggests the immobility of Internet spectatorship and the limits placed on the viewing body.

The spectator's investment in individual and unique artworks is also disturbed by the varied ways that *D-TOY 2.502.338* can be viewed. The "final" work may seem to be an abstract composition, which is framed by white. However, the work's edges or limits become increasingly hard to delineate as viewing continues. Through the "zoom in," "zoom out," "play," and other Flash Player menu options, the work can be changed into a series of similar pieces. For instance, the zoom in option produces what could be called "micro" works, since it is clear that this is an enlargement of a section, but these images are the same size as the first view. They are both details and completely different works. Each view presents an abstract composition that is reminiscent of Kenneth Noland's and Ellsworth Kelly's paintings. However, these net art

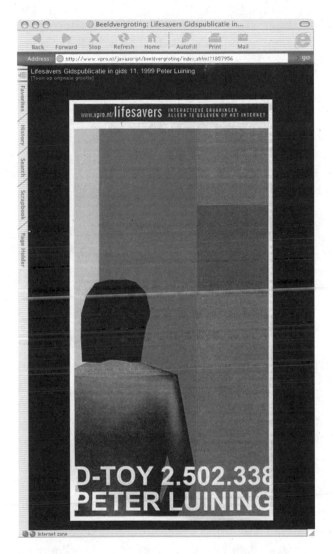

Figure 4.4
Peter Luining, "VPRO Aflevering," VPRO, 3 Dec. 2003, <http://www.vpro.nl/javascript/beeldver groting/index.shtml?1857956>.

images have no autonomy outside the spectator's manipulation. This browser-based spectatorship is related to André Malraux's "Museum without Walls," which is produced through photographic books and other reproduction technologies, and delivers "'fictitious' arts," which render misleading information about an object's scale and other attributes.[87] In Internet settings, there is also no constancy to a work's measurements. The dimensions of the screen and computer options, as well as the aspects of the work, determine the spectator's view.

Luining also alters his art by changing the display mechanisms. By presenting the work in alternative ways, he indicates that spectatorship provides different views.[88] Net art is often difficult to detach from its supporting display structure in the same way that site-specific installations are difficult to distinguish from their surroundings. Presenting the work differently allows Luining to further destabilize the coherence and constancy of individual net artworks. By shifting the display, Luining also highlights how the interface functions as a meaning producing system. His quotation of disparate styles disturbs the spectator's ability to read these works as original and authentic. Luining cites but does not deliver the expected conventions of art, browsers, and computer games and puts pressure on a variety of irreconcilable aesthetic styles or "movements" so that their codes fail. His aesthetic may avoid the canonization and institutionalization of other Internet works if the display mechanisms, through which spectators encounter these works, continue to evolve. However, the spectator's views of the more stable VPRO interface, where the site design remains the same, suggests that this aesthetic of disorientation, misquotation, and spectatorial limitations is also being incorporated into a net art canon.

Michaël Samyn

Michaël Samyn's *The Fire from the Sea* is more visually complex than Jodi's or Luining's net art.[89] His depictions of running children, walls of fire, and fluttering butterflies appear to be aligned with a romantic vision and a more traditional kind of art production (figures 4.5–4.6). However, Samyn's work also acknowledges its means of delivery and critiques the properties of the computer. *The Fire from the Sea*, like Jodi's work, begins with a warning. The spectator is informed that this "piece is not user friendly and deliberately counter-intuitive: roll over to load, click to unload. It can even bring a fast computer to its knees."[90] Samyn combines images and employs subtle colors but the stated intent of his net art is to produce spectatorial and computer failure. Renderings of failure also occur in hypertext literary works where, according to Moulthrop, "profound shock" describes what these works consider and render so that

Figure 4.5
Michaël Samyn, *The Fire from the Sea*, Lifesavers, 26 Jan. 2000, 28 Nov. 2003, <http://www.vpro.nl/data/lifesavers/16/index.shtml>.

hypertext "may be a technology of trauma, reflexively figuring its own assault on the textual corpus in terms of insults to the physical body."[91] Moulthrop's indication that aggressions are aimed at the spectator's body as well as the text also occurs in Samyn's net art intervention against the computer, which is brought to its "knees" and metaphorically disrupts the spectator's body, position, and engagement.

Experiences and renderings of shock also happened in earlier engagements with technology. Benjamin indicates that shock is related to modernist industrialization, being a part of the crowd, and viewing the conveyor belt rhythms of films; Wolfgang Schivelbusch describes the embodied discomfort and alarm that accompanied early train travel; and Tom Gunning notes that the frenzies of early cinema viewing reflect experiences with urban life.[92] Gunning describes how early film spectators eagerly shifted between fearfully reacting to the depicted things, as if they were real, and pleasurably noting the illusions. The spectator of *The Fire from the Sea* also enjoys the

Figure 4.6
Michaël Samyn, *The Fire from the Sea*, Lifesavers, 26 Jan. 2000, 25 May 2000, <http://www.vpro
.nl/data/lifesavers/16/index.shtml>.

illusion and notes computer failures and codes because Samyn does not let the viewer master the interface. Even the instructions are unreliable because the spectator must
"click" rather than "roll over" the word "Enjoy" in order to engage the piece and its
promised programming. Despite Samyn's warning about spectatorial disturbances,
some spectators insist that the instructions provide the correct way to begin.[93] This can
lead to a frustrated reloading of the opening screen. It is during these moments of irri-
tation, shock, and confusion, according to Benjamin, that aura and references to art
fail.[94]

The spectator's experiences with unpleasant interfaces and disintegrating aura are
particularly pronounced in *Sixteenpages*, which Samyn produced with Auriea Harvey
(figure 4.7). *Sixteenpages* offers an unusual version of the search engine, which references such popular forms as the Shell gas station sign, winning points in computer
games, and search terms.[95] In this work, the spectator struggles to manipulate an
avatar through a depicted maze, and works with keyboard and mouse to gather information. When the avatar—a representation of a fleshy and naked body—is steered

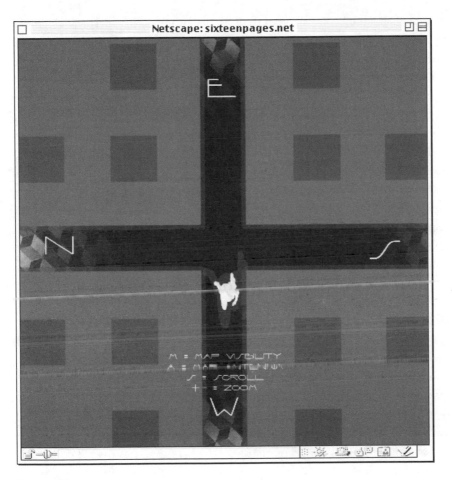

Figure 4.7
Michaël Samyn and Auriea Harvey, "sixteenpages.net," *Sixteenpages*, 10 Apr. 2002, <http://sixteenpages.net/>.

into the "wall" of the maze, it makes strange sounds of pain and despair. This suggests spectatorial limitations. Samyn's work critiques and even occasionally sabotages the expectations of spectators with expensive and high-bandwidth technologies, but his work is even more frustratingly difficult to view for spectators with outdated equipment. For instance, *The Fire from the Sea* has a tendency to stall slow computers and dial-up connections even though it can also delay computers with faster processors and connections. His depiction of the vulnerable Internet spectator in *Sixteenpages* still renders a white and walking male spectator. Unfortunately, Samyn's critique is most readily available to those who are already acknowledged as a part of the system.

Samyn's visual effects operate through traditional aesthetic criteria. *The Fire from the Sea* employs a rendering of translucent layers and a dark ground as a way of depicting depth. The browser window acts as a frame through which the spectator gains access to this rendition of a spatial world. Points of light seem to depict a night sky that is seen through the browser window. However, the spectator is forced to contend with the means of delivery as well as the content. The spectator must engage with the illusion of a window into another world, a familiar painting and web convention, which supports an "erect human posture," and with the computer's mouse navigation and menu-based controls, which suggest different bodily orientations.[96] The diverse elements of *The Fire from the Sea* place the subject in different positions and produce a version of Leo Steinberg's "flatbed" subject position. This flatbed position, which disorders the traditional vertical relationship between viewer and art object, renders such unconventional spectatorial positions as appearing to float over flat icons and topographical maps.

The spectator cannot engage with the coherent narrative that Samyn's animation implies or even manipulate the elements according to a familiar set of computer codes. Of course, this spectatorial displacement has already been foregrounded by his warning at the beginning of *The Fire from the Sea*. Rolling over what seems to be a translucent torso allows the spectator to manipulate a series of visual and sound elements, which includes a tangle of what seems to be octopus tentacles. However, this "bodily" control quickly changes into a representation of a throbbing organlike mass of flesh that is covered in bloodred spots (figure 4.6). This image is one of the many evoked failures and "insults" to the corporeal body that Samyn renders. The pulsing image suggests the catastrophic toll of AIDS more than it does computer viruses or codes. The spectator only gains some level of control over the piece by "touching" each mark, engaging on some metaphorical level with the viral body, and changing its sores from dark burgundy to a bright bloodred.

The Fire from the Sea presents a series of complex visual and auditory elements. The bottom register of marks allows the spectator a small amount of agency in choosing the kinds of images that are being portrayed. It provides a fairly clear set of effects that include (from left to right) clouds, a pair of woman's lips, butterflies, and a wall of flames. A layered soundtrack, which includes ocean noises and a woman's slow melodic singing, accompanies these images. The date stamp, which appears on some of the images, contradicts the complexity of the design because it evokes the low tech of camera snapshots. Playing children, fluttering butterflies, and other captured "instamatic" moments may seem to provide the spectator with a nostalgic past, but manipulating the effects means that an animated wall of flame or a scorching sun often burns out these possibilities. The subtle qualities and non-narrative composition of

Samyn's *The Fire from the Sea* encourage engagement without providing the spectator with a final destination.

Samyn's work is distinctive because he renders both aesthetically attractive compositions and some kind of critique of the medium. He works to keep his identity between the expected positions by describing himself as a "bad designer and an ex-artist."[97] Samyn and Harvey sometimes resist their individual authorial roles by identifying their combined projects as entropy8zuper.org. Samyn borrows from the computer vernacular but his work has some critical and aesthetic interests that are not shared by many other net artists. He uses these differences to distinguish and establish a position for his work. In an interview with Alex Galloway, Samyn indicates that he is surprised that individuals at Rhizome appreciate his work. It seems to him that "Rhizome is interested in a totally different kind of Art, you know the kind of art that *looks* conceptual and only uses code as an aesthetic element and is never about anything but itself."[98] By making these comments, Samyn differentiates himself from the formalist aspects of net art.

Samyn's critique of net art also suggests that politics and critical projects are linked to an aesthetic. He indicates that during the period when people were reacting to the Communication Decency Act, "when every website made its homepage black as a protest against censorship, I made the homepage of FFF black too with the text 'This page is black as a result of aesthetic considerations.'"[99] Samyn provides an important reminder of how aesthetics operate along with political projects. However, he does not consider in any depth the various ways that aesthetic strategies can be political. Samyn critiques "the typical 'blinking pixel' net artists," but they all render an aesthetic of failure.[100] Samyn may state that his critical project is "to make something poetic and beautiful that is about human things rather than machines."[101] However, Samyn's opening warning in *The Fire from the Sea* and rendering of interface breakdowns in *Sixteenpages* demonstrate that he is also engaged with the computer machine and aesthetic of code. Samyn's aesthetic of failure, which includes misusing computer conventions, both engages and resists the aspects of other net art.

Conclusion: The Limits of Failure and Repetition

In the work of Jodi, Luining, Samyn, and some other net artists, clear links and instructions about the interface are replaced by glitches and misleading directions that only certain spectators can still understand. Turning the ruptures in this work into more elaborate site-wide, browser, or system failures is a problem because at least some spectators must engage in order for net art to maintain an audience. Net art quotes and performs failures while keeping a precarious relationship with functionality. The net artworks of Jodi, Luining, and Samyn render a version of Barthes' punctum. These works render "that accident which pricks," "bruises," and is "poignant."[102] However, the poignancy and pain of interacting with net art works eventually dissipate as the spectator grows acclimated to sites and discovers the highly constructed aspects of the failures. This may even be necessary in order for net art to function.

In *Camera Lucida*, Barthes indicates that no punctum can persist over time or be shared by viewers. The shocks and moments of intimate engagement, which he experiences through aspects of photographs, eventually dissipate. Some other point of interest may replace these moments, but there is no way to recapture the initial flashes of blindness and confusion that occur when first viewing an image. In the case of net art, changing sites and aspects of the work can keep the spectator in a more prolonged period of blundering. However, as the spectator becomes more familiar with the work, a clear and less critically oriented engagement replaces an attention and consideration of particular interface tools and representations. Net art most clearly engages with "accomplished" Internet spectators and those who are familiar with art conventions. These spectators can find a way to engage with and understand the quotations of the sites. However, these spectators are also most likely to quickly decode all the failures. Sadly, spectators who engage are most safe from the destabilizing effects of these works.

All of this suggests that there is a problem with the kinds of failures that net artists employ and the forms of repetition used to achieve these effects. Butler indicates that repetition can be used to unravel dominant cultural beliefs. However, the kinds of repetition that occur in these net artworks and the ways they have become institutionalized suggest that repetition may also reproduce traditional categories and forms of power. This problem with the politics of repetition is indicated by the ways Jodi's repetitions have become a stylistic convention rather than encouraging further interrogations of programming and technology. Repetition of particular phrases and ideas, which may admittedly be different than Butler's repetition of the law, also negates the political messages in other net artworks. For instance, Jennifer Ley's *Catch the Land Mine!* quotes a "click" and "catch" form of Internet advertising campaign in order to call attention to the catastrophic loss of life and body parts that has occurred with the proliferation of land mines.[103] However, the initially disturbing experience of being informed that "you" have lost limbs and received other injuries, after trying to "catch" a mine, is not intensified with repetition. The recurrence of the same images and texts causes apathy rather than concern after any lengthy engagement.[104]

The Mongrel collective also uses repetition as part of its political strategy.[105] Their *Natural Selection* web site looks like and appears to work in the same ways as Internet search engines unless racist terms are employed.[106] When a search for a racist term is initiated, the spectator is offered URLs to sites with confusing rants and images that repeat aspects of hate. The Mongrel simulation functions differently than Samyn and Harvey's *Sixteenpages* search engine, which does not look like or operate in the same ways as Google and Yahoo! *Natural Selection* is likely to raise questions about search engine reliability, authority, and "guiding" among spectators familiar with Mongrel's work and those viewers who notice that the URLs for the racist sites are part of the Mongrel site.[107] However, the repetitions that Mongrel employs also rely on knowing spectators for the critique to operate and there are some representational problems with the work. For instance, the images of naked women, which they employ in their fake sites, are objectifying and degrading rather than clearly operating as part of their critical practice. Spectators who are not familiar with Mongrel and net art are likely to experience *Natural Selection* in much more uneasy and unproductive ways. For instance, when briefly engaging with *Natural Selection* in the classroom, students expressed extreme discomfort with Mongrel's representations, which may be useful, and concern that these materials extended the presence of hate.

There are certainly situations in which repetition and the related performative moments can be a research and political strategy. Nevertheless, the ongoing viability of such instances remains unclear. According to Christine Ross, the recent trend among media artists to focus on "insufficiency" and "fallible corporeality" indicates the limits of the performative as a political tactic.[108] Ross suggests that Butler's performative repetition is not a successful strategy for producing political works. The ways repetition functions in net art also indicates that the relationship between disruptive reiteration and reinscription needs to be more carefully articulated. This might be achieved by considering spectators' initial reactions to repetition and the ongoing results of such tactics. In the meantime, political groups and theoreticians should have concerns about organizing their work solely around such effects.

Despite critical and theoretical arguments about the political effects of failure, this strategy also presents some problems. Spectator's increasing recognition of net art and the growing interest of many traditional art institutions indicate that the aesthetic of failure will continue to become more stylistic. The institutionalization of the aesthetic of failure as a common kind of Internet style threatens to compromise its "wrongness" and provide instructions for spectators who previously engaged with the strange and unfamiliar properties of these works. The challenge for net artists, software producers, technology critics, and other spectators may be finding new critical strategies rather than relying on repetition to highlight the ways that technologies have been constructed. Perhaps with such effects and aesthetics, spectators can continue to read carefully as well as differently.

Introduction

There are many Internet sites where spectators uphold setting-specific aesthetics, reading skills, and artistic practices. Virtual Places or VP, which is a web-based graphical communication setting that has been supported by Excite and a variety of other companies, is difficult to understand without knowledge of the system and its aesthetics.[1] Excite describes VP as "a community strategy that focuses on bringing people together online," and makes it seem like a material environment in which people achieve physical connections and move through an environment.[2] An important part of the VP setting is synchronously typed messages that other participants read. There is also a visual emphasis and an elaborate system for producing and understanding graphical avatar representations as both the spectator and original artworks. The visual depictions, synchronous texts, and other aspects of the setting are employed in order to render a VP user who is engaged in communicating with other people. However, an attention to avatars and the ways that these images are understood indicates that VP also produces spectators who look at, evaluate, and erotically enjoy visual material. These aesthetic practices are as integral an aspect of VP as the aesthetic of failure is to net art sites.

The narratives about VP interactivity, and Excite's indication that the software "allows people to navigate the Web with others while chatting at each page they visit," make it seem as though critical concepts of spectatorship cannot usefully address this setting.[3] Spectatorship has productively articulated visual experiences and viewing positions. However, theories about the ways spectators are acted upon, produced by varied settings, regulated, and sometimes even rendered passive may seem to limit the effectiveness of these discourses in considering engagements with graphical communication settings. Spectatorship has mistakenly been conceived of as the antithesis of activity. However, the spectator always has some ability to move

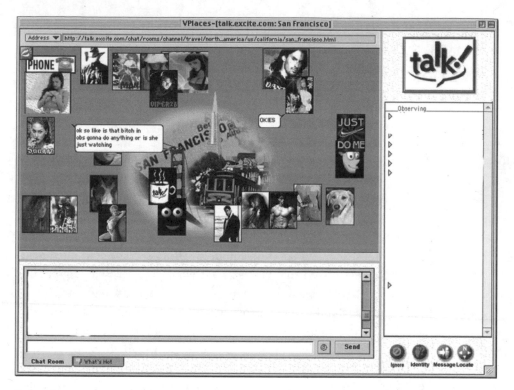

Figure 5.1
Excite, "VPlaces-[talk.excite.com: San Francisco]," 31 May 2000, <http://talk.excite.com/chat/rooms/channel/travel/north_america/us/california/san_francisco_html>.

in relation to contemplated works and to communicate with other viewers. The concept of the spectator is meant to suggest the ways a variety of mechanisms act upon and help construct viewing and reading engagements. These issues are particularly useful in considering sites like VP.

Avatar identification is an important part of VP spectatorship and a whole culture has been shaped around the ways that VP avatar images are manufactured and exchanged. Avatars are made from previously produced material—mostly from music, movies, and erotic magazines and web sites (figure 5.1). The avatar images are gleaned from popular sources and render familiar subjects and styles, but VP spectators articulate setting-specific functions and understandings of them. VP presents some uncommon concepts of authorship, cultural works, and the ways that previously produced materials should be identified and treated. For instance, VP producers who are often described as "artists" and "painters" identify avatars as their own original work because of the time spent selecting, copying, and cropping images. These practices conflict with Benjamin's indication that reproductions undermine aura. VP painters use a variety of strategies to relate their avatars to traditional artistic production.[4] Nevertheless, the artistic methods that painters employ, in order to render avatars as originals, indicate their ideological differences from critical considerations of reproductions and unintentionally distinguish them from net art and traditional forms of art production.

VP specific web sites address ethical and authorial concerns about the replication of avatars on other VP sites. The legitimacy of VP painters and their claims to own work are threatened by avatar "thefts" that put avatar images back into a public sphere of unidentified and incorrectly attributed exchange. Fan producers and web jewel designers, who are considered later in this chapter, also express concerns about the correct reuse of copied texts.[5] These ideas and anxieties about artistic work should encourage researchers and academics to read this material as system participants and to acknowledge the complex ethics involved in images and authorship. Setting-specific meanings and values are displaced when this material is simply viewed as an example of derivative work. However, addressing this material as a participant may not always be so easy.

VP avatars become "original" and "alive" through the production and reading practices of informed spectators. Yet it is difficult to determine how this occurs because VP producers and spectators rarely explain their aesthetic criteria. This creates a setting-specific knowledge that prevents some spectators from understanding, in ways that are similar to net art practices. The dearth of explanations in VP about aesthetic criteria, reading, and viewing may not be surprising since worth is often presumed rather than articulated in more traditional settings as well. Barthes indicates that "knowing *how to read* can be determined, verified at its inaugural stage, but it very quickly becomes a knowledge without basis, without rules, without degrees, and without end."[6] Barthes suggests the possibilities for reading differently. However, individual readings and experiences are often controlled by societal beliefs about cultural production. For instance, Elizabeth Long maintains that reading has to be taught and that instruction in particular ways of reading and evaluating always occur within communities and social structures.[7] Feminists and cultural critics continue to question how the age, class, gender, race, and sexuality of producers are regulated through aesthetic codes and conceptions of mastery.[8]

The theories of Roland Barthes, Umberto Eco, and Michel Foucault indicate that there are no cohesive authors and that the literary intentions of a particular producer can never be fully known.[9] They have looked to "writerly" or "open" works that emphasize reading processes, acknowledge that different forms of meaning are produced from texts, and provide readers with more control. More recent works on cultural appropriation and borrowing by authors like Camille Bacon-Smith, Rosemary Coombe, Henry Jenkins, and Constance Penley also focus on the ways individuals read and remake texts. They indicate that people can use these activities to bring texts closer, achieve political ends, and make subcultures and minorities visible.[10] For instance, Bolter and Landow consider how new forms of electronic cultural production challenge traditional authorship and the relationship between reading and writing.[11] They locate this disruption of dominant culture, which would ordinarily render a hierarchical division between consumers and producers, in hypertext and computer writing.

Theories of reading, fan culture, and hypertext offer vital methods to understand how texts are remanipulated in VP and other settings. However, there is also an ongoing tension in VP between the employment of unconventional reading and authorial strategies and the transformation of these practices into a hierarchical culture that regulates meaning making. An examination of VP indicates that current theories of alternative authorship and readership do not fully explain Internet production. Admittedly, VP is not exactly the same as the fan cultures or hypertexts that these authors describe. However, VP culture does include designing web sites, reworking texts, and producing avatars that are based on movie actors, rock stars, and other public figures. These similarities indicate that there are some problems with current ideas about fan culture and hypertexts. Unconventional reading practices can also reinscribe romantic notions of authorship.

Internet settings provide increased opportunities to engage with and even remake media texts but it is too soon to imagine that oppositional strategies, which question media messages, are no longer required. Jenkins argues that the Internet destroys the structures that differentiate between media consumers and producers so that certain forms of politics or the "old rhetoric of opposition and co-option" are no longer necessary.[12] Landow encourages individuals to resist considering and critiquing culture through the concepts of "center, margin, hierarchy, and linearity."[13] However, the collaborations and serial production strategies, which these authors consider, sometimes require a critical resistance that cannot operate in alliance with texts. An appreciation of alternative reading and production practices should be tempered with critical considerations of the less positive aspects of these cultures. For instance, the intervention of spectators and producers into media texts sometimes reproduces or even increases the stereotyped renderings of age, class, ethnicity, gender, race, and sexuality that can accompany these forms.

Critical writing on hierarchy and power by such authors as Nancy Hartsock, Trinh T. Minh-ha, Edward Said, and Eve Kosofsky Sedgwick can be used along with theories of authorship in order to indicate how Internet production renders new forms of power.[14] The work of Carol Duncan, Linda Nochlin, Griselda Pollock, and other feminist art historians are also useful in considering the ways older cultural narratives about individual authorship and artistic mastery operate in Internet settings. These critical works help explain how VP spectators write about avatar production, present graphical material on web sites, and make work into something more than copying. The introductory sections in this chapter provide a context for considering VP's setting-specific reading practices, the position of other spectators, the rendering of stereotypes, and the ways feminist and postcolonial theory can offer critical tools to address VP and other Internet sites. Without such theoretical combinations and the analysis of Internet sites, theories of alternative authorship cannot provide a way of analyzing the whole system.

Virtual Places

VP was designed by Ubique and first hosted by GNN, an Internet service provider, in Berkeley, California, in 1995. America Online also hosted a version at about the same time.[15] Excite began to host VP on 12 May 1997 and has called the software "Talk!" and more recently "Super Chat."[16] There are also versions of VP supported by Halsoft (also known as VPchat), Voodoo Chat, and other companies.[17] Some of these alternatives appeared when Excite was restructuring its version. Excite's support of different software builds, and its willingness to rectify varied system problems, has shifted over time and made some participants uneasy. VP spectators persistently refer to this group of interfaces as "VP," VPlaces," and "Virtual Places" despite different providers, problems with the availability of some versions, and changes in software.

Spectators engage with VP through a browser-based client that provides views of the web. The browser's functions and visual design are similar to Microsoft Internet Explorer, Netscape Navigator, Opera, and other browsers. The familiar features include a main screen in which web sites are downloaded, a menu-driven toolbar across the top of the browser, and a series of graphical "buttons." The repetition of familiar icons and options from other browsers allows the spectator to easily employ this software and to continue comprehending the web through already established conventions. Excite changed its software so that VP could be embedded in the Microsoft Internet Explorer browser. However, the artistic practices and conceptions of avatars, which are considered in this chapter, continue to function in the same way.

Both the stand-alone and embedded browsers offer features that are specific to VP. Web browsers are designed to give ready access to varied forms of information by allowing the spectator to easily download and decode data. For most web spectators, the quick manipulation of representations and the ability to change between varied browser frames are important. However, the stand-alone version of VP only provides one available frame. Another browser must be employed when the spectator wants to simultaneously view other sites. The Super Chat version, which is incorporated into the browser, allows the spectator to view VP as well as other web sites with the same software. However, Super Chat spectators are also more likely to unintentionally view another site with the VP screen and logout of the system. VP browsers are not that useful in reading web sites because the viewing frame is so much smaller than that of other browsers.[18] This is because much of the frame is filled with setting-specific options.

The VP software enables an engagement and view of the social setting rather than an examination of the web. VP browsers can download any web site, but avatars are most likely to be visible in the varied "rooms" offered by the sponsoring company (Excite, Halsoft, or Voodoo Chat) and at sponsor-specific "paint shops," where avatars can be downloaded.[19] The software provides a frame where spectators input texts, read other spectator's messages, consult a list of spectators who are looking at the same web site, and view visual versions of avatars and web sites. The browser allows the spectator to privately communicate through instant messaging options and to access information about other avatars. Some of the VP browsers also allow spectators to hear and speak through a voice option and to join a group "tour" of the web. The design of the browser encourages the visual examination of avatar representations as well as the reading of VP-generated texts. Through these devices, VP shifts the individual-oriented viewing structure of the web browser toward one of mutual display.

Avatars

The term "avatar" describes the visual representations that are employed in such graphical communication settings as VP. Avatars are believed to be a version of the self that exists "within" the interface. Varied dictionaries and other guides not only define the term "avatar" for Internet spectators but also suggest how avatars should be employed and rendered. Spectators are advised to "just be aware" that avatars "represent" the spectator, let "you role play and interact with people you meet online," and are "a real person in a cyberspace system."[20] These definitions instruct the spectator to carefully consider the kinds of representations that are chosen and to develop a direct form of identification where "you are your avatar."[21] The "avatar" is often conceptualized as a visual image. However, the name or "nick," spectator's messages, and visual aspects produce the avatar. Delphica indicates that many spectators select nicknames that are a form of their own name in order to invite spectators "to see more of the real you."[22] Graphical avatars, and MOO characters, are made into what appear to be people and a living essence through such tactics. Even avatars that are not being manipulated are sometimes described as alive.[23]

The VP browser allows spectators to choose from a number of "stock" avatar images, but most spectators make or download their own representations. Many of these personally produced and downloaded avatars are erotic. For instance, images of young white women, which are the most common form of avatar offered by paint shops, often have large breasts, long legs, scanty clothes, tousled hair, and highly made-up faces. The numerous spectators who choose to self-represent with these sexual images indicate the societal fascination with certain types of bodies, show how individuals would like to present themselves, and send cultural messages about appropriate representations. Despite some individuals' pleasure in viewing countless available erotic images and the promised correlation of these representations to spectators who appear to be equally available, there are some problems with such avatar representations. The gender that is visually depicted by avatars does not always correlate with the gender listed in the "My Identity" form, which other spectators can view through the VP browser. This gender correlation becomes even more confusing when these erotic representations are a kind of advertisement for the bodies that spectators desire rather than the body that they claim to have.

A variety of academic and popular texts associate avatar identification with the postmodern conception of fragmented selves.[24] MOOs are also thought to facilitate "readily interchangeable parts" and a "hybrid generation."[25] In VP, spectators often change their avatar image and choose different images to represent themselves, in a process that is related to morphing, rather than making their different representations appear to be one person. VP spectators represent a particular gendered position instead of a uniform physiognomic identity. Feminist theorists indicate that such fragmented positions, which suggest conflicting identities and desires, can disturb conceptions of cohesive identity that would otherwise authorize some individuals—particularly white heterosexual men—and validate their right to power.[26] However, multiple Internet positions can also suggest that spectators have power in different settings. The articulated connections between the spectator and VP avatar seem to place the individual simultaneously inside the screen and in the physical world. Employing the term "avatar" also supports the idea of an empowered spectator because it has been defined as a "god."[27] The tendency to refer to system administrators as "wizards" or "gods" in such synchronous settings as MOOs, MUDs, and The Palace suggests the severe power differences that persist.

Stephenson considers the relationship between power inequities and avatar-based computer use in his novel *Snow Crash*. He depicts a setting where "people are pieces of software called avatars" and they communicate in the virtual metaverse.[28] His descriptions of the social ranking of avatars by complexity suggest that computer systems replicate rather than alleviate hierarchy. On the low end, and ostracized by many through "dirty looks," are off-the-shelf avatars and the grainy "black-and-white" people who use public terminals.[29] The regulatory looking of avatars, which makes it clear to the spectator that an avatar is generic, also indicates that virtual settings have a class structure.[30] Stephenson's narratives about Internet differences, which are enforced by the gaze as well as other processes, are related to incidents in MOOs, net art sites, VP, and other Internet settings.

Programmers and synchronous communication setting spectators have adopted Stephenson's narrative. For instance, Bruce Damer's consideration of graphical communication settings describes *Snow Crash* as the "Bible of the avatar Cyberspace movement" and indicates that if "you haven't read it, you haven't seen the light, brother!"[31] Stephenson suggests some of the problems with Internet communication, but many of his readers have not acknowledged his consideration of hierarchical computer settings. In fact, comments about the significance of Stephenson's book helped establish its place in the cyberpunk and graphical communication hierarchy. For instance, Damer's comments "speak" to a reader who may not have received the "light," and he assures this Internet "brother," who he has gendered as male, that knowledge is available through the text. Such comments may not be surprising since Stephenson has also tried to establish his place in an Internet and science fiction canon by claiming that he coined the term "avatar."

Stephenson indicates in the acknowledgments to his book that the "words 'avatar' (in the sense used here) and 'Metaverse' are my inventions."[32] Such a territorial claim to terms is not surprising since Gibson is credited with and continues to receive great acclaim for creating the term "cyberspace," although "cyber" has a much longer history. Stephenson indicates it was only after publishing *Snow Crash* that he discovered that Randy Farmer and Chip Morningstar used the term "avatar" to describe characters in Habitat, an early Internet setting that they designed in 1985.[33] Stephenson does not mention that the term also appears in Poul Anderson's *The Avatar*, which was published in 1978.[34] *Snow Crash* is important to graphical communication spectators because it articulates avatar-based communication and the relationship between avatars and spectators. However, the "history" of the term is more multifaceted than most spectators acknowledge, and Stephenson's position as its inventor is more tentative.

Stephenson's novel represents the appeal of being visible in graphical settings. However, it is not clear what becomes visible when spectators employ VP. Amateur photographic images by VP spectators rarely appear, and claims that the avatar is a digital photograph of the spectator are even less common. Interestingly, the VP and LambdaMOO settings still suggest that there is a correlation between representations and physical bodies and a sort of visual and textual trace of the physical person. Nevertheless, the elements that constitute the VP avatar are largely unexplored by spectators. It is not clear if the avatar is only the picture or some conjunction of image, name, and textual comments. In either case, visual representations in VP produce a kind of "speaking." They stand in for ideas about what bodies are, describe the physiognomy of the spectator, represent what spectators are seeking, and present a form of art that can only be read by some spectators.

Painters and Avatar Galleries

The availability of thousands of VP "galleries," where spectators can view and select avatars, indicate the pleasure in visualization and the appeal of making avatar images. Self-identified artists freely offer preproduced avatar images on web site "paint shops." On these web-based sites, spectators can also get avatars made specifically for them by "painters." "Painting" is the personalization of scanned photographs and other images by changing the background, layering images, adding highlights, or appending the spectator's alias.[35] "Paint shop" and "painter" refer to Jasc's Paint Shop Pro software, which is a popular application among VP artists. However, the terms "paint shop" and "painter" also render VP as high culture. The value of avatar production is underscored by painters who use aggrandizing terms like "mastery," describe grids of avatar images as "galleries," and establish shop rules that often distinguish between how VP painters and spectators can behave. Spectators are warned not to bother the artists, make unauthorized avatars while using the paint shop site (spectators cannot function as artists), and create lag by following the artists' habit of showing their different avatars in rapid succession. The production of avatars is part of a whole VP network in which participants vie for rankings on "top 100" sites, have a "featured" artist of the month, boast about the skill of their artists, and compete for awards.[36]

There are numerous paint shop ranking contests and painting awards where painters may either compete in real time or submit images in response to a set of parameters. Synchronous painting contests are announced on site pages and can be watched by any spectator. Contests and awards determine what sites look like and how they function. Paint shops have hyper-visible awards notices, or a series of banners that display their rankings, and present most of the awards. Contests articulate VP artistry and the intellectual property of painters. For instance, Hey Baby Grafx's criteria for awards are "ORIGINAL DESIGN! and ORIGINAL CONTENT!!"[37] Contests try to define, at least for the spectators, judges, and participants who watch them, what a winning image and masterful authorship looks like. Contests are both participatory and regulatory events. They "instruct" users in reading practices, canonize certain painters, and establish aesthetic criteria. What remains unclear are how other spectators, who do not participate in this economy, can understand and read avatar images. VP practices do not provide much education or explanation about paint shop practices. However, this elision is not designed to produce the forms of spectatorial failure that happen in net art, which encourage the spectator to examine the properties of the Internet and computer. Instead, VP painters articulate their identity through the production of difference and even the withholding of setting-specific knowledge.

The setting-specific conventions and reading practices of VP make appropriated images into unique forms of artistry. Painters and paint shops employ framing texts about artistic excellence and "talent" to connect their production to the fine arts. For instance, the Image Reflections paint shop claims that spectators use the site because of "the astounding talent of our artists."[38] VP Essentials describes an "Artist of the Month . . . who has proven time after time that talent comes from within."[39] The Society of Gesture Makers encourages the spectator to "learn from the masters!"[40] VP artists produce a version of the "typical art historical narrative" that Griselda Pollock and other feminists critique. This narrative renders "a gifted individual creating out of his (sic) personal necessity a discrete work of art."[41] In VP, the idea of individual and aura-imbued work is supported by site design, which often incorporates images of paintbrushes, palettes, and other emblems of artistry. Of course, these tools are depicted in order to indicate the artistic aspects of paint shop sites, and such equipment is not employed in producing avatars.

The statements on paint shop web sites reproduce traditional ideas about art production in order to provide a history and justification for avatar painting. In these accounts, creativity is conceptualized as magical and coming from within. For instance, Av Illusionz describes an artistic process in which the producer transcends the ordinary and potentially derivative aspects of VP work. This personal "vision" allows the artist to reach "beyond the thing that is, into the conception of what can be. Imagination gives you the picture. Vision gives you the impulse to make the picture your own."[42] Through this description, Av Illusionz represents the VP process of changing copied images, or the "picture," into something that is culturally valuable, individually rendered, and owned. Such narratives suggest that VP painters use copies in distinctly different ways than Benjamin envisioned, and that these technologically facilitated copies encourage rather than reduce the need for original and aura-imbued works. In this VP narrative, there is no need to consider how skills, aesthetics, and genres are culturally produced and shared because creativity remains a largely unknowable aspect of the individual. Such VP processes also elide the socially constructed reading and viewing skills that are required to understand.

Nochlin indicates that the tendency to resist articulating the criteria for "great art," which occurs in VP and a variety of other settings, is intentional and has political implications. She notes that there are few considerations of how aesthetics are established and that the critical research done in this area is often dismissed as unscholarly, unfocused, and inappropriate for the discipline of art history, which is an obvious field for such considerations. This is because such investigations "would reveal the entire romantic, elitist, individual-glorifying, and monograph-producing structure upon which the profession of art history is based" and how certain forms of art and artists are protected.[43] In VP, considering such aesthetic criteria would indicate the conflicts in paint shop practices. VP painters reinscribe traditional values and art-historical discourses even though participants in these other systems would not recognize the culture. VP producers conceptualize images differently than intended and read them inventively. However, as the narratives of VP and other Internet settings are accepted, they produce new hierarchical forms of cultural production rather than alternative types of reading and producing. VP spectators read images differently than do viewers in other settings, but there are also VP codes on how to read.

All cultural producers borrow images, themes, and genre conventions from other work. However, the appropriated and remanipulated aspects of cultural production are not acknowledged to the same degree. Coombe suggests that legal institutions regulate and legitimize some forms of "meaning-making" by envisioning them as authorship, while other activities are understood as illegitimate and derivative and thus denigrated.[44] Peter Jaszi indicates that copyright law, and I think that social conceptions of authorship could be added to his argument, have "lost sight of the cultural value of what might be called 'serial collaborations'—works resulting from successive elaborations of an idea or text by a series of creative workers."[45] VP engages in serial production and collaborative authorship in a number of ways. The use of the paint shop metaphor suggests salons and schools of artistic production rather than acts of individual authorship. Shops usually present avatars as the work of a particular painter, but there are some sites that present their avatars as part of a larger shop practice.

What Coombe and Jaszi have not discussed are the ways that subcultural producers, such as VP painters, participate in serial production and then authorize their work by repeating discourses about traditional authorship. VP paint shops continue to present statements that support notions of individual authorship even though there are many instances of collaborative production within the system. VP producers and spectators—and individuals often shift between these roles—conceptualize paint shop work as artistry and authorship rather than as the deeply intertextual (referencing multiple kinds of texts as part of the work), quotational, and postmodern ways images circulate. VP images have obvious source material, which is acknowledged and then displaced, but when one considers how these images are read within the system, the conception of derivative works and postmodernism may not apply.

VP spectators acknowledge that their production, reading, and meaning-making practices are different than those performed in other settings. However, this admission is often connected to explanations of why VP production is better than other practices. For instance, Ink describes a process of viewing in which a "priceless work of art" is incomprehensible to spectators but a drawing from a comic book "blows their mind." Ink concludes by noting, "We are all different & appreciate different things in life."[46] In this narrative of difference, the popular comic book, which can be equated with VP production, is both accessible and elevated to an art context through mind expanding and transcendental viewing. There are some less elevating depictions of VP. The Crackhouse paint shop presents an alternative or "freakish" membership and derides VP practices.[47] A participant in a Crackhouse contest suggested that "there are no winners . . . only least crappy."[48] Yet even this description demonstrates that quality is determined through visual evaluation. Paint shop texts and contests indicate how spectators should view avatars and inform spectators, including viewers who do not participate and who are new to the culture of avatar production, that this material is important. However, most paint shop sites and producers do not explain how artistry, originality, and talent are determined. Nevertheless, conflicts and ethical debates about painters reusing each other's images abound.

Owning Texts

"Theft" and "copy" as well as such terms as "artist," "painter" and "original" have setting-specific meanings in VP that are based on the ways that the images are made, used, and circulated. Bruce Ziff and Pratima V. Rao indicate that the "breach" of copyright or theft of work is an "appropriative act" and that we can describe the involved authors and producers but this also articulates the "rights of *individuals* based on views of authorship."[49] As they suggest, narratives about appropriation can establish traditional versions of authorship and creativity by indicating that a unique and individual idea has been taken. For instance, VP authorship is established through the numerous narratives about theft and the copyright notices that appear on many paint shop sites. These copyright notices provide instructions on how the spectator should view avatar images.

Landow considers the ways images, textual passages, motifs, and genre conventions are continually recycled and wonders how society assigns "legal, commercial, and moral rights" when the author is more fragmented.[50] These problems also occur in VP where copyright, according to ...ThunderCat_22..., is "the most bitched about topic."[51] VP authorship is dispersed because painters tend to self-represent with multiple avatars, there are differences between spectator and avatar, some spectators employ the same avatar image, and there are also similarities among avatar names. VP producers have reacted to the problems of serial production and fragmented authorship by providing narratives of individual inspiration, creativity, and ownership. Paint shops include declarations about copyright protection and complaints about avatar thefts, but comments about painters' appropriation of other sources are rare. VPlaces is unusual in indicating that it does not credit sources because the available size of the avatar, which has a "restricted space of *48x64*[,] *leaves no possibility* for a *visible copyright quote*."[52] Of course, VPlaces does not explain why sources are not cited in paint shops where there is more room for such texts. Such VP statements about avatar thefts articulate an ethics of appropriation even if the conception of intellectual property and copyright is unusual.

Painters employ images without crediting the author, but posting avatar images on other web sites is highly discouraged. Many paint shops have notices that inform spectators about expected behavior, VP netiquette, and the ethics of avatar production. Silent Lucidity's Avatars notes, "As usual don't steal the avs from this page and post them as your own work. Trust me, if you made your own avs you would not want someone claiming your hours of hard work!!!"[53] Eternal.Goku indicates that everything in VP is "from a magazine or something" but "to make those pics original ,,, Is a task."[54] Expressions is "very tired of seeing my work on other pages" because "The Internet Gods Do Not Poof Up at the Snap of Their Fingers Content for Websites. Somebody a Real Person Worked Very Hard to Create the Items."[55] These notices and comments indicate that a significant part of the VP criterion for intellectual property is "work." This work makes the material useful in VP rather than changing the ways images appear. In other words, VP ethics suggest that these images belong to painters because they spent time on them.

VP work processes include selecting, scanning, and cutting. Callisto describes their offerings as "original avatars" that were "made using scanned images."[56] Jennifer S. notes that her avatars are made from images "copped from the net, original scans or original graphics."[57] In VP, scanning is more than the reproduction of images. The conceptual substitution of "original scan" for "copy," like the discourse about work, makes appropriated material unique. Selecting, scanning, and cutting produces originals. Avatars are "Originals Cut & Made By Us From Pictures We Scanned Or Found On The Web" and "hand selected and cut."[58] Xtreme Grafix Paintshop lists "how good the cut is" as its first criteria for paint shop awards.[59] The cut may even be more important for VP painters than their use of software-facilitated painting techniques. The cut allows painters to remove the image from its previous context and encourages spectators to read it differently. There may be "Similar Avatars Cut From The Same Pictures," but it is unlikely that two painters will put the cut in exactly the same place.[60] This emphasis on the cut suggests that there is a relationship between VP and traditional photographic practices. Stanley Cavell indicates that the cut, the "implied presence of the rest of the world, and its explicit rejection, are as essential in the experience of a photograph as what it explicitly presents."[61] The originality and worth of cutting may be dismissed in some cultural settings, but Cavell's comments indicate that the cut is as important as traditional manipulations of art materials.

The Society of Gesture Makers has a list of "Black-Listed Sites" and chronicles "stolen avatars."[62] While most paint shops discourage avatar "thefts," some painters still take avatars and justify their actions. For instance, Wicked Creations indicates that "these avs were all 'stolen' from av sites that they themselves 'stole' from photographers images in magazines."[63] Silent Lucidity, who posted a warning about stealing avatars, has more recently indicated that originality and theft are inextricably intertwined in VP and that there are problems with an image culture where representations are constantly being reconfigured. "Silent" notes that "I used images everyone else does and called them Original. . . . You see, I scanned, sized, formatted, and erased text . . . so yeah, I think I did make these and they are originals . . . lol. All images herein are copyrighted to their respective owners."[64] In a "confession" about being "an avatar thief," Swooz also suggests that there are problems with VP notions of originality and mocks claims to authorial mastery, which are based on the idea that the work of "stealing" images justifies claiming them.[65] However, a variety of strategies and warnings are deployed in order to indicate that downloading avatars and then presenting them in another paint shop is theft. The .::Erotic-BDsM::. paint shop indicates that the practice of downloading and posting avatars with a notice that indicates, "These Are NOT Mine I Just Collected Them From Other Sites," or "We Take No Credit For Making These," should be questioned and "Aren't Really Class Avatar Sites."[66] The conception of "class" is used to regulate painter and spectator behavior. Such posted comments are meant to repress other opinions about avatar production and to protect sites from spectators' alternative readings and uses of avatars.

Painters describe their avatars as alive and situated in order to indicate that there are ramifications to taking them. Theft is rendered as a disruption of the avatar's placement and agency as well as of the painter's authorial control. For instance, the Avatar Factory states that its avatars "live here, feel free to use them, but please do not post them to other avatar pages."[67] Shadow-Wolf implores, "Please Do Not Post These Avatars To Anyother Gallery. They Live Here, And I Worked Hard To Make Them."[68] Narratives about Internet representations being alive are also employed in telepresence art sites and webcams. In these settings, liveness is used to make renderings seem less mediated. In VP, this discourse about liveness is even more complicated because painters describe avatars living in a particular setting in order to emphasize creative ownership and to show that theft disturbs the avatar's life. Suggesting that spectators "wear" avatars also connects or even conflates the spectator and avatar. Even though The Crackhouse derides VP production practices, it still advises spectators that "these avs are all originals . . . wear, dont post."[69] Quality and artistry are also rendered through the clothing metaphor. Lil.voodoo encourages the spectator "who wears our creations" to "be proud and wear them with STYLE!!!"[70] There are also indications that "your 'closets' will be filled with VP attire" and that "only the best dressed VPsters shop here."[71] Paint shop texts indicate the quality, worth, and originality of painters without explaining their criteria for these judgments.

Criteria for Originality

Xtreme Grafix Paintshop is one of the few sites that articulate criteria for awards, which are "based on creativity and artistic ability."[72] The shop looks "at: a) How good the cut is. b) The effects that were applied. c) The originality of the background. d) Coloring techniques. e) The ability to read the name. f) The overall look of the AV."[73] Of course, most of Xtreme Grafix's criteria are still based on personal taste. Painters rarely provide information or discuss their criteria for originality in paint shops. When I raised this topic, poor.lady was one of the few VP painters who articulated an aesthetic. She presented her "tubalicious av," which she previously made as a joke about bad painting, and it produced a visual conversation (figure 5.2).[74] Through the avatar,

Figure 5.2
poor.lady, "Excite Chat—[Excite Talk!: Ing's AV and Gesture Links—Over 2100 Links!!!]," 13 Mar. 2001, <members.aol.com/cowtowning/AVlinks.htm>.

poor.lady and other shop painters explained that excessively decorated avatars are scorned. They are simple to produce with the "tubes" and other software that are available from paint shop sites. Painters appreciate designs that make VP work easier to determine because it is so simple to produce many avatar effects. This is one reason that the cut is appealing.

Many VP spectators also distinguish between regular avatars and those painted specifically for another spectator. Man indicates that painted avatars are very popular, observing: "Good av painters really have a good sense of art, and great perceptional vision. Av painting takes patience and talent, but if you have the time and quality of work to take up av painting, it's rewarding, almost everyone likes a well-painted avatar.[75] Man's comments about avatar painting suggest that a "well-painted" avatar will be easily recognized and its quality admired by all VP spectators. The belief in the universal aspects of art and aesthetics also continues in physical communities. In all these instances, there is a conviction that artistic production improves and develops over time. Blue Rhino Avatars has been "trying to adjust" its "av making techniques to the current trends."[76] Sen notes that in 1998 "painting was a simplified method of basically putting names on Avs," but she has "changed with the times" and so have her "techniques."[77] With these comments, Blue Rhino and Sen render art as a linear and developmental process. These narratives about progress, style, and development are also an important part of establishing artistic worth in other markets. For instance, Carol Duncan indicates that, in the nineteenth century, progress in art was believed to be "progress toward an ideal that, brilliantly realized in the past, could now measure the achievements of the present."[78] These ideas about artistic development continue in contemporary art markets and VP settings.

Avatar production methods are justified by connecting them to the types of copying that happen in more traditional art forms. For instance, xX_Ms_Mike_T.. suggests that "a real painting comes from an image inside someone else so whose to say" and that high culture should not be allowed to argue "that they're not copyin' what they see."[79] Despite such allusions to the serial aspects and borrowing that happen in all art forms, recent examples of cultural appropriation, which include rap musicians' quotations of earlier songs and David Salle's and Jeff Koons's references to popular imagery, are not mentioned. XxX_Golden_XxX argues that there is no difference between avatar production and "real painting," which means "manipulating the image and adding it to other images," and all painters manipulate "shapes, colors, transparency, and text."[80] Despite such descriptions, the idea that the painter individually crafts an avatar for another spectator is not always accepted. For instance, Southern was disturbed by XxX_Golden_XxX's account of being the sole producer. Southern selected the image and wanted to make it clear that this was a part of the process.[81] This reaction may not be surprising since the selection of materials is articulated on many VP sites as a key aspect of avatar production. For instance, UniQue Avatars describes its avatars as "UN-i-Q-ue" because each "is carefully selected for the most discriminating of tastes."[82] The ideas about originality and ownership, which are established in paint shops, may be part of an attempt to regulate spectators who would otherwise see their selections of avatars from paint shops as painting. Shop rules always distinguish between painters and those who are waiting for painted avatars.

Images of the shop painters are clearly displayed on web sites in order to reinforce the unique identity of the artists and shops (figures 5.3–5.4). These images of muscled men and large-breasted women probably do not portray the physical bodies of most painters. However, the style of the work and the gender of the avatar are meant to render an identity for them. These images cannot make the painters recognizable since they often employ multiple avatars. Yet, concerns that imposters will inappropriately paint at shops abound. For instance, Pixelbox indicates, "Our staff members reside in Halsoft Chat. Anyone painting here other than in Halsoft does not work here!"[83] Some shops advertise that they are looking for painters and encourage the submission of avatars as part of the application. However, the ability to paint at a particular shop is always regulated.

VP sometimes appears to be the logical outcome of postmodernist art practices because of the copying. A cursory examination suggests that VP avatars seem like the

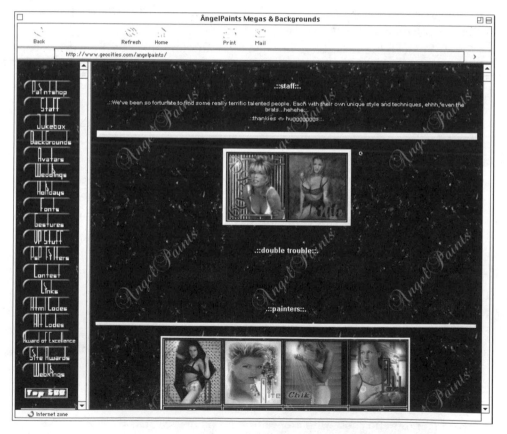

Figure 5.3
AngelPaints, "AngelPaints Megas & Backgrounds," 25 June 2003, <http://www.geocities.com/ angelpaints/>.

Theories of Internet Authorship

VP paint shops maintain ideas about originality and individual authorship that are different than those suggested by theories of Internet and computer production. Hypertext theories indicate that technologies and communities have changed the role of the author and reading processes. For instance, Landow notes that "terms such as text and distinctions such as originality do not make much sense" with the computer.[85] Bolter presents similar ideas about computer production and argues that an "electronic text cannot pretend to be an 'original' work in the conventional sense."[86] According to him, visual and literary forms of electronic writing emphasize the transience and mutability of texts and reduce distinctions between readers and authors by "turning the reader into an author."[87] These academics suggest that traditional notions of authorship are no longer possible.[88]

Studies of fan cultures also describe an empowered reader who intervenes in and even becomes the producer of new forms of cultural production. Computers, technological operations, and Internet settings mediate some forms of fan culture. For instance, Bacon-Smith indicates that digital technologies allow members of science fiction, fantasy, and horror cultures to produce work through "consensus" and "connections."[89] These connections happen within the fluid communities of producers, consumers, and fans where, according to Jenkins, "every reader was understood to be a potential writer."[90] Jenkins studies the "collaborative enterprise" of science fiction and fantasy authors and fans and the ways they find value and make meaning from cultural texts that others condemn for being trivial. [91] Jenkins's consideration extends to Internet-based fan communities that are "focused around the collective production, debate, and circulation of meanings, interpretations and fantasies in response to various artifacts of contemporary culture."[92] Penley also describes the active work of fans and how they "are producing not just intermittent, cobbled-together acts, but real products."[93] All of these studies of fan culture indicate that particular reading skills are needed to understand fan-produced texts. However, they do not address the political implications of these fan-produced systems of knowledge.

There are some writers who indicate that the Internet and computer have not reconfigured the relationship between artists/authors and viewers/readers, question the privileged discourse that accompanies originality, and note that these technologies have yet to democratize society. Charles Ess considers the utopian claims for hypertext and provides a more complex understanding of what Internet democracy might mean.[94] Aarseth argues that hypertext theory is a form of "technological determinism" that does not acknowledge how authorship is challenged in a variety of forms.[95]

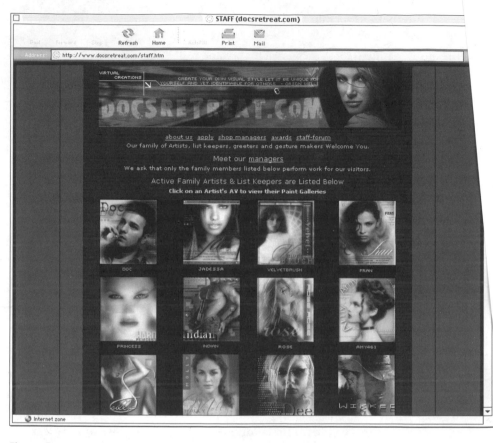

Figure 5.4
Docs Retreat, "STAFF (docsretreat.com)," 22 Nov. 2003, <http://www.docsretreat.com/
staff.htm>.

work of Barbara Kruger, Sherrie Levine, Richard Prince, and other artists who recycle
contemporary advertising and other forms of cultural production. However, VP's paint
shop codes are very different from the appropriation, conceptual, and painterly art
that is privileged in the contemporary art markets in Los Angeles, New York, and
Europe. In VP, the authenticity of avatar representations and the authority of painters
are underscored, with no visible irony, by the claim to be "the original vp avatar site .
. . since 1996" and to have achieved other firsts.[84] The elitist conceptions of avatar
painting and shops suggest that VP painters want to engage with spectators in other
systems. However, VP painters and spectators do not articulate their relationship to
postmodern appropriation and other terms in ways that cultural sympathizers would
understand.

Andrea MacDonald provides a brief introduction to how hierarchy operates within fan cultures and how media outlets regulate meaning through Internet settings. She indicates that the celebrated participation of science fiction authors and television writers in Internet-facilitated "group discussions" results in a situation where "authors are able to jump in and correct fan interpretations."[96] MacDonald notes that Internet technologies allow fans to maintain exclusive fan email lists, "reread a text and synthesize with many minds," and "gatekeep meaning making," but she never addresses the political significance of authorial control.[97]

Theories about the radical possibilities of Internet and computer reading tend to indicate that digital technologies facilitate the critical theories of Barthes, Deleuze and Guattari, and Eco. For instance, Landow suggests that Barthes' discussion of the active or "writerly" reader in S/Z "precisely matches" computer hypertext.[98] Barthes differentiates between "readerly" texts, which provide traditional reading experiences, and writerly texts, which allow the reader to intervene and render a more empowered position.[99] Stam, Burgoyne, and Flitterman-Lewis indicate that the readerly text "posits authorial mastery" while the writerly text "provokes an active reader, sensitive to contradiction and heterogeneity, aware of the work of the text."[100] Writerly texts change the passive consumer into a producer. Barthes indicates that such things as tables of contents, footnotes, and particular ways of writing provide the reader with a sense of agency and encourage a more self-directed engagement with the text. Images offer different kinds of reading and viewing experiences than do written texts. Nevertheless, all written texts can be read visually and some, such as concrete poetry, may actually call for this approach. With single visual images, pages and information cannot be skipped over in the same way that they can be in a written text. However, the spectator's ability to examine visual works through a series of looks and glances also facilitates writerliness.

The avatars produced by VP painters and the ways they are understood offer both readerly and writerly aspects. VP spectators read avatar images in different ways than other populations do. The writerliness of avatars only engages certain viewers, and avatars require certain kinds of viewers in order to be activated in a writerly way. This may be because readers are also producers who can, when they are empowered by a community or organization, still regulate the ways that meaning is understood. Barthes indicates that the reader also "*overcodes*; he does not decipher, he produces."[101] Coombe argues that "through irony mockery, parody, pastiche, and even alternative modes of appreciation, activities of creative appropriation enable fans to comment indirectly not only on gender ideology, but on law, culture, authorship, authority, and the commodity form."[102] However, VP painters and spectators often produce traditional meanings and disturbing politics through unlikely sources.

Despite the claims of these critics, the "death" or reconfiguration of the author and rise of the reader may not always bring positive political change.[103] Norma Broude and Mary D. Garrard indicate that the death of the author is likely to lead to the death of feminism as a facilitator of positive political and art-historical change.[104] This is because feminist investigations into the reasons that so few women are recognized as authors and artists no longer apply with these methods. It is certainly worth noting that theories about the death or revision of authorship, by Barthes, Foucault, and others, appeared at about the same time as women were establishing their own subjectivity and authorial voice. Second-wave feminists and poststructuralists were interested in questioning the role of modern authors and artists because these producers were deified, attributed great powers of creativity and originality, deemed to be larger than life, and often presumed to be male.[105] However, attempts to reverse the power structure and provide the critic and reader with more control may have only resituated the attributes previously ascribed to authors and artists. Calls for the death of the author and the rise of the reader too often establish forms of reading that the critic personifies. Within these models, there are still ideal readers.

VP and other Internet settings model and regulate alternative readings. In some cases, it is the community rather than the author that sets specific reading codes and languages. For instance, VP Headquarters indicates that new spectators go through a kind of initiation process where they begin to understand setting- and Internet-specific texts. They "learn the talk," which includes "OMG, LMAO, WB, WTF," "sentences get shorter," punctuation disappears, and then the spectator is "fittin right in!"[106] A variety of academics and theorists indicate that alternative readings allow the reader to have more control. However, the replacement of the controlling author with a regulating community, which authorizes some reading and spectatorial strategies over those of other individuals, does not necessarily provide a better political position. The death of the author and rise of the reader and viewer may need to be replaced by critiques of how we read, view, and produce.

Gender, Race, Sexuality, and the Avatar

Setting-specific reading and production practices are an important part of paint shops. VP and its accompanying paint shop structure allow producers, who would not be accepted by more traditional art markets, to display, boast about, and provide VP spectators with their work. The varied ways VP and other Internet settings help cultural producers find an appreciative audience and market for their work are encouraging. Hypertext and fan theories emphasize these positive aspects of Internet settings and suggest how VP painters can become artists as well as viewers, the ways appropriated work becomes important, and the different meaning making and social systems that occur. However, an examination of VP texts also indicates that participants in this setting tend to institute traditional notions of authorial and artistic mastery, which have historically regulated what work looked like and who could produce it. VP supports the ideology of more traditional art markets and education institutions where the white male privilege of both artists and spectators is still established.

Artistic movements and the accompanying critical and historical discourses tend to privilege the work of white heterosexual men and celebrate erotic images of women. In Pollock's consideration of art-historical engagements with postimpressionism, which also applies to other artistic movements, she indicates that "patriarchal versions" of gender, sexuality and sexual difference are instituted because of the glorification of mastery and identification with the sexualities of the art and artists.[107] Broude and Garrard provide a similar critique of abstract expressionism and indicate that this movement celebrated a "'virile' art" in which the "potency" of the practicing artists depended on their transcending a female-gendered natural world.[108] The numerous cultural critics, feminists, and Marxists working in art history provide ongoing critiques of art representations, art historical narratives, and gallery and museum practices. However, narratives about male genius have not dissipated with time. Guerilla Girls documents the ways art institutions privilege white male artists and indicates, for instance, that the Museum of Modern Art should change the title of a 1997 contemporary still-life show to "The Objects of MOMA's Desires are Still White Males" because there were so few other artists represented.[109] VP also provides more images of white artists and representations of white spectators. While there are many images of women in this setting, they tend to institute patriarchal visions of gender, sexual difference, and sexuality and do not render empowered forms of identity for women.

VP paint shop galleries are often composed of grids of representations of women and offer the spectator a variety of menu and submenu options (figure 5.5). The Image Reflections paint shop presents organized avatar grids of "types" such as "Blondes," "Brunettes," "Redheads," "Ebony," "Asian," "Hispanic," "B & W," "MiddleEast," "Misc," and "In Art." under the "Females" category.[110] The inclusion of the grid within the VP structure, which is designed to render original and masterful work, is interesting because the grid is a conventional device and, as Krauss notes, *can only be repeated.*[111] Thus, when interrogated, the grid indicates the repetitive aspects of paint shop practices and how these settings articulate woman as a category. This challenge to notions of originality is not what VP painters want. Nevertheless, each attribute of

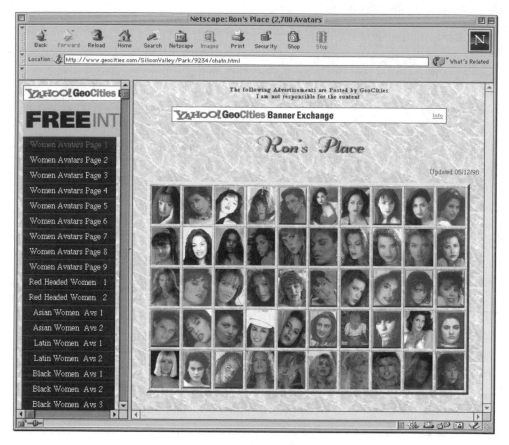

Figure 5.5
Ron's Place, "Ron's Place (2. 700 Avatars," 15 Apr. 2000, <http://www.geocities.com/
SiliconValley/Park/9234/chatn.html>.

Image Reflections' and other paint shops' grids is translated into a series of cut and cat-
egorized representations that are available for the spectator's selection. The grids make
it seem as if representations of women, which are the largest number of images, are
physically available for the taking.

The organization of women's bodies into available types, including mappings of
skin and hair color, too easily evokes a history of racial and ethnic intolerance in
which the charting and mapping of bodies were used as scientific proof of differences.
The grid suggests that the body is knowable and controllable. Jennifer Gonzalez critiques the practice of providing grids of avatars and indicates that "the interdependent
histories of colonialism and collecting (especially for museums of anthropology)"

should encourage viewers to ask "*who* is collecting *whom* online" and what kinds of bodies are put on display.[112] As Gonzalez suggests, the large number of women's images on these sites and the organization of certain bodies are not surprising. Nevertheless, these images render a culture of collecting, classifying, and objectifying that is not equally available or comfortable for all spectators.

The fantasy of possessing and even digitally correcting women's naked bodies is rendered by painters and offered to spectators. Such commodifying practices are supported by the paint shop texts, which encourage spectators to "wear" and "own" avatars of women. There are an excessive number of women avatars available at most paint shops. These images almost always portray young, glamorous, fully made-up, light-skinned women who strike erotic poses for the spectator. Such elements as tousled hair, sultry looks, and scanty clothing that barely covers the women's breasts repeat themselves with striking regularity. Paint shop representations are influenced by traditional painting and sculpture conventions, in which the gaze of the artist and spectator are overtly male and the object viewed is female, and the continuance of such viewing positions in museums.[113] For instance, Guerilla Girls indicates that "85% of the nudes are female" in the modern sections of the Metropolitan Museum of Art.[114] VP representations of women are usually cropped above the waist so that the mobile body is made into a series of parts that are contained by the frame. Representations of women in museums, MOOs, and technology advertisements also tend to be looking down, reading, or otherwise passive and available to the spectator's gaze.

VP representations offer a strikingly limited notion of what a woman can be even though the goal of avatar selection, as described by a variety of Internet dictionary and VP sites, is to represent a unique self. Women avatars tend to be passive and contained by the frame, but men are represented in motion, wielding bloodied swords, generating power from their wizened hands, and comfortably presenting erotic sexuality and grotesque physiognomy. The male grids read like a list of possibilities, while the female grids present a limited vernacular.[115] Feminist art historians have critiqued such visually produced differences between women and men. For instance, Nochlin argues that artists' representations of women are based upon and reproduce cultural beliefs that men are different from and superior to women.[116] The articulation of such gender differences in VP is particularly disturbing because spectators are informed that avatars provide information about physical attributes.

Paint shop mottoes connect avatar representations to a core body and identity by making claims such as "We make you look good" and "Our labor makes you look beautiful."[117] Todd Beaulieu even advises VP spectators that the gender "choices are simple, look down, check your genitalia and make a choice."[118] Beaulieu's comments suggest that identity and self-representation are based on genital distinctions and that looking at avatars is the same, or at least provides the same information, as does looking at a spectator's physical genitalia. He describes avatar selection as a "simple" process, but these choices and representations render complex and unstable effects. VP provides overt messages about the gender and sex of avatars and spectators, but age, sex, and location (ASL) inquiries, which are often directed at these representations, indicate that there are still problems with identification. The ASL question limits the kinds of desires and aspects of identity that are acknowledged as important, or even existent, because spectators almost always presume the heterosexuality of other spectators.[119] However, directing the ASL question at avatars with overtly represented gender also expresses anxiety about the possible differences between material bodies and virtual representations.

Beaulieu's narrative about avatar selection indicates that there are some "problems" with sex identification because looking down and verifying are required in order to correlate spectator and representation. The kind of genital verification that Beaulieu encourages is rare even in physical settings. Anne Fausto-Sterling indicates that presumptions about genitally based sex are usually rooted in cultural perceptions rather than visible "proof."[120] Anne Fausto-Sterling's as well as Suzanne J. Kessler and Wendy McKenna's work suggests that physical and Internet presumptions about genitals and other sex traits should be called "cultural genitals" because they are societally rendered rather than physically verified.[121] The indication in VP and other Internet communication settings that there is an inextricable link between physical bodies and virtual descriptions makes avatars into a form of cultural genitals, displaces the many spectators who masquerade, and ignores the academic and popular literature on Internet gender transgressions.[122]

Both self-identified women and men use female avatars. It appears that the intent of "male" spectators is to represent what they want while women are representing a version of what they offer. This use of representational masquerade is different from MOO settings where male spectators seem to employ female characters to gain attention and erotic encounters. Of course, there is rarely a correlation between VP images and the embodiment of spectators. These representations become a way of offering images of women's bodies to the male gaze. They are a form of "picture exchange" or a way of trading erotic images. The availability of these erotic images and their coding through a variety of setting-specific practices render VP as a deeply gendered setting and mark its spectators as male. Of course, some of this material is gleaned from beauty magazines and other sources where women would be looking pleasurably and imaginatively at women.[123] This homosocial if not homoerotic gaze is also rendered by the ways women webcam operators watch each other.

A number of possible explanations exist for the abundant representations of women that are on display in VP paint shops. It is possible that more women than men use VP. Certainly, these images are offered for the pleasurable contemplation of other spectators. It also seems likely that male painters are uncomfortable making erotic male avatars. Homophobia is rampant in VP, and intolerance is even expressed in settings that are advertised as gay. It is unfortunately the case that some male-identified artists refuse to paint male avatars that they find suggestive. There is a disturbing belief that homosexuality is contaminating and proximity, even though exact distance between characters in the VP browser setting can never be determined, is incriminating. For instance, when a spectator employed an unusual representation of shaved male genitals, which were "tattooed" with a comic character, other spectators reacted in an extremely negative manner. The spectator was told to move the avatar so that it was not "too close," to "GET OFF ME," and to "move to the right or change that thing . . . not into dick on my shoulder."[124] The avatar was illegally "booted" or removed from the setting even though it was further from the avatars than in many situations. Confusion and hostile confrontations over erotic male avatars suggest that the varied representational strategies employed in displaying female avatars, including the use of these images by self-identified men, should also be a point of conflict. However, these avatars seem to produce less negative reaction than erotic male images.

The visual notions that are established in VP include an idea of what homosexuality looks like. Punky advises men in her "So you wanna be a Cyberstud" article that if "you are trying to attract women/girls stay away from the 'all naked spread out guy view av or any kind of ass bent over'" avatar.[125] According to her, there is a correlation between depictions of more passive men and homosexuality that makes certain types of avatars, which include figures that are lying down and available to the gaze, unappealing to women. Of course, many women "slash" fiction writers identify as heterosexuals and enjoy creating erotic gay images and narratives about their favorite male characters.[126] Unfortunately, Punky's argument is supported by the comments from male avatars. For instance, on one occasion a full-length nude male avatar, which was depicted from the rear, was labeled a homosexual and asked "aren't you embarrassed to wear an AV that goes for GAY" and are you "one of the village people, uh . . . ??"[127]

VP images are believed to provide information about sexual availability, since erotic images of women are read as a form of heterosexual invitation and naked or back views of men are believed to indicate a spectator's homosexuality. This spectatorial engagement is quite different from textual renderings of erotic female characters on MOOs, which are often attributed to men. For instance on LambdaMOO, Cyberfemme felt that she needed to nuance her description of "a blonde woman from California" by noting,"And no, I'm not a guy in disguise."[128] Setting-specific knowledge informs such readings. Spectators only know that there is a need to clarify their representations when they have been initiated into the codes and limits of these systems.

Making Differences in Virtual Places

The setting-specific skills needed to understand avatar representations render informed readers, who seem to be "inside" the setting, and uninitiated readers, who are kept "outside" of VP systems of knowledge. Individuals who do not have the correct computer and software cannot see the avatars and alternative ways that web sites are being employed. Since VP and other browser-based synchronous communication clients can be used to view any web site, the possibility always exists that alternative reading and participatory cultures are invisibly occurring. Different visual and textual cultures are also a part of VP. For instance, with the stand-alone software, a mug avatar represents spectators who are logged into the system with a different client and have a text-only interface. "Mugs" or "muggies" have a particularly beleaguered position in VP. One user complained, "hopefully i wont be mug forever . . . god it's like having a disease."[129] Spectators that employ the more graphics-intensive interface expect mugs to behave as invited guests that could be expulsed at any time. Of course, some individuals who manipulate mugs have spent more time using the system than have spectators with elaborate avatar representations. The ostracizing of mugs suggests the importance of the visual within VP. It indicates that VP participants expect particular readings or at least the possibility of reading in a visual way. However, the codes that allow some spectators to produce setting- specific meanings prevent other individuals from understanding.[130] The rejection of mugs, visually rendered homosexuality, avatars that spectators believe to be gay, and other "outsider" categories are used to produce the culture of VP.

The work of a variety of academics indicates how binary oppositions are used to perpetuate dominant society and the belief that certain centered individuals have a right to power. The writing of Foucault suggests how rules are designed to render power rather than legislate particular behaviors; Said shows how the concept of the Orient allows for the articulation of an Occident with a very different culture and right to power; Sedgwick indicates how the category of the homosexual has been instrumental in articulating heterosexuality and consolidating normative power; and Minh-ha considers how margins are necessary in order for the center to persist. The theories of these authors can provide an additional critical component to studies of hypertext and fan cultures. They offer ways to address the binary logic and setting-specific knowledge that operate in VP and other Internet settings.

As the problem of mug avatars indicates, the strategies that allow some spectators to write into culture and make the setting their own also denigrate other spectators and prevent them from participating. For instance, the particular writing practices of leet or elite, which includes substituting numerals for letters, are used "to create group identity, and to obscure meaning from outsiders, especially 'newbies.'"[131] Terms like "newbie" and "muggie" designate spectators who seem unfamiliar with Internet systems, act as a form of diminutive, and are derogatory. The instructions to read netiquette guidelines and FAQs, and the suggestion that "newbies can become an online nuisance when they do not lurk," encourage conformity, an acknowledgement of status, and keeping textually quiet.[132] Netiquette and other guidelines are produced more for social norming than out of necessity. For instance, the direction not to capitalize whole words, which is conceptualized as shouting, further ostracizes the elderly and other people with vision problems and has no effect on the technical functioning of the system. Foucault indicates that it is the mechanisms of exclusions and prohibitions that are necessary. Social issues are often a means to gain power.[133] In VP and other Internet settings, spectators also employ guidelines and rules to gain authority and control.

The forms of setting specific knowledge and regulation that occur in VP and other Internet settings can also be understood through Said's work.[134] He considers the ways European cultures have produced narratives about the Orient as "other," exterior, and different in order to mark the European writer's power and position. Hartsock employs Said's theory in her consideration of women and power, and she indicates that out of the same process that creates an opposite or "other" comes "a being who sees himself as located at the center and possessed of all the qualities valued in his society."[135] In VP, this opposition is rendered through distinctions between avatar thieves and original painters, mugs and visual avatars, and erotic male and female avatars. VP culture is articulated by describing the unacceptable behaviors of other spectators. The cultural construction of such undesirable positions as "muggies," who are "outside" or marginal, allows VP spectators to enforce their own position of power and centrality. As Min-ha indicates, without the margin "there is no center, no heart."[136] VP and other Internet settings become legitimate cultural entities at the expense of spectators who are conceptually kept outside of the setting.

Conclusion: Authorship in Other Internet Settings

Many Internet settings attempt to maintain authority over cultural work and spectators. Certainly, sites that sell net art want to retain individual ownership and validate the work's originality despite the difficulty of such practices. Web jewel designers offer some of their graphics for free, but they also attempt to determine how collections of web page elements are used through elaborate "terms of use" agreements, "watermarking," and other digital tracking methods. Moyra employs the metaphor of the museum in order to contextualize her project and indicate that the visual elements visible on the site and available for download always belong to her. She states that her designs "are on loan to you, just as museums across the world loan each other special pieces."[137] Even after removing most of her site in 2002, Moyra thanked spectators for their "patronage."[138] By using the museum analogy, Moyra declares that her graphic elements are a fine art that is worthy of canonization. The Museum of Counter Art, which makes note of its connoisseurs and has a "visitor survey" and "exhibit rooms," also uses the museum to provide a context for its products.[139] Other web jewel designers evoke similar effects, and share some conventions with VP, by using the term "gallery," depicting paintbrushes and other art tools, and describing themselves as artists.[140]

The elaborate rules about how web jewels can be employed, which appear on the sites of most designers, are justified by asserting value.[141] In order to use the web jewels, spectators must agree to the "terms of use," credit the artist, provide links that reference the web jewels site (these graphics are often referred to as "linkware"), not make any changes to graphics because it "hurts to see them deformed," download graphics rather than "stealing" the designer's bandwidth, only use the designs for personal and nonprofit sites, and not have any representations of intolerance or erotic content on the site.[142] Spectators are also repeatedly warned about the legal ramifications of copyright infringement. For instance, Silver asks spectators to "look but don't steal," and sites include special links to report thefts.[143] Web jewel sites, as well as some VP paint shops, include numerous links to copyright information. Of course, these web jewel designers have already borrowed from art and design conventions.

Fan fiction readers and producers also present rules and have frequent discussions about maintaining authorial control. For instance, a prolonged debate occurred in the LiveJournal forum when a group of well-known fan vidders discovered that another fan had manipulated their images and then claimed authorship.[144] Some of these vidders implemented the Grey Day action—the "day that fandom artists all over the web take back their creative rights."[145] On this day, they removed the material from web sites that were participating in this action and replaced it with a notice about fan practices. Their mission was as follows:

1.) To help educate fans in order to diminish the occurences of plagiarism of fannish works, and theft of bandwidth. 2.) To support an online environment in which fannish artists can be encouraged to share and feel secure in posting their derivative works without fear of having them altered or re-distributed without their permission. 3.) To help prevent art theft in as many fandoms as possible by sharing information with fellow artists and fans.[146]

As this statement indicates, fans believe that their remanipulations of images and texts from advertisements, films, television shows, and other popular sources are unique and their practices are distinctly different than the reuse of fan-produced works.[147]

Fan practices are related to the customs of VP painters. Fans produce setting-specific understandings of texts and connections among time, work, and uniqueness. For instance, Sisabet indicates that a great deal of "time and effort was invested" in her vids in order to "create something unique."[148] Fans and VP painters believe that work is a significant part of what makes an image belong to someone. VP painters also participate in a kind of fandom when they remake and use images of their favorite actors, musicians, and sports figures in avatars. Not all fandoms are the same, but many of these cultures agree that fans should not steal or manipulate elements of other fan works. According to taraljc, "fandom functions on the idea of borrowing canon—but not stealing from your fellows."[149] Different rights are articulated for "The Powers That Be," or the writers and producers of popular media texts, and "the li'l fanfic writer/artist" because there are few economic rewards for reworking media texts.[150] Fan work is also justified because it provides narratives about homoerotic relationships between characters and other ideas that have been denied or repressed by the media producers.[151]

Fan producers, net artists, VP painters, and web jewel designers employ varied tactics to validate their practices and indicate the value of their work. These alternative forms of production could provide an antidote to the hierarchical, stereotyped, and regulatory aspects of more traditional forms of culturally approved art. Unfortunately, many practitioners regulate meaning and behavior through pronouncements and threats. There are indications that appropriating fan work is "JUST NOT DONE in this community . . . It's socially unacceptable."[152] VP and web jewel sites have lists of "thieves," and fans have considered a similar process of providing the "names, screennames, email addies, LJ addies, URL's of personal sites, and any other information we can get our rightous little hands on about the thieves."[153] Fan, VP, and web jewel narratives about originality and authorial control indicate that these producers employ traditional art as a way of asserting their importance. Net artists may use the notion of appropriation to achieve similar effects. As they are currently articulated, the concepts of derivative work, the conflation of reader and author, writerly modes, and postmodern practices do not fully explain fan, VP, and web jewel cultures. Hypertext and fan theories offer some important ways to understand these systems, but few critical tools to articulate the political problems that persist.

Whether writing about, participating in, or viewing Internet settings, academics and other individuals have a responsibility to understand how they operate. Shoshana Green, Cynthia Jenkins, and Henry Jenkins suggest that when studying fan cultures, academics must be more aware of the multiplicity and interconnected aspects of fandom and read the cultures more carefully.[154] Their study includes the incorporation of a large amount of fan-produced texts. However, the close readings that they advocate do not address the hierarchical practices and stereotyped conventions that persist in these settings. In order to consider these inequities, there needs to be a process that combines close reading, the investigation of subcultural works, and the critical evaluation of the power structures and representations instituted in these settings. As indicated by the application of feminist and postcolonial theory in this chapter, critical works on power and mastery provide a very different understanding of Internet settings and their politics. It is only when reading as a VP spectator and critically attending to setting politics that it is possible to see what the images and cultures look like. Attempting to engage as an informed spectator and as a spectator who may not have the power to use all aspects of the setting, while difficult to practice, provides a more complex understanding of Internet systems and enculturation. Such a hybrid critical approach indicates the importance of Internet subcultural practices and the ways traditional values and stereotyped perceptions sometimes accompany new production strategies.

6 This Is Not Photography, This Is Not a Cohesive View: Computer-facilitated Imaging and Fragmented Spectatorship

Introduction

The spectator is encouraged to view realistically rendered web site images as if they were photographs, a trace of the real, or a doorway into the natural world. Art renderings on museum web sites, depictions that accompany eBay listings, images on news sites, and a variety of other visuals are presented in ways that downplay their constructed aspects. The spectator is persuaded to find photographic elements and even to view these images as photographs because they are commonly referred to as "photography," "digital photography," or "post-photography." Internet and computer-facilitated images are produced through processes that diverge from lens-based and chemical photography, but the visual and conceptual aspects of these differences are rarely addressed. Despite these tendencies, it is possible to emphasize the deeply constructed aspects of these representations by using the terms "computer-facilitated" and "digital imaging," reading these images carefully, and discussing the technologies through which they are produced and delivered. When the constructed and mediated aspects of these representations are highlighted, they offer a unique site from which to investigate spectatorship and the ways that other forms of digital imaging are employed. The computer-facilitated works of Carol Selter, Susan Silton, and Ken Gonzales-Day, which are presented on the web, are particularly productive sites from which to begin this consideration because they foreground aspects of photographic and digital production, the ways that bodies are commonly represented, and viewing positions.[1]

Many spectators equate photographs and photolike forms with what they represent. The conflation of representation and object occurs because photography is believed to be light's direct transcription of objects, which were once in front of the camera, onto film and paper. "Post-photography," and other computer-facilitated processes that look like photography, are produced through a very different set of technologies. However, spectators still tend to engage with these images as if they were an exacting document or even a conduit to real things. There are traditional photographs and photolike works that address the inherent problems in reading images as truth. Some postmodern photographers, photo critics, and academics continue to resist the social inscription of photographic representations as real.[2] Many individuals describe the visual and ideological differences that distinguish photography from computer-facilitated images. This work remains theoretically provocative, but it has also been largely unsuccessful as a political strategy.

One solution to this dilemma is to focus on the spectator and to propose theories based on viewing positions. In this chapter, I rethink the spectator's situation and role in producing meaning. This offers some unique opportunities to engage with cultural conceptions of computer-facilitated images in alternative ways. It also presents different methods for considering how photographs become conflated with the material things that they depict. There needs to be a more complex theory of digital imaging than current proposals, which indicate that computer-manipulated images have resulted in the "death" of photography and the disengagement of photographic and photolike images from truth.[3] Any examination of the ways that images function in Internet and computer settings indicates that the understanding of photography as a trace, or indexical sign of a particular object, and the conflation of digital images with photography persist. Theories of photography offer important ways to address digital imaging, but they also make it difficult to indicate that photography and digital imaging have distinct qualities and social implications. Rethinking these theories can allow for a critique of traditional engagements with photographs and digital images, provide the opportunity to differentiate between the aspects of photography and digital imaging, and propose alternative forms of viewing. This is an important shift since spectators are rarely provided with different models for viewing images.

The critical literature about photography offers meaningful ways to engage with digital images. However, most critiques of photography fail to address the mutable aspects of spectatorship and the ways that individuals do not or cannot follow the spectatorial directions provided by images and cultural ideals. The usual photographic point of view, where the spectator gazes at highly constructed images and sees them as natural, limits the critical interventions that can be performed. This makes Selter's, Silton's, and Gonzales-Day's disruptions of traditional spectatorial engagement worth noting.[4] In this chapter, these issues are addressed by considering how photography and digital imaging spectators are constructed, cultural notions of these forms, and the ways that web sites mediate the spectator's experience of digital images. Sections on Selter's, Silton's, and Gonzales-Day's work demonstrate how photographic theory can enable a more precise understanding of spectatorship and images. Barthes' theories and the concept of morphing are particularly important to this analysis because they present a model of fragmented spectatorship.[5] Through these critical strategies, a different spectator can be suggested and further inquiries can be made about the ways all sorts of images become real and true.

Making the Digital Imaging Spectator

Social forces as well as the organizing influences of representations and interfaces produce spectators. Steinberg argues that artworks produce spectators by articulating the particular attributes of viewers and where they are located.[6] Annette Kuhn indicates that "the family is actually in [the] process of making itself" when engaging with photographs, which includes such obvious processes as exposing film to light and chemically developing pictures as well as selecting, ordering, writing titles, framing, and displaying images.[7] Kuhn's proposal may seem to indicate that individuals can construct any identity. However, the standard array of photographic images that are usually available for this identity production, which include school pictures, studio portraits, professional and amateur images of family events, and travel snapshots, tend to provide deeply constructed notions of the family and individual.[8] Combining these materials in albums, scrapbooks, wall arrangements, and CDs is also likely to produce traditional visions of the family and its roles. By accepting varied reading and viewing cues, the spectator enables such positions. For example, the mandate to view artworks, photographs, and films from a particular distance and be quiet is conveyed by aspects and objects in the museum and the cinema.

Photography and film spectators are produced and aligned with the camera technology as well as the cultural work. The relationship between the film spectator and apparatus provides a useful model to start conceptualizing other forms of camera identification. The film and photography spectator's identification with the apparatus have been traced back to Renaissance perspective and earlier devices like the camera obscura, which had a small hole or lens that reflected a version of the scene into a dark box or space.[9] Jean-Louis Baudry, André Bazin, and Siegfried Kracauer mention photographic forms as part of their cinema prehistories.[10] Jacqueline Rose indicates that the "photographic image is seen as a norm to which the cinema conforms," and Christian Metz suggests that both are "*prints* of real objects" and render images through the actions of light and chemicals.[11] In considering how apparatus and photography theory might be newly applied to the cinema, Mulvey notes that digital technologies facilitate a certain stillness in films and allow the spectator more control over the speed of images, which means that photography and film are now more interrelated.[12] Mulvey's proposal also encourages a consideration of the ways Internet and computer-facilitated "photography" are like the cinema, because the presumed stillness of the image is undone by the cycling of the screen, flashing banners, and shifting of the depiction as it downloads.

Apparatus theory provides some useful ways to understand current conceptions of the still camera and spectator when adjustments are made and its limitations are acknowledged.[13] The forms of identification that occur in film and photography tend to produce centered spectators who appear to have power over image production. When traditional narrative films are shown, the optical apparatus of the cinema, as well as what is portrayed on the screen, establish the spectator as the center and originator of meaning. Baudry indicates that the "monocular vision" of the camera specifies the "very spot" that the subject must occupy.[14] Metz notes that identification is conceptually split between the projector and screen. The spectator releases the film and is situated with the projector and receives it and is the screen.[15] In both cases, the spectator becomes integrated with the apparatus and identifies with the camera.[16]

Identification with the photography apparatus also locates the spectator conceptually and ideologically within space, provides instructions for ways to view the photograph, and makes certain kinds of spectators. Photographers have sometimes employed nontraditional and even destabilizing viewpoints such as the worm's-eye and bird's-eye view. However, the photographer's traditional bodily position when using the camera is usually clearly conveyed. The spectator engages with photographic images by literally and conceptually taking the position of the photographer. There may be exceptions in the photomontages of Claude Cahun, Hannah Höch, and Pierre Molinier, which cut up the body, render composite images, and produce a "range of identifications."[17] Nevertheless, in all these instances, gallery and museum presentations encourage the spectator to be physically arranged in front of the image. Albums, boxes of snapshots, flipbooks, and stereoviews also render different arrangements between the physical body and the image, while still addressing centered subjects and presenting traditional ideas about bodies, identity, and spectatorial engagements. Some painters have also highlighted their bodily position in front of the canvas by rendering a body or object that represents them within the painting. Fried refers to this composite position as the "painter-beholder."[18] The position of the photographer or painter may be very different from the embodied existence of the individual, but the image and cultural conceptions provide varied effects to stabilize these differences.

Apparatus theory suggests how spectators are constructed by certain viewing structures. However, most of it fails to address the role that difference plays in viewing, and it does not provide sites of resistance. Mulvey's account of visual pleasure, and indication that there are no empowered ways for women to view films, has encouraged feminists to continue to address the ways cultural production, including apparatus theory, renders sexual difference. Such feminist theorists as de Lauretis indicate apparatus theory's "phallic premise" and its failure to consider the possibility of other viewing positions for women.[19] Feminists also note that while apparatus theory and psychoanalysis explain the structures of film, this does not indicate that such positions should be supported or perpetuated. Apparatus and feminist psychoanalytic film theory also help articulate aspects of Internet spectatorship and are vital to my analysis of how these settings operate, but my intent is to render hybrid theories and consider forms of cultural production that can explain and potentially change current viewing positions.

It may be difficult for the spectator to identify differently with Internet and computer representations, but these instances are worth noting. The work of artists like Selter, Silton, and Gonzales-Day highlight how spectators are set up to see images and indicate what photography and digital imaging processes render. In the work of these artists, the breakdown of a unified point of view and coherently imaged body can challenge the idea of the spectator as a singular, empowered, vertical, and columnar individual with the power to be situated directly in front of works of art. Their images encourage an interrogation of normative spectatorial positions by demonstrating that the body of the spectator can never fully correlate to the position articulated by the work. Their references to photography and use of scanners and other technologies encourage an acknowledgment of the partial and fragmented engagements that are produced by such devices and can make the varied relationships between images and spectatorial bodies more apparent.

Photography

An understanding of photography, digital imaging, and web "display" is useful in formulating a theory of the spectator's alternative engagements with such digital images as Selter's Animalia Series, Silton's Self Portraits, and Gonzales-Day's Skin Series. The societal structures that make photographs seem real and the ways spectators are instructed to engage need to be examined. Not surprisingly, strategies that reveal the technologies by which meaning is instituted and the formats that produce spectators are resisted. Gonzales-Day notes that the photograph as "a verifiable fact or document continues to linger with contemporary viewers despite the radical impact of digital technology on photographic practice."[20] His comment suggests that social inscription and the willingness of the spectator to perform in front of works in particular ways repress the constructed aspects of computer-facilitated and camera-generated images.

There continues to be a societal tendency to emphasize photography's referential aspects and to describe the things depicted by photographs as if they were real. Photography is believed to be a simple and unmediated process of permanently recording an image on light-sensitive film, paper, or another surface.[21] The photographic image is rarely conceived of as handmade.[22] A variety of photography critics, historians, theorists, and viewers connect photographs through a mythic shared materiality to the things that they represent. Barthes indicates that photographs are never distinguished from their referents or the objects that they represent.[23] This is supported by Sontag's suggestion that photography is more than a rendered image or interpretation; "it is also a trace, something directly stenciled off the real, like a footprint or a death mask."[24] Krauss describes some instances in which the constructed aspects of photographs are underscored. However, she also describes photography as an "imprint or transfer off the real."[25] This consistent correlation of the image with the artifact makes the surface of the photograph and its constructed aspects difficult to detect. There should be great concern that, as Barthes indicates, the "photograph is always invisible: it is not it that we see."[26] If people do not see the specificity of photography and the surface is not interrogated, then processes that seem to be photographic (such as digital imaging and realist computer graphics) can also be engaged with as a trace or "deposit" of the real, and the underlying presumptions that accompany these images can be supported.[27]

Photography is believed to be not only a trace of the material artifact but also a deposit of a particular time. Bazin establishes a relationship between stillness and photography with his indication that photography "embalms time."[28] The use of such terms as "snapshot" and "instamatic" underscore the idea that photography renders an instant. The photograph's link to objects, which appears to be supported by the actions of light and chemicals, makes the image an "imprint" of a past moment and, according to Doane, promises to rematerialize time.[29] The veracity of photography is supported by the idea that it "captures" a moment and pictures are "taken," which suggests that segments of the real and time are seized and embedded in the photographic artifact.[30] However, much more mutable kinds of photographic time are indicated by the special cages used to stabilize the sitter's body in early photography, blurred and repetitive images from people and other things mistakenly moving while being photographed, and the conflation of divergent individuals, places, and periods through varied photographic techniques. Even the fastest of photographic exposures occurs within a period of lived time.

It is difficult to examine the surface and the ways photographs and digital images are mediated and produced because the spectator is instructed to engage with images as a series of objects.[31] Photography critics like Alan Trachtenberg indicate that the processes of photographic production and spectatorship are not "innocent acts."[32] Images, whether facilitated by an optical technology or produced by other means, always convey varied ideological messages, but the spectator is usually encouraged to ignore how this happens. Some photographic practices as well as academic and popular writing have questioned the idea that photography is unmediated. Bolter and Grusin wonder how the processes of photographic production, which include exposing film to light, developing the negative with chemicals, using the negative and light to transfer the image to light-sensitive paper, and developing the positive with more chemical baths, can be an unaltered and immediate image.[33] Selecting and cropping always occur when making and printing images. According to John Tagg, these mediated aspects can be noted when attention is paid to the production processes because photographs are not based on the model of the eye, although this is often suggested, but rather on conveying space on a two-dimensional surface.[34] Seeing the altered aspects of images requires a reconfiguration of spectatorial behavior, which includes refusing to identify with the apparatus and resisting the empowered position.

The possibility of such reconfigured engagements is suggested by Barthes' personal viewing of photography in *Camera Lucida*, which provides a unique opportunity to consider different forms of spectatorship. He focuses on the viewer's relationship to images, desires, and experiences rather than the photographer's, or "operator's," practices. His theory of punctum, which relies on the varied evanescent details or flaws in the image, indicates that viewing can be structured by the spectator as well as the photograph.[35] However, Barthes is believed to have a "realist attitude," to poignantly reassert "the realist position," and to depict the camera and photography as "an instrument of evidence."[36] Barthes begins *Camera Lucida* with a discussion of the referential aspects of photography, but his use of punctum goes beyond the evidential.[37] Barthes' emphasis on individual spectatorial engagements with detailed aspects of the image, rather than unified social conventions, indicates some ways to rethink spectatorship.

Barthes associates the realist aspects of photography with studium, which the viewer is culturally trained to read, and individual photographic instances with punctum, which disrupt these larger cultural conceptions. Studium occurs when spectators only "take a kind of general interest" in images and engage through "the rational intermediary of an ethical and political culture."[38] Punctum is "the detail" that disrupts the cohesive photographic trace and the uniform cultural effects of photography. Barthes' discussion of punctum, which produce a visceral response in the spectator, can offer a personal idiosyncratic engagement with photographic surface. Punctum suggests an ever-shifting experience with some photographic images, individual rather than shared experiences, and the replacement of the photographer's ability to convey factual evidence with the spectator's reading. Punctum can be the basis for a theory of computer-facilitated spectatorial engagement because of this focus on position. As suggested by my application of Barthes' theories to net art, punctum is also useful in highlighting the distinct differences in digital processes because it addresses individual experiences with images rather than cultural beliefs about images

Digital or Post-photography

Digital camera "snapshots," photographs that are computer-manipulated or "corrected," multiple camera pictures that are combined with the use of a computer into a synthetic whole, scanner images, and photorealistic computer graphics are produced under specific conditions and have a different relationship to material views. Most individuals still group these images with photography and describe them as photographs, despite how the information is recorded and which technologies are employed.[39] It is becoming even more difficult to describe the attributes of digital images because film-based photographs are often partially produced and conveyed through digital means and digital images are printed on paper. Spectators usually have an extremely hard time detecting the specific production processes of digital images. Popular accounts do not help resolve this confusion because digital camera techniques are ordinarily described as a kind of traditional photography that offers increased convenience and faster image delivery.

These descriptions, while still relating digital to light and chemical photography, indicate that digital processes are better than "straight" or "traditional" photography because the "flexibility" of the rendering techniques allows formal aspects to be changed and images combined.[40] There is also an occasional indication that digital processes have a looser relationship to the material world than does photography and, as Michelle Pacansky indicates in her comments about the Scanner as Camera webwork, are "like a wet painting."[41] Unfortunately, the important connections between computer-facilitated imaging, collage, and painting remain largely unexplored. While digital processes tend to produce a certain fluidity and have a more tenuous relationship to material views, it is a mistake to assume that photography, which is produced with light-sensitive materials and chemicals, is not flexible, that all photographs have the same indexical relationship to the material world, and that different photographic practices resist malleability to the same degree. Undeveloped photographic film and negatives have developing and printing potentialities, while the paper print is more fixed. Of course, even the print can be cut, painted on, displayed differently, and rephotographed.

Some critics indicate that photography and computer-facilitated imaging have distinct properties. William J. Mitchell argues that digital images often look like photographs, particularly when they are presented in such venues as newspapers, but they are profoundly different.[42] According to him, "analog" photographs have an indefinite amount of information, and more detail is available when they are enlarged, but digital images have a definite amount of information.[43] Of course, enlargements offer different views and "details," even if this depiction is the visual breakdown that occurs when there is no more recorded information. Mitchell also indicates that film and paper photographs degrade when reproduced, but a digital copy is "absolutely indistinguishable from the original."[44] However, concerns about ownership, which are expressed by fans, net artists, VP painters, and web jewel designers, indicate that the term "original" is not always easy to apply to Internet and computer-facilitated technologies. With traditional photography, it is also difficult to argue that the negative, first print, photographer's arrived upon image, or series of differently produced versions is the original. Geoffrey Batchen highlights the problems with computer-facilitated originality and reliability by describing digital imaging as "an overtly fictional process" that "abandons even the rhetoric of truth."[45] Yet digital images, which may be digital corrections of photographic material, are often employed in academic conferences, books, news shows, and newspapers as proof and truth.

Despite the ongoing employment of digital imaging as a form of traditional photography, a great deal of the critical literature suggests that digital imaging will destabilize photographic truth when its constructed aspects and troubled referential connections are highlighted. Timothy Druckrey and Fred Ritchin both argue that the "tenuous" connection between photography and digital imaging will be "shattered," there will be "a profound undermining of photography's status as an inherently truthful pictorial form," and this will cause a "tremendous shift" in society.[46] There is also an indication, according to Anne-Marie Willis, that in "some ways we are facing the death of photography" and, as William J. Mitchell notes, that since "its sesquincentennial in 1989 photography was dead—or, more precisely, radically and permanently displaced."[47] These claims are understandable since photography's reliability is consistently called into question by manipulations and the malleability of its every aspect. However, the continued use of the term "photography" when referring to a variety of image-making practices, the cultural investment in camera-produced images as truth, and governmental and individual embarrassments over what is shown in images indicate that photography and its connection to the documentary are not dead for most individuals.

Photography's and computer-facilitated imaging's association with unmediated truth and proof provides authority and power to the depictions and producers. There are ever-increasing possibilities of changing images, but there is still no distinct way to recognize altered images. This should be cause for concern. Said calls for the elimination of repressive "systems of representation" that have authority and do not allow individuals to intervene in the ways they are represented.[48] As digital imaging and generation techniques improve, the represented individuals have increasingly less control over how their bodies are portrayed and conflated with other images. Repressive systems of representation also occur when gender and racial categories are articulated and when grids of bodies seem available to view and collect in web sites for VP avatars, dating, and "most wanted" criminals. Without interventions, popular images tend to produce normative forms of spectatorship and encourage the viewer to accept the image as the truth about individuals.

The photograph usually directs spectators away from its constructed aspects in order to function as evidence.[49] However, Selter's, Silton's, and Gonzales-Day's works foreground production processes. Of course, such disturbances have also been intentionally and mistakenly produced in traditional photography. Some digital videos, films, and television programs also address the constructed aspects, ideological biases, seeming transparency, and unreliability of these forms. Critical discussions of film and literary reflexivity consider what happens when the technology and produced parts of the text are revealed.[50] Despite these disturbances to narrative flow and indexical connections, photography and digital imaging continue to be associated with the real. This suggests that new strategies are needed in order to read images differently. Rethinking spectatorship can provide one such approach because it is the viewer who accepts cultural conventions or produces different meanings. While the role of the spectator has been constructed along with photography, this position has not been as culturally recognized or enforced. This suggests that it may be possible to reconceptualize representations through spectatorship rather than through the image.

The Scanner as Camera

Structured spectatorial positions and alternative forms of image production may also work at cross-purposes, as they do in the California Museum of Photography's Scanner as Camera webwork, which offers images by Carol Selter, Susan Silton, and Darryl

Curran and an essay by Michelle Pacansky (figure 6.1–6.5).[51] Pacansky distinguishes between photography and digital images in the essay and the artists do similar things through their work, but the design of the site directs spectators to read this material as photographs.[52] There is a constant emphasis on the Scanner as Camera and that the scanner is somehow still a camera because the site essay and most of the images are bracketed under the title. The font, which is executed as if a shape had been removed from stiff gray paper and the white ground revealed underneath, also renders Selter's, Silton's, and Curran's representations as material objects. A version of Gibson's space behind the screen is suggested by shadowing the white part of the letters, so that the gray appears to project further forward.[53] The thin white border, which appears around each of the Scanner as Camera images, evokes the tendency in photography to leave a white margin around the print, encourages the spectator to relate these computer-facilitated images to photography, and implies that the images should be engaged with in more traditional ways. These renderings prevent the spectator from experiencing the site as extremely thin, flat, or virtual.

Pacansky indicates that the correlation of images with objects, which usually occurs in photography, is undone in digital imaging.[54] However, museum and gallery web sites, including the California Museum of Photography's site, often reinforce the cultural association of photography and digital imaging with materiality and use varied computer-facilitated images to represent their collections.[55] The Scanner as Camera site also tends to suggest traditional spectatorial engagements, with a centered body in front of art, by presenting a single image at a time. Other compositions might offer the opportunity to reconsider spectatorial positions and to theorize an engagement that is not based on the body's orientation with physical things. For instance, Selter and Silton encourage a rethinking of spectatorship by indicating how photography has been associated with the real, materiality, and embodiment and the ways these connections fail. Selter, Silton, and Gonzales-Day provide a kind of morphology or articulation of the characteristics of digital image production. They consider digital imaging's gridlike aspects, easily manipulated data, usual composition from parts, and relationship to becoming more than being.

Carol Selter's Animalia and Punctum

Selter's Animalia Series indicates how digital and photographic images become connected to material realities and contends that these connections are always contradictory. A perfunctory examination of Selter's work may suggest that her images, which are produced by scattering live animals on a flatbed scanner, portray such animals as chicks, ducklings, iguanas, silkworms, and toads. However, her images clearly portray screen-mediated bodies. The depictions of animal bodies are misshapen, and parts are not represented because the bodies were pressed against the scanner's glass surface during the production process. There is no clear formula that encourages the spectator to correlate animal bodies with the depictions. Sometimes the weight of the animal and its materiality erased significant aspects of its embodiment; there are also doubled and multiplied representations and flashes of glare where no body is depicted. These elements are not mistakes in the imaging process, and they do not remain at a remove from the representation. Instead, Selter uses the aspects of scanner- and computer-facilitated imaging to indicate how photography conveys materiality and to disrupt the spectator's sense of individual mass and body.

In Selter's images, an understanding of three-dimensional form and specific environment are disturbed by the jagged and seemingly folded forms and the dark surface that depicts no "natural" place. For instance, *Desert Iguana* depicts distorted representations of iguanas that appear to be embedded in the black "ground" (figure 6.1). Almost-white glare, which reads like unprinted parts more than any form, intensifies the unreal aspects of the images. There is no simply recorded whole because the computer encodes information as the scanner's optical head moves across the glass and the animals move. The image is a product of multiple positions, temporalities, and points of view, which are consolidated into an image, rather than a singular body or time. Selter highlights the impossibility of articulating the represented numbers of animals or parts by entitling an image of more than three partial toad renderings *Toad*. The consolidation of multiple views into the image provides the spectator with a kind of view into the scanner apparatus, when the technology records vertical bands, and an image of the glass screen, at the points where animal bodies dissolve into glare. This makes the spectator attend to the photographic plane and the scanner process instead of just "looking through" images and at "real" animals.

The depiction, rather than the animals, seems to stretch out of shape, compress, turn inside out, and get pulled through rents in the image. At these junctures, there is a radical destabilization of the surface and photography seems to be literally and conceptually turned inside out. The spectator's engagement with these gaps in the indexical aspects of the images, which "pricks" and "bruises," is different from being directed to material objects and provides a version of Barthes' punctum.[56] Photographs, or in this case digital images, are "punctuated, sometimes even speckled with these sensitive points; precisely, these marks, these wounds are so many *points*."[57] There are renderings of holes, bloated and distended forms, hollowed out bodies, and breaks where the depiction abruptly stops. For instance, in *Ducklings*, dark lines and smears

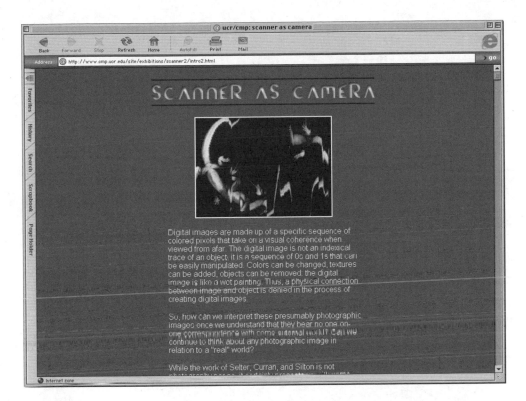

Figure 6.1
Carol Selter, *Desert Iguana*, "UCR/CMP: Scanner as Camera," UCR California Museum of Photography, 1998, 27 Sept. 2004, <http://www.cmp.ucr.edu/site/exhibitions/scanner2/intro2.html>.

of color appear where part of the image seems to have been folded away (figure 6.2). Punctum prevents a familiar cultural engagement and renders a kind of violence to the viewer's optical processes when the missing aspects of Selter's images and the visual incomprehension of webcams are noted. Punctum forces the spectator of the *Animalia Series* to address the seamed, unexpected, and difficult aspects of the representation.

Punctum occurs, according to Jane Gallop, when an aggressive aspect of the photograph "penetrates the viewer" and, as Roger Warren Bebe notes, "creates an intense affect."[58] For Barthes, punctum collapses the distinction between the centered spectator and object because it "rises from the scene, shoots out of it like an arrow, and pierces" and penetrates the viewer.[59] In such cases, spectatorship is not about stable culturally proscribed positions and the unnoticed processes that shape desires. There is pleasure, pain, and bodily fragmentation when punctum undoes traditional forms

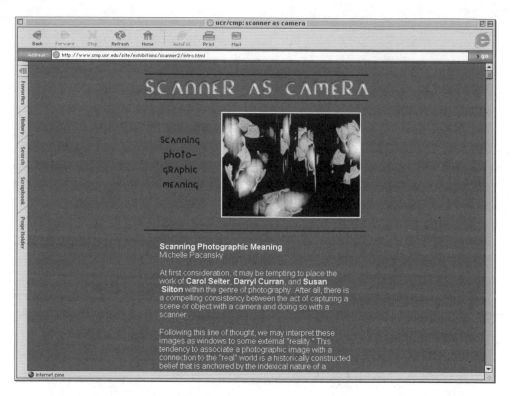

Figure 6.2
Carol Selter, *Ducklings*, "UCR/CMP: Scanner as Camera," UCR California Museum of Photography, 1998, 27 Sept. 2004, <http://www.cmp.ucr.edu/site/exhibitions/scanner2/intro.html>.

of spectatorship. Studium and traditional forms of spectatorship render a form of "enclosure," and, according to Gallop, breaking or opening something up allows "seepage" and renders punctum.[60] In the Animalia Series, there is "seepage" between elements, a shifting point of view, and a kind of breach of the uniform spectator.

The omnipresence of other kinds of bodies and positions is difficult to ignore in Selter's work. The spectator is virtually lying down, looking "up" at representations of animal anuses, and seeing the "dirty" underside of the picture. For instance, the animals in *Chicks* appear to be looking down at the spectator, so that the spectator is virtually below the chicks' bodies, and at the same time looking directly at representations (figure 6.3). The spectator's torqued position, which does not provide the usual empowered view of distant objects, is underscored by the ways animals appear to gaze back. Mikhail Bakhtin suggests that such improperly embodied arrangements "transfer top to bottom, and bottom to top," place the face where the buttocks should be, and

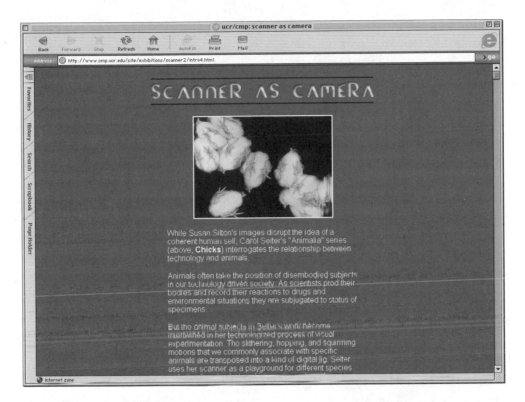

Figure 6.3
Carol Selter, *Chicks*, "UCR/CMP: Scanner as Camera," UCR California Museum of Photography, 1998, 27 Sept. 2004, <http://www.cmp.ucr.edu/site/exhibitions/scanner2/intro4.html>.

use misplacement and disorientation to undo norms and ordinary roles.[61] The spectator of Selter's work cannot occupy one position, since the view and material body present different positions, or one time, because different temporal states are encapsulated in the jagged half-images of moving animals. There are multiple positions rather than a singular viewpoint because the computer encodes information as the scanner's optical head moves across the glass. Reading practices are disturbed, and the meaning of the image is changed because Selter situates the spectator in difficult positions and emphasizes the screen.

Susan Silton's Self Portraits and Images of the Partial Self

Silton also employs a scanner in order to make her images and shifts positions as the optical head of the scanner moves across the glass. This produces distorted images that make particular aspects of the body difficult to identify. Silton uses these practices to indicate how difficult it is to rely on recorded data as an exacting representation. It would be incorrect to suggest that this is Silton, that the subject is Silton in any traditional sense, or even that she represents herself. Her images portray a kind of liquidity or dissolution of the self rather than any consolidated view. Silton uses these elements to address the genre of self-portraiture and the improbable belief that it captures the whole view. By recombining features and rendering amorphous flesh, Silton denies the spectator a unified point of view or articulated relationship to the artist. Through such processes, Silton encourages spectators to reconceptualize their relationship to imaging technologies.

Cultural conceptions of photography encourage the spectator to use words like "flesh" and "face" when describing Silton's *Self Portrait No. 21* (1995), which presents a twisted column that stretches diagonally from lower left to the upper right and connects the representation of the mouth to the eye (figure 6.4). The detailed folds in the nose destabilize what would otherwise seem like a record of sagging flesh and creases and the indexical aspects of the image. The spectator of *Self Portrait No. 21* and other images from this series will also have difficulty with such terms as "size" and "shape." However, the Scanner as Camera site suggests a stable viewing experience by stating that all of the "Silton images in this exhibition are Iris prints, 4 7/8" x 8", created in 1995."[62] The notation about the printing technology produces an authoritative language and suggests that the spectator will experience a physical object. Silton's scanner images are output using an exacting jet printer and the detail and texture are implied, but there is no way for the spectator to experience these images as a paper print or process. It is difficult to articulate what the spectator is viewing because successive reproductions have irrevocably combined different print and computer generations of this image. The notation about physical dimensions also provides an inaccurate measure since browser settings and screen size determine the spectator's engagement and the size of the Selter and Curran images are not specified.

The Scanner as Camera site design, with its attempt to establish stable images and viewing positions, is contrary to Selter's and Silton's spectatorial disturbances. The unruliness conveyed by these artists is related to the feminist project of demonstrating how bodies are constructed and identity is mutable. Silton's Self Portraits series is part of her ongoing examination of "the perception of lesbian as mutant" and "mutation."[63] She employs morphing and multiplication to explore the "possibilities for transformation or variation" that resist the societal privileging of normative bodies and desires.[64] The morph addresses fears about unnatural and easily transformed bodies, but it also indicates that bodies are reshaped through contact with technology, flesh, surfaces, and time. Jeanette Winterson describes the pleasurable processes of

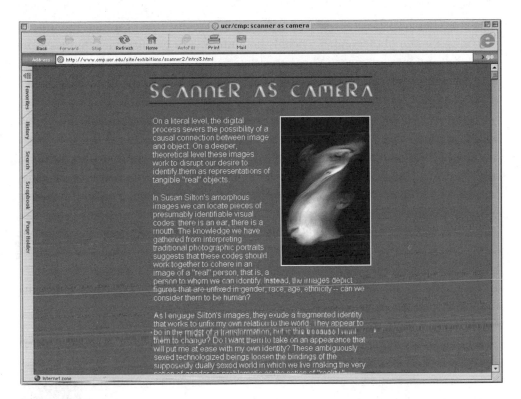

Figure 6.4
Susan Silton, *Self Portrait No. 21*, 1995, "UCR/CMP: Scanner as Camera," UCR California Museum of Photography, 1998, 27 Sept. 2004, <http://www.cmp.ucr.edu/site/exhibitions/scanner2/intro3.html>.

bodies drawn into temporary shape through optic and haptic engagement, where fingers "become printing blocks" and "tap meaning" into the body.[65] Winterson and Silton indicate that the spectator makes meaning out of other bodies and that it is through viewing that bodies are produced. Bodies are "pliable to power," as Elizabeth Grosz indicates, and rendered through varied forms of cultural writing and inscriptions, which include Internet and computer spectatorship, wearing clothing and makeup, and driving and identifying with a car.[66] The body is not a preproduced and stable position but rather a mutating structure that is always reading, being read, and produced by other individuals.

The body is the product of external forces and relationships rather than an authentic and consolidated self. Barthes indicates that physically and conceptually considering the self through photography produces a different body. According to him, the spectator changes when observed by the lens and is constituted through the process of posing for the photograph.[67] There is no authentic or genuine view but a deeply structured and inexact image. When using the scanner and engaging with the camera, the spectator makes "another body" and is transformed "in advance into an image."[68] Photography encourages the observed and the observer to become a representation, but even this image does not provide a consolidated identity. Barthes' writing and Silton's images suggest that the processes of portraiture disturb the possibility of being a unified subject and remaining the same. In the Self Portraits series, Silton considers her "own mutated selves, physical and psychological, with the intention of challenging what we know to be human, to be ourselves."[69] A confused body rifting and even horrific encounter occurs when engaging with such twisted and malleable images of the self. Spectators may want the mobile image of multiple photographs, scans, or other imaging technologies to "always coincide with" the "profound 'self.'"[70] However, the spectator's self will never exactly coincide with the image. The photographic portrait is a "*disturbance,*" as Barthes notes, in the cultural construction of the individual and "the advent of myself as other."[71]

Through backdrops, composition, lighting, posing, cropping, and printing, camera-based imaging technologies tend to produce an "other" or perceptions about cultural groups rather than any true or exacting account of traits. The work of Edward Said, Nancy Hartsock, and Andrew Edgar and Peter Sedgwick indicate that this "projection constructs the identities of cultural *subjects* through a relationship of power in which the Other is the subjugated element."[72] Describing the supposed characteristics of the other—what is external and different about avatars, newbies, people of color, photographic subjects, and women—is an attempt to articulate normative culture, the self, and to maintain power in such arrangements. The construction of the other is usually a way to assert self-identity. However, when the other is also a version of the self, it can render a disconnection from identity and crisis. Views of the spectator, which are facilitated through photography, digital imaging, or some other means of reproduction, present a situation in which self is turned into selves that hover among external, internal, distant, close, and the same.

Society may have "repressed the profound madness" of the way photography produces our double but there is still, according to Barthes, a "faint uneasiness" that occurs when looking at the "self" on paper.[73] All recorded representations repeat this confusion by addressing the spectator in front of the image and rendering a double. Silton's scanner images increase the uneasiness of engaging with doubles because they are recognizable but not anatomically understandable. She emphasizes such conflicts by wondering how conjoined twins mediate ideas about the stable and singular self.[74]

Silton produces multiple recordings that have been inexactly condensed into one image and offers an engagement with monstrous bodies that should not and cannot be. However, even less manipulated scanner images condense multiple times and image fragments. The visions of self provided by photography, computer imaging, and other copying systems are some of the only ways to access full views of "your" body. According to Barthes, you "are the only one who can never see yourself except as an image."[75] This body, which is supposed to be intimately known, can only be seen in pieces.

Silton renders a disturbing resolution to this fragmentation of the self, visibility, and spectatorial positions in *Self Portrait No. 20*, which she has labeled as a "cyborg," or a combination of technological and animate components (figure 6.5).[76] The image depicts an eye that seems capable of looking at the rest of the body. There is a high level of continuity between the rendering of the cheek, lips, and nose and the "knowable" body, but the eye is not so easily placed. It is abnormally large, blurry, lit so that it appears wet or weeping, and twists or falls away from the rest of the depicted face. The position of the eye suggests that spectators may be able to see a version of their whole body but the view will be different from what was expected. Silton's images are horrific because they offer too much of the body and leave the processes of sight in some disrepair. The spectator can no longer engage with the image as a window onto three-dimensional space or as a reflection of the spectator's own body because the body is in pieces, flattened, and pulled out of shape. By disturbing the usual viewing positions, she puts a great deal of pressure on familiar understandings of spectatorship. Silton indicates that society tends to resist bodies that fold when in contact, morph, and mutate, and she demands that the viewer find a vocabulary to speak about the spectator as selves. Such an engagement and language, as it is posited in Silton's image, highlights the precarious place of the spectator and the inadequate terms of spectatorial understanding.

Ken Gonzales-Day's Skin Series and the Cut

Gonzales-Day's images are also clearly produced through varied processes. He indicates that they "are photographed, scanned, altered, fragmented, and recombined."[77] His Skin Series comprises close-up representations of skin that are distorted, arranged in a grid, and veiled with diagrams of skin structure (figures 6.6–6.7). He blends the camera-produced and digital images so that the constructed state of these images is obvious but the precise aspects of mediation are impossible to locate. This undermines the referential aspects of these representations, which would otherwise encourage the

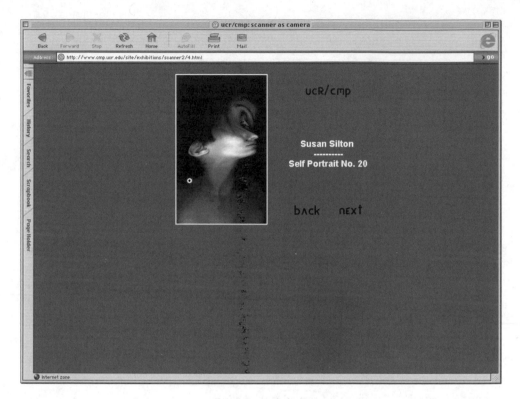

Figure 6.5
Susan Silton, *Self Portrait No. 20*, 1995, "UCR/CMP: Scanner as Camera," UCR California Museum of Photography, 1998, 27 Sept. 2004, <http://www.cmp.ucr.edu/site/exhibitions/scanner2/4 .html>.

spectator to engage from a particular position and correlate them to photographic truth. The spectator is presented with a different kind of identification and point of view because of the fusion of camera-based and digital processes, uneasy states of the referent, and juxtaposition of different forms of rendering.

Gonzales-Day's images are available in varied combinations on the web. The most extensive group is on his site.[78] However, there are other sites that provide more textual materials. For instance, the Sweeney Art Gallery site, which is also part of the University of California Riverside, presents digital images from Epidermal Interventions, which was shown in 1999 as part of their Projects Series (figure 6.7).[79] The site presents four images from his Skin Series, which are combined with links and an essay by Gonzales-Day, and organized into a formal arrangement of vertical and horizontal bands. The site design, with its minimal black lines that separate the images

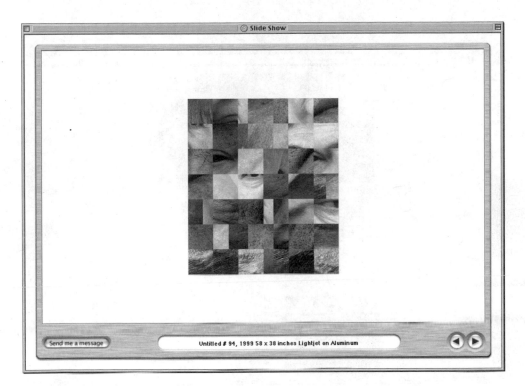

Figure 6.6
Ken Gonzales-Day, *Untitled # 94*, 1999, "Slide Show," 27 Sept. 2004, <http://homepage.mac.com/
kengonzalesday/PhotoAlbum9.html>.

from the rest of the material, suggests a spectatorial engagement with images and
words. Three of Gonzales-Day's images are arranged in a horizontal band near the top
of the site. In most monitors, the spectator would not be able to obtain a full view of
the fourth image without scrolling. The cropping of the fourth image suggests that
spectatorship is a continuous process of reading and arranging the body in front of
works rather than a centered engagement. The design is different from that of the
Scanner as Camera site because it does not construct a spectator in front of a singular
work. The scrolling view and the long column of Gonzales-Day's statement suggest
vertical forms of reading or a horizontal reading of sentences that has its counterpoint
in a strong vertical block of text. The site can also be frustrating because the viewer
cannot engage with the "whole" view.

The four images on the Sweeney Gallery site only become identifiable representations of skin because their striated pattern and pinky-brown hues provide reading

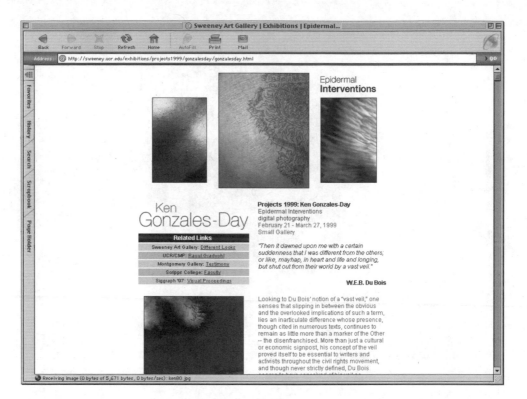

Figure 6.7
Ken Gonzales-Day, "Sweeney Art Gallery | Exhibitions | Epidermal," Sweeney Art Gallery, 1999, 27 Sept. 2004, <http://sweeney.ucr.edu/exhibitions/projects1999/gonzalesday/gonzalesday.html>.

cues. The middle image encourages the spectator to read the mottled surfaces on the left as pimples and the polyplike nodes and dark lines of the bottom image as skin and hair. Constructed aspects of the left, right, and bottom image prompt the spectator to question what appear to be direct references. Through this organization, Gonzales-Day and the site designers begin to provide reading indications that are absent in net artworks and VP web sites. Gonzales-Day suggests that there are always "shifts and slippage" between the constructed and referential aspects of photography and digital imaging.[80] For instance, by combining medical diagrams of skin with photographic processes, Gonzales-Day shows that these images are intentional drawings. His depictions come with such "flaws" as deep lines and creases, tattoos, scars, and eruptions that encourage the spectator to attend to the inscribed surface and the ways photography, digital imaging, and the body are produced through accidental and purposeful writing. He indicates that photography is "a language," which is related to the deeply mediated process of writing. With this photographic language, "your adjectives could be printing or cropping," and there are both "evocative statements" and "ideological constructs."[81] In order to understand the ideological intents of photography and computer-facilitated images, spectators must develop reading skills.

Gonzales-Day uses a cubic grid to evoke the pixels of computer rendering and to suggest that arbitrary numerical information rather than an indexical relationship undergirds computer-facilitated representations. A great deal of the material is garnered from images of Gonzales-Day and his parents, but these do not read as self-portraits or family photos. He "builds" grids of eyes, cheeks, and lips from computer-manipulated squares of different individuals. These "pixels" are not color building blocks, and they do not combine into a unified digital whole. Instead, he mixes cubes of race and gender "components" so that the categories, which are ordinarily enforced on varied bodies, become confused. His works suggest "modernist aesthetic principles," the continued employment of the grid in art works, and "photography's history of racial analysis and classification," which employed the seemingly unbiased qualities of the medium to record aspects of the body. Such "scientific" images were then read for "evidence" of differences in intelligence, race, and sexuality.[82] Gonzales-Day's images function differently from those of scientists and avatar painters because he uses the grid, as Krauss theorizes its function, as "antinatural" and "antireal."[83] His grids remind spectators about systems of classification. However, he undermines the naturalistic and evidential aspects of photography, does not objectify the body, and clearly manipulates skin color and point of view. Through such practices he indicates that race and identity are also produced through reading and writing.

Gonzales-Day's cubic grids render the folding of one body into another. Sometimes a part of one cube seems to have been generated by a part of another sequence. At other times, there is a kind of bleeding from one compartment or area of the image to another. These renderings of morphed bodies, with their stretching and folding at the seam, connect varied identities together so that there cannot be an articulation of the unified self. Each cropped square of these images shifts the viewer between the flatness of the modernist grid, and a representation of a particular angled, although sometimes impossible to identify engagement with the body. While Cavell indicates that implying and rejecting the presence of the world through cropping is as important to photography as what it portrays, Gonzales-Day uses the crop in order to make it impossible to engage with images as a unified worldview.[84] These internal crops produce a shifting position. Gonzales-Day's works do not provide the optical viewpoint and identification that are available with traditional photography or Hollywood film. The spectator cannot achieve identification with the singular lens, camera, photographer, or even an arrangement that is like that of the double viewer/viewed cinema structure that Metz describes because portions of individuals are constantly being grafted onto and morphed into other things.[85]

The spectator's engagement with film can ordinarily be understood through the concept of suture, or the processes through which texts provide subjectivity to viewers. Suture can also be used when considering the spectator's engagement with photographic and computer-facilitated images.[86] Suture occurs when spectators accept a character to act as their stand-in, or allow a point of view to articulate what they see. Suture is successful, according to Silverman, when "the viewing subject says, 'Yes that's me' or 'That's what I see.'"[87] Suture gives the "subject the illusion of a stable and consistent identity" and rearticulates "the existing symbolic order in ideological orthodox ways."[88] It is designed to produce passive subjects who are aligned with the codes of traditional media rather than critical spectators. While film theory, and more particularly apparatus theory, offers the most elaborate theorization of suture, Fried's work on the painter-beholder also suggests a similar understanding of how spectators are connected to texts.[89]

The spectator of photographic and digital works also tends to identify with the position of the image producer and text.[90] However, when Gonzales-Day is "fragmenting" his "own subjectivity with each blemish, scar and line," he is also disturbing such spectatorial positions.[91] The spectator is not sutured and cannot see and be positioned in the uniform ways that are articulated by the text. This presents an intriguing opportunity to retheorize the kind of spectatorial engagements that occur with imaging technologies. In a physical sense, the spectator is still arranged somewhere in front of the image in order to gain a view of the work. However, this position is no longer authorized or empowered by the knowledge that camera and photographer were once set up in this exact position to the referent. This disjunction leaves the spectator in an uneasy position of having no articulated place from which to engage.

The New Media Grid

Other new media artists also misuse the grid in order to consider the relationship between spectatorship and difference.[92] For instance, Keith Piper's Internet-based *Relocating the Remains/Excavating the Site* suggests that grids facilitate classification, collecting, and surveillance (figure 6.8).[93] Anthropological images of "native" bodies, medical drawings, and seemingly scientific information about "the size of" and "weight of" bodies are mapped against a grid.[94] However, these diagrammed parts do not cohere into a consolidated subject or position for the spectator. Piper irreparably

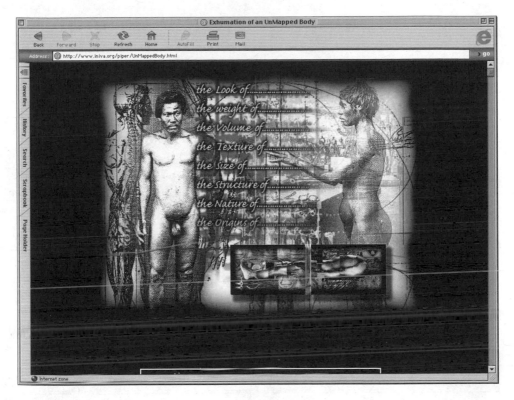

Figure 6.8
Keith Piper, "Exhumation of an UnMapped Body," *Relocating the Remains/Excavating the Site*, 27 Sept. 2004, <http://www.iniva.org/piper/UnMappedBody.html>.

alters the legible body promised by da Vinci's and the AAAS's *Vitruvian Man* by removing most of the rational shapes (figure I.1).[95] In another part of his work, a black male body replicates the position of the *Vitruvian Man* within the circle, square, and grid.[96] However, the blurring of the images, disparate elements, and citation of the systems of knowledge that produce such bodies, which he indicates include "anthropology," "craniology," "ethnology," and "technology," suggest how the "other" is produced. Through such strategies Piper renders multiple readings, spectatorial positions, and articulations of race.

Piper uses grids of overlapping gold frames and other art references to indicate that the bounded histories of people of color are also produced by the museum. Piper and the Mongrel collective subversively repeat aspects of the museum while exhibiting within its structure.[97] For instance, the Tate commissioned Mongrel's Graham

Figure 6.9
Graham Harwood, *Uncomfortable Proximity*, "Harwood De Mongrel Tate Collection," 27 Sept. 2004, <http://www.tate.org.uk/netart/mongrel/collections/mong8.htm>.

Harwood to produce a net art "versioning" of its web site (figure 6.9).[98] His *Uncomfortable Proximity* offers deeply manipulated grids of images from the collection, links to other aspects of the site, and commentary on the racial and class issues of the museum where "British Modernism" is exhibited "in one of the lowest waged areas of Britain" and black subjects are reconstituted in stereotyped ways.[99] Harwood references the museum's site design, web frame, and art frames in a tactic that is similar to Mongrel's simulation of the browser in *Natural Selection*.[100] In his version of the Tate, aesthetic objects and a comfortable spectatorial distance are replaced with disturbingly close images of paintings, oozing sores, and the scummy water of *Uncomfortable Proximity*.

Harwood repeats and revisions the museum's structure in ways that evoke other net art practices. He uses such failures as broken links and empty art frames in order to invite different forms of Internet and web museum spectatorship. Harwood's disturbing visuals, which make the spectator look away, direct attention to the structure of the museum and the kinds of spectatorship it ordinarily facilitates. However, Harwood's production of uncomfortable viewing does not change the rest of the Tate site and may even alleviate the museum from having to critically examine its role in shaping cultural norms and perceptions. By including net art critiques in clearly demarcated sections of web sites, museums may be able to perform a kind of self-examination while remaining largely the same. Artists like Piper and Mongrel are in a difficult position because they critique and exhibit in museums. Their appropriation of the modernist grid as a way of deforming linear narrative and imaging other bodies is a political act. However, their misuse of the grid within technological settings also remains uneasy because, as Mongrel indicates, "Hierarchically ordered technology and structural racism mesh too easily together."[101] These connections should encourage critical examinations of the ways the grid and interface support classification, power structures, and control. One possible resistance to the hierarchical and consolidating tendencies of technology is the process of morphing.

Conclusion: The Morphed Spectator

Selter's, Silton's, and Gonzales-Day's deliberate acts against the wholeness of the represented subject suggest how identity is produced through crops and other forms of photographic and computer-facilitated writing, and they encourage the spectator to see photography as a meaning-making system. Their destabilization of the traditional unified spectatorial engagement with images encourages viewers to address the ways they are structured to look. Theories of folding and morphing by such authors as Vivian Sobchack offer further methods for articulating fragmented and disempowered viewing. These theories suggest that digital imaging spectatorship is not like the immobile view, or the one time, that is associated with photography or the linear flow of time that the spectator is supposed to receive with traditional Hollywood film. The digital image and morph offer times that are reversible and outside lived experience, according to Sobchack, because of their "supernatural" and accelerated processes of change and transformation.[102]

Morphing, or changing a picture from one image to another through a succession of fleeting phases, is a useful way to address temporality and Internet spectatorship.[103] The temporal aspects of the Internet, which the spectator engages with, include flashing banners, animated sequences, streaming media (such as RealAudio), the continued emphasis on QuickTime and Flash (which also render certain kinds of time through product names), image and file downloads, software installations, scrolling synchronous communication sessions and web browsers, clocking varied activities, spacing out while gaming and "surfing," and the cycling of the screen.[104] Such experiences as lags and crashes seem to prevent or stall the real time of computer processing. These temporal aspects of the Internet emphasize the spectator's experience of waiting, encourage the assessment that nothing is happening, and produce a fragmented shifting or morphing that represents changes but does not usually have a clear beginning and end.

Digital imaging technologies can never be relied on to provide a consistent and invariable image. They always have the potential to morph because of their easy transformability at the level of the pixel, which means that the image retains a level of formlessness.[105] Morphing and the shapeless aspects of computer-facilitated imaging are also rendered by Apple's OS X operating system, which depicts web browsers and other software windows twisting and melting into the "dock" when they are temporarily removed from view. The fluid and sequential aspects of Selter's, Silton's, and Gonzales-Day's works morph or change images of people and animals into other things through phases that are visible in the jagged composites of the scanner images and leaking grids. When the spectator engages with images, through the images' point of view, then morphing also affects or even changes the spectator.

Cinematic morphing sequences represent contemporary concerns and interests in such medical technologies as plastic surgery, sex changes, and genetic manipulation. These filmic practices recraft bodies and erode the possibility of uniqueness, a stable other, and a consistent list of differences. The morphing of film characters in *Alien Resurrection* (Jean-Pierre Jeunet, 1997), *Mimic* (Guillermo del Toro, 1997), and *Species* (Roger Donaldson, 1995) addresses concerns about genetic or technological experiments that have gone wrong. Liquidity is also used to visibly articulate a character's shiftiness in *Hollow Man* (Paul Verhoeven, 2002), *The Mask* (Chuck Russell, 1994), and *Terminator 2: Judgment Day* (James Cameron, 1991). The "mercurial shape" in such films is threatening at least in part because of what Mark Dery describes as its "polymorphous perversity."[106] The shock of recognition in morphing sequences is related to the unstructured and unexpected failures of Internet and computer technologies but morphing's fluidity makes it conceptually different than the coded, planned, and deeply referential aspects of net art failures. Technology is a site of new anxiety and uneasiness because, as Scott Bukatman argues, "it cannot even be relied upon to keep its shape."[107] Film morphing provides the viewer with a fascinating spectacle that diverges from narrative conventions, a liquidity that can never be fully mapped and traced, and a warning that there are dangers in embracing such positions.[108]

The constant doubling and folding of the morph/body into itself, which is figured quite specifically in the works of Selter, Silton, and Gonzales-Day, evoke the spectator's fragile and folded body and self-engagement while in front of the screen. Digital imaging and cinematic morphing render a spectator who is close to the screen because the image cannot be read coherently.[109] Folded positions, which are explored in more detail in the afterword, are without central coherence, a unified point of view, or a core embodiment. Morphing suggests liquidity, or what Sobchack calls the "quick change," and an unknowable time when images are compressed and distorted beyond physical possibility.[110] It offers a folding, unfolding, and twisting of time. For instance, Amelia Jones indicates that Silton's images are "portraits of motionless motion."[111] Computer-facilitated images and film morphing articulate the process of becoming, which can also be a type of motionless motion.

Morphing does not render the same experience as the theorized immobility of photography or the lived time of traditional Hollywood film. Barthes distinguishes between the "immobility" of photography, where the thing posed in front of the camera "has remained there forever," and the movement of film, where "the pose is swept away and denied by the continuous series of images."[112] The traditional narrative film experience, which is often associated with the long shot, is linear, developmental, and not reversible.[113] The temporality that narrative films convey, like the rendering of real time in television, telepresence artworks, and webcams, is articulated so that the spectator associates these representations with the embodied experiences of lived time and change. Morphing operates quite differently than traditional narrative film because it offers a time that is outside lived experience and is reversible. The scanner also renders distorted and compressed duration because different times are encoded as the head moves across the glass. The scanner's representation of time without traditional sequence often remains unacknowledged so scans can be instantaneous and seamless images. By eliding these shifting temporalities, digital images are associated with photography and cinema. According to Metz, photography and cinema render a space that *"was*, but no longer *is."*[114] Through spectatorial identification, they also offer an inhabitable space and a real view. However, the morphed image renders nonlinear time rather than space.

The digital image and the morph may remain outside lived time because they have what Spielmann describes as a "permanent instability."[115] This instability renders forms of spectatorship that are fragile and not validated by identification and direct correspondence with the screen. The continued liquidity and shifting of morphing, which tend to render different spectatorial positions, make this experience different from net art failures, which usually provide the same image and stylistic conventions with subsequent viewing. However, morphing's instability, which is part of its theoretical value, may also be its undoing as a critical model. The lack of constancy of such experiences allows spectators to enjoy moments of disruption and loss, to select the more traditional aspects of the images and engagement, and to remain the same. The challenge for media producers and critics, who want to interrogate spectatorship and representations, is to find forms of morphing that cannot be overwritten or displaced by traditional models. When spectatorship cannot be fixed, and the spectator is not fully recognized or formed by the screen, then processes of viewing have to be considered in order to engage with and understand images.

Afterword | **The Flat and the Fold: A Consideration of Embodied Spectatorship**

Introduction

Spectators are often conceived of as unified, empowered, and directly if not erectly positioned in front of objects and screens.[1] Internet sites as well as academic and popular narratives also privilege a commanding spectator. As the chapters in this book demonstrate, there are many ways sites and interfaces suggest that spectators have power and control. However, there are also renderings of cramped and bent bodies, bloated forms, errant flesh, static positions, and aches and pains that occur because of the computer, keyboard, and screen. Some of these images and narratives provide a negative image of the common spectator that is then contrasted with a more skilled and disciplined programmer position.[2] Renderings of an impotent body are also designed to motivate spectators to gain control over body and interface. However, a close reading and critical rethinking of these images and narratives, like the one performed in this afterword, indicate that Internet and computer spectators fail to achieve an ideal position. An examination of these positions can also suggest alternative ways to theorize spectatorship.

Spectators worry about their "extra" flesh, experience of being creased, and sweaty engagement with chairs and other computer technologies. The bending of the body because of poor posture, unusual seating positions, and repetitive tasks of mousing, typing, and other computer work are painful and inane. The writings of Bordo, Deleuze, Irigaray, and Theweleit offer ways to critically consider this folded body.[3] Deleuze's theoretical work on the fold suggests the critical possibilities of becoming, which render a different subject position than conceptions of uniform being, and latent "virtualities" that will, according to Grosz, never be realized as a solid or centered form.[4] Morphing also renders fluidity rather than a stable state.[5] The fold and the morph suggest more precarious forms of viewing and can be used to theorize the fleshy position of the body in front of the computer screen.

Internet spectators and researchers cannot see specific individuals by looking at writings and representations, but depictions of seated and folded viewers offer a way to theorize the body of the Internet and computer spectator, resist some of the narratives about empowered computer users, and consider how other forms of spectatorship are less vertical than expected. For instance, self-identified male programmers—who should be understood as Internet and computer spectators despite their resistance to being associated with "common" users—write in a variety of Internet forums about their long periods of time in front of the computer and personal concerns about body size and shape. Male programmers' overt fascination and concern with their own flesh contradicts cultural presumptions that the body is a woman's issue. These narratives offer an opportunity to rethink the gender representations that are presented in a variety of settings. In this afterword, I address the fold in digital imaging, the desire to leave the body behind, the repetitive strain of computer work, attempts to control computer-related pain, programmers' concerns about fat, the erotic of doubled flesh, and the bodily risks in disassembling computers. By considering versions of the body that are different from those usually addressed, I hope to encourage a more careful interrogation of the Internet and computer spectator's position.

Carol Selter, Susan Silton, Ken Gonzales-Day, and the Fold

Selter, Silton, and Gonzales-Day provide ways to consider the Internet and computer spectator's bodily arrangement (figures 6.1–6.7). Their depictions of doubled and folded bodies suggest the spectator's seated and bent position, self-contact with flesh, and erotic engagement. The spectator's position, which might otherwise be envisioned as masculine and somehow standing erectly in front of the screen, is feminized by these representations of intimacy and self-touching. This overt embodiment is related to the spectator's closeness to the screen. However, the spectator cannot read Selter's depictions as a material reality because of the temporal folding of different animal moments and movements into one image. Form is folded in such a way that individual animals cannot always be recognized. A folding of one body into another and distortions in time are also suggested by Silton's representations of her body. In her images, the doubled or multiple aspects of the folded body confuse cultural conceptions of the individual because they are produced from the same person. Selter's and Silton's images are a picture of the technology and a folding of the inside of the scanner mechanism into the outside of the picture (figures 6.1–6.5). In Gonzales-Day's *Untitled # 94* (1999), some sections of the cubic-grid of skin seem to have been generated by other sequences, there is a kind of bleeding between compartments, a folding over onto adjacent rectangles, and a stretching and folding at the seams (figure 6.6).[6] Through such devices, he also suggests the folding of one body into another. The fold moves the viewer between recognition and loss of the photographic surface as representations of bodies appear and dissolve in these works.

Craig Owens indicates that doubling, or the internal duplication that occurs in some photographs—and we could add digital images by Selter and Silton to this category—suggest "a literal folding back" of the image "upon itself."[7] The fold can be a kind of duplicative or photographic process because it touches and imprints. However, these repeats suggest formal comparisons of similar shapes and arrangements rather than rendering exacting copies. They foreground photography's and other reproductive technologies' discourse about verisimilitude as well as the failures of exacting repetition. This technologically facilitated double is not necessarily a trace of the real. Deleuze indicates that the double does not have to be a copy of the same or something completely different: "It is not a doubling of the One, but a redoubling of the Other. It is not a reproduction of the Same, but a repetition of the Different. It is not the emanation of an 'I,' but something that places in immanence an always other or a Non-Self."[8] As Deleuze suggests, the in-between state of the fold and the double indicate that there are problems with binary logic and the articulation of a stable and unified self.

The doubling and persistent folding of the inside and outside, which according to Deleuze "resembles exactly the invagination of a tissue in embryology" and the "doubling in sewing," is rendered by the elasticity of Selter's animal representations, the twisting of Silton's self-portraits, and the shifting status of Gonzales-Day's skin images. These artists' renderings of other positions and Deleuze's theory of the fold, which he relates to women's bodies and production, suggest femininity, feminist politics, and other relationships to body and society. As Joan Key indicates, folding breaks down categorizations and the subject positions that rely on such oppositions as "the included and the excluded, the abject and the desirable, the obscene and the seen."[9] Folding prevents the articulation of distinctions between subjects and objects and a cohesive spectatorial position. Deleuze's emphasis on "what resists assimilation, what remains foreign even with a presumed identity" and other theories of the fold are useful in articulating fragmented and resistant spectatorial engagements and a feminist politics that thinks through the folded body to other positions.[10]

The Body Folded and Evacuated

The bodies of Internet spectators and many other contemporary individuals are conceptually and physically folded. Jaron Lanier describes a material folding where individuals "live in this constant sort of fetal position" and "are seated in a soft chair looking at a world through a glass square, be it the windshield of the car or the screen of a television or computer."[11] The presumed stasis and softness of the Internet and computer spectator are often parodied. For instance, Irongull indicates, "By eliminating solid food, and using a catheter, I never have to leave the warm comfy cradle of my recliner."[12] The "evolution of mankind" illustration, which appears on a number of web sites, depicts the folded body and lapse from an erect stance of Internet and computer spectators (figure A.1).[13] In the image, "man" has given up such powerful tools as the jackhammer and is hunched in a decidedly delicate position on a computer chair. His body is no longer depicted as impermeable or differentiated from the environment.

Debates about comfortable chairs and computing positions regularly appear in such Internet forums as Slashdot, which is described as "News for Nerds. Stuff that matters." However, there is also a resistance among forum readers to the "typical" programmer's soft and folded form that would link them to static spectatorship. By interrogating such differences in this afterword, I hope to uncover the desires, visions, and disparate cultural forces at work on the body. While academics and popular writers often indicate that spectators achieve power through their Internet and computer engagements, the bodies of spectators are also depicted as excessively soft. This may not be as contradictory as it seems because early cyberpunk fiction writers equated the skill of male computer programmers with the pure mind. For instance, Case and other hackers in Gibson's *Neuromancer* disparagingly refer to the body as "meat" and much prefer the "bodiless" state of cyberspace. When Case's nervous system is damaged, he falls into a "prison of his own flesh."[14] In the words of another Gibson character, who is quite accepting of this position, "somewhere we have bodies, very far away."[15] This distance from the body also occurs in Tom Maddox's literature when George feels "like somebody else was at home" in his body.[16] The material conditions, which encourage Stephenson's character Hiro to spend a lot of time in virtual reality because it "beats the shit out of the U-Stor-It" where he lives, echo the rotting infrastructure of inner cities and the inadequate conditions of people working with and producing computer technologies on assembly lines.[17]

The cyberpunk fiction of a number of men, and the continuing narratives about Internet and computer use, suggest that the female body is unimportant and to be left behind in a world that increasingly privileges pure mind.[18] Kevin Robins critiques such positions and indicates that the promise that new technologies can free individuals from the constraints of the physical body also implies that there is no reason to consider current ecological, material, and political conditions.[19] At the same time, Internet

Figure A.1
"Evolution of mankind!!!," 27 Sept. 2004, <http://www.angelfire.com/ri/cardzzz/joke2.html>.

spectators who self-identify as women are never allowed to leave their bodies behind because they continue to be deluged with questions about their physical attributes and sexual availability. Feminist cyberpunk writers like Pat Cadigan and Melissa Scott present a more body-centric computer engagement. However, the expressed desire to leave the body behind, which appears in much of this fiction, is not surprising since the body continues to be dismissed within Western tradition.[20]

Narratives about rejecting the body while maintaining the mind are also part of academics' and inventors' considerations of artificial intelligence, or AI. For instance, Ray Kurzweil indicates that it makes sense to replace or dispose of material bodies because individuals identify with the mind.[21] He suggests that this "Evolution of Mind," where brains will be downloaded into personal computers and other containers, can allow people to overcome death and allow for mind expansion, since the growth limits dictated by cranium size will no longer apply.[22] Kurzweil believes that the process of downloading someone's brain "won't be perfect at first," "small imperfections" will not be noticeable because people are always changing, and eventually "the newly emergent 'person' will appear to other observers to have very much the same personality, history, and memory."[23] Hans Moravec also associates identity with the mind and argues that the individual can soon become a "living brain in a vat."[24] He rejects critical and feminist indications that identity is interconnected with the body, suggests that this incorrectly "assumes that a person is defined by the stuff of which a human body is made," and proposes the model of "pattern-identity," which defines the person as "the *pattern* and the *process* going on" in the "head and body, not the machinery supporting the process."[25] Moravec wants to preserve the mind and thinking processes, but the "rest is mere jelly" and "so messy" that it should be discarded.[26]

Kurzweil's and Moravec's rejection of the fleshy body and insistence that corporeality has no effect on the subject is argued from a centered and empowered position where experiences are culturally validated as "normal" and body identity has remained largely unlabeled. However, Butler reminds us that gender and other cultural conceptions of the body produce individuals.[27] Kurzweil's and Moravec's beliefs are supported by Western understandings of the individual, which encourage them to reject embodiment as messy and feminine. When Kurzweil describes bodies, they are frivolous, resistant to change, and female. For example, his character Molly has "switched to nonfat muffins" because she needs to "drop at least half a dress size," and Nellie asks for but is denied evidence of her lover's "real" body.[28] Kurzweil's depiction of a gambler and "problem solver," which is meant to represent him, exists in a world where he gazes upon and garners attention from "beautiful women" but is not fully satisfied.[29] These writings, like the work of many cyberpunk fiction authors, offer very different subject positions for men and women. Male readers, who can identify with Kurzweil and Moravec, are promised whatever "mind-hosting bodies" that they choose to inhabit as well as the heterosexual "right" to gaze upon women.[30] Kurzweil's and Moravec's celebration of particular kinds of intelligence indicates that they intend mind-prolonging procedures for traditionally conceived scholars and visionaries. Class and race are not directly addressed and their intentions for the futures of other individuals are less clear.

Feminists have critiqued the tendency among philosophers and Western subjects toward a mind/body split and the persistent association of the devalued body with the feminine. This consideration continues with new technologies.[31] For instance, Hayles indicates how the erasure of embodiment is common to both the "liberal humanist subject and the cybernetic posthuman," who is envisioned leaving the body behind or melding with the machine.[32] The liberal subject was imagined as a rational mind that *"possessed* a body but was not usually represented as *being* a body."[33] In this case, the body was an object to control rather than an intrinsic part of the self. The body is also made into an "excluded other," according to Morse, when male program- mers form elaborate identifications with machines and computer processes.[34] Such dualistic approaches, which presume that mind can be detached from body, ignore the integral place of sustenance and repair. Eating is rarely incorporated into narratives about cyborgs.[35] Morse indicates that the individuals who are attached to computers and disengaged from the organic body "have, in fact, at least one body too many—the one now largely sedentary carbon-based resting at the control console that suffers hunger, corpulence, illness, old age, and ultimately death."[36] Kurzweil, Moravec, and a variety of other technology-oriented writers want to escape this folded and painful body. Their desire to leave the body behind is not surprising since the conditions that Morse describes are culturally coded as undesirable. However, academics, hackers, programmers, and spectators also note that material experiences are not so easily displaced.

Hierarchy and Control

The bending of the body and the repetitive tasks of computer work can be painful and dull. Technology people express concern about "long boring meetings," "particularly boring meetings," and "the over night shift for an ISP" with its "long and boring shift."[37] The Work or Spoon web site indicates that on some days, "gouging your eye out with a spoon would be so much less painful than going to work."[38] This psycho- logical pain may be understandable since Work or Spoon, FuckedCompany.com, and Fuck That Job chronicle the disappearance and downsizing of Internet- and comput- er-based companies. These web sites also describe instances of employee anger, despair, and boredom that accompany these economic developments.[39] A critical consideration of these sites indicates how the position of programmers and other well- paid technology workers are changing. It also suggests varied attempts to maintain the more respected identities of programmers by producing hierarchy.

Work or Spoon, FuckedCompany.com, and Fuck That Job readers are understand- ably disgusted with the changes in pay and job requirements that have appeared in advertisements for computer programming and design work after the demise of any start-up companies. However, employees who word process, input information, use computers as part of customer service positions, and manufacture hardware are usual- ly even more poorly paid and culturally dismissed. Morse indicates that workers are despairing over the growing reliance on automation, "devaluation of labor," and "global job crisis," which has them being monitored and competing with machines that have "far greater capacities for repetition, speed, and endurance" than they possess.[40] The indication that endurance has been reached is represented by the angry responses in many Internet forums. For instance, shanga-langa-lang notes, "$6ph? To do repetitive data entry? Fuck this asshole."[41] Despite such dismissals, many workers remain unsure of what to do about the depreciation of their skills and career opportunities.

Computer programmers and designers render hierarchy as well as manifestos about appropriate pay and work conditions at these job sites. They angrily compare the pay offered in advertisements for "skilled" computer work with what is deemed to be less desirable employment. Site participants often presume that service and sales workers should make less money. One job seeker demeans the skills and hard labor of food service employees when arguing, "I would take the McDonalds Job. You don't need to think nearly as much."[42] Other workers and positions are dismissed with comments like "Damn. That's almost as much as a manager makes at Mikki D's," "Maybe I should aply for a mikki d's manager position," and "I hear Starbucks give.you full health bennies."[43] Administrative assistants, clerical workers, and support staff are labeled as merely a "toady" and "lackie" for higher management and thus not worthy of consideration.[44] Dismissing these forms of work articulates an identity, resists a perceived status shift, dislocates technology positions from the computers that are increasingly employed in service and sales work, and counteracts any association with the bodily humiliation and control that accompany these other forms of technological employment.

The resistance of computer programmers and designers to being associated with administrative, assembly, and service work is not surprising. Engagements with computerized production lines and other machines are sometimes intolerable. A Reuters news article suggests that "supermarket cashiers in Argentina are being forced to wear diapers to keep them from taking toilet breaks at work."[45] Tom indicated on Fuck That Job that he was also "assigned to a work station" where he could not leave unless someone covered for him.[46] Since that required his "having to go up to 4 or 5 hours without a bathroom break," he "used to have to wear diapers." Marc Linder studies the ways that companies sometimes regulate and control workers' bodies, and the resultant lack of "pee breaks."[47] He describes the "significant problem" of workers being denied access to bathrooms, the unnecessary medical risks of not being able to evacuate, and the excessive expense of having to buy adult diapers because employers do not acknowledge workers' needs.[48] These problems persist in computer-facilitated telemarketing companies and some other settings because there are very strict rules about workers leaving their assigned positions.

Describing the relationship between these technologies and Internet spectatorship is not easy. A variety of workers engage with computers and computerized technologies but have no connectivity on the job or can only view Internet sites that are related to work. For some workers, Internet and computer time has become more regulated as employers develop concerns about productivity. For instance, the mobile phone retailer Phones 4U banned email to "boost production."[49] As such corporate decisions suggest, employers sometimes conceptualize telemarketers and other individuals as a kind of machine that performs tasks but has no needs. However, the bodies of workers do not always respond positively to intense, repetitive, and lengthy interactions with computers. Cindy Brown indicates that her cashier job, which includes engaging with computers, "consists of working for six hours, repetitively greeting customers, scanning groceries, taking money, thanking the customer." She notes that this may seem easy but adds that standing "for six hours straight is no small feat—between knee aches, back aches and headaches, six hours can feel like an eternity."[50] Moise's account of academic work indicates that her "aching body is physically bound to the computer."[51] In both these descriptions, the worker's body is captured and held by the technology and services it. When production, service, and telemarketing jobs, and the oppressive and painful conditions that they sometimes require, are removed from common conceptions of the Internet and computer, it is easier to support contemporary narratives about positively reconfigured bodies and minds.

The Spectator in Pain

Some feminist science fiction novelists highlight how the bodies of Internet and computer spectators become doubled and cramped. In Scott's *Trouble and Her Friends*, Internet and computer spectators are reminded of their fragile and easily damaged state. Bodies are foregrounded rather than transcended when characters engage for any length of time. During one computer session, Trouble's fingers cramped so extremely "inside the tight shell of the metal-bound glove" that she "winced" and "straightened slowly" when disengaging.[52] In Cadigan's *Dervish Is Digital*, Konstantin constantly addresses her flesh and the ways "the stretch waist band of her trousers seemed close to the limit."[53] Her body also cramps and folds. After Konstantin disengages from the interface, her "left foot seized up and she fell over onto the carpet, rubbing her instep and pushing her toes back hard." Her "cramp ebbed, renewed, ebbed again."[54] Scott's, Cadigan's, and other feminist science fiction writers' descriptions of folded and mutable bodies, which are physically and psychically damaged, may be acceptable or even expected because they are incorporated into female subjects.

Descriptions of pain also appear in Slashdot, Ars Technica, and other web-based forums, which display writings from programmers and computer technology workers that often self-represent as male. There are concerned posts about how "games always cause some pain," the "long-lasting (and intense) pain in my right index finger, the only finger I used for mouse navigation," and "experiencing near constant excruciating pain in my arms, hands, and wrists."[55] The descriptions of pain that appear regularly in such forums indicate that bodies are being put under extreme strain. Internet and computer engagement needs to be drastically redesigned and rethought for these technologies to continue as an element of daily life. However, programmers who post about pain usually want to maintain a lifestyle that includes long periods of programming and gaming. Ergonomic and technological suggestions are provided so spectators can continue or even expand their Internet and computer use. For instance, Syncophant-16 recommends a product that allows him to play longer. He used to "play civ3 for about 3 straight hours . . . before being out of commission for a couple of days." Now he "can do about 16 hours straight and . . . play again the next day— huge improvement."[56] Other programmers switch the mouse to the other hand or take breaks in order to be "at the computer constantly, 12–14 hours a day."[57] While Ashtrashe expresses amazement that there are people who "play a lot of games despite having problems with their wrists and hands" and wonders if it is worth it, blasikov insists, "Of course it is!"[58] For some individuals, a certain amount of pain and bodily damage is an acceptable trade-off in order to continue using the computer. Others make distinctions between intermittent and unbearable pain that will permanently prevent programming, gaming, and money making.

Some programmers make the body into a technology and describe arms and hands as "tools" in order to reconceptualize pain.[59] Relgar notes, "It's the nastiest scare for techie types to have random pains in what amounts to the tools of the profession."[60] These programmers acknowledge pain at the same time that they displace weak or soft flesh, evoke narratives about humanist and posthuman subjects, and control bodies while not wanting to be bodies. For instance, a dieting programmer transforms the body into a version of the computer when suggesting that "you too can lose that 'Server Case' and bring it down to a slim 'Mini Tower.'"[61] In a technology review, Adam "Stone Table" Israel offers IMAK Smart Gloves as a hardware solution that will make the body "stone" hard and resolve pain. Israel casts himself as a soldier, overcoming weakness through determination, and indicates that he has "fought recurring problems with both wrists over the years."[62] He also notes that "inflamed, weak wrists may be a source of ridicule for some, but it's nothing to laugh at when it happens to you."[63] Programmers' pains are sometimes dismissed as unmanly because weak wrists are coded as gay and effeminate.[64] Technology forums rarely mention alternative sexualities in a positive way, and pain in the arms and hands is believed to be an aspect of a "less successful" male programmer's lifestyle where sex with women is replaced with masturbating and pornography. Requests for help in dealing with hand pain receive suggestions to "jerk off less" and indications that posters are "resisting" porn, or "pr0n," and "one-handed-typing" jokes, which obviously allow them to humorously comment on masturbating.[65] These responses occur because pain suggests a lack of personal control.

Male programmers, or at least individuals representing themselves and accepted by other readers as male, present stories about conquering pain, containing and solidifying the body, and resisting flows, fat, and other soft states. Critical considerations of masculinity, including Theweleit's study of German soldiers, provide ways to understand these concerns. Theweleit indicates that one type of soldier, or the "man of steel," wants to "dam in, and to subdue any force that threatens to transform him back into the horribly disorganized jumble of flesh, hair, skin, intestines, and feelings."[66] Bordo notes that the "ideal" body is firm, contained, and "bolted down" because this protects "against eruption from within" and verifies the individual.[67] This desire to become a "man of steel" is also present in the cyberpunk fiction of Gibson, with its aversion to "meat," and the AI theories of Kurzweil and Moravec, which want to excise the "jelly." Programmers are also interested in gaining control over messy and easily damaged bodies because its "jumble" links them to the feminine. They idealize a mechanized body, which displaces internal functions, and imagine that when the "correct" keyboard, mouse, computer, screen, chair, and desk are purchased and set up properly they can transcend the limits of the corporeal body. There is a desire to control pain, according to Kim Sawchuck, Cathy Busby, and Bill Burns, because it indicates that there is no independent agent who is in complete and absolute control.[68] Programmers and other Internet spectators try to establish their knowledge of a series of technologies, including the body, and authority so there is no invalidating pain.

The Fat and the Fold

Many programmers are interested in having a firm and coherent body, but they also present narratives about soft male flesh, in part because they are considering their inability to reach a hard and solid state. These representations cannot reveal the material body of any individual, but they do suggest that Internet spectators represent male flesh in ways that are quite uncommon in physical settings. Critically examining these narratives should offer some ways to rethink the relationship between body and

gender and be equally productive for other individuals. Silverman argues that bringing about "a large-scale reconfiguration of male identification and desire would, at the
very least, permit female subjectivity to be lived differently."[69] As it is currently
employed, "feminine" can be attached to almost anything, but it always evokes
woman.[70] Male programmers' tales about their bodies offer examples of men rendering feminine behaviors and indicate that equating women to femininity and men to
masculinity does not provide a complete understanding of individual bodies and
behaviors. Considering these representations can make alternative representations of
the male body visible, rather than allowing culture to continue associating men with
the mind. As Silverman indicates, critically engaging with these narratives about fat
should help society rethink the female as well as the male spectator's position.

Narratives about nerds and geeks in text-based communication settings, usenet,
cyberpunk literature, and films like *War Games* (John Badham, 1983) and *Thomas in
Love* (Pierre-Paul Renders, 2000) depict pasty-faced and asocial men languishing in the
monitor's glow.[71] The programmer Sir_Timothy humorously and ambivalently
describes his lifestyle as "get up, walk to computer, use computer, eat, go to the bathroom."[72] Charles Arthur describes the attendees of a hacker conference as "about 20
pounds overweight. It's all those hours at the keyboard."[73] Society tends to associate
computer workers with large and unexercised bodies. There are pronouncements that
"*geekus midwestus*" has "rolls and rolls of fat" and that the Internet is "full" of "fat ass
ugly guys."[74] Negative and harassing posts suggest that some male programmers are
unable to control their bodies. There are suggestions that you can lose weight if you
were to get "off your lazy ass and do something," instructions to "get off your ass, stop
watching >4 hours of TV, eating a bucket of crap (chips, popcorn, burgers, whatever),"
and contentions that "eating is about self control and not being a child."[75] This lack
of control is usually coded as feminine and associated with women. However, the bodies of women programmers are rarely mentioned in these discussions, and women
seem less likely to post in these forums on body issues, perhaps because they already
encounter so many comments and social pressures in other situations. Men are the
intended targets of these comments, which provide moral superiority to those with
bodily control and render larger individuals as weak and indolent.[76]

Comments about getting up indicate that the chair and sitting are sometimes perceived as negative aspects of the male computer programmer's lifestyle. TobyWong
notes the problems facing programmers because of the cultural tendency to equate sitting with "goofing off" and the fact that computer work requires a certain amount of
stasis and focus on the screen.[77] Programmers indicate that they are "sitting and
slouching" and "sitting at computers for 8, 10, 12, even 24 hours at a time."[78]

Programmers joke about needing to be "surgically removed from" their chairs; observes one of them, "I have been sitting at my PC so long that my fat has curled around the posts on my chair and I can't get out."[79] Their comments indicate concerns about embodied positions and the sense that many male spectators cannot detach from the screen and its representations.[80] Bodily folding is incorporated into computer spectatorship with these descriptions of programmers losing their male form. Some programmers accept or even ambivalently celebrate their soft state and sedentary lifestyle, but others fear that such behaviors are a "recipe for obesity," "muscle loss," and disrespect.[81] Testimonials and requests for diets appear in a number of forums.[82]

Individuals who self-present as male programmers in Internet settings write about the male body, concerns about weight, and fear of fat in ways that feminize them. Ironic commentary on the lifestyles and eating habits of male programmers and other intensive computer users abound. This fascination with the male body is notable. While men are traditionally expected to view the female form—a problem that feminists have addressed—such Internet stories indicate that men are often considering the bodies of other men. Their focus suggests a homosocial or even homosexual setting and system of desire. However, this male-centric setting, which certainly presents problems for other gender-representing individuals, does not inherently lead to a consolidation of power. These men are coded as feminine because they seem to exist within an excessively meaty and embodied state.

Feminist scholars indicate how intense views and intimate engagements with the body are usually associated with women and femininity. However, society continues to attribute women's interest in clothing, home decorating, thinness, and youth, which are obviously encouraged through a variety of cultural processes, to an essential femininity. Instances of male programmers' "endless obsession about 'weight,'" as Doom describes it, make it more difficult to render the body as a "woman's domain" and indicate the need for society to address the continued proliferation of body insecurities.[83] Something happens to the male spectator's position and the category "man" because, as Bordo indicates, the "man who cares about his looks the way a woman does, self-esteem on the line, ready to be shattered at the slightest insult or increase in weight gain, is unmanly; sexually suspect."[84] Male programmers, whose sexuality and ability to attract women are already questioned by the popular media, become even more suspect and complicated when they spend time focusing on male bodies. Male programmers' ironic comments about bodies are an attempt to detach them from cultural evaluation by indicating that they do not care, expressing what would otherwise be said about them, retaining power despite differences, and denying their underlying concerns about physiognomy.

Men and the Weight Loss "Challenge"

An ongoing thread on Ars Technica, which is entitled "Ars Weight Loss Challenge," presents numerous thoughts about the weight, body shape, clothing issues, diet, and exercise routines of male programmers. The thread represents men oscillating between despair and fascination with their physique. The participation of women is fairly minor, and women's bodies are represented in disappointingly traditional ways by men. However, a close examination of this Internet forum still offers the opportunity to consider detailed renderings of men's bodies. These descriptions provide some uneasy reading because it is difficult to detach unfamiliar representations of the body from invasive viewing even though similar expressions from women are common. I have had more ethical concerns about this chapter than other materials in this book, perhaps because it provides descriptions of less normative male bodies.[85] Many of these programmers are attached to their Internet representations and concerned about their bodies. However, there are also aspects of the challenge that follow already established Internet conventions. Such familiar themes as the inactive lifestyle of computer workers, feelings of abjection, identifying as fat, and issues of control are presented.

Men's descriptions of physicality, which appear in a variety of Internet forums, indicate their discomfort with being embodied and in contact with their own skin. There are descriptions of being "a big, fat, ballooned caricature of myself" and having a "sandbag around my waist."[86] An uneasiness with being visible and the object of the gaze is indicated by unhappy descriptions of when "your shirt doesn't hide your real body form anymore, IIIEEEHHHHH!!! YUCK!"[87] These expressions of detachment, body loathing, and being "bummed" about the "mushy" parts of the body are not surprising.[88] Moira Gatens and other recent feminist researchers indicate that discomfort and repulsion toward the body accompany Western thought and society.[89] These posts about male bodies also render "somatophobia" or fear of the body and apprehension about women. However, this body loathing is not solely about a morbid fear and hatred of women, as Gatens indicates is often the case. The writings of male programmers indicate that they also have a deep dislike of their own bodies.

Programmers also express concerns about being displaced from normative masculinity. This results in a desire to "reduce the man-tits" and a belief that there is "nothing worse than man-tits."[90] Male programmers' aversion to roundness, softness, and accentuated breasts may be particularly pronounced because these characteristics are all associated with women. Iris Marion Young notes that "breasts are the most visible sign of a woman's femininity."[91] Men and women are encouraged to regulate their breasts in ways that enforce traditional gender positions. For example, Bordo indicates the "deep political meaning" in women's refusal to "discipline" the breasts for the visual pleasure of other individuals in the 1960s.[92] While it is more rarely discussed, men usually strive to render their breasts so that they are culturally acceptable. Men use differentiating terms such as "pecs" or "chest" to produce bodies that appear to be different from what has been culturally understood as woman. Such concepts also allow men to distance themselves from breasts' "fluid being," amorphous aspects, and indefinite shape, which may be carried over into a general body image and identity.[93]

When joining the Ars Technica thread, male programmers represent themselves as overweight. The terms used in their self-descriptions are often brutal. Dave88 identified as "a fat bugger," and Ferret was "tired of my geek pudgyness."[94] However, this focus on body image, which feminizes the participants, often leads to stories about "successfully" exercising, dieting, and improved appearance. Detailed information about weight and body mass, calorie intake, foods eaten, and exercise practices provide ways to tabulate and graph the body. These accounts are accompanied by indications that "my torso looks better, and my shirt hangs off my chest and shoulders instead of pooching out around my belly" and that "the veins in my arms are begin ning to show again, faintly. Proof positive that the fat is melting away."[95] Participants use this "evidence," which is sometimes accompanied by "before and after" images, to act as authorities about weight loss and exercise. They argue about the benefits of different programs, provide encouragement and advice to others, and use weight loss as an example of their knowledge. The authority asserted in other technology forums, which provide details on the attributes and specifications of computer technologies, is also established in these discussions about male bodies.

As the challenge thread continues, the narratives increasingly emphasize individual control and stamina. For instance, MrDetermination renders perseverance and other traits that are traditionally associated with masculinity through his user name and posted comments. He suggests that "pain, suffering, commitment, endurance . . . these things are always hard, always. . . . Overcome the pain."[96] His ideas about pain are particularly striking since the men who participate in this forum frequently have to stop exercising and body improvement regimens because of injuries. MrDetermination's instructions to overcome pain are connected to traditional conceptions of what it means to perform masculinity appropriately and to the transformation of the body into a machine. The writings of male programmers, which appear in such forums, often repeat aspects of the liberal humanist and posthuman narratives about controlling the body. There is little interest in just being a body but a great deal of concern with tabulating and ordering every aspect of embodiment, which includes food intake, exercise, and weight, and developing the body into an ideal male form.

MrDetermination encourages the production of a hard male body, but narratives about being "out of control" and having less than an ideal body continued to appear.[97] For instance, Kraicat describes his food intake as "2 pieces of pizza, a pack of cookies and root beer for breakfast" and asks for "HEEELLLPPP!!!"[98] There is a sense that being larger is "all your fault," according to Carol Squires.[99] The challenge thread supports this idea with indications that "discipline ALWAYS = results."[100] The belief that anyone can lose weight and develop a muscular physique means that any inability to achieve the norm indicates that "you're a failure because you can't control your body, can't keep the discipline, can't fit the standard."[101] Nevertheless, it is not surprising that many male programmers are unable to achieve a hardened and less fluid state. Theweleit notes that the ideal of the steel figure, which the soldier wished for and was expected to achieve, was barely approximated.[102] The media condemnation of large bodies and the United States' declarations about rising obesity articulate normative physiognomy and indicate that many individuals are not achieving cultural expectations. Aspects of this standard are reinforced by the challenge, but male programmers' focus on their bodies also indicates some conflicts in current conceptions of masculinity. Their writings present bodies that fold, curl around chairs, persist in a "half melted" state, and rest between varied subject positions.[103]

Erotic Folding

Society indicates that men achieve a more ideal physical and intellectual distance from screen representations. However, the overinvolvement of male programmers and other spectators with body image contradicts these narratives and makes them more feminine. As I have already suggested, society relates the close connection between body and screen to feminine and female positions. Doane has shown how intimate, passive, and undesirable viewing positions are all associated with women.[104] Luce Irigaray uses cultural conceptions of women's nearness to the body and self-contact with flesh to propose a positive form of women's embodiment, which constantly folds, and Laura U. Marks suggests that there are haptic as well as optic viewing engagements.[105] These positions are employed as feminine and feminist political strategies. They emphasize embodied differences—shifts in body position—as parts of the object are touched and experienced, and tactile forms of seeing that are contrary to the controlling gaze. The spectator's tactile relationship with body, chair, and other aspects of the local environment encourage very different narratives about embodiment and viewing.

The experience of a folded, seated, and self-touching body is described as both erotic and abject. For instance, dhamsaic notes that one thing he hates about "being a computer geek" is the "*sweaty-ass*™" where "you've been sitting in the same chair for 6 hours coding or browsing or quaking or whatever and the heat and humidity make for a relatively uncomfortable rear."[106] This is because, as Bordo indicates, we "bend over, we sit down, and the flesh coalesces in spots."[107] Male programmers' descriptions of sticking to chairs, back and arm pain, abrasions from fabric, and the weight of flesh highlight the body rather than allowing a transcendental collapse with the computer screen. As the work of Irigaray and Marks suggests, this conjunction and folding of the body is not always rejected. Sedgwick imagines a purpose for this flesh and a "use to being fat" because it seemed that no one "could come to harm" when "enfolded" in her touch.[108] Bernadette Bosky argues that "all that flesh and skin is there to be enjoyed."[109] Sites about big beautiful women, bears, and belly builders offer ways to enjoy flesh and provide a corollary to the dominant position on body size.[110]

Some Internet spectators also note that flesh can be arranged in unexpected ways. Wraithlyn indicates that there are Internet and computer spectators who "don't walk erect at ALL,"[111] She encourages a consideration of the "wheelchair bound reader" and the "child who hasn't learned to walk yet, but sits on a parent's lap and stares at the screen." Nancy Mairs contemplates being a wheelchair user, "the discomfort and even distaste that a misshapen body arouses," and the personal pleasures of her body in contact with fabric and skin.[112] She provides an embodied erotic that embraces wheelchair users' bodies, the "corporeal conversation" with her caregiving partner, and seated positions.[113] It may not be the typical conception of computer-facilitated erotic, but the seated body is in a constant process of readjusting and self-touching. This frottage includes the slide of moist flesh and the overlapping of skin. Depending on the desired position, the multiple folds of the computer spectator can render a horror of flesh or engage the whole body in pleasurable self-controlled sensation.

It is tempting to argue that the intimate bodily contact of Internet and computer spectators will have a radical effect. Mairs notes that the "world you see" and experience while sitting "is definitely different from the one you see when you're standing."[114] Her writings and the postings of programmers also indicate that people view seated spectators differently. However, cultural messages about ideal bodies and viewing positions often prevent any recognition of these states. Such cultural engagements as reading, theater, film, and television offer a history of seated spectatorial positions, but the details of folded bodies have rarely been addressed.[115] Instead of acknowledging the properties of seated bodies, our ideals for bodies have become even more stringent, as Bordo indicates, and Western society rejects the slightest softness and bulge as revolting and disorderly, even though folded bodies cannot achieve a streamlined shape.[116] An erotic of seated Internet and computer spectatorship offers a way to render and appreciate different kinds of bodies and to resist empowering narratives about computer use. Without alternative models of seated and soft bodies, we are encouraging a technology of waste in which individuals are encouraged to overdiet and overexercise and to try to reach impossible ideals of sitting without folding.

Conclusion: A Technology of Waste

The narratives about Internet and computer use, which indicate that they empower individuals and free them from unpleasant material conditions, are contradicted by the ways that some workers must engage. The Internet and computer also place individuals, particularly those in developing countries, at risk and produce a technology of waste. Toby Miller describes how the obsolescence of television monitors affects the ecology and health of individuals.[117] He notes that they are made under dangerous conditions by Chinese, Indian, and Mexican women who leave family and relocate to manufacturing areas in their respective countries. When these monitors are discarded, they are sent back to China and other developing countries. Young children and other people take this electronic equipment apart without appropriate protection from the toxic substances they contain, and in a much less organized production process than was used in the manufacture of this equipment. The associated health and environmental risks of electronic waste disposal, which include audio and stereo equipment, cell phones, digital and video cameras, computers, computer peripherals, DVD players, fax and copying machines, television and computer monitors, VCRs, video-game consoles, and other wireless devices, are much larger than even Miller indicates. In 1998, more than 20 million personal computer processors became obsolete in the United States but only about 13 percent were recycled or reused.[118] More than 3.2 million tons of electronic waste is put into landfills each year in the United States.[119] In the European Union, electronic equipment comprised 4 percent of the municipal waste in 2000, and it increases by 16–28 percent every five years.[120]

The correct handling and disposal of these electronic products needs to be addressed because about "40% of the heavy metals, including lead, mercury and cadmium, in landfills come from electronic equipment discards."[121] However, many consumers, technology workers—including those who take equipment apart after it is discarded, and even landfill employees are unaware that cathode ray tubes (CRTs) and some other electronic materials contain large amounts of lead and other harmful materials and qualify as toxic waste.[122] While the dismantling of electronic equipment is often described as "recycling," a report from The Basel Action Network (BAN) and Silicon Valley Toxics Coalition (SVTC) indicates that this term elides such unhealthy behaviors as smashing cathode ray tubes and other parts, shredding, and burning.[123] In such places as Guiyu, China, adults and children demanufacture computers and other electronics for about $1.20 a day in unregulated, unsafe, and disorganized conditions.[124] Leaving scrap outside, using open vats of acid to reclaim precious metals, and burning electronic parts has released so many toxins into the environment that water now has to be shipped in from other sources.[125] Workers suffer a variety of chronic illnesses because of these practices, and there are high incidences of birth defects and infant mortality.[126] Prisoners in the United States, who were employed by companies like Dell, also disassembled products without proper equipment and safety precautions because there were concerns about making dangerous tools available to them.[127]

The involvement of developing countries, people of color, and other populations in the demanufacturing of television and computer equipment is significantly different from the happy and well cared for global computer-facilitated workforce that IBM, Microsoft, and other computer and software companies depict. The news coverage after the release of the BAN and STVC report spurred some companies to move their disassembly operations to more sophisticated facilities in the United States.[128] Dell also announced in July 2003 that it would not longer be using prisoners and initiated a recycling program for U.S. consumers.[129] Retailers have also offered recycling events in connection with computer manufacturers.[130] However, this has not completely stopped the shipping of materials to developing countries for demanufacturing. Design practices continue to be part of the problem because they require toxic materials in computer and other electronic equipment manufacturing, make it extremely difficult to take systems apart, prevent people from knowing what is inside this equipment, and demand time-intensive and risky disassembly practices.[131]

These histories, which are also the current future for all electronic products, present different connections between technology and society than most current representations of the Internet and computer. For instance, advertisements for new monitors promise a verdant place that the spectator can access inside the screen, but upgrading computers and other technologies increases the toxic materials in the environment. The representations of natural untouched places, where computers have disappeared, are contrary to the current visibility of these technologies in home spaces, workplaces, and the outdoors. Cyberpunk authors tend to provide fascinated descriptions of an environment littered with technological waste at the same time that they envision "cyberspace" as a way of escaping the more unpleasant aspects of this material condition. However, there are exceptions to these narratives about leaving the body behind.

Stephenson describes a "Group of Environmental Extremists" tracking business and industrial polluting in *Zodiac: The Eco-Thriller*.[132] Sterling's *Heavy Weather* portrays a world where escalating levels of pollutants in the atmosphere have increased the greenhouse effect and done irreparable harm.[133] Margaret Atwood's *Oryx and Crake*, Octavia Butler's *Parable of the Sower*, Sheri S. Tepper's *The Fresco*, and many other works depict worlds that are unpleasantly reconfigured by escalating greed, hate, inequities between rich and poor, and industrial pollutants.[134] Combining these narratives with current conceptions of Internet and computer use would provide a much more complicated portrayal of how technologies function in contemporary society.

Sterling has also been active in encouraging other understandings of the Internet and computer. He helped start the Dead Media Project, which provides information about previous media failures in the hopes that society can avoid repeating previous mistakes, and proposed and implemented the Viridian design movement, which addresses the greenhouse effect and other unsustainable aspects of the world's material infrastructure.[135] Sterling calls for a new relationship between humans and objects where "spimes" make current industrial processes explicit and allow consumers or "end-users" to understand the aspects of products, reuse parts and information, and safely dispose of things that no longer work.[136] He argues that current forms of consumption, where things are constantly discarded and replaced, are reaching their limits; there are no longer any unused and unpopulated areas where things can be thrown away; and the current processes of disposal are doing serious harm. Sterling wants a system where it is possible to "locate valuable objects that are dead, and fold them back into the product stream."[137] Sterling's spime suggests processes of folding bodies, culture, the environment, and technologies in ways that inform and make obvious all the aspects and stakes in the system.

Academics and spectators should consider these ecological issues and how celebrating Internet and computer technologies without noting the accompanying problems can support unethical industrial practices. Miller indicates that these environmental issues have not been addressed in media studies because most television scholars are concerned with "female subjectivities."[138] His descriptions of the ecological risks that accompany computer and television technologies are notable. However, his dismissal of television and other media theories may be premature. A number of academic disciplines, which include but are not limited to television studies, offer methods to consider the systems of power and knowledge that have produced this economy. Feminist theories of spectatorship and theories of female subjectivities also present critical strategies to oppose the representations of the "other" that often accompany these reports. Postcolonial and critical race studies and a variety of other critical strategies can indicate how populations are made to seem dispensable because of their age, class, gender, global position, race, or sexuality. Engaging with the varied aspects of the Internet and computer requires the adoption of critical strategies from different disciplines. Despite Miller's dismissal of certain forms of media analysis, a critical engagement with Internet and computer spectatorship and the environmental issues that accompany digital technologies could start with the kinds of strategies proposed in this book.

Critical approaches to the Internet and computer should address the interrelated practices that work on bodies, produce spectators and screen representations, and render certain understandings of the world. These theories might also provide ways to correlate the constructed aspects of the Internet and computer, narratives about empowered users, and descriptions of fleshy programmers. I am resistant to understanding Internet and computer representations as "people" because this tends to make a variety of stereotypes real. However, there are reasons to attend to what Hayles describes as "mindbody." She encourages the academic and spectator to understand "the body and embodiment in relational terms, as processes emerging from complex recursive interactions rather than as pre-existing entities."[139] The challenge in investigating the Internet and computer is to engage with the so-called mindbody, identities that emerge from complex technological systems, and computer-facilitated interactions while interrogating rather than accepting the narratives that accompany such positions. This practice could productively adopt the fold as its critical model, acknowledge how varied social forces are in conversation, and resist imagining that everything is the same.

Acknowledgments

On the verge of completing this book, and accompanying my excitement and pleasure at finishing a long and challenging project, I continue to be confronted with images that provide detailed messages about my body and its cultural and physical position. When I am lucky, I work with colleagues, family, friends, and students to collaboratively question the structured and regulatory positions that Internet settings produce. There are also more ambivalent moments. For instance, I received a Hallmark birthday "E card" that indicates a "wish" to "reach through the computer screen," depicts hands emerging from the computer and pulling "me" against the monitor, and shows the aftermath of this engagement where "I" wipe greasy marks from the screen.[1] It is not always easy to indicate how these humorous narratives, which suggest that the computer delivers real bodies and tactile engagements, also elide the ways that Internet settings render traditional roles and positions. While viewing the card again, I remain unsure whether to appreciate the research materials, enjoy the birthday greetings, or accept the card's representation of computer-facilitated embodiment and dirty bodies and wash my face. As I contemplate male programmers' accounts of the "extra" flesh that can accompany computer work and their belief that among the "rewards" of firmer bodies is dating thin young women who make their peers jealous, another advertising email arrives and indicates that I can still lose ten pounds.

These narratives and representations indicate that the Internet is a place where bodies exist. However, as Butler has suggested about other settings, only certain bodies are deemed to matter and have worth.[2] Butler was asked to reprieve a material body, which was "free" of social discourse and cultural values, as she expanded her thesis on the ways that gendered bodies were produced and experienced through language. Internet sites also ask about the material body and the cultural worth of our embodiment. They make it difficult to speak or engage with Internet and computer settings without accepting stories about the ability to move within the Internet space. I am grateful that my colleagues, family, friends, and students have helped me question the ways the Internet simultaneously produces bodies and limits ideas about how we should look, feel, and understand our self and individuals within the world.

I was not expecting this insistent articulation of Internet spaces, bodies, and positions in the early 1990s, when I began hearing accounts about how the Internet challenged current conceptions of age, gender, race, and sexuality. These narratives indicated that the Internet and computer were facilitating a societal shift in the ways that identities and selves were understood. As a feminist with postmodernist leanings, I was thrilled to imagine another site where such actions were occurring. After some gopher searching and other inquiries, I signed up for a LambdaMOO text-based synchronous communication setting character. I was immediately fascinated by the narratives and representational possibilities of such sites. However, I also noticed that very different cultural forces were at work in Internet settings. Age, gender, race, and sexuality still had stable meanings because some individuals reinstituted traditional aspects of identity through programming, designing, and using sites. They made cultural positions real and necessary in Internet and computer settings.

This engagement occurred while I was in the doctoral program in art history at the Graduate School and University Center of the City University of New York and in the MFA program in creative arts at Hunter College. This book is not a product of my course work or resultant dissertation, which was about the virtual museum, but many professors provided an environment where I could do intensive research on Internet and computer settings. Particular thanks are owed to Bill Agee, Carol Armstrong, Rosemarie Haag Bletter, Andrea Blum, William Boddy, Joel Carreiro, Patricia Clough, Susan Crile, Mark Feldstein, Peter Hitchcock, Valerie Jaudon, Stuart Liebman, Rose-Carol Washton Long, Setha Low, Linda Nochlin, Jane Roos, Jim Saslow, Eve Kosofsky Sedgwick, Ella Shohat, Chris Straayer, Lisa Vergara, Michelle Wallace, Tom Weaver, Sandy Wurmfeld, and Sharon Zukin. Some of these individuals offered Internet and new media courses, which were vital to my understanding of this developing area and set of academic fields, and others welcomed my questions within their curriculum. I am also indebted to the Grad Center for its early acknowledgment that critical work in Internet and new media studies is important and its generous funding, which included a Geoffrey Marshall Dissertation Fellowship.

My ongoing consideration of Internet settings has also been supported by academic journals and the outstanding editors and referees who sustain this intellectual community. My study of how the museum was represented in Internet settings was encouraged by *Convergence: The International Journal of Research into New Media Technologies* and the generous editing commentary of Alexis Weedon. Maggie Morse reviewed this article, provided a welcoming environment at the University of California–Santa Cruz, and continues to offer mentoring advice and intellectual conversations. Alison Adam and Eileen Green included my initial consideration of MOO looking and gazing in *Information, Communication, and Society* and the *Virtual Gender: Technology, Consumption and Identity* anthology. Gary Banham commented on an early version of the net art chapter, included it in a special issue on aesthetics for *Angelaki: Journal of Theoretical Humanities*, and suggested that the material on VP was worthy of its own exploration. Nick Jankowski provided a great deal of support and published some of my webcam research in *New Media & Society*. My continued research in Internet and new media studies has been informed and improved by their careful mentoring and commentary.

Colleagues have also introduced me to important issues and methods. Helen Nissenbaum encouraged me to consider Internet research ethics. Helen Nissenbaum and Charles Ess also graciously obtained a grant from the National Science Foundation, which funded my travel to the Computer Ethics: Philosophical Enquiries Conference at the University of Lancaster and supported a special issue of *Ethics and Information Technology*. This has informed my discussion of Internet research issues and guidelines in this book. Ess also supported my membership in the Association of Internet Researchers' Ethics Working Group. Through this group, I continue to discuss the ways humanities methods apply to Internet research and the need to consider a variety of disciplinary practices and Internet spectators when establishing recommendations and guidelines.

My ability to spend time researching Internet settings has been supported by generous grants from a number of institutions. The School of Social Science at the Institute for Advanced Study (IAS) expressed interest in this project at a very early stage. I am grateful to Adam Ashforth for running the IAS seminar on information technologies; Joan Wallach Scott for expressing an interest in the ways that Internet and new media studies are connected to feminist theory; Clifford Geertz, Eric Maskin, and Michael Walzer for their interest in my work; and the National Endowment for the Humanities (NEH) for helping fund this vital experience. Michael Fortun, Joan Fujimura, Maggie Morse, Helen Nissenbaum, Monroe Price, Sylvia Schafer, and Tom Streeter were particularly helpful with their research suggestions during my year at IAS. The NEH also funded the incredibly vital summer seminar on Literature in Transition: The Impact of Information Technologies, which Kate Hayles led at the University of California–Los Angeles. Hayles is a supportive mentor, colleague, and a vital scholar with a wide knowledge of new media practices. I appreciate her including me in this invigorating seminar, which all of the participants still speak about with great enthusiasm. Other seminar participants, including Jenny Bay, Kathleen Fitzpatrick, William Gardner, Tara McPherson, Rita Raley, and David Silver, read drafts of my work and continue to be an important part of my intellectual development and community.

Colleagues at my academic institutions have also supported technology expenses and travel and, more important, included me in their intellectual conversations. While I was only there for a year, the University of California–Santa Cruz offered an invigorating environment and array of programs where I could consider the Internet and related technologies and social practices. My colleagues, including Dilip Basu, Raoul Birnbaum, Sharon Daniel, Carolyn Dean, Carla Freccero, Donna Haraway, Donna Hunter, Jennifer Gonzalez, John Hay, Virginia Jansen, David Evan Jones, Maggie Morse, Keith Muscutt, Catherine Soussloff, and Shelley Stamp provided invaluable assistance. While at Bowling Green State University, I found a lively group of academics interested in discussing how the Internet, new media, feminism, and postcolonial theory interrelate. Ellen Berry, Rachel Buff, Heather Elliott-Famularo, Radhika Gajjala, and Jeannie Ludlow have been particularly encouraging. Many of my recent conference trips, which have allowed me to participate in ongoing conversations about Internet and new media studies, were supported by Wellesley College. Lilian Armstrong, Becky Bedell, Pat Berman, Judy Black, Margaret Deutsch Carroll, Lee Cuba, Carlos Dorrien, Peter Fergusson, Alice Friedman, Jeanne Hablanian, Brooke Henderson, Miranda Marvin, Phyllis McGibbon, Qing-Min Meng, Mary Pat Navins, James Rayen, and John Rhodes have been particularly kind. I also owe a debt of gratitude to the Mellon Foundation for its postdoctoral fellowship, which brought me to Wellesley. During my time at the University of Connecticut–Storrs, Anne D'Alleva, Margo Machida, Marita McComiskey, and Judith Thorpe were very supportive. While I have barely started my position at Tulane University, my colleagues in the Department of Communication, including Constance Balides, Joy Fuqua, Gaye LeMon, Ana Lopez, Jim Mackin, Vicki Mayer, John Patton, Mauro Porto, Carole Spitzack, Karen Taylor, and Frank Ukadike, have been wonderfully gracious and encouraged my research.

I also owe a debt of gratitude to the colleagues and friends who have invited me to present my work, offered their time and effort in locating sources and other materials, commented on drafts and presentations, enthusiastically discussed spectatorship and Internet settings, and helped me tell other stories about the body. I want to extend a special thanks to these individuals, including Bryan Alexander, Monica Amor, Nancy Baym, Sandra Braman, Janne Bromseth, Laurie Beth Clark, Sabrina DeTurk, Sara Diamond, Mary Ann Doane, Greg Elmer, Nathan Epley, Anna Everett, Ken Gonzales-Day, Stine Gotved, Liz Greene, Nancy Gunn, Louise Harter, Marta Hanson, Vinzenz

Hediger, Devorah Heitner, Janet Hess, Ken Hillis, Nalo Hopkinson, Amelia Jones, Steve Jones, Marc Linder, Alec Macleod, Thomas Malaby, Molly McCarthy, Sally McCorkle, Katie Mondloch, Kate O'Riordan, Bill Pallack, Michael Petit, David Phillips, Adrian Piper, Erica Rand, Alan Rosenberg, Ellen Fernandez Sacco, Steve Shaviro, Marg Suarez, Fred Turner, Debbie Wacks, Heather Waldroup, Mark Williams, Ken Wissoker, and David Valilee. I also owe a great deal to Kathy Caruso, Valerie Geary, and Doug Sery at MIT Press for their support, enthusiasm, and thoughtful questions through the writing and editing process. Finally, I want to thank my family. This book would never have been completed without the feminist and intellectual mentorship of Stephanie White and Pauline Farbman.

Notes

The Body, the Screen, and Representations: An Introduction to Theories of Internet Spectatorship

1. ICQ, "Welcome—ICQ Universe—ICQ.com," <http://universe.icq.com/universe/welcome/>; Cheap Tickets, "Cheap Tickets—Flights, Hotels, Cars, Cruises," 28 Aug. 2004, <http://www.cheaptickets.com/trs/cheaptickets/home/index_01.xsl>; and "~*Frock*Candy*Baby*~," 9 Jan. 2003, 31 Jan. 2004, <http://frockcandy.net>. The date listed before the URL is the last time that the site was viewed in the format described. Some sites with dates before 2004 are no longer available, while others have just changed and no longer offer the text or image that I describe. In instances where I include two dates, the first date indicates when the current configuration of the site was first available, according to the site designers, or the date on which the Internet "article" was offered. The texts quoted from those Internet sites, which appear throughout this book, also include unconventional capitalizations. This means that link titles and other short quotations often include divergent forms of capitalization. Formatting these diverse texts was difficult because evaluative implications accompanied each decision. The titles of Internet sites are not italicized because distinguishing between Internet journals and web sites created a hierarchy. Since titles are traditionally italicized in print literature, titles of articles that were available in print but accessed from a database or web site are italicized. The constant reconfiguration of Internet representations and changes in Internet service providers make it difficult to find previously quoted material and important to chronicle the kinds of depictions that happen in Internet settings.

2. Mark S. Frankel and Sanyin Siang, "Ethical and Legal Aspects of Human Subjects in Cyberspace," American Association for the Advancement of Science, 1999, 14 Aug. 2004, <http://www.aaas.org/spp/dspp/sfrl/projects/intres/main.htm>.

3. Gateway, "Gateway Computers & Home Electronics," 14 Aug. 2004, <http://gateway.com/index.shtml>, and Crockett Johnson, *Harold and the Purple Crayon* (New York: HarperCollins, 1955). More recent versions of this Gateway image depict the same child drawing a series of laptops and a desktop computer, monitor, and printer. Gateway, "Gateway Computers & Home Electronics," 14 Sept. 2004, <http://gateway.com/index.shtml>.

4. IBM, "IBM United States," 14 Aug. 2004, <http://www.ibm.com/us/>.

5. Logitech, "Logitech—Leading Web Camera, Wireless Keyboard," 15 Aug. 2004, <http://www
.logitech.com/index.cfm?countryid=19&languageid=1>.

6. Dell, "Dell Home & Home Office," 14 Aug. 2004, <http://www1.us.dell.com/content/default
.aspx?c=us&l=en&s=dhs&cs=19>.

7. Asians are more likely to be depicted in relationship to computer technologies than are individuals from the African diaspora, Latinos/as, or other people of color.

8. Microsoft, "Microsoft Corporation," 14 Aug. 2004, <http://www.microsoft.com/>.

9. ATI Technologies Inc., 13 Aug. 2004, <http://www.atitech.ca/>.

10. NewTek, "SIGGRAPH 2004–NewTek," 14 Aug. 2004, <http://www.newtek.com/shows/
siggraph/2004/index.html>.

11. NVIDIA, "NVIDIA Home," 14 Aug. 2004, <http://www.nvidia.com/page/home>. While
these images make some sort of connection between women and technology and indicate that
the characteristics that comprise "woman" are produced, their sexist and racist portrayals of bodies limit the possibility of using them as part of a political project.

12. Representations of nearly naked women are also handed out as part of promotional materials, featured in giant advertising banners, and presented in animated shorts and marketing videos
at conferences and trade fairs. For instance, at SIGGRAPH 2004, a conference and trade show for
computer graphics, Harry Dorrington and ATI's *Ruby: The DoubleCross* animation presented more
detailed images of Ruby in the curated Animation Theater event. In front of the exhibition hall
and at a key entrance to the Los Angeles Convention Center, a gigantic ATI banner featured Ruby
with her large breasts, thrusting hips, and stiletto heels.

13. Robert Stam, Robert Burgoyne, and Sandy Flitterman-Lewis, *New Vocabularies in Film
Semiotics: Structuralism, Post-structuralism, and Beyond* (New York: Routledge, 1992), 147.

14. Judith Mayne, "Spectatorship as Institution," in *Cinema and Spectatorship* (London:
Routledge, 1993), 31.

15. Mary Ann Doane, *The Desire to Desire: The Woman's Film of the 1940s* (Bloomington: Indiana
University Press, 1987); Mary Ann Doane, *Femmes Fatales: Feminism, Film Theory, Psychoanalysis*
(New York: Routledge, 1991); Laura Mulvey, *Visual and Other Pleasures* (Bloomington: Indiana
University Press, 1989); and Christian Metz, *The Imaginary Signifier: Psychoanalysis and the Cinema*,
trans. Celia Britton, Annwyl Williams, Ben Brewster, and Alfred Guzzetti (Bloomington: Indiana
University Press, 1982).

16. For instance, cultural studies and related ethnographic methods were developed because
academics felt that theories of spectatorship did not adequately address the specifics of an individual's experiences.

17. A variety of political events, which included the May 1968 uprising, civil rights, war resistance, the women's movement, and gay and lesbian rights produced an environment in which
film and other popular forms could be considered.

18. Mayne, *Cinema and Spectatorship*; Stam, Burgoyne, and Flitterman-Lewis, *New Vocabularies in Film Semiotics*; and Kaja Silverman, *The Subject of Semiotics* (New York: Oxford University Press, 1983).

19. Film theorists indicate that it is no coincidence that film and psychoanalysis developed at the same time and that the theorization of psychoanalysis within a capitalist consumer society makes it particularly productive as a way of interrogating film. Their site of investigation was often the "classical cinema" institution, which included the Hollywood film system after the employment of sound in the late 1920s and before the demise of the studio system in the 1950s.

20. E. Ann Kaplan, "Introduction," in *Women and Film: Both Sides of the Camera* (New York: Methuen, 1983), 1–20.

21. Apparatus and feminist psychoanalytic film theory were also deeply informed by the work of Louis Althusser and his concept of ideology. Louis Althusser, "Ideology and Ideological State Apparatuses (Notes toward an Investigation)," in *Lenin and Philosophy, and Other Essays*, trans. Ben Brewster (New York: Monthly Review Press, 1972), 85–126. For a discussion of ideology as it applies to film theory, see Kaplan, "Introduction," in *Women and Film*.

22. Mayne, "Subject of Spectatorship," in *Cinema and Spectatorship*, 33.

23. However, their understanding of the cinema apparatus can be quite different. Baudry's indication that cinema viewing is a form of regression to an earlier developmental stage is quite different than Mulvey's concerns with the ways male spectators of the classical cinema identify with the male screen protagonist and are empowered. For Metz, the primary identification is with the projector, the screen, and the process of looking. Projection renders a position for the spectator as unified, rational, and coherent. Jean-Louis Baudry, "The Apparatus," in *Apparatus: Cinematographic Apparatus: Selected Writings*, ed. Theresa Hak Kyung Cha (New York: Tanam Press, 1980); Jean-Louis Baudry, "Ideological Effects of the Basic Cinematographic Apparatus," in *Narrative, Apparatus, Ideology: A Film Theory Reader*, ed. Philip Rosen (New York: Columbia University Press, 1986), 286–298; Metz, Imaginary Signifier; and Mulvey, *Visual and Other Pleasures*.

24. Laura Mulvey, "Visual Pleasure and Narrative Cinema," *Screen* 16, 3 (Autumn 1975): 6–18.

25. Mulvey's theory of identification was based on gender similitude, so that the male spectator identified with the male protagonist. The only positions for women were as the passive receiver of the male look or a transvestism where she identified with the male protagonist. The concept of an empowered male gaze, theorized by Mulvey, Metz, and others, is a reconceptualization of Jacques Lacan's theory in which the gaze is not associated with a unified subject or desire and everyone is subjected to an outside gaze that cannot be possessed. Jacques Lacan, *The Four Fundamental Concepts of Psycho-analysis*, trans. A. Sheridan (New York: W. W. Norton, 1981). Doane indicates that feminist film theory made the gaze more subjective because Lacan's theory of the gaze is not useful in considering sexual difference and the unequal positions of mastery and subjection. Doane, "Film and Masquerade," in *Femmes Fatales*, 17–32. A number of scholars, including Mulvey, have reconsidered the early feminist film theory that described the gaze as a totalizing and purely patriarchal structure. Laura Mulvey, "Afterthoughts on 'Visual Pleasure and Narrative Cinema' inspired by *Duel in the Sun*," *Framework* 15–17 (1981): 12–15.

26.   Doane, "Film and Masquerade" and "Masquerade Reconsidered," 33–43, in *Femmes Fatales*.

27.   See, for instance, Mieke Bal, "Reading the Gaze: The Construction of Gender in 'Rembrandt,'" in *Vision and Textuality*, ed. Stephen Melville and Bill Readings (Durham, NC: Duke University Press, 1995), 147–173; Norman Bryson, "The Gaze in the Expanded Field," in *Vision and Visuality*, ed. Hal Foster (Seattle: Bay Press, 1988), 87–114; and Griselda Pollock, *Vision and Difference: Femininity, Feminism and the Histories of Art* (London: Routledge, 1988).

28.   Writings that equate spectatorship with the eye include Michael Fried, *Three American Painters: Kenneth Noland, Jules Olitski, Frank Stella* (Cambridge, MA: Fogg Art Museum, 1965), and Clement Greenberg, "Master Léger," "Abstract, Representational, and So Forth," and "The New Sculpture," in *Art and Culture: Critical Essays* (Boston: Beacon Press, 1961).

29.   John Berger, *Ways of Seeing* (London: Penguin Books, 1972), 49, 47. Berger's analysis predates Mulvey's theory of spectatorship and sexual difference and provides a less psychoanalytically inflected reading. However, it does not offer as complete an analysis of the gaze. A discussion of this appears in Linda Williams, "Introduction," in *Viewing Positions: Ways of Seeing Film*, ed. Linda Williams (New Brunswick, NJ: Rutgers University Press, 1995), 1.

30.   Griselda Pollock, "Beholding Art History: Vision, Place, and Power," in *Vision and Textuality*, ed. Melville and Readings, 41. Women were depicted looking down and looking away. However, they also worked as artists and models and looked at and produced images of women. For other discussions of this, see Anne Higonnet, "Secluded Vision: Images of Feminine Experience in Nineteenth-century Europe," in *The Expanding Discourse: Feminism and Art History*, ed. Norma Broude and Mary D. Garrard (New York: HarperCollins Publishers, 1992), 171–186; Patricia Simons, "Women in Frames: The Gaze, the Eye, the Profile in Renaissance Portraiture," in *Expanding Discourse*, ed. Broude and Garrard, 39–58; Craig Owens, "The Discourse of Others: Feminists and Postmodernism," in *Expanding Discourse*, ed. Broude and Garrard, 487–502; and Abigail Solomon-Godeau, *Photography at the Dock: Essays on Photographic History, Institutions, and Practices* (Minneapolis: University of Minnesota Press, 1991).

31.   Fried, *Three American Painters*, 14.

32.   Teresa de Lauretis notes the "phallic premise" of apparatus theory, Joan Copjec indicates that it constructs a phallic machine that only produces male spectators, and Constance Penley suggests that it may repeat some of the desires of male theorists when explaining how the male subject is centered and unified. Teresa de Lauretis, "Through the Looking Glass," in *Narrative, Apparatus, Ideology*, ed. Rosen, 367; Joan Copjec, "The Anxiety of the Influencing Machine," October 23 (Winter 1982): 43–59; and Constance Penley, "'A Certain Refusal of Difference': Feminism and Film Theory," in *The Future of an Illusion: Film, Feminism, and Psychoanalysis* (Minneapolis: University of Minnesota Press, 1989), 41–56.

33.   Doane, "Desire to Desire," in *Desire to Desire*, 9.

34.   Discussions about ways psychoanalytic film theory may prevent considerations of physical viewers have appeared in the *Camera Obscura* issue on the "spectatrix" as well as in other journals and conferences. Responses to apparatus theory occur, as Mayne notes, because there is a

difference between the ideal subject position, which the apparatus promises, and the spectator's imperfect experiences. Alternative engagements may also occur in different genres. Doane provides extensive analysis of "women's films," their address to women, and the kinds of spectatorial positions that they render. Other forms of difference and histories of the gaze also need to be considered because, as bell hooks notes, there is a relationship among slave owners punishing black enslaved individuals for looking at whites, black parents disciplining their children for looking back, and deploying the "oppositional gaze." *Camera Obscura* 20–21 (May–Sept. 1989); Mayne, "Paradoxes of Spectatorship," in *Cinema and Spectatorship*, 79; Doane, *Desire to Desire*; and bell hooks, "The Oppositional Gaze," in *Black Looks: Race and Representation* (Boston: South End Press, 1992), 115–131.

35. For instance, Williams notes that "gaze theory" articulates a much too limited way of seeing, but it also indicates the importance of analyzing spectatorship in "an era of both visual narrative and visual attractions." Williams, "Introduction," in *Viewing Positions*, 19.

36. Kaplan, "Introduction," in *Women and Film*, 1–20.

37. Anne Friedberg, "The End of Cinema: Multi-media and Technological Change," in *Reinventing Film Studies*, ed. Christine Gledhill and Linda Williams (London: Arnold, 2002), 448.

38. What Is, "Lurking—A SearchWebServices Definition," 30 July 2001, 31 Aug. 2004, <http://searchWebServices.techtarget.com/sDefinition/0,,sid26_gci213740,00 .html>, and CCI Computer, "High-tech Dictionary Definition," 31 Aug. 2004, <http://www.computeruser.com/resources/dictionary/definition.html?lookup=7695>. Lurking usually indicates a questionable form of Internet use. However, some computer dictionaries suggest that it "is not pejorative and indeed is casually used reflexively: 'Oh, I'm just lurking.'" The Jargon Dictionary, "'L' Terms [The Jargon Dictionary]," 20 Aug. 2000, 24 Mar. 2003, <http://info.astrian.net/jargon/terms/l.html #lurker>. Sites and netiquette manuals also recommended lurking to spectators who are unfamiliar with settings.

39. Mayne, "Introduction," in *Cinema and Spectatorship*, 4.

40. Net Lingo, "NetLingo Dictionary of Internet Words," 31 Aug. 2004, <http://www.netlingo .com/lookup.cfm?term=user>.

41. Espen Aarseth, "Ruling the Reader: The Politics of 'Interaction,'" in *Cybertext: Perspectives on Ergodic Literature* (Baltimore, MD: Johns Hopkins University Press, 1997), 173–174.

42. George P. Landow, "Hypertext: An Introduction," in *Hypertext 2.0: The Convergence of Contemporary Critical Theory and Technology* (Baltimore, MD: Johns Hopkins University Press, 1997), 273.

43. Friedberg, "The End of Cinema," in *Reinventing Film Studies*, ed. Gledhill and Williams, 448.

44. Mayne, "Introduction," in *Cinema and Spectatorship*, 1.

45. Diane Carr, "Play Dead: Genre and Affect in *Silent Hill* and *Planescape Torment*," Game Studies: The International Journal of Computer Game Research 3, 1 (May 2003), 31 Aug. 2004, <http://gamestudies.org/0301/carr/>.

46. See, for instance, Amy Bruckman, "Ethical Guidelines for Research Online," 4 Apr. 2002, 31 Aug. 2004, <http://www.cc.gatech.edu/~asb/ethics>; Charles Ess and the AoIR Ethics Working Committee, "Ethical Decision-making and Internet Research: Recommendations from the AoIR Ethics Working Committee," Ethics Report/Association of Internet Researchers, approved by AoIR, 27 Nov. 2002, 31 Aug. 2004, <http://www.aoir.org/reports/ethics.pdf>; and Mark S. Frankel and Sanyin Siang, "Ethical and Legal Aspects of Human Subjects in Cyberspace," American Association for the Advancement of Science, 1999, 14 Aug. 2004, <http://www.aaas.org/spp/dspp/sfrl/projects/intres/main.htm>.

47. For discussions about the current limits of Internet research guidelines, see Charles Ess, ed., *Ethics and Information Technology* 4, 3 (2002). Also available at <http://www.nyu.edu/projects/nissenbaum/projects_ethics.html>.

48. Charles Ess and the AoIR Ethics Working Committee, "Ethical Decision-making and Internet Research: Recommendations from the AoIR Ethics Working Committee," Ethics Report/Association of Internet Researchers, approved by AoIR, 27 Nov. 2002, 31 Aug. 2004, <http://www.aoir.org/reports/ethics.pdf>.

49. Mary Ann Doane, "Misrecognition and Identity," *Cine-Tracts* 11 (Fall 1980): 25–32; Doane, *Femmes Fatales*; Judith Mayne, "Feminist Film Theory and Criticism," in *Multiple Voices in Feminist Film Criticism*, ed. Diane Carson, Linda Dittmar, and Janice R. Welsch (Minneapolis: University of Minnesota Press, 1994), 48–64; Mulvey, "Afterthoughts on 'Visual Pleasure and Narrative Cinema' Inspired by *Duel in the Sun*," *Framework*; Mulvey, "Visual Pleasure and Narrative Cinema," *Screen*; Renata Salecl and Slavoj Žižek, 'Introduction," in *Gaze and Voice as Love Objects*, ed. Renata Salecl and Slavoj Žižek (Durham, NC: Duke University Press, 1996), 1–6.

50. Noël Burch, *Theory of Film Practice*, trans. Helen R. Lane (New York: Praeger Publishers, 1973); Doane, "Film and Masquerade" and "Masquerade Reconsidered," in *Femmes Fatales*; and Metz, *Imaginary Signifier*.

51. Jodi, *%20Wrong*, 31 Aug. 2004, <http://404.jodi.org/>; Jodi, *%20Wrong*, Rhizome, 1 Jan. 1996, 31 Aug. 2004, <http://rhizome.org/artbase/1678/wrong.html>; Peter Luining, *D-TOY 2.502.338*, Lifesavers, 9 Mar. 1999, 31 Aug. 2004, <http://www.vpro.nl/data/lifesavers/10/index.shtml>; and Michaël Samyn, *The Fire from the Sea*, Lifesavers, 26 Jan. 2000, 31 Aug. 2004, <http://www.vpro.nl/data/lifesavers/16/index.shtml>.

52. Judith Butler, "The Force of Fantasy: Feminism, Mapplethrope, and Discursive Excess," *Differences: A Journal of Feminist Cultural Studies* 2, 2 (Summer 1990): 105–125; Jonathan Crary. "Eclipse of the Spectacle," in *Art after Modernism: Rethinking Representation*, ed. Brian Wallis (New York: New Museum of Contemporary Art, 1984), 282–294; Stuart Moulthrop, "Traveling in the Breakdown Lane: A Principle of Resistance for Hypertext," 3 July 2004, <http://iat.ubalt.edu/moulthrop/essays/breakdown.html>; Stuart Moulthrop, "Traveling in the Breakdown Lane: A Principle of Resistance for Hypertext," *Mosaic* 28, 4 (1995): 55–77; and Stuart Moulthrop, "Error 404: Doubting the Web," in *The World Wide Web and Contemporary Cultural Theory*, ed. Andrew Herman and Thomas Swiss (New York: Routledge, 2000), 259–276.

53. Roland Barthes, *The Pleasure of the Text*, trans. Richard Miller (New York: Hill and Wang, 1975); Roland Barthes, *S/Z: An Essay*, trans. Richard Miller (New York: Hill and Wang, 1974); Jay David Bolter, *Writing Space: The Computer, Hypertext, and the History of Writing* (Hillsdale, NJ: Lawrence Erlbaum Associates, 1991); Rosemary J. Coombe, *The Cultural Life of Intellectual Properties: Authorship, Appropriation, and the Law* (Durham, NC: Duke University Press, 1998); Henry Jenkins, *Textual Poachers: Television Fans and Participatory Culture* (New York: Routledge, 1992); and Landow, *Hypertext 2.0.*

54. Nancy Hartsock, "Foucault on Power: A Theory for Women?," in *Feminism/Postmodernism*, ed. Linda J. Nicholson (New York: Routledge, 1990), 157–175; Trinh T. Minh-ha, "No Master Territories," in *The Post-colonial Studies Reader*, ed. Bill Ashcroft, Gareth Griffiths, and Helen Tiffin (London: Routledge, 1995), 215–218; Edward Said, *Orientalism* (New York: Random House, 1979); and Eve Kosofsky Sedgwick, *Epistemology of the Closet* (Berkeley: University of California Press, 1990).

55. The work of Carol Selter and Susan Silton is available at "UCR/CMP: Scanner as Camera," California Museum of Photography, 1998, 16 Aug. 2004, <http://www.cmp.ucr.edu/site/exhibitions/scanner3/>, and Ken Gonzales-Day at "Ken Gonzales-Day: On-line Portfolio," 16 Aug. 2004, <http://homepage.mac.com/kengonzalesday/Menu16.html>.

56. Roland Barthes, *Camera Lucida: Reflections on Photography*, trans. Richard Howard (New York: Hill and Wang, 1981), and Roland Barthes, *Roland Barthes by Roland Barthes*, trans. Richard Howard (Berkeley: University of California Press, 1977).

57. Gilles Deleuze, *Foucault*, trans. Sean Hand (Minneapolis: University of Minnesota Press, 1988), and Vivian Sobchack, ed., *Meta-morphing: Visual Transformation and the Culture of Quick Change* (Minneapolis: University of Minnesota Press, 2000).

58. Susan Bordo, *Unbearable Weight* (Berkeley: University of California Press, 1993); Luce Irigaray, *This Sex which Is Not One*, trans. Catherine Porter (Ithaca, NY: Cornell University Press, 1985); and Klaus Theweleit, *Male Fantasies, Male Bodies: Psychoanalyzing the White Terror*, vol. 2 (Minneapolis: University of Minnesota Press, 1989).

59. The hand-pointer is related to a variety of advertising and book conventions. These images derive from the pointing hands in manuscript books, newspapers, and other print media, which direct readers to information that is of interest. When it is used in manuscript books and printed literature, the pointing hand is also known as a fist, hand director, indicator, indicator mark, index, manicule, and printer's fist. In a discussion about this image on SHARP-L, which is sponsored by the Society for the History of Authorship, participants shared this list of terms and made connections between drawings of hands in manuscripts, the carrying over of this tendency in printed literature, and the computer hand-pointer. SHARP-L, "Pointing Hand," 30 June 2004, 27 Sept. 2004, <https://listserv.indiana.edu/cgi-bin/wa-iub.exe?A1=ind0406&L=sharp-l?>. The hand-pointer is also associated with the advertisements for yellow pages, with an image of a hand, that indicate information can be retrieved when you "let your fingers do the walking." This phrase is now also commonly used to refer to Internet searching and viewing. IBM used Charlie Chaplin's white-gloved little tramp to promote its early personal computers with a com-

mand line interface in about 1981. Apple represented Chaplin in its "Macintosh for the rest of us" campaign with his hand positioned like the hand-pointer in order to reference the graphical user interface. Macintosh has continued to use the figure of Chaplin in its "Think Different" campaign, which began in 1997.

60.   While it has been denied by Ask.com, the "Jeeves" butler appears to be modeled after P. G. Wodehouse's butler character, who appears in a number of his novels.

61.   Ask Jeeves, "Ask Jeeves Search Smarter," 27 Aug. 2004, <http://sp.ask.com/docs/announcements/searchsmarter.html>.

62.   It is tempting to argue that the gloved hand suggests that the spectator is a form of servant who responds to the Internet and to the computer's commands. However, the many depictions of the spectator controlling aspects of the interface through the hand-pointer make this reading unlikely.

1   Making Internet and Computer Spectators

1.   This incorporation of the computer into the lived experience of the spectator also occurs with television. See, for instance, James Friedman, ed., *Reality Squared: Televisual Discourse on the Real* (New Brunswick, NJ: Rutgers University Press, 2002). The desktop metaphor is considered in Steve Johnson, *Interface Culture: How New Technology Transforms the Way We Create and Communicate* (San Francisco: HarperEdge, 1997).

2.   Friedberg, "The End of Cinema," in *Reinventing Film Studies*, ed. Gledhill and Williams, 451n7.

3.   Ken Hillis, "Identity, Embodiment, and Place—VR as Postmodern Technology," in *Digital Sensations: Space, Identity, and Embodiment in Virtual Reality* (Minneapolis: University of Minnesota Press, 1999), 189.

4.   Garnet Hertz, "Desktop_10jpg. 832x264 Pixels," 31 Aug. 2004, <http://www.conceptlab.com/desktop/img/desktop_10.jpg>, and Desktop Is, "DESKTOP IS *DESKTOPS*," 31 Aug. 2004, <http://www.easylife.org/desktop/desktops.html>.

5.   For a longer discussion of the ways Internet settings operate by creating an "insider" and "outsider," see chapter 5 on the Virtual Places graphical communication setting.

6.   Anna Everett, "The Revolution Will Be Digitized: Afrocentricity and the Digital Public Sphere," Special Issue on Afrofuturism, ed. Alondra Nelson, *Social Text* 71, 20, 2 (Summer 2002): 125.

7.   Obviously, male or even indeterminately gendered individuals were often the target of the finger command. However, The Jargon Lexicon reinscribes the gendered and sexist aspects of this term by providing the following example of finger: "OK, finger Lisa and see if she's idle." The Jargon File, "The Jargon File," 4.4.7, 29 Dec. 2003, 1 Sept. 2004, <http://www.catb.org/~esr/jargon/html/F/finger.html>.

8.   Paul Dourish, "Where the Footprints Lead: Tracking Down Other Roles for Social Navigation," in *Social Navigation of Information Space*, ed. Alan J. Munro, Kristina Höök, and David Benyon (London: Springer-Verlag, 1999), 27.

9. Esther Dyson, "Introduction," in *Release 2.0: A Design for Living in the Digital Age* (New York: Broadway Books, 1997), 2.

10. Luciano Paccagnella, "Getting the Seats of Your Pants Dirty: Strategies for Ethnographic Research on Virtual Communities," Journal of Computer Mediated Communication 3, 1 (June 1997), 1 Sept. 2004, <http://www.ascusc.org/jcmc/vol3/issue1/paccagnella.html>.

11. Alan J. Munro, Kristina Höök, and David Benyon, "Footprints in the Snow," in *Social Navigation of Information Space*, 2.

12. Bruce Damer, "DigitalSpace: Avatars Book Home Page and Teleport," 1 Sept. 2004, <http://www.digitalspace.com/avatars/index.html>.

13. Jennifer Gonzalez, "The Appended Subject: Race and Identity as Digital Assemblage," in *Race in Cyberspace*, ed. Beth E. Kolko, Lisa Nakamura, and Gilbert B. Rodman (New York: Routledge, 2000), 27–28.

14. Sherry Turkle, *Life on the Screen: Identity in the Age of the Internet* (New York: Simon & Schuster, 1995). She also explores aliveness in Sherry Turkle, "Who Am We?," *Wired Magazine* 4.01 (Jan. 1996), 1 Sept. 2004, <http://www.wired.com/wired/archive/4.01/turkle.html?pg=1&topic=&topic_set=>.

15. Norman K. Denzin, "Cybertalk and the Method of Instances," in *Doing Internet Research: Critical Issues and Methods for Examining the Net*, ed. Steven G. Jones (Thousand Oaks, CA: Sage Publications, 1999), 109.

16. Luciano Paccagnella, "Getting the Seats of Your Pants Dirty: Strategies for Ethnographic Research on Virtual Communities," Journal of Computer Mediated Communication 3, 1 (June 1997), 1 Sept. 2004, <http://www.ascusc.org/jcmc/vol3/issue1/paccagnella.html>.

17. "I Robot, You Jane," *Buffy the Vampire Slayer*, written by Ashley Gable and Thomas A. Swyden, dir. Stephen Posey, Season 1, Episode 9, 1997. Fritz is scorned for his description of the Internet. However, his vision of live information is monstrously fulfilled.

18. Bruce Sterling defined cyberpunk as "a new alliance is becoming evident: an integration of technology and the Eighties counterculture. An unholy alliance of the technical world and the world of organized dissent—the underground world of pop culture, visionary fluidity, and street-level anarchy." Bruce Sterling, "Preface," in *Mirrorshades: The Cyberpunk Anthology*, ed. Bruce Sterling (New York: Ace Books, 1988), xii–xiii.

19. William Gibson is credited with coining the term "cyberspace." William Gibson, *Neuromancer* (New York: Ace Books, 1984). A variety of writers have connected cyberpunk fiction to Internet developments. See, for instance, Michael Benedikt, ed., *Cyberspace: First Steps* (Cambridge, MA: MIT Press, 1992); Scott Bukatman, *Terminal Identity: The Virtual Subject in Postmodern Science Fiction* (Durham, NC: Duke University Press, 1993); and Peter Fitting, "The Lessons of Cyberpunk," in *Technoculture*, ed. Constance Penley and Andrew Ross (Minneapolis: University of Minnesota Press, 1991), 295–315.

20. Melissa Scott, *Dreamships* (Alexandria, VA: Tor Books, 1993); Gibson, *Neuromancer*; and Pat Cadigan, *Synners* (New York: Bantam Books, 1991).

21. Blue Mountain, "I Heard Your Computer Had a Bug," 5 Feb. 2000, <http://www2 .bluemountain.com/eng3/daphne/COMputer.html>, and Geek Culture, "iMac Geek e-Occasion Card!," 5 Feb. 2000, <http://www.geekculture.com/occasioncards/newicam.html>.

22. Gibson, *Neuromancer*, 3.

23. William Gibson quoted in Larry McCaffery, "An Interview with William Gibson," *Mississippi Review* 16, 2/3 (1996), 1 Sept. 2004, <http://www.mississippireview.com/1996/9602gibs.html>.

24. Gretchen Barbatsis, Michael Fegan, and Kenneth Hansen, "The Performance of Cyberspace: An Exploration into Computer-mediated Reality," Journal of Computer Mediated Communication 5, 1 (Sept. 1999), 1 Sept. 2004, <http://www.ascusc.org/jcmc/vol5/issue1/barbatsis.html>.

25. Jan Fernback, "There Is a There There: Notes toward a Definition of Cybercommunity," in *Doing Internet Research*, ed. Jones, 206, 218.

26. Jonathan G. S. Koppell, "No 'There' There: Why Cyberspace Isn't Anyplace," *The Atlantic Monthly* 286, 2 (Aug. 2000), 28 May 2002, <http://www.theatlantic.com/issues/2000/08/ koppell.htm>.

27. Ibid.

28. Henry Jenkins, "Games, The New Lively Art," forthcoming in *Handbook for Video Game Studies*, ed. Jeffrey Goldstein (Cambridge, MA: MIT Press), 1 Sept. 2004, <http://web.mit.edu/ 21fms/www/faculty/henry3/GamesNewLively.html>.

29. Gwen, "Gwencam," 19 Oct. 2000, <http://gwen.webica.com/cam/>, and Cindy "Intro," 13 Jan. 2001, <http://www.summer-web.com>.

30. The Art Institute of Chicago, 15 Nov. 2003, <http://www.artic.edu/>.

31. NetLingo, "NetLingo Dictionary of Internet Words," 1 Sept. 2004, <http://www.netlingo .com/lookup.cfm?term=navigate>.

32. Lev Manovich, "The Operations," in *The Language of New Media* (Cambridge, MA: MIT Press, 2000), 164.

33. Frank Odasz, "Issues in the Development of Cooperative Networks," in *Public Access to the Internet*, ed. Brian Kahin and James Keller (Cambridge, MA: MIT Press, 1995), 120. Odasz's comments are related to descriptions of the Internet as the "information superhighway," a concept that Al Gore supported. For a discussion of the highway metaphor, see Steven G. Jones, "Understanding Community in the Information Age," in *CyberSociety: Computer-mediated Communication and Community*, ed. Steven G. Jones (Thousand Oaks, CA: Sage Publications, 1995), 10–35.

34. Tarrek, "Painless Chairs?," Slashdot, 16 July 2003, 27 Aug. 2004, <http://ask.slashdot.org/ article.pl?sid=02/07/15/2323238&tid=99&tid=4>, and mantid, "In Search of the Perfect Computer Chair," Slashdot, 26 Oct. 2000, 27 Aug. 2004, <http://ask.slashdot.org/article.pl?sid =00/10/26/175245&tid=159>.

35. TobyWong, "Aeron Chairs as Stupidity Barometers," Slashdot, 8 Aug. 2001, 27 Aug. 2004, <http://slashdot.org/comments.pl?sid=20145&threshold=1&commentsort=0&tid=159&mode=thread&cid=2148026>.

36. Andrew L. Shapiro, "The Control Revolution: How the Internet Is Putting Individuals in Charge and Changing the World We Know," 23 Mar. 2003, <http://www.controlrevolution.com/microsoft.html>. The limits of Microsoft's interest in this question are highlighted in an urban legend that claims that the company was inundated with cryptic answers to their question, which they did not understand, and requested an end to these correspondences.

37. Alain J-J. Cohen, "Virtual Hollywood and the Genealogy of its Hyper-spectator," in *Hollywood Spectatorship: Changing Perceptions of Cinema Audiences*, ed. Melvyn Stokes and Richard Maltby (London: British Film Institute, 2001), 160–161.

38. For a discussion of this, see Liz Kotz and Judith Butler, "The Body You Want," *Artforum* (Nov. 1992): 82–89.

39. Free On-Line Dictionary of Computing (FOLDOC), "Surfing from FOLDOC," 6 Sept. 2004, <http://foldoc.doc.ic.ac.uk/foldoc/foldoc.cgi?surfing>.

40. Justine Cassell and Henry Jenkins, "Chess for Girls? Feminism and Computer Games," in *From Barbie to Mortal Kombat*, ed. Justine Cassell and Henry Jenkins (Cambridge, MA: MIT Press, 1998), 12.

41. Susan Herring, "Gender and Power in Online Communication," Center for Social Informatics, SLIS, Indiana University-Bloomington, Oct. 2001, 6 Sept. 2004, <http://www.slis.indiana.edu/CSI/WP/WP01–05B.html>, and Anne Rickert and Anya Sacharow, "It's a Woman's World Wide Web," Media Metrix and Jupiter Communications, 2000, 6 Sept. 2004, <http://www.beachbrowser.com/Archives/News-and-Human-Interest/August-2000/web-la-feminine.pdf>.

42. hhsb, "*Silly/Stupid/Salacious-Guest-Descriptions," LambdaMOO, 4 Jan. 2000, <telnet://lambda.moo.mud.org: 8888>. Such narratives about unappealing ages and abject body types, which I will examine in the afterword of this book, are notable. Not only do they represent disturbing forms of intolerance, but they also suggest that narratives about empowered programmers are riddled with negative attributes and internal doubts.

43. Yahoo! Greetings, "Three Catastrophies," Yahoo!, 24 Mar. 2003, <http://send.greetings.yahoo.com/greet/send?.id=152006022&.catu=/browse/Any_Occasion/Computers_and_Internet/>; Yahoo! Greetings, "Troubleshooting Win98," Yahoo!, 24 Mar. 2003, <http://send.greetings.yahoo.com/greet/send?.id=152005462&.catu=/browse/Any_Occasion/Computers_and_Internet/>; and John Macpherson, "Technology Is Your Friend," Yahoo!, 24 Mar. 2003, <http://send.greetings.yahoo.com/greet/send?.id=152035618&.catu=/browse/Any_Occasion/Computers_and_Internet/>.

44. Robert C. Allen, "Audience-oriented Criticism and Television," in *Channels of Discourse, Reassembled: Television and Contemporary Criticism*, 2nd ed., ed. Robert C. Allen (Chapel Hill: University of North Carolina Press, 1992), 118.

45. Ibid., 102.

46. Yahoo!, 6 Sept. 2004, <http://www.yahoo.com/>; Travelocity, "Travelocity.com—Go Virtually Anywhere!," 23. Mar. 2003, <http://www.travelocity.com/?Service=TRAVELOCITY>; and Cheap Tickets, "Cheap Tickets—Flights, Hotels, Cars, Cruise," 23 Mar. 2003, <http://www.cheaptickets.com/trs/cheaptickets/home/index_01.xsl>.

47. Amazon, "Amazon.com—Earth's Biggest Selection," 23 Mar. 2003, <http://www.amazon.com/exec/obidos/subst/home/gateway.html/104-6162359-2625559>.

48. Allen, "Audience-oriented Criticism and Television," in *Channels of Discourse Reassembled*, 119.

49. Lev Grossman, "Salon 21st | Terrors of the Amazon," Salon, 2 Mar. 1999, 6 Sept. 2004, <http://archive.salon.com/21st/feature/1999/03/02feature2.html>.

50. Amazon, "Amazon.com: The Page You Made," 23 Mar. 2003, <http://www.amazon.com/exec/obidos/tg/new-for-you/pym/home/-/0/ref=pd_nfy_gw_rv_a/104–6162359-2625559>.

51. The often-quoted statement "On the Internet, nobody knows you're a dog" accompanied a *New Yorker* cartoon. Peter Steiner, *The New Yorker* 69, 20 (5 July 1993), 61. This statement and the cartoon are often reproduced on various web sites.

52. See, for instance, Yahoo!, "Yahoo! Greetings," 7 June 2004, <http://www.yahoo.americangreetings.com/display.pd?bfrom=3&prodnum=2011789&Searchstr=internet&path=42809&st=t&>, and Blue Mountain, 7 June 2004, <http://www.bluemountain.com/display.pd?bfrom=1&prodnum=3032990&Searchstr=computer&path=35616&st=t&>.

53. Virginia Shea, "Core Rules of Netiquette," *Netiquette* (San Francisco: Albion Books, 1994), 40, and Virginia Shea, "Rule 5: Make Yourself Look Good Online," The Core Rules of Netiquette, 7 June 2004, <http://www.albion.com/netiquette/rule5.html>.

54. "Gender and Ethnicity," The Jargon File 4.4.7, 29 Dec. 2003, 7 June 2004, <http://www.catb.org/~esr/jargon/html/demographics.html>.

55. CCI Computer, "High-tech Dictionary Definition," 6 Sept. 2004, <http://www.computeruser.com/resources/dictionary/definition.html?lookup=6686>, and NetLingo, "NetLingo Dictionary of Internet Words," 6 Sept. 2004, <http://www.netlingo.com/lookup.cfm?term=portal>.

56. Amazon, "Amazon.com—Earth's Biggest Selection," 23 Mar. 2003, <http://www.amazon.com/exec/obidos/subst/home/gateway.html/104–6162359-2625559>.

57. NetLingo, "NetLingo Dictionary of Internet Words," 6 Sept. 2004, <http://www.netlingo.com/lookup.cfm?term=portal>. According to *PC World*, "AltaVista, Excite, Infoseek, Lycos, Microsoft's Internet Start, Netscape's Netcenter, Snap, and Yahoo" are the "eight major portal contenders." M. Lake, "The New Megasites: All-in-one Web Supersites," *PC World* (Aug. 1998), 6 Sept. 2004, <http://www.pcworld.com/reviews/article/0,aid,7202,00.asp>.

58. Yahoo!, "Yahoo! Wallet," 6 Sept. 2004, <http://wallet.yahoo.com/>.

59. A spectator who provides a "wrong" name and information will constantly be addressed and produced through those terms.

60. Yahoo!, "Yahoo!," 23 Mar. 2003, <http://www.yahoo.com/>.

61. Yahoo!, "Welcome to Yahoo!," 6 Sept. 2004, <http://edit.yahoo.com/config/eval_register ?.v=&.intl=&new=1&.done=&.src=ym&.partner=&.p=&promo=&.last=>.

62. Of course, physical experiences have already instituted a gendered position.

63. Yahoo!, "Yahoo! Profile," 6 Sept. 2004, <http://profiles.yahoo.com>.

64. Yahoo!, "Yahoo!—Yahoo! Profiles," 6 Sept. 2004, <http://help.yahoo.com/help/us/profiles/ profiles-20.html>.

65. Yahoo!, "Yahoo! Member Directory," 15 Sept. 2004, <http://members.yahoo.com/interests ?.kw=will&.oc=t&.sb=1&.cb=1>.

66. Yahoo!, "Yahoo! Terms of Service," 6 Sept. 2004, <http://docs.yahoo.com/info/terms/>.

67. MSN, "MSN Member Directory—Create Your Profile Settings," 17 Mar. 2003, <http:// members.msn.com/edit.msnw>.

68. Lycos, "Member Registration—Terra Lycos Network, 6 Sept. 2004, <http://ldbreg.lycos.com/ cgi-bin/mayaRegister?m_RC=32&m_NP=FREE_Mail&m_PR=27&IC=1>.

69. GeoPortals.com, "GeoFreeMail.com—Free Email from GeoPortals.com," 17 Mar. 2003, <http://geoportals.mail.everyone.net/email/scripts/joinuser.pl?EV1=10478565594700259>.

70. Delphi Forums, "Quick Registration," 6 Sept. 2004, <http://login.prospero.com/ dir-login/index.asp?webtag=mainconf&lgnDST=http%3A%2F%2Fforums%2Edelphiforums %2Ecom%2Fmy%2Dforums>.

71. ICQ, "About the Web's Largest Community—ICQ," 6 Sept. 2004, <http://www.icq.com/ products/whatisicq.html>, and ICQ, "Enter Your Details—Web Registration—ICQ.com," 6 Sept. 2004, <http://web.icq.com/register/attach?jc=433f31697f54ea94900808c0d3a69f26eefe056f 17430890f743cc576c5ecbf8c882359f25ed1668bb197d61387addc0ca4f3785f9fbca57c2a1333241 135d87a71f9959x1921>.

72. Yahoo!, "Welcome to Yahoo!," 1 July 2000, <http://edit.yahoo.com/config/eval_register? .intl=&new=1&.done=&.src=ym&partner=&promo=&.last=>, and Yahoo!, "Welcome to Yahoo!," 6 Sept. 2004, <http://edit.yahoo.com/config/eval_register?.intl=&new=1&.done=&.src=ym&.part ner=&.p=&promo=&.last=>.

73. ICQ, "About the Web's Largest Community—ICQ," 17 Mar. 2003, <http://www.icq.com/ products/whatisicq.html>; ICQ, "Enter Your Details—Web Registration—ICQ.com," 17 Mar. 2003, <http://web.icq.com/register/attach?jc=433f31697f54ea94900808c0d3a69f26eefe056f1743 0890f743cc576c5ecbf8c882359f25ed1668bb197d61387addc0ca4f3785f9fbca57c2a1333241135d 87a71f9959x1921>; and ICQ, "License Agreement—Web Registration—ICQ.com," 19 Jan. 2001, 17 Mar. 2003, <https://web.icq.com/register/license/1,,,00.html?email=touchtype%40hotmail %2Ecom>.

74. Ken Goldberg, "Ouija 2000," *Ouija 2000*, 6 Sept. 2004, <http://ouija.berkeley.edu/register.html>. A notable exception to this limiting format is the optional part of the registration form provided by the Rhizome art site. The site offers the choice of "Male," "Female," or "in Transition" and the explanation that it uses "demographic information about [its] members in grants and other fundraising activities." Rhizome, "Rhizome.org: User Info," 12 Sept. 2004, <http://rhizome.org/preferences/user.rhiz>.

75. See, for instance, Judith Butler, *Bodies that Matter: On the Discursive Limits of "Sex"* (New York: Routledge, 1993); Judith Butler, *Gender Trouble: Feminism and the Subversion of Identity* (New York: Routledge, 1989); Teresa de Lauretis, *Alice Doesn't: Feminism, Semiotics, Cinema* (Bloomington: Indiana University Press, 1984); and Diana Fuss, *Essentially Speaking: Feminism, Nature, and Difference* (New York: Routledge, 1989).

76. Yahoo!, "Yahoo!," 20 Apr. 2003, <http://www.yahoo.com/>.

77. Ibid.

78. According to Pat Kirkham and Judy Attfield, the gendered use of pink and blue for these purposes was only established in the 1930s. Pat Kirkham and Judy Attfield, "Introduction," in *The Gendered Object*, ed. Pat Kirkham (Manchester and New York: Manchester University Press, 1996), 5.

79. Trendmaster, 21 Aug. 1998, <http://www.trendmaster.com>.

80. Playmates, "Girls' Toys," 16 Mar. 2003, <http://www.playmatestoys.com/html/sec_girls_toys.html>.

81. Toys "R" Us, "Toysrus.com/Amazon.com," 6 Sept. 2004, <http://www.amazon.com/exec/obidos/tg/browse/-/171280/ref%3Drd%5Ftru%5Fhp/102–5833799-5064166>.

82. The Right Start, "The Right Start—Babies to Kids," 6 Sept. 2004, <http://www.rightstart.com/global/Store/Home/Default.cfm?TID=037016241946579303160357758&Site=gift>.

83. Playmates, "Girls' Toys," 16 Dec. 1999, <http://www.playmatestoys.com/html/girls_toys.html>.

84. Teresa de Lauretis, *Technologies of Gender: Essays on Theory, Film, and Fiction* (Bloomington: Indiana University Press, 1987), 11–12.

85. Ibid., 12.

86. Yahoo!, 7 July 2004, <http://yahoo.com>.

87. Wikipedia, "Chat—Wikipedia," 6 Sept. 2004, <http://www.wikipedia.org/wiki/Chat>.

88. Free On-Line Dictionary of Computing (FOLDOC), "Chat from FOLDOC," 6 Sept. 2004, <http://foldoc.doc.ic.ac.uk/foldoc/foldoc.cgi?chat>.

89. iVillage, "About Chat," 18 Mar. 2003, <http://www.ivillage.com/ivillage/chat/articles/0,12426,262598_289955,00.html>.

90. William J. Mitchell, "Replacing Place," in *The Digital Dialectic: New Essays on New Media*, ed. Peter Lunenfeld (Cambridge, MA: MIT Press, 1999), 199, 19 Mar. 2003, <http://emedia .netlibrary.com/reader/reader.asp?product_id=9304>.

91. CSG Network and Computer Support Group, "Computers, Telephony, and Electronics Glossary," 6 Sept. 2004, <http://www.csgnetwork.com/glossaryc.html#chat>.

92. Delphi Forums, "Welcome to Delphi Forums," 17 Mar. 2003, <http://www.delphiforums .com/>.

93. @ourplace.com, "@ourplace.com," 18 Mar. 2003, <http://www.ourplace.com/>; The Chat House, "Chat at the Chat House: Chatroom.com Chathouse," 6 Sept. 2004, <http://www2 .chathouse.com/>; ChatSpot.net, "ChatSpot.net | Live Teen Chat Rooms," 18 Mar. 2003, <http:// www.chatspot.net/>; ChaTTown, "Chattown—The Internet's Coolest Free Chat," 6 Sept. 2004, <http://www.chattown.com/>; Habbo Hotel, "Habbo Hotel—Home Page," 6 Sept. 2004, <http://www.habbohotel.com/habbo/en/>; iVillage, "Chat," 6 Sept. 2004, <http://www.ivillage .com/chat/>; and Link Room, "LinkRoom," 18 Mar. 2003, <http://www.linkroom.com/>.

94. Club Gabbay, "Club Gabbay::Index," 6 Sept. 2004, <http://www.clubgabbay.com/>.

95. TG Chat, "Welcome to TG Chat!," 18 Mar. 2003, <http://iseek.com/TheGathering/front door.htm>, and TG Chat, "WELCOME to The Gathering Chat!," 18 Mar. 2003, <http://iseek.com/ TheGathering/>.

96. Cynthia Haynes and Jan Rune Holmevik, "Lingua MOO Homepage," 13 June 2004, <http://lingua.utdallas.edu/>.

97. ICQ, "ICQ.com—Get ICQ Instant Messenger, Chat," 17 Mar. 2003, <http://web.icq.com/>.

98. Ibid.

99. ICQ, "About the Web's Largest Community—ICQ," 17 Mar. 2003, <http://www.icq.com/ products/whatisicq.html>, and ICQ, "About THE Web's Community—What Is ICQ?," 10 Sept. 2004, <http://www.icq.com/products/whatisicq.html>.

100. *The Oxford English Reference Dictionary*, ed. Judy Pearsall and Bill Trumble (Oxford: Oxford University Press, 1996), and xrefer, "xrefer-telepresence n.," 26 Jan. 2003, <http://xrefer.com/ entry.jsp?xrefid=428449&secid=.-&hh=1>.

101. Eduardo Kac, "Teleporting an Unknown State," 6 Sept. 2004, <http://www.ekac.org/ teleptrvl.html>.

102. Eduardo Kac, "Teleporting an Unknown State," 6 Sept. 2004, <http://www.ekac.org/ teleptrvl.html>, and Eduardo Kac, "Teleporting an Unknown State," 26 Jan. 2003, <http://www .ekac.org/teleporting.htm>.

103. Ken Goldberg and Joseph Santarromana, "The Telegarden," 6 Sept. 2004, <http:// telegarden.aec.at/index.html>. The garden "went offline" in August 2004.

104. Ken Goldberg and Joseph Santarromana, "About the Tele-Garden," 26 Jan. 2003, <http:// telegarden.aec.at/html/intro.html>.

105. Ibid.

106. Ken Goldberg, "Introduction: The Unique Phenomenon of a Distance," in *The Robot in the Garden: Telerobotics and Telepistemology in the Age of the Internet*, ed. Ken Goldberg (Cambridge, MA: MIT Press, 2000), 3, 13.

107. Manovich, "Screen and the User," in *Language of New Media*, 94.

108. Thomas J. Campanella, "Be There Now," Salon, 7 Aug. 1997, 31 Aug. 2004, <http://www.salon.com/aug97/21st/cam970807.html>.

109. DuPont, "Flat Panel Displays," 14 Sept. 2004, <http://www.dupont.com/mcm/new/flatpanel.html>.

110. Computer Bargains, "Flat Screen," 16 Jan. 2003, <http://www.computerbargains.net/h530.htm>.

111. Mike Godwin, "Foreword," in *High Noon on the Electronic Frontier: Conceptual Issues in Cyberspace*, ed. Peter Ludlow (Cambridge, MA: MIT Press, 1996), 20 Mar. 2002, <http://semlab2 .sbs.sunysb.edu/Users/pludlow/foreword.html>, and David Silver, "Looking Backwards, Looking Forward: Cyberculture Studies, 1990–2000," *Web.studies: Rewiring Media Studies for the Digital Age*, ed. David Gauntlett (Oxford University Press, 2000): 19–30, 20 Mar. 2002, <http://www.com .washington.edu/rccs/>.

112. Guillermo Gomez-Peña, "The Virtual Barrio @ The Other Frontier (Or the Chicano Interneta)," Jan. 1997, 6 Sept. 2004, <http://www.zonezero.com/magazine/articles/gomezpena/gomezpena.html>.

113. James T. Costigan, "Introduction: Forest, Trees, and Internet Research," in *Doing Internet Research*, ed. Jones, xx.

2 Visual Pleasure through Textual Passages: Gazing in Multi-user Object-oriented Settings (MOOs)

1. Jan Rune Holmevik, "How to Design, Set Up, and Manage an Educational MOO," in *High Wired: On the Design, Use, and Theory of Educational MOOs*, 2nd ed., ed. Cynthia Haynes and Jan Rune Holmevik (Ann Arbor: University of Michigan Press, 2001), 108.

2. The MOO spectator types commands in order to engage with the character and read setting-specific texts. Commands allow characters to "speak," "move," "look," access information, and interact with other characters in a variety of ways.

3. Webopedia, "What Is MUD?," 2 Sept. 2004, <http://www.pcwebopaedia.com/TERM/M/MUD.html>, and Wikipedia, "MUD—Wikipedia," 25 Oct. 2003, 30 Oct. 2003, <http://en.wikipedia.org/wiki/MUD>.

4. These settings are distinguished by differences in programming and the ways that they are employed.

5. Free On-Line Dictionary of Computing (FOLDOC), "Multi-user Dimension from FOLDOC," 2 Sept. 2004, <http://wombat.doc.ic.ac.uk/foldoc/foldoc.cgi?Multi-User+Dimension>.

6. LambdaMOO, type "help theme," 2 Sept. 2004, <telnet://lambda.moo.mud.org: 8888>. Many of the quoted LambdaMOO system-generated texts have remained the same over many years. All typos and misspellings are from the "original" texts.

7. Pavel Curtis, "Not Just a Game: How LambdaMOO Came to Exist and What It Did to Get Back at Me," in *High Wired: On the Design, Use, and Theory of Educational MOOs*, ed. Cynthia Haynes and Jan Rune Holmevik (Ann Arbor: University of Michigan Press, 1998), 25–44. See also Ken Schweller, "Pavel and MOO," MOO-cows Mailing List Archive, 4 Nov. 1996, 2 Sept. 2004, <http://www.elilabs.com/mcarc/11-96/msg00014.html>.

8. Pavel Curtis, "Mudding Social Phenomena in Text-based Virtual Realities," paper presented at the conference on Directions and Implications of Advanced Computing, sponsored by Computer Professionals for Social Responsibility, 1992, 2 Sept. 2004, <http://www.eff.org/Net_culture/MOO_MUD_IRC/curtis_mudding.article>.

9. Pavel Curtis, "Muds Grow Up: Social Virtual Reality in the Real World," 5 May 1993, 2 Sept. 2004, <http://www.eff.org/Net culture/MOO_MUD_IRC/muds_grow_up.paper>.

10. Christina Allen, "Virtual Identities: The Social Construction of Cybered Selves" (Ph.D. dissertation, Northwestern University, 1996); Richard Bartle, "Interactive Multi-user Computer Games," Electronic Frontier Foundation, Dec. 1990, 2 Sept. 2004, <http://www.eff.org/Net_culture/MOO_MUD_IRC/>; Amy Bruckman, "Community Support for Constructionist Learning," *Computer Supported Cooperative Work* 7 (1998): 47–86, 2 Sept. 2004, <http://www.cc.gatech.edu/fac/Amy.Bruckman/papers/cscw.html>; Lynn Cherny, *Conversation and Community: Chat in a Virtual World* (Stanford, CA: CSLI Publications, 1999); Julian Dibbell, *My Tiny Life: Crime and Passion in a Virtual World* (New York: Holt, 1998); Julian Dibbell, "A Rape in Cyberspace; or, How an Evil Clown, a Haitian Trickster Spirit, Two Wizards, and a Cast of Dozens Turned a Database into a Society," *The Village Voice*, 21 Dec. 1993, 36–42; Stephen Doheny-Farina, *The Wired Neighborhood* (New Haven, CT: Yale University Press, 1996); Cynthia Haynes and Jan Rune Holmevik, "Lingua Unlimited: Enhancing Pedagogical Reality with MOOs," Kairos 1, 2 (1996), 6 Sept. 2004, <http://english.ttu.edu/kairos/1.2/binder2.html?coverweb/HandH/start.html>; Haynes and Holmevik, eds., *High Wired*, 2nd ed.; Beth E. Kolko, "Intellectual Property in Synchronous and Collaborative Virtual Space," in *Cyberethics: Social and Moral Issues in the Computer Age*, ed. Robert M. Baird, Reagan Ramsower, and Stuart E. Rosenbaum (Amherst, MA: Prometheus Books, 2000), 257–282; Howard Rheingold, *The Virtual Community: Homesteading on the Electronic Frontier* (Reading, MA: Addison-Wesley, 1993); Allucquère Rosanne Stone, *The War of Desire and Technology at the Close of the Mechanical Age* (Cambridge, MA: MIT Press, 1995); Turkle, *Life on the Screen*; Michele White, "Cabinet of Curiosity: Finding the Viewer in a Virtual Museum," *Convergence: The International Journal of Research into New Media Technologies* 3, 3 (Autumn 1997): 28–70; and Michele White, "Regulating Research: The Problem of Theorizing Community on LambdaMOO," *Ethics and Information Technology* 4, 1 (2002): 55–70.

11. LambdaMOO, login screen, 2 Sept. 2004, <telnet://lambda.moo.mud.org: 8888>.

12. Wikipedia, "Object-oriented Programming—Wikipedia," 1 Mar. 2003, <http://www.wiki pedia.org/wiki/Object-oriented>.

13. LambdaMOO, type "help objects," 2 Sept. 2004, <telnet://lambda.moo.mud.org: 8888>.

14. LambdaMOO, login screen, 2 Sept. 2004, <telnet://lambda.moo.mud.org: 8888>.

15. The idea that characters are unread is ironically performed in the following guest character description: "Hi! My name's Tiffany. I read a book once. It was pretty cool, full of words n stuff." Loki, "*Silly/Stupid/Salacious-Guest-Descriptions," LambdaMOO, 6 Dec. 1998, <telnet://lambda.moo.mud.org 8888>.

16. Merriam-Webster Dictionary, "Merriam-Webster Online," 2003, 6 Sept. 2004, <http://www .m-w.com/cgi-bin/dictionary?book=Dictionary&va=look>.

17. Ibid.

18. He notes: "Even a rapid glance at the language we commonly use will demonstrate the ubiquity of visual metaphors. . . . Depending, of course, on one's outlook or point of view, the prevalence of such metaphors will be accounted an obstacle or an aid to our knowledge of reality. It is, however, no idle speculation or figment of imagination to claim that if blinded to their importance, we will damage our ability to inspect the world outside and introspect the world within. And our prospects for escaping their thrall, if indeed that is ever our foreseeable goal, will be greatly dimmed." Martin Jay, *Downcast Eyes: The Denigration of Vision in Twentieth-century French Thought* (Berkeley: University of California Press, 1994), 1.

19. Merriam-Webster Dictionary "WWWebster Dictionary—Search Screen," 1998, 6 Sept. 2004, <http://www.m-w.com/cgi-bin/dictionary?book=Dictionary&va=gaze>.

20. Salecl and Žižek, "Introduction," in *Gaze and Voice as Love Objects*, 3.

21. Mulvey, "Visual Pleasure and Narrative Cinema," *Screen*.

22. The classical cinema is usually associated with the Hollywood system between the time that sound was employed in the late 1920s and the demise of the studio system in the 1950s.

23. Mulvey, "Visual Pleasure and Narrative Cinema," in *Visual and Other Pleasures*, 19.

24. Metz, *Imaginary Signifier*, and Lacan, *Four Fundamental Concepts of Psycho-analysis*.

25. Doane, "Remembering Women," in *Femmes Fatales*, 86.

26. Mulvey, "Afterthoughts on 'Visual Pleasure and Narrative Cinema' Inspired by *Duel in the Sun*," *Framework*.

27. Doane, "Film and Masquerade," in *Femmes Fatales*.

28. Doane, "Masquerade Reconsidered," in *Femmes Fatales*.

29. Mayne, "Feminist Film Theory and Criticism," in *Multiple Voices in Feminist Film Criticsm*, ed. Carson, Dittmar, and Welsch, 50.

30. The "Spivak" gender is named after Michael Spivak because of the extensive work that "e" has done with pronouns. The Spivak pronouns as defined by the help system are E (subjective), Em (objective), Eir (possessive-adjective), Eirs (possessive-noun), Emself (reflexive). LambdaMOO spectators can obtain a definition of the Spivak gender and a list of pronouns by typing "help Spivak." The characters Velvet and Nosredna worked on this definition. The other intergender categories remain undefined. LambdaMOO, type "help spivak," 6 Sept. 2004, <telnet://lambda .moo.mud.org 8888>.

31. Stam, Burgoyne, and Flitterman-Lewis, *New Vocabularies in Film Semiotics*, 166.

32. For instance, in *Six Feet Under*, the character David instructs Arthur in how to appropriately perform his duties in a funeral home and act. When we see Arthur repeating David's instructions, we know that he is acting, but this is explained and still has meaning within the narrative. "Parallel Play," *Six Feet Under*, written by Jill Soloway, dir. Jeremy Podeswa, Season 4, Episode 42, 2004.

33. Stam, Burgoyne, and Flitterman-Lewis, *New Vocabularies in Film Semiotics*, 166.

34. CCI Computer, "High-tech Dictionary Definition," 6 Sept. 2004, <http://www.computeruser .com/resources/dictionary/definition.html?lookup=3109>.

35. These problems with identification are considered in more depth in chapter 3, which is about webcams, and chapter 6, which considers digital imaging.

36. Michel Foucault, *Discipline and Punish: The Birth of the Prison* (New York: Vintage Books, 1995).

37. In the work of contemporary theorists, including Tony Bennett and Lisa Cartwright, Foucault's model of the panopticon is altered to include panoptic social regulation by community surveillance. In other words, community codes are maintained by a mutual understanding of social standards and the knowledge that the community itself is or could be watching. Tony Bennett, *The Birth of the Museum: History, Theory, Politics* (New York: Routledge, 1995), and Lisa Cartwright, *Screening the Body: Tracing Medicine's Visual Culture* (Minneapolis: University of Minnesota Press, 1995).

38. Mark Winokur considers how the Internet prevents spectators from thinking outside of its structure and encourages self-regulation. Mark Winokur, "The Ambiguous Panopticon: Foucault and the Codes of Cyberspace," CTheory, 13 Mar. 2003, 16 July 2004, <http://www.ctheory.net/ text_file.asp?pick=371>.

39. Abraxas, character description, type "look ~Abraxas," LambdaMOO, 21 Dec. 1998, <telnet:// lambda.moo.mud.org: 8888>.

40. Olive_Guest, character description, LambdaMOO, 22 June 2004, <telnet://lambda.moo.mud .org: 8888>.

41. Brown_Guest, character description, LambdaMOO, 11 July 2004, <telnet://lambda.moo .mud.org: 8888>.

42. LambdaMOO, type "help @describe," 6 Sept. 2004, <telnet://lambda.moo.mud.org 8888>.

43. There are a number of ways guests can also be used to establish a fixed identity. Some guests choose to employ the same description every time that they log in. Other spectators simply label the guest with a name like Sue or Ben that makes it seem as if this is their name.

44. LambdaMOO, type "help @describe," 6 Sept. 2004, <telnet://lambda.moo.mud.org: 8888>.

45. Characters can morph or change into different names, descriptions, and genders. Characters may morph into a different body construct, but they always have the same object number.

46. Infrared_Guest, character description, LambdaMOO, 10 July 2004, <telnet://lambda.moo.mud.org: 8888>.

47. Beige_Guest, character description, LambdaMOO, 10 July 2004, <telnet://lambda.moo.mud.org: 8888>.

48. Jorge R. Barrios and Deanna Wilkes-Gibbs, "How to MOO without Making a Sound: A Guide to the Virtual Communities Known as MOOs," in *High Wired*, ed. Haynes and Holmevik, 51.

49. Allen, "Audience-oriented Criticism," in *Channels of Discourse, Reassembled*.

50. LambdaMOO type "help character," LambdaMOO, 6 Sept. 2004, <telnet://lambda.moo.mud.org: 8888>.

51. Jenkins, *Textual Poachers*.

52. The genwho feature provides information about the gender of all characters with spectators who are currently using the MOO. Stetson, "@addfeature #1017," type "genwho," LambdaMOO, 24 June 2004, <telnet://lambda.moo.mud.org: 8888>. The spectator must add the appropriate feature object before genwho will function.

53. Spectators who do not set their character's gender by typing "@gender <gender>" will have their gender remain as "neuter." If spectators set their character gender to something other than one of the ten gender choices, then the system uses neuter pronouns. A few spectators have circumvented the neuter pronominal markers by programming their own set of gender pronouns.

54. LambdaMOO, type "help theme," 6 Sept. 2004, <telnet://lambda.moo.mud.org: 8888>.

55. Ibid.

56. It is possible that spectators could employ "@examine <object name or number>." However, most spectators, at least when they seek information about other characters, use the "look" command. I have determined this by using a program to record all the times that characters look at my character as well as the type of command that they employed.

57. LambdaMOO, type "help introduction," 6 Sept. 2004, <telnet://lambda.moo.mud.org: 8888>. These commands, which are listed in the order in which they appear, are "look," "say," "@who," "movement," and "@quit."

58. Guest, LambdaMOO, 1 June 1999, <telnet://lambda.moo.mud.org: 8888>.

59. The spectator must add the appropriate feature object before most of these commands will function.

60. Foucault, *Discipline and Punish*, 197.

61. See, for instance, David Lyon, "Surveillance as Social Sorting: Computer Codes and Mobile Bodies," in *Surveillance as Social Sorting: Privacy, Risk, and Digital Discrimination*, ed. David Lyon (London: Routledge, 2003).

62. Barrios and Wilkes-Gibbs, "How to MOO," in *High Wired*, ed. Haynes and Holmevik, 66.

63. I employed a programmed feature that recorded the commands characters used when they "looked" at my character.

64. LambdaMOO, type "help read," 6 Sept. 2004, <telnet://lambda.moo.mud.org: 8888>.

65. Rusty, type "help #24262," LambdaMOO, 6 Sept. 2004, <telnet://lambda.moo.mud.org :8888>.

66. @kgb lists the character's name, object number, last logout, amount of time logged out, last login, amount of time logged in, amount of time idling, current time, MOO age, seniority among all MOO characters, real life time zone (if set by the spectator) and current time in that zone, gender, name of player class (each player class provides the character with a slightly different set of capabilities), programmer status (characters must request to be programmers), number of feature objects used (features can be added in order to increase the character's functionality), MOO home, current location and list of other characters in that room, shortest alias or other names for the character, number and names of morphs (other names, genders, and descriptions that the character can change into), current description, LambdaMOO club memberships, currently held objects, total amount of quota (the amount of database space that the character can use to do such things as write descriptions, copy objects from preexisting programs, or program), total quota used, quota still available, and relationship to the character (this may show that the character lists them as a "pal" or uses their feature objects). "@kgb <character name>," LambdaMOO, 1 Sept. 2004, <telnet://lambda.moo.mud.org: 8888>.

67. GreyDruid, type "help #49074," LambdaMOO, 6 Sept. 2004, <telnet://lambda.moo.mud.org :8888>.

68. Guest as quoted in Hammer, "*Silly/Stupid/Salacious-Guest-Descriptions," LambdaMOO, 6 Dec. 1998, <telnet://lambda.moo.mud.org: 8888>. The existence of salacious guest descriptions has become such a regular part of MOO systems that a MOO mailing list was formed in order to post these descriptions. It is my belief that some of these descriptions are written solely for the entertainment of the list readers. This position was performed by Plaid_Guest's description: "Hi! I am Loki. I logged on as a guest and entered a goofy description just so I could post it here for all to see! Thanks!" Plaid_Guest, character description, LambdaMOO, 7 Dec. 1998, <telnet:// lambda.moo.mud.org: 8888>. Spectators can also read all of the current guest descriptions by typing "@od." jowl, "@addfeature #72280," LambdaMOO, 6 Sept. 2004, <telnet://lambda .moo.mud.org: 8888>.

69. Guest as quoted in Krys, "*Silly/Stupid/Salacious-Guest-Descriptions," LambdaMOO, 4 June 2002, 23 June 2004, <telnet://lambda.moo.mud.org: 8888>.

70. Teal_Guest, character description, LambdaMOO, 1 Dec. 1998, <telnet://lambda.moo.mud.org: 8888>.

71. Red_Guest, character description, LambdaMOO, 31 May 1999, <telnet://lambda.moo.mud.org: 8888>.

72. Mulvey, "Visual Pleasure and Narrative Cinema," in *Visual and Other Pleasures*, 25.

73. Beige_Guest, character description, 3 Mar. 2003, <telnet://lambda.moo.mud.org: 8888>, and Guest, character description, 6 Dec. 1998, <telnet://lambda.moo.mud.org: 8888>.

74. Technicolor_Guest, character description, LambdaMOO, 3 Mar. 2003, <telnet://lambda.moo.mud.org: 8888>; Pink_Guest, character description, LambdaMOO, 17 Mar. 2003, <telnet://lambda.moo.mud.org: 8888>; and Guest, character description, LambdaMOO, 6 Dec. 2003, <telnet://lambda.moo.mud.org: 8888>.

75. Mulvey, "Visual Pleasure and Narrative Cinema," in *Visual and Other Pleasures*, 19. In some descriptions, it is also possible to imagine other gendered positions for the empowered spectator. However, the articulated gender representations of characters and the overt heterosexuality of many performances decrease the likelihood or expectations for such dynamics.

76. Ibid.

77. Periwinkle_Guest, character description, LambdaMOO, 2 Mar. 2003, <telnet://lambda.moo.mud.org: 8888>.

78. Ebony_Guest, character description, LambdaMOO, 2 Mar. 2003, <telnet://lambda.moo.mud.org: 8888>.

79. Kaja Silverman, *Male Subjectivity at the Margins* (New York: Routledge, 1992), 152.

80. Purple_Guest, character description, 4 June 1999, <telnet://lambda.moo.mud.org: 8888>, and Guest, character description, 4 June 1999, <telnet://lambda.moo.mud.org: 8888>.

81. There is a higher proportion of both male and female erotic descriptions on some small "adult-oriented" MOOs.

82. Renfair, type "help #67671," LambdaMOO, 2 Jan. 1999, <telnet://lambda.moo.mud.org :8888>.

83. Silver_Guest, character description, LambdaMOO, 3 Mar. 2003, <telnet://lambda.moo.mud.org: 8888>.

84. Create, character description, type "look ~Create," LambdaMOO, 11 Mar. 2003, <telnet://lambda.moo.mud.org: 8888>.

85. Silver_Guest, character description, LambdaMOO, 25 June 2004, <telnet://lambda.moo.mud.org: 8888>.

86. Technicolor_Guest, character description, LambdaMOO, 11 June 1999, <telnet://lambda.moo.mud.org: 8888>.

87.   A number of intergender characters, which include the character Irradiate, have shared their experiences on this topic with me. An informal study supports these claims. My intergender character was looked at twenty-two times by male characters, ten times by female characters, and four times by intergender characters between 3 Mar. 1999 and 1 June 1999.

88.   Doane, *Femmes Fatales*, 20–21.

89.   Plaid_Guest, character description, LambdaMOO, 27 Dec. 1998, <telnet://lambda.moo.mud .org: 8888>.

90.   Khaki_Guest, character description, LambdaMOO, 7 July 2004, <telnet://lambda.moo.mud .org: 8888>. This guest description and some others appear regularly. I first noticed it on 17 Mar. 2003.

91.   Beige _Guest, character description, LambdaMOO, 23 Jan. 1999, <telnet://lambda.moo.mud .org: 8888>.

92.   Periwinkle_Guest, "Quoted-Out-Of-Context," LambdaMOO, 10 Aug. 1995, <telnet:// lambda.moo.mud.org: 8888>.

93.   Phaedrus, "The -Official- SpivakFAQ," 1 June 1999, <http://www.jacksonville.net/~phaedrus /spivak.html>.

94.   Lemi, "*Best of the Lists," LambdaMOO, 13 Jan. 1997, <telnet://lambda.moo.mud.org : 8888>.

95.   Rog, type "@go #116," "look useless mirror," LambdaMOO, 6 Sept. 2004, <telnet:// lambda.moo.mud.org: 8888>.

96.   Bewitch, character description, type "look ~Bewitch," LambdaMOO, 21 Dec. 1998, <tel net://lambda.moo.mud.org: 8888>.

97.   Lacan, *Four Fundamental Concepts of Psycho-analysis*.

98.   Doane, "Misrecognition and Identity," *Cine-Tracts*, 28.

99.   Diversity University, 13 June 2004, <http://moo.dumain.du.org:8000/>, and LinguaMOO, 13 June 2004, <http://elsie.utdallas.edu:7000/>.

100.   Jan Rune Holmevik and Cynthia Haynes, "enCore Home Page," 19 Jan. 2004, 6 June 2004, <http://lingua.utdallas.edu/encore/>. Diversity University offers a different graphical user inter- face.

101.   LinguaMOO, 12 June 2004, <http://elsie.utdallas.edu:7000/>. The Trace Online Writing Centre has ongoing dialogues that are facilitated by LinguaMOO. Dene Grigar defended her dis- sertation using the setting in 1995. Dene Grigar and John F. Barber, "Defending Your Life in MOOspace: A Report from the Electronic Edge," in *High Wired: On the Design, Use, and Theory of Educational MOOs*, ed. Cynthia Haynes and Jan Rune Holmevik (Ann Arbor: University of Michigan Press, 1998), 192–231.

102.   Characters can also be customized with an image that is supported by the spectator's web site. These images have largely been conceptualized as a photograph of the spectator. For instance, a LinguaMOO announcement notes that all "registered players can now have their photo show up under their name." Jan Rune Holmevik, "WWW + MOO = WOO!! (LinguaMOO)," 13 June 2004, <http://elsie.utdallas.edu:7000/519>.

103.   Cynthia Haynes and Jan Rune Holmevik, "LinguaMOO Beginner's Guide to MOOing," LinguaMOO, 6 June 2004, <http://129.110.23.73:7000/xpress_misc/guide.html>.

104.   Ibid.

105.   Erin Karper, "A Guide to enCore MOOs: Getting Around," AlaMOO User's Guide, 2002, 7 June 2004, <http://www.accd.edu/sac/english/lirvin/AlaMOO/AlaMOOGuide/getting.htm>.

106.   Barrios and Wilkes-Gibbs, "How to MOO," in *High Wired*, ed. Haynes and Holmevik, 66.

107.   These other MOOs include AcadeMOO, 7 June 2004, <http://academoo.cl.msu.edu :8000/>; AlaMOO, 7 June 2004, <http://ranger.accd.edu:7000/>; BC-MOO, 23 Mar. 2000, 7 June 2004, <http://josiah.letu.edu/moofiles/howto.html>; cmcMOO, 2 May 2002, 7 June 2004, <http://purlmoo.uib.no:8000/>; DartMOO, 7 June 2004, <http://dartmoo.dartmouth .edu:7000/>; forMOOsa, 7 June 2004, <http://formoosa.fl.nthu.edu.tw:7000/>; MiamiMOO, 7 June 2004, <http://moo.muohio.edu:7000/>; OldPuebloMOO, 7 June 2004, <http://oldpueblo moo.arizona.edu:7000/>; ProNoun MOO, 7 June 2004, <http://linnell.english.purdue.edu :7000/>; Project Achieve, 7 June 2004, <http://achieve.utoronto.ca:2221/>; Texas Tech English MOO, 7 June 2004, <http://moo.engl.ttu.edu:7000>; U-MOO, 7 June 2004, <http://umoo.uncg .edu:7000/>; and VRoma MOO, 7 June 2004, <http://www.vroma.org:7878/>.

108.   LinguaMOO settings with a rendering of a figure include the C-Fest Forum, Collaboratory, First Dimension, Help Kiosk, Library, Libris, Poetry Room (rendered by Mark Tansey), The Studio, and Scriptorium. The figure in some of these representations works more successfully as a stand-in for the spectator and some of the images repeat.

109.   LinguaMOO, 25 June 2004, <http://elsie.utdallas.edu:7000/>.

110.   LinguaMOO, "Courtyard," 6 June 2004, <http://129.110.23.73:7000/Xpress_Client/verti cal_layout>.

111.   Mulvey, "Visual Pleasure and Narrative Cinema," in *Visual and Other Pleasures*, 19.

112.   Matte_Guest character description, LambdaMOO, 5 June 1999, <telnet://lambda.moo .mud.org: 8888>, and Copper_Guest character description, 6 June 1999, <telnet://lambda.moo .mud.org: 8888>.

113.   Salecl and Žižek, "Introduction," in *Gaze and Voice as Love Objects*, 1–6.

3 Too Close to See, Too Intimate a Screen: Men, Women, and Webcams

1.   Mulvey, "Visual Pleasure and Narrative Cinema," *Screen*.

2. Mulvey, "Afterthoughts on 'Visual Pleasure and Narrative Cinema' Inspired by *Duel in the Sun*," *Framework*.

3. Doane, "Film and Masquerade" and "Masquerade Reconsidered," in *Femmes Fatales*.

4. Salecl and Žižek, "Introduction," in *Gaze and Voice as Love Objects*, 3.

5. Jesse Berst, "Around the World in Eight E-Links," ZDNeT, 24 Dec. 1998, 30 June 2002, <http://www.zdnet.com/anchordesk/story/story_2908.html>.

6. John Dvorak, "Little Brother Is Watching," ZDNet, 20 Nov. 2000, 6 Sept. 2004, <http://zdnet.com.com/2100-1107-503080.html>.

7. Howard A. Landman, "Sonnets to JenniCam," I, 7, 25 Jan. 1999, 30 June 2002, <http://www.polyamory.org/~howard/Poetry/jennicamI07.html>.

8. John Dvorak, "Little Brother Is Watching," ZDNet, 20 Nov. 2000, 6 Sept. 2004, <http://zdnet.com.com/2100-1107-503080.html>.

9. Thomas J. Campanella, "Eden by Wire: Webcameras and the Telepresent Landscape," in *Robot in the Garden*, ed. Goldberg, 23.

10. Thomas J. Campanella, "Who Says the Net Makes Cities Obsolete," Salon, 7 Aug. 1997, 6 Sept. 2004, <http://www.salon.com/aug97/21st/cities970807.html>.

11. Simon Firth, "Live! From My Bedroom," Salon, 8 Jan. 1998, 6 Sept. 2004, <http://www.salon.com/21st/feature/1998/01/cov_08feature.html/>.

12. Steven Shaviro, "Seen," Stranded in the Jungle, 14 July 2004, <http://www.dhalgren.com/Stranded/29.html>.

13. Thomas J. Campanella, "Be There Now," Salon, 7 Aug. 1997, 6 Sept. 2004, <http://www.salon.com/aug97/21st/cam970807.html>.

14. Sandra Blessum, "AfriNews: Remember when . . . ," Africam, 5 Nov. 1999, <http://main.africam.co.za/afrinews/contents.html>.

15. Katharine Mieszkowski, "Candy from Strangers," Salon, 13 Aug. 2001, 6 Sept. 2004, <http://www.salon.com/tech/feature/2001/08/13/cam_girls/index.html>, and Steven Shaviro, "Seen," Stranded in the Jungle, 14 July 2004, <http://www.dhalgren.com/Stranded/29.html>.

16. Kristine Blair and Pamela Takayoshi, "Navigating the Image of Woman Online: Whose Gaze Is It, Anyway?," Kairos 2, 2 (Fall 1997), 6 Sept. 2004, <http://english.ttu.edu/kairos/2.2/coverweb/invited/kb3.html>.

17. Victor Burgin, "Jenni's Room: Exhibitionism and Solitude," *Critical Inquiry* 27, 1 (Autumn 2000): 77–89.

18. Free On-Line Dictionary of Computing (FOLDOC), "Webcam from FOLDOC," 11 Jan. 1999, 2 Sept. 2004, <http://wombat.doc.ic.ac.uk/foldoc/foldoc.cgi?webcam>.

19. What Is, "What Is Streaming Video," 2 Sept. 2004, <http://searchNetworking.techtarget .com/sDefinition/0,,sid7_gci213055,00.html>.

20. Webopedia "Real Time—Definitions and Links," 2 Sept. 2004, <http://www.pcwebopaedia .com/TERM/r/real_time.html>.

21. What Is, "What Is Real Time," 2 Sept. 2004, <http://searchSmallBizIT.techtarget.com/ sDefinition/0,,sid44_gci214344,00.html>.

22. Margaret Morse, "Virtualities: A Conceptual Framework," in *Virtualities: Television, Media, Art, and Cyberculture* (Bloomington: Indiana University Press, 1998), 22–23.

23. Dictionary.com, "Dictionary.com/webcam," June 2002, <http://www.dictionary.com/ cgi-bin/dict.pl?term=webcam>.

24. Barthes, *Camera Lucida*, 77.

25. Rosalind E. Krauss, "The Photographic Conditions of Surrealism," in *The Originality of the Avant-garde and Other Modernist Myths* (Cambridge, MA: MIT Press, 1994), 110.

26. MOOs and other text-based settings try to render a version of this technologically facilitated visual correspondence.

27. Quentin Stafford-Fraser, "Trojan Room Coffee Pot Biography," 3 May 2001, <http://www.cl .cam.ac.uk/coffee/qsf/coffee.html>.

28. Worldwide Webcam Sites, 5 May 1999, <http://www.webcamsearch.com>; Worldwide Webcam Sites, "Webcam Search.com—A Complete Directory to Over 26,000 Webcam Related Sites Throughout the World," 21 Dec. 2000, <http://www.webcamsearch.com/>; and Worldwide Webcam Sites, "WebcamSearch.com—A Complete Directory to Over 42,000 Webcam Related Sites Throughout the World," 2 Sept. 2004, <http://www.webcamsearch.com/>. This growth seems to have tapered off.

29. JennyLee, "Fneu Cam," 9 Dec. 2000, <http://jennylee.warped.com/>.

30. Christopher R. Smit, "Fascination: The Modern Allure of the Internet," in *Web.studies*, ed. Gauntlett, 133.

31. What Is, "What Is . . . a Cam, Homecam, Livecam, or Webcam (A Definition)," 5 May 1999, <http://whatis.com/cam.htm>, and Wikipedia, "Jennicam—Wikipedia, the Free Encyclopedia," 14 July 2004, <http://en.wikipedia.org/wiki/JenniCam>.

32. Teresa Senft, "Dissertation Proposal," Homecam Heroines: Auto-Performance, Gender and Celebrity on the World Wide Web, Jan. 2000, 2 Sept. 2004, <http://www.echonyc.com/ %7Ejanedoe/diss/dissprop.html>.

33. Chris Taylor, "Jenni and the Bishops," Time Daily, 27 Mar. 1998, 14 July 2004, <http://www .time.com/time/search/article/0,8599,10769,00.html>.

34. Wikipedia, "Jennicam—Wikipedia, the Free Encyclopedia," 14 July 2004, <http://en .wikipedia.org/wiki/JenniCam>.

35. See, for instance, Claudia Cowan, "Turning Off the Jennicam," Fox News, 31 Dec. 2003, 12 July 2004, <http://www.foxnews.com/story/0%2C2933%2C107105%2C00.html>, and "R.I.P. Jennicam," BBC News, 1 Jan. 2004, 12 July 2004, <http://news.bbc.co.uk/2/hi/uk_news/maga zine/3360063.stm>.

36. What Is, "What Is . . . a Cam, Homecam, Livecam, or Webcam (A Definition)," 5 May 1999, <http://whatis.com/cam.htm>.

37. Jennifer Ringley, "JenniCam: Life, Online," 15 May 2001, <http://www.jennicam.com/ j2kr/faq.html>.

38. Alicia Grace, "Alicamdotorg," 25 Mar. 2001, <http://www.geocities.com/alicamlive/ files/about.htm>.

39. Katharine Mieszkowski, "Candy from Strangers," Salon, 13 Aug. 2001, 6 Sept. 2004, <http:// www.salon.com/tech/feature/2001/08/13/cam_girls/index.html>.

40. Aimee, "Aimee's Official Freak of the Week Page," 27 Apr. 1999, 15 July 2004, <http:// www.acamgirl.com/freaks/freak1.html>.

41. Messy "Voyeurism," 25 June 2002, <http://www.craptabulous.com/voyeurism.html>.

42. Julie, "JulieCam Profile—Internet Conferencing," About, 25 June 2002, <http://netconfer ence.about.com/library/cammers/blcammer079.htm>.

43. Justice, "Home," 25 Oct. 2000, <http://justice9.homestead.com/home.html>.

44. Cindy, "Intro," 13 Jan. 2001, <http://www.summer-web.com>.

45. Kathy, "About Kat Scan," 3 Jan. 2001, <http://www.members.home.net/webwoman/kat cam.htm>.

46. Elektric, "ElektriCam—Elektric's WebCam Page," 3 Jan. 2001, <http://www.elektricam.com/ faq.html>.

47. Aimee, "Aimee Live Profile—Internet Conferencing," About, 1 Apr. 2001, <http://net conference.about.com/internet/netconference/library/cammers/blcammer002.htm>.

48. Saski, "SaskiWatch Livecam Profile—Internet Conferencing," About, 1 July 2002, <http:// netconference.about.com/library/cammers/blcammer097.htm>.

49. Andi, "AndiCam Profile—Internet Conferencing," About, 5 June 2002, <http://netcon ference.about.com/library/cammers/blcammer069.htm>, and Julie, "JulieCam: About Me," 14 July 2004, <http://juliecam.net/about.html>.

50. Messy, "Voyeurism," 25 June 2002, <http://www.craptabulous.com/voyeurism.html>.

51. Messy, "FAQ," 15 July 2004, <http://www.craptabulous.com/background.html>, and Aimee "Freaks," 2 Sept. 2004, <http://acamgirl.com/main.php>.

52. Damian Tambini, "New Media and Democracy: The Civic Networking Movement," New Media & Society 1, 3 (1999), 2 Apr. 2002, <http://www.sagepub.co.uk/frame.html?http://www.sage pub.co.uk/journals/details/j0182.html>.

53.   This reflects the ongoing problems that spectators have with harassment and other forms of Internet provocation. Some spectators perpetuate these unpleasant dynamics because they cannot stop engaging. There always appears to be one synchronous communication participant who must respond to extreme examples of homophobia, racism, and sexism even though these statements are clearly designed as a way of gaining attention.

54.   Aimee, "Freaks," 2 Sept. 2004, <http://acamgirl.com/main.php>.

55.   Susan Herring argues, "One of the most striking characteristics of CMC, in my experience, is the extent to which it is a locus of conflict. . . . Whatever its explanation, the prevalence of conflict has as a consequence that users, even those subscribed to special-interest discussion groups, cannot reasonably be considered homogeneous populations with respect to their interests and social/political agendas." Susan Herring, "Critical Analysis of Language Use in Computer-mediated Contexts: Some Ethical and Scholarly Considerations," *The Information Society* 12, 14 (1996), 2 Sept. 2004, <http://venus.soci.niu.edu/~jthomas/ethics/tis/go.susan>.

56.   Cindy, "Intro," 13 Jan. 2001, <http://www.summer-web.com>.

57.   Amy, "Amycam . . . Live, Fun, Free, Girl WebCam site (The Lifecam of a Camgirl)," 25 Dec. 2000, <http://www.theworldiknow.com/index2.html>.

58.   Aimee, "A Cam Girl Dot Com, a Free Live Web Cam Site & More," 24 Mar. 2001, <http://members.aol.com/heyaimee/cam.html>, and Cindy Roberts, "Cincam," 13 Jan. 2001, <http://www.geocities.com/SoHo/Coffeehouse/1769/Cam/index2.html>.

59.   Simon Firth, "Live! From My Bedroom," Salon, 8 Jan. 1998, 2 Sept. 2004, <http://archive.salon.com/21st/feature/1998/01/cov_08feature2.html>.

60.   Barthes, *Pleasure of the Text*, 10.

61.   Leo Bersani, *The Freudian Body: Psychoanalysis and Art* (New York: Columbia University Press, 1986).

62.   About: The Human Interface, "Women Webcam Profiles," About, 1 Apr. 2001, <http://netconference.about.com/internet/netconference/library/blwcammers.htm>.

63.   About: The Human Internet, "Men Profiled Cam Stars A-B," About, 1 Apr. 2001, <http://netconference.about.com/internet/netconference/cs/mencamprofilesi/index.htm>.

64.   Cindy Roberts, "Hit Sluts," 1 Jan. 2001, <http://www.themestream.com/gspd_browse/browse/view_article.gsp?c_id=244997&id_list=273480,272511,271105,269288,269292,267443,267485,267499,266258,263922,262528,262626,258565,251437,244997,241948,240772,233763,234286,225715>.

65.   About: The Human Internet, "Women Webcam Profiles," About, 1 Apr. 2001, <http://netconference.about.com/internet/netconference/library/blwcammers.htm>.

66.   Turkle indicates that the Internet provides a setting in which spectators can explore problems and issues that they face in the material world. Turkle, *Life on the Screen*.

67. Jennifer Ringley, "JenniCam: Life, Online," 15 May 2001, <http://www.jennicam.com/j2kr/faq.html>.

68. Aimee, "FAQ," 2 Sept. 2004, <http://acamgirl.com/main.php>.

69. Amy, "Amycam Profile—Internet Conferencing," About, 5 June 2002, <http://netconference.about.com/library/cammers/blcammer041.htm>, and Mandy, "MandyCam FAQ," 25 June 2002, <http://www.mandycam.tv>.

70. Ali, "Ali-Cam Profile—Internet Conferencing," About, 5 June 2002, <http://netconference.about.com/library/cammers/blcammer091.htm>.

71. Mandy, "MandyCam FAQ," 25 June 2002, <http://www.mandycam.tv>, and Karen Ann, "Karen Ann's Moments in Time Cam Profile—Internet Conferencing," About, 26 June 2002, <http://netconference.about.com/library/cammers/blcammer076.htm>.

72. Cindy Roberts, "Cindy and Jesse Cam Profile—Internet Conferencing," About, 1 Apr. 2001, <http://netconference.about.com/internet/netconference/library/cammers/blcammer092.htm>.

73. Amy Scislowicz, "Amycam . . . Live, Fun, Free, Girl WebCam Site (The Lifecam of a Camgirl)—FAQ," 25 Mar. 2001, <http://www.theworldiknow.com/faq/faq.html>.

74. Izzi, "Izzicam Guests," 26 Mar. 2001, <http://www.izzicam.com/faqs.html>.

75. Aimee, "Aimee Live Profile—Internet Conferencing," About, 1 Apr. 2001, <http://netconference.about.com/internet/netconference/library/cammers/blcammer002.htm>.

76. Cindy Roberts, "Cindy and Jesse Cam Profile—Internet Conferencing," 1 Apr. 2001, <http://netconference.about.com/internet/netconference/library/cammers/blcammer092.htm>.

77. Foucault, *Discipline and Punish*, 202.

78. Carol Clover, *Men, Women, and Chain Saws: Gender in the Modern Horror Film* (Princeton: Princeton University Press, 1992).

79. Elektric, "ElektriCam—Live Amateur Streaming Webcam, Photo Gallery, Videos, and More!," 26 Mar. 2001, <http://www.elektricam.com/faq.html>.

80. LiveJournal, "1st Golden Goat Awards: LiveJournal," 2 Sept. 2004, <http://www.livejournal.com/users/goldengoat>.

81. About: The Human Interface, "Women Webcam Profiles," About, 1 Apr. 2001, <http://netconference.about.com/internet/netconference/library/blwcammers.htm>.

82. Jennifer Ringley, "JenniCam: Life, Online," 21 Nov. 2003, <http://www.jennicam.com/>.

83. Gwen, "Top Girls Cams," 14 Jan. 2001, <http://www.todocamaras.com/cgi-bin/topgirlscams/out.cgi?id=gwen00&url=http%3a%2f%2fgwen.webica.com>, and Mandy, "Mandy—Cam FAQ," 25 June 2002, <http://www.mandycam.tv>.

84. Amy Scislowicz, "Amycam . . . Live, Fun, Free, Girl WebCam Site (The Lifecam of a Camgirl)—FAQ," 25 Mar. 2001, <http://www.theworldiknow.com/faq/faq.html>.

85. Aimee, "A Cam Girl Dot Com, a Free Live Web Cam Site," 14 July 2004, <http://www.acam girl.com/>.

86. Ana Voog, "Anacam," 14 July 2004, <http://www.anacam.com/>.

87. Marius as quoted in "R.I.P. Jennicam," BBC News, 1 Jan. 2004, 12 July 2004, <http://news .bbc.co.uk/2/hi/uk_news/magazine/3360063.stm>.

88. Steven Shaviro, "Seen," Stranded in the Jungle, 14 July 2004, <http://www.dhalgren.com/ Stranded/29.html>.

89. Izzi, "Izzicam Guests," 9 Dec. 2000, <http://happy.izzicam.com:81/last24.html>.

90. See, for instance, Mulvey, *Visual and Other Pleasures*.

91. Sobchack, "Introduction," in *Meta-morphing*, xi–xxiii.

92. Metz, "Passion for Perceiving," in *Imaginary Signifier*, 60.

93. Burch, "Editing as a Plastic Art," in *Theory of Film Practice*, 35.

94. For a discussion of this, see Doane, *Femmes Fatales*.

95. Susan Sontag, "In Plato's Cave," in *On Photography* (New York: Penguin Books, 1977), 13.

96. Bolter, "Writing Culture," in *Writing Space*, 227.

97. Metz, "Passion for Perceiving," in *Imaginary Signifier*, 60.

98. Stam, Burgoyne, and Flitterman-Lewis, *New Vocabularies in Film Semiotics*, 160.

99. Messy, "Voyeurism," 15 July 2004, <http://www.craptabulous.com/voyeurism.html>, and Gwen, "Gwencam," Oct. 2000, <http://gwen.webica.com/cam/>.

100. Campanella, "Eden by Wire," in *Robot in the Garden*, 32, and Mike Musgrove, "Jennicam Voyeur Web Site Closing," MercuryNews.com, 1 Jan. 2004, 27 Sept. 2004, <http://www.dfw.com/ mld/ledgerenquirer/business/technology/7612474.htm?template=contentModules/emailstory .jsp&1c>.

101. Wikked, "Live: The View Out of My Monitor (20 Second Updates) Brought to You by Big Brother," 18 June 1999, <http://www.idiosyncratic.com/cam.html>.

102. CamGirls Ring, 21 Nov. 2003, <http://www.camgirlsring.com>.

103. Stam, Burgoyne, and Flitterman-Lewis, *New Vocabularies in Film Semiotics*, 160–161.

104. Aimee, "Top Girls Cams," 14 Jan. 2001, <http://www.topgirlscams.com/>, and Abalee, "Top Girls Cams," 14 Jan. 2001, <http://www.topgirlscams.com/>.

105. Mulvey, "Visual Pleasure and Narrative Cinema," in *Visual and Other Pleasures*, 19.

106. Roger Ebert, "Rear Window Is Alive on the Web: Watching Is Weird, but So Is Being Watched," *Yahoo! Internet Life*, Nov. 2000, 30 Oct. 2000, <http://www.zdnet.com/yil/stories/fea tures/0,9539,2644881,00.html>.

107. Jennifer Ringley, "JenniCam: Life, Online," 21 Nov. 2003, <http://www.jennicam.com/>.

108. Aimee, "A Cam Girl Dot Com, a Free Live Web Cam Site & More," 24 Mar. 2001, <http://members.aol.com/heyaimee/cam.html>.

109. Ana Voog, "Anacam," 14 July 2004, <http://www.anacam.com/>.

110. Alicia and Fabiana, "2Garotas Webcam Site," 24 Mar. 2001, <http://www.2garotas.com.br/2camgirls/>.

111. Doane, "Film and Masquerade," in *Femmes Fatales*, 26–27.

112. Pat Cadigan, "Icy You . . . Juicy Me," *The Register*, 3 Sept. 2001, 15 July 2004, <http://www.theregister.co.uk/content/6/17497.html>.

113. Mandy, "MandyCam FAQ," 25 June 2002, <http://www.mandycam.tv>.

114. For a discussion of Internet surveillance and the production of data images see Lyon, ed., *Surveillance as Social Sorting*.

115. Bagu, "Bagu's World Profile—Internet Conferencing," About.com, 24 Sept. 2001, <http://netconference.about.com/library/cammers/blcammer030.htm>. Obviously, men are prominently featured on top site listings of male webcam operators.

116. "Mylivewebcam.com Top 100," 10 June 2004, <http://www.mylivewebcam.com/topguys/index4.html>, and Just a Guy with a Webcam, 10 June 2004, <http://www.mancamz.net/pg/>.

117. Chris, "This Is Me," 10 June 2004, <http://christophersmall.com/MyFramePage.htm>, and NetGod's Media Network Webcam Ring, "Webring: Hub," 10 June 2004, <http://M.webring.com/hub?ring=2307>.

118. This occurs even though women post to these webcams and write about viewing in blogs and other forums.

119. Kenny, "Kennys Cam," 10 June 2004, <http://www.kennys-cam.com/main.php?location=bio.html>.

120. Chad, "Chad's Cyberspace Hangout Profile," About, 27 Sept 2001, <http://netconference.about.com/library/cammers/blcammer026.htm>.

121. Chris, "Fish Cam," 9 June 2004, <http://www.christophersmall.com/FishCam.htm>.

122. Chris, "ChristopherSmall.com," 10 June 2004, <http://christophersmall.com/main.htm>.

123. Ana Voog as quoted in Bingo Barnes, "I'll Show You Mine," *Las Vegas Weekly*, 9 Dec. 1999, 2 Sept. 2004, <http://www.lasvegasweekly.com/features/ill_show_you_mine.html>.

124. Christine Humphreys, "Meet the Star of Jennicam," ABCNews.com, 30 Oct. 2000, <http://abcnews.go.com/sections/tech/DailyNews/jennicam980422.html>.

125. Jennifer Ringley, "Reallifemacs: Jennifer Ringley," MacAddict.com, 1 Nov. 2000, 2 Nov. 2000, <http://www.macaddict.com/community/reallifemac/jenni3.shtml>.

4 The Aesthetic of Failure: Confusing Spectators with Net Art Gone Wrong

1. Jodi, *%20Wrong*, 6 Sept. 2004, <http://404.jodi.org/>; Jodi, *%20Wrong*, Rhizome, 1 Jan. 1996, 6 Sept. 2004, <http://rhizome.org/artbase/1678/wrong.html>; Peter Luining, *D-TOY 2.502.338*, Lifesavers, 9 Mar. 1999, 6 Sept. 2004, <http://www.vpro.nl/data/lifesavers/10/index.shtml>; and Michaël Samyn, *The Fire from the Sea*, Lifesavers, 26 Jan. 2000, 6 Sept. 2004, <http://www.vpro.nl/data/lifesavers/16/index.shtml>.

2. Walter Benjamin, "The Work of Art in the Age of Mechanical Reproduction," in *Illuminations*, ed. Hannah Arendt, trans. Harry Zohn (New York: Schocken Books, 1969), 217–251.

3. James A. H. Murray, Henry Bradley, W. A. Craigie, and C. T. Onions, eds., *Oxford English Dictionary*, vol. 1 (Oxford: Clarendon Press, 1961), 148.

4. xrefer, "xrefer-Aesthetic," *The Thames and Hudson Dictionary of Art Terms* (London: Thames and Hudson Ltd, 1984), 24 May 2001, <http://www.xrefer.com/entry.jsp?xrefid=647986&secid=.->.

5. Mary Devereaux, "The Philosophical Status of Aesthetics," 6 Sept. 2004, <http://www.aesthetics-online.org/ideas/devereaux.html>.

6. Sarah Worth, "Feminist Aesthetics," in *The Routledge Companion to Aesthetics*, ed. Berys Gaut and Dominic McIver Lopes (London and New York: Routledge, 2001), 437.

7. Immanuel Kant, *Critique of Judgment*, trans. J. H. Bernard (New York: Haffner Press, 1951), and Hal Foster, ed., *The Anti-aesthetic: Essays on Postmodern Culture* (Port Townsend, WA: Bay Press, 1983).

8. Not all of these lists consider net art in the same way. Josephine Bosma has argued that nettime has largely evacuated net artists from its forum and disrupted critical exchanges: "Now that nettime has chosen to mostly close the door to art, the development of net art has lost a central point for critical cross disciplinary thought from a multicultural perspective." Josephine Bosma, "Text for Moscow: Between Moderation and Extremes. The Tensions Between Net Art Theory and Popular Art Discourse," Switch 6, 1, 6 Sept. 2004, <http://switch.sjsu.edu/web/v6n1/article_b.htm>.

9. Some critics have suggested that the terms used to describe Internet artworks have political implications. Bosma argues that "replacing the term 'net art' by 'web art' causes a negligence of art history within a political and economic environment. The radical implications of net art are replaced by the much less threatening aspects of web art." Josephine Bosma, "Text for Moscow: Between Moderation and Extremes. The Tensions Between Net Art Theory and Popular Art Discourse," Switch 6, 1, 6 Sept. 2004, <http://switch.sjsu.edu/web/v6n1/article_b.htm>.

10. Brett Stalbaum also argues that it "is both productive and ironic that these sites turn to a specific historical manifestation of modernism as an escape avenue." Brett Stalbaum, "Conjuring Post-Worthlessness [excerpt]," Rhizome, 20 Aug. 1999, 6 Sept. 2004, <http://rhizome.org/object.rhiz?1543&q>.

11. Steve Dietz, "Why Have There Been No Great Net Artists?," Webwalker 28, 23 Apr. 2000, 6 Sept. 2004, <http://www.walkerart.org/gallery9/webwalker/index.html>.

12. Jay David Bolter and Richard Grusin, "Digital Art," in *Remediation: Understanding New Media* (Cambridge, MA: MIT Press, 1999), 142.

13. Alexei Shulgin and Moscow WWWArt Centre, "WWWArt Award," 6 Sept. 2004, <http://www.easylife.org/award/>.

14. Vuk Cosik and Alexei Shulgin, "Who Drew the Line?," Net Criticism, ZKP2 Proceedings, June 1996, 6 Sept. 2004, <http://www.nettime.org/desk-mirror/zkp2/theline.html>.

15. Benjamin Weil, "Untitled (äda'web)," Walker Art Center: Gallery 9, 6 Sept. 2004, <http://www.walkerart.org/gallery9/dasc/adaweb/weil.html>.

16. äda'web, "äda'web, Engage," Walker Art Center, 6 Sept. 2004, <http://adaweb.walkerart.org/home.shtml>.

17. Rhizome, "Rhizome.org Info," 22 July 2000, <http://rhizome.org/info/>. Rhizome's artbase is described as "an online archive of Internet art projects. The goal of Rhizome is to preserve Internet art projects for the future, and to provide a comprehensive resource for those who are interested in experiencing and learning more about Internet art." Rhizome, "Rhizome Artbase: The Net Art Resource," 22 July 2000, <http://rhizome.org/artbase/>.

18. See, for instance, Cyber-Kitchen, "The Cyber-kitchen," 6 Sept. 2004, <http://www.the-cyber-kitchen.com/>, and Turbulence, 6 Sept. 2004, <http://www.turbulence.org/>.

19. Rhizome, "Rhizome.org: Info—About Us," 6 June 2004, <http://rhizome.org/info/index.php>, and Gilles Deleuze and Félix Guattari, *A Thousand Plateaus: Capitalism and Schizophrenia*, trans. Brian Massumi (Minneapolis: University of Minnesota Press, 1987).

20. Mark Tribe, "Membership Fee?," Rhizome, 24 Oct. 2002, 5 June 2004, <http://rhizome.org/thread.rhiz?thread=5289&text=10852>. Rhizome also instituted a free day on Fridays. This continues the connection with traditional museums because they also offer a free evening admission—often on Fridays—to visitors.

21. See, for instance, Pall Thayer, "Rhizome, Membership Fee?," 25 Oct. 2002, 5 June 2004, <http://rhizome.org/thread.rhiz?thread=5289&text=10852>. The web-based survey that was employed to determine support of a Rhizome membership fee indicated less support than the list-based discussions. Of the 1,632 respondents between 24 October and 4 November 2002, 847 indicated that they would not pay and the rest supported varied membership fees. Mark Tribe, "Results of Membership Fee Survey," Rhizome, 4 Nov. 2002, 5 June 2004, <http://rhizome.org/thread.rhiz?thrcad=5528&text=11434>.

22. John Hopkins, "Re:, <nettime> Rhizome: Burn Rate," nettime, 21 Jan. 2003, 5 June 2004, <http://amsterdam.nettime.org/Lists-Archives/nettime-l-0301/msg00098.html>, and Vladimir Kovacevic, "Art Rhizome Critique," 11 Mar. 2003, 5 June 2004, <http://www.geocities.com/afterrhizome/AfterRhizomeCritique.htm>. Robert M. Tynes angrily declared that "your body reeks of organs" in order to suggest that Rhizome was not aligned with the politics of Deleuze and Guattari and their theories of the body without organs. Robert M. Tynes, "<nettime> Rhizome Nettime Flame," nettime, 30 Jan. 2003, 6 June 2004, <http://amsterdam.nettime.org/Lists-Archives/nettime-l-0301/msg00165.html>.

23. Rhizome is defined as "a horizontal, root-like stem that extends underground and sends out shoots to the surface." Rhizome, "Rhizome.org: Info—About Us," 6 June 2004, <http://rhizome .org/info/index.php>.

24. Peter Luining, "<nettime> Free Accessable Copy Rhizome's Artbase Now Online," nettime, 16 Jan 2003, 6 June 2004, <http://amsterdam.nettime.org/Lists-Archives/nettime-l-0301/msg00162.html>; Net.Art Connexion, 6 June 2004, <http://netartconnexion.net/>; and Peter Luining, "netartreview.net," Net Art Review, 12 Feb. 2004, 6 June 2004, <http://www.netart review.net/logs/2004_02_08_backlog.html>. This site slyly promises an engagement with Rhizome by claiming that "any resemblance to an existing database is purely coincidental!" Despite its claims, Net Art Connexions does not offer all of the links in Rhizome's artbase.

25. Rhizome, "About the New Museum of Contemporary Art," 5 June 2004, <http://rhizome .org/info/new_museum.php>.

26. t.whid, "Rhizome Needs to Drop Its Membership Fee and Free Its Content," Rhizome, 18 May 2004, June 5 2004, <http://rhizome.org/thread.rhiz?thread=13229&text=25312>. While individual artbase objects or articles can be linked, it is no longer possible to reference Rhizome with an emailed URL or to view the site without a membership. Curt Cloninger, "Rhizome Needs to Drop Its Membership Fee and Free Its Content," Rhizome, 20 May 2004, June 5 2004, <http:// rhizome.org/thread.rhiz?thread=13229&text=25351>.

27. Rob Myers, "Rhizome Needs to Drop Its Membership Fee and Free Its Content," Rhizome, 18 May 2004, 5 June 2004, <http://rhizome.org/thread.rhiz?thread=13229&text=25312>, and Edward Tang, "Rhizome Needs to Drop Its Membership Fee and Free Its Content," Rhizome, 19 May 2004, 5 June 2004, <http://rhizome.org/thread.rhiz?thread=13229&text=25328>.

28. Benjamin, "Work of Art in the Age of Mechanical Reproduction," in *Illuminations*, ed. Arendt, trans. Zohn, 221.

29. Guggenheim Museum, "Guggenheim Museum—Exhibitions—Virtual Projects," 7 Sept. 2004, <http://www.guggenheim.org/exhibitions/virtual/index.html>; San Francisco Museum of Modern Art, "SFMOMA | e.space | Main," 7 Sept. 2004, <http://www.sfmoma.org/espace/espace _overview.html>; Walker Art Center, 16 June 2003, <http://www.walkerart.org/jsindex.html>; and Whitney Museum of American Art, "Whitney ARTPORT: The Whitney Museum Portal," 7 Sept. 2004, <http://www.whitney.org/artport/>. A variety of Internet constituencies, including members of the Rhizome lists, have questioned the Walker Art Center's commitment to net art after it fired Steve Dietz, who was the Director of New Media Initiatives.

30. David Ross as quoted in Reena Jana, "David Ross: Director, San Francisco Museum of Modern Art," *Flash Art International* (Jan./Feb. 1999): 34. David Ross was director of SFMOMA from June 1998 to Aug. 2001. San Francisco Museum of Modern Art, "Museum History Overview," 7 Sept. 2004, <http://www.sfmoma.org/info/mushist_overview.asp>.

31. Luther Blissett, "0100101110101101.ORG—art.hacktivism," Rhizome, 26 June 1999, 7 Sept. 2004, <http://rhizome.org/thread.rhiz?thread=463&text=1486>.

32. For a press release from the first SFMOMA prize in May 2000, see SFMOMA, "SFMOMA Press Release," 5 Aug. 2000, <http://www.sfmoma.org/info/press/press_webby.html>.

33. SFMOMA, "SFMOMA Press Release," 14 June 2001, <http://www.sfmoma.org/info/press/press_webby.html>.

34. Art.Teleportacia, "FIRST AND THE ONLY REAL NET ART GALLERY," 7 Sept. 2004, <http://art.teleportacia.org/>.

35. Art.Teleportacia, "FAQ," 17 July 2000, <http://art.teleportacia.org/art-ie4.html> and Artcart, "Artcart—Be Avantgarde—Buy Net.art," 3 Aug. 2000, <http://artcart.de/>. Artcart offers works by Peter Luining and a number of other net artists. Artcart, "Artcart—Be Avantgarde—Buy Net.art," 7 Sept. 2004, <http://artcart.de/>.

36. Douglas Crimp, *On the Museum's Ruins* (Cambridge, MA: MIT Press, 1993), 112.

37. Artcart, "Artcart.de—Be Avantgarde—Buy Net.art," 18 July 2004, <http://www.artcart.de/index4.html>.

38. Bill Nichols, "The Work of Culture in the Age of Cybernetic Systems," *Screen* 29, 1 (Winter 1988): 23.

39. Discussions about this issue happened at a SFMOMA panel on net art and in other forums: "One of the most forward-thinking SFMOMA curators, Betsky came under fire for his 'butterfly-pinning' method of archiving websites, in which he burns them onto a CD and renders links dead. While Betsky said that the work maintains its beauty without active links, artists and new media enthusiasts in the audience expressed their discontent with giving privilege to form over function." Marisa S. Olson, "Weighing In on Net Art's Worth," Wired News, 15 May 2000, 7 Sept. 2004, <http://www.wired.com/news/culture/0,1284,36320,00.html>.

40. Art.Teleportacia, "FAQ," 9 Sept. 2000, <http://art.teleportacia.org/art-mac.html>.

41. Michaël Samyn as quoted in Art.Teleportacia, "Under Construction," 17 July 2000, <http://art.teleportacia.org/art-ie4.html>.

42. For a discussion of this issue, see Luther Blissett, "0100101110101101.ORG—art.hacktivism," Rhizome, 26 June 1999, 7 Sept. 2004, <http://rhizome.org/thread.rhiz?thread=463&text=1486>.

43. This site was a parody of Britanica.com, which offered content from the *Encyclopedia Britannica* even though "Britannica" was spelled incorrectly. 0100101110101101.org, "Britannica.com," 2 Aug. 2000, <http://www.britannica.com/bcom/original/article/0,5744,8800+2,00.html>.

44. Free On-Line Dictionary of Computing (FOLDOC), "Surfing from FOLDOC," 7 Sept. 2004, <http://foldoc.doc.ic.ac.uk/foldoc/foldoc.cgi?surfing>.

45. Landow, *Hypertext 2.0*.

46. Ibid., 118. Of course these connections are also an attempt to relate computer-based works to more canonical forms of production.

47. Crary, "Eclipse of the Spectacle," *Art after Modernism*, ed. Wallis, 290. See, for instance, Paul Virilio, *Open Sky*, trans. Julie Rose (London: Verso, 1997), and Paul Virilio, *The Lost Dimension*, trans. Daniel Moshenberg (New York: Semiotext(e), 1991).

48. Crary, "Eclipse of the Spectacle," *Art after Modernism*, ed. Wallis, 291. See, for instance, Philip K. Dick, *Do Androids Dream of Electric Sheep?* (New York: New American Library, 1968); David Cronenberg, *eXistenZ*, 1999; and David Cronenberg, *Videodrome*, 1983.

49. Cyberpunk novels that articulate this difference between mind and body include Gibson, *Neuromancer*; Neal Stephenson, *Snow Crash* (New York: Bantam Books, 1992); and Bruce Sterling, *Holy Fire: A Novel* (New York: Bantam Books, 1996).

50. Kim Cascone's article and my chapter share some of the same concerns, which include an overlap in our titles, and were originally written at about the same time. Kim Cascone, "The Aesthetics of Failure: 'Post-digital' Tendencies in Contemporary Computer Music," *Computer Music Journal* 24, 4 (Winter 2000): 12–18, 11 Sept. 2004, <http://0-lysander.ingentaselect.com .luna.wellesley.edu:80/vl=8538791/cl=14/nw=1/fm=docpdf/rpsv/cw/mitpress/01489267/v24n4/ s4/p12>.

51. For a discussion of this, see Laura U. Marks, "Video's Body, Analog and Digital," in *Touch: Sensuous Theory and Multisensory Media* (Minneapolis: University of Minnesota Press, 2002), 158.

52. Lee Bul, "Beauty and Trauma," *Art Journal* 59, 3 (Fall 2000): 106.

53. For instance, the work of James Der Derian highlights such "accidents" as "A U.S. EP-3E Aries II aircraft on a routine reconnaissance flight is in a mid-air collision with a Chinese fighter plane" and a "CIA-contracted surveillance plane [that] detects a suspicious plane flying over the Amazon and alerts the Peruvian Air Force, which shoots down a Cessna carrying not drugs but U.S. Baptist missionaries and their two children." James Der Derian, "Global Events, National Security, and Virtual Theory," in *Information, Technology, and Society: Proceedings*, Institute for Advanced Study, 8–10 June 2001, 2.

54. For a discussion of this issue, see Christine Ross, "The Insufficiency of the Performative: Video Art at the Turn of the Millenium," *Art Journal* 60, 1 (Spring 2001): 29.

55. Terry Winograd and Fernando Flores, *Understanding Computers and Cognition: A New Foundation for Design* (Reading, MA: Addison-Wesley Publishing Company, 1985), 77–78.

56. Dirk Paesmans as quoted in Josephine Bosma, "Interview with Jodi," nettime, 16 Mar. 1997, 7 Sept. 2004, <http://www.ljudmila.org/nettime/zkp4/38.htm>.

57. Eyebeam, 16 June 2003, <http://www.eyebeam.org/divisions/curatorial_jodi.html>.

58. Ibid.

59. Peter Lunenfeld, "The World Wide Web: In Search of the Telephone Opera," in *Snap to Grid: A User's Guide to Digital Arts, Media, and Cultures* (Cambridge, MA: MIT Press, 2000), 84.

60. Jodi as quoted in Tilman Baumgärtel, "Interview with Jodi," Telepolis, 10 June 1997, 7 Sept. 2004, <http://www.heise.de/tp/english/html/result.xhtml?url=/tp/english/special/ku/6187/1 .html&words=Baumgaertel>.

61. Send Coffee, "404 Error," 28 Sept. 2004, <http://www.sendcoffee.com/minorsage/404error .htm>; Jenni Ripley, "404 Research Lab," Plinko.Net, 7 Sept. 2004, <http://www.plinko.net/ 404/>; and "404 Not Found Homepage," 31 July 2000, <http://www.mindspring.com/~isixty five/404page/404.html>.

62. Moulthrop, "Error 404," in *World Wide Web and Contemporary Cultural Theory*, ed. Herman and Swiss, 261.

63. "Sarah Papesh, "sarahpapesh.com :: online portfolio :: 404," 7 Sept. 2004, <http://sarah papesh.com/404.html>.

64. Terry Harpold, "The Contingencies of the Hypertext Link," in *The New Media Reader* CD, ed. Noah Wardrip-Fruin and Nick Montfort (Cambridge, MA: MIT Press, 2003), and Terry Harpold, "The Contingencies of the Hypertext Link," 7 Sept. 2004, <http://www.newmediareader.com/ cd_samples/WOE/Harpold.html>.

65. What we read is not on the screen, under the glass, or distinctly located on the hard drive.

66. Barthes, *Pleasure of the Text*, 9.

67. Ibid., 12.

68. N. Katherine Hayles, "Virtual Bodies and Flickering Signifiers," in *How We Became Posthuman: Virtual Bodies in Cybernetics, Literature, and Informatics* (Chicago: University of Chicago Press, 1999), 30.

69. Ibid.

70. All mistyped addresses on a specific site will usually produce the same 404 message.

71. Jodi, *%20Wrong*, Rhizome, 1 Jan. 1996, 6 Sept. 2004, <http://rhizome.org/artbase/1678/ wrong.html>.

72. Jodi as quoted in Tilman Baumgärtel, "Interview with Jodi," Telepolis, 10 June 1997, 7 Sept. 2004, <http://www.heise.de/tp/english/html/result.xhtml?url=/tp/english/special/ku/6187/1 .html&words=Baumgaertel>.

73. Butler, "Force of Fantasy," *Differences*, 121.

74. Strangely, Butler's call to performativity always seems best resolved by her critical practice and repetition of texts.

75. Butler, "Force of Fantasy," *Differences*, 124n7.

76. Alex Galloway observes, "Immitators of the Jodi style abound. From Hotwired's recent RGB feature (www.hotwired.com/rgb/opp/++++++++++++++++++/) to the design group e13 (www.e13.com), from San Francisco's superbad.com to Brooklyn's experimental performance space Fakeshop (www.fakeshop.com), net art these days is taking a giant step away from print-oriented graphic design and toward an aesthetic of the machine, of code, of the crash." Alex Galloway, "Browser.art," Rhizome, 30 Jan. 1998, 7 Sept. 2004, <http://rhizome.org/ thread.rhiz?thread=43&text=1040>.

77.   Eryk Salvaggio, "Absolut Net.Art: Project Description," Rhizome, 5 Nov. 1998, 7 Sept. 2004, <http://rhizome.org/object.rhiz?1690&q>.

78.   Jodi as quoted in Tilman Baumgärtel, "Interview with Jodi," Telepolis, 10 June 1997, 7 Sept. 2004, <http://www.heise.de/tp/english/html/result.xhtml?url=/tp/english/special/ku/6187/1.html&words=Baumgaertel>.

79.   Jodi, %20Wrong, Rhizome, 1 Jan. 1996, 6 Sept. 2004.

80.   Eyebeam, 16 June 2003, <http://www.eyebeam.org/divisions/_curatorial_jodi.html>, and Peter Luining, "Peter Luining Interviewed by criticalartware," criticalartware, 7 Sept. 2004, <http://www.criticalartware.net/conversions/basichtml/pl.html>.

81.   For a discussion of originality, see Krauss, "Originality of the Avant-garde," in Originality of the Avant-garde and Other Modernist Myths, 157.

82.   Peter Luining, D-TOY 2.502.338, Lifesavers, 9 Mar. 1999, 6 Sept. 2004, <http://www.vpro.nl/data/lifesavers/10/index.shtml>.

83.   Peter Luining, "Works," 28 Sept. 2004, <http://works.ctrlaltdel.org/>.

84.   AllWords.com, "AllWords.com—Dictionary, Guide, Community and More," 14 July 2001, <http://www.allwords.com/query.php?SearchType=3&goquery=Find+it%21&Language=ENG&Keyword=morphing>.

85.   VPRO, "VPRO Aflevering," Lifesavers, 3 Sept. 2004, <http://www.vpro.nl/data/1832158/extern-aflevering.shtml?1961723>.

86.   VPRO, "VPRO Aflevering," Lifesavers, 3 Sept. 2004, <http://www.vpro.nl/data/1832158/extern-aflevering.shtml?1961723>, and Peter Luining, "Beeldvergroting: Lifesavers Gidspublicatie in gids 11, 1999," Lifesavers, 1999, 3 Sept. 2004, <http://www.vpro.nl/javascript/beeldvergroting/index.shtml?1857956>.

87.   André Malraux, "Museum without Walls," in The Voices of Silence: Man and His Art, trans. Stuart Gilbert (Garden City, NY: Doubleday, 1953), 24.

88.   Peter Luining as quoted in Josephine Bosma, "Interview with Peter Luining," Rhizome, 3 May 2000, 7 Sept. 2004, <http://rhizome.org/thread.rhiz?thread=649&text=2798>.

89.   Michaël Samyn and Auriea Harvey often work together and present multimedia works on their collaborative web site. They won the first SFMOMA Webby Prize for Excellence in Online Art in May 2000. Michaël Samyn and Auriea Harvey, "if (1+1==1) {e87=true;}," 24 Sept. 2000, <http://www.entropy8zuper.org/>; Michaël Samyn and Auriea Harvey, "If (1+1==1) {e87=true;}," 7 Sept. 2004, <http://www.entropy8zuper.org/>; and Glen Helfand, "Net Work: The SFMOMA Webby Prize and the State of Online Art," Open: The Magazine of the San Francisco Museum of Art (Fall 2000), 7 Sept. 2004, <http://www.entropy8zuper.org/godlove/closer/pop/200009_sfmoma-open.jpg>.

90.   Michaël Samyn, The Fire from the Sea, 26 Jan. 2000, 6 Sept. 2004, <http://www.vpro.nl/data/lifesavers/16/index.shtml>.

91. Stuart Moulthrop, "Traveling in the Breakdown Lane: A Principle of Resistance for Hypertext," 3 July 2004, <http://iat.ubalt.edu/moulthrop/essays/breakdown.html>, and Moulthrop, "Traveling in the Breakdown Lane," *Mosaic*.

92. Benjamin, "On Some Motifs in Baudelaire," in *Illuminations*, 155–200; Wolfgang Schivelbusch, *The Railway Journey: Trains and Travel in the 19th Century* (New York: Urizen Books, 1979), 114–133; and Tom Gunning, "An Aesthetic of Astonishment: Early Film and the (In)Credulous Spectator," in *Viewing Positions: Ways of Seeing*, ed. Linda Williams (New Brunswick, NJ: Rutgers University Press, 1995), 114–133. For a consideration of Benjamin's discussion of shock, see Miriam Hansen, "Benjamin and Cinema," in *Benjamin's Ghosts: Interventions in Contemporary Literature and Culture*, ed. Gerhard Richter (Stanford, CA: Stanford University Press, 2002), 41–73.

93. I encountered this insistence while presenting *The Fire from the Sea* to students in the classroom. This "problem" with the instructions has also produced interesting conversations.

94. Benjamin indicates that shock disintegrates aura. Benjamin, "On Some Motifs in Baudelaire," in *Illuminations*, 194.

95. Michaël Samyn and Auriea Harvey, "sixteenpages.net," *Sixteenpages*, 7 Sept. 2004, <http://sixteenpages.net/>.

96. Leo Steinberg, "Other Criteria," in *Other Criteria: Confrontations with Twentieth-century Art* (New York: Oxford University Press, 1972), 82.

97. Michaël Samyn and Auriea Harvey, "*g*c*n*c*s*i*s*," 28 Sept. 2004, <http://www.entropy8zuper.org/godlove/fuxation/>.

98. Michaël Samyn as quoted in Alex Galloway, "A Dream Come True—Interview with Michael Samyn," Rhizome, 18 Apr. 2000, 7 Sept. 2004, <http://rhizome.org/thread.rhiz?thread=643&text=1660>.

99. Michaël Samyn as quoted in fokky, "Art and Design—An Interview with Michael Samyn," Rhizome, 3 Oct. 1997, 7 Sept. 2004, <http://rhizome.org/thread.rhiz?thread=912&text=871>.

100. Michaël Samyn as quoted in Alex Galloway, "A Dream Come True—Interview with Michael Samyn," Rhizome, 18 Apr. 2000, 7 Sept. 2004, <http://rhizome.org/thread.rhiz?thread=643&text=1660>.

101. Ibid.

102. Barthes, *Camera Lucida*, 27.

103. Jennifer Ley, "Catch the Land Mine!!—Win a Free Prosthetic . . . ," *Catch the Land Mine!*, 2001, 4 Sept. 2004, <http://www.heelstone.com/banner/>.

104. My observation of people using this net artwork in lab situations suggests that engagement escalates in attempts to "win" the game. The important meaning of the texts is displaced in favor of having a more game-oriented experience.

105. Mongrel's core members are Matsuko Yokokoji, Mervin Jarman, Richard Pierre-Davis, and Graham Harwood. Mongrel, "About Mongrel," 8 Apr. 2004, <http://www.mongrelx.org/About/>.

106. Mongrel, "Natural Selection," 21 July 2004, <http://www.mongrel.org.uk/>.

107. Mongrel uses an image of a man falling from a building, which evokes Yves Klein's faked jump, to represent their *Natural Selection* search engine's lack of stability and reliability. They ask, "Who will guide me through the Internet?," Mongrel, "Project," 9 June 2004, <http://www.mongrelx.org/Project/projects.html#natural>.

108. Ross, "Insufficiency of the Performative," *Art Journal*, 33.

5 Can You Read Me? Setting-specific Meaning in Virtual Places (VP)

1. Excite stopped supporting VP on 2 Feb. 2005. Excite, "Excite Super Chat Download," 2 Feb. 2005, 10 Apr. 2005, <http://chat.excite.com/noncached/download.html>. However, a number of VP servers continue to be available. These include Halsoft (also known as VPchat) and Voodoo Chat. VPchat, "Chat Rooms—Chat Games—Avatar Chat," 10 Apr. 2005, <http://vpchat.com/>, and Voodoo Chat, "Voodoo Chat," 10 Apr. 2005, <http://www.voodoochat.com/index.php>. Since individuals continue to engage with VP, I have left the descriptions in the present tense.

2. Excite, "Excite, Inc. Builds Consumer Interaction within Channels as Part of New Community Strategy," 17 Apr. 2000, <http://www.home.net/news/excite/051297chat.html>.

3. Excite, "Excite, Inc. Builds Consumer Interaction within Channels as Part of New Community Strategy," 17 Apr. 2000, <http://www.home.net/news/excite/051297chat.html>.

4. Benjamin, "Work of Art in the Age of Mechanical Reproduction," in *Illuminations*.

5. Fans of literature, film, television shows, and other popular forms remake texts into such things as stories, images, LiveJournal icons, and video compilations. Web jewel designers produce graphic elements that other Internet producers can employ for their web sites.

6. Roland Barthes, "On Reading," in *The Rustle of Language*, trans. Richard Howard (New York: Hill and Wang, 1986), 35.

7. Elizabeth Long, "Textual Interpretation as Collective Action," in *Viewing, Reading, Listening: Audiences and Cultural Reception*, ed. Jon Cruz and Justin Lewis (Boulder: Westview Press, 1994), 192.

8. See, for instance, Norma Broude and Mary D. Garrard, eds., *The Power of Feminist Art* (New York: Harry N. Abrams, 1994), and Carol Duncan, *Civilizing Rituals: Inside Public Art Museums* (London: Routledge, 1995).

9. Roland Barthes, "The Death of the Author," in *Image/Music/Text*, trans. Stephen Heath (New York: Hill and Wang, 1977), 142–148; Barthes, *Pleasure of the Text*; Barthes, *S/Z*; Umberto Eco, *The Open Work* (Cambridge, MA: Harvard University Press, 1989); and Michel Foucault, "What Is an Author?," in *The Art of Art History: A Critical Anthology*, ed. Donald Preziosi (Oxford: Oxford University Press, 1998), 299–314.

10. Camille Bacon-Smith, *Science Fiction Culture* (Philadelphia: University of Pennsylvania Press, 2000); Coombe, *Cultural Life of Intellectual Properties*; Henry Jenkins, "Interactive Audiences? The 'Collective Intelligence' of Media Fans," in *The New Media Book*, ed. Dan Harries (London: BFI Publishing, 2002), 157–170; Jenkins, *Textual Poachers*; and Constance Penley, "Brownian Motion," in *Technoculture*, ed. Penley and Ross, 135–162.

11. Bolter, *Writing Space*; Landow, *Hypertext 2.0*; and George P. Landow, *Hypertext: The Convergence of Contemporary Critical Theory and Technology* (Baltimore, MD: Johns Hopkins University Press, 1992).

12. Jenkins, "Interactive Audiences?," in *New Media Book*, ed. Harries, 167.

13. Landow, "Hypertext and Critical Theory," in *Hypertext*, 2.

14. Hartsock, "Foucault on Power," in *Feminism/Postmodernism*, ed. Nicholson; Minh-ha, "No Master Territories," in *Post-colonial Studies Reader*, ed. Ashcroft, Griffiths, and Tiffin; Said, *Orientalism*; and Sedgwick, *Epistemology of the Closet*.

15. Bruce Damer, "Virtual Places: Cruisin' the Web Cosmos," in *Avatars! Exploring and Building Virtual Worlds on the Internet* (Berkeley, CA: Peach Pit Press, 1998), 239.

16. Excite, "Excite Super Chat," 23 July 2004, <http://chat.excite.com/noncached/frameset.html>.

17. VPchat, "Chat Rooms—Chat Games—Avatar Chat," 10 Apr. 2005, <http://vpchat.com/>, and Voodoo Chat, "Voodoo Chat," 10 Apr. 2005, <http://www.voodoochat.com/index.php>.

18. This size is further decreased by banner advertisements.

19. Since the server database supports information about avatars, a spectator who is logged into the Halsoft setting will only be able to see and communicate with others using the Halsoft software. Other VP spectators remain invisible and unavailable even if they are looking at the same URL.

20. NetLingo, "NetLingo: The Internet Language Dictionary," 7 Sept. 2004, <http://www.netlingo.com/lookup.cfm?term=avatar>; Learn the Net: An Internet Guide and Tutorial, "Learn the Net: Glossary: Avatar," 7 Sept. 2004, <http://www.learnthenet.com/english/glossary/avatar.htm>; and Webopedia, "What Is Avatar?," 7 Sept. 2004, <http://www.pcwebopaedia.com/TERM/a/avatar.html>.

21. Vpchat, "Virtual Places Chat—Avatars and Gestures," 7 Sept. 2004, <http://www.vpchat.com/avatars_and_gestures>.

22. Delphica, "VP Nicknames . . . What's in a Name?," VP on the Wire, 12 Oct. 2000, 18 Oct. 2000, <http://vpwire.vdirect.com/>.

23. For instance, a site that offers avatars for spectators to download indicates that the "avatars found on this site live here . . . this is their home." VPChat, "!VPChat: Avatar Shoppe: 2400 Avatars & Gestures!," 14 Apr. 2000, <http://www.vpchat.com/avatars/index.html>.

24. See, for instance, Allucquère Roseanne Stone, "Virtual Systems," in *Incorporations*, ed. Jonathan Crary and Sanford Kwinter (New York: Zone Books, 1992), 608–621, and Turkle, *Life on the Screen*.

25. Shannon McRae, "Coming Apart at the Seams: Sex, Text and the Virtual Body," in *Wired Women: Gender and New Realities in Cyberspace*, ed. Lynn Cherny and Elizabeth Reba Weise (Washington: Seal Press, 1996), and Shannon McRae, "Coming Apart at the Seams: Sex, Text and the Virtual Body," 7 Sept. 2004, <http://www.usyd.edu.au/su/social/papers/mcrae.html>.

26. See, for instance, Diana Fuss, "Fashion and the Homospectatorial Look," in *Identities*, ed. Kwame Anthony Appiah and Henry Louis Gates, Jr. (Chicago: University of Chicago Press, 1995), 90–114; Marjorie Garber, *Vested Interests: Cross-dressing and Cultural Anxiety* (New York: Routledge, 1992); and Linda Hutcheon, "Postmodernism and Feminisms," in *Postmodern Debates*, ed. Simon Malpas (New York: Palgrave, 2001), 101–109.

27. Allword.com, "Allwords.com—Dictionary, Guide, Community and More," 7 Sept. 2004, <http://www.allwords.com/query.php?SearchType=3&goquery=Find+it%21&Language=ENG& Keyword=avatar>. A connection between religious manifestations and virtual settings is established in a number of the classic cyberpunk books. In Gibson's *Neuromancer*, as well as a number of his other works, noncorporeal godlike entities inhabit the Internet setting. In Stephenson's *Snow Crash*, religious texts and software change the ways that such "systems" as brains and computers function. Gibson, *Neuromancer*, and Stephenson, *Snow Crash*.

28. Stephenson, *Snow Crash*, 35–36.

29. Ibid., 220.

30. The articulation of an inside and outside also renders the Internet as space.

31. Bruce Damer, "Bibliographies and Articles," 7 Sept. 2004, <http://www.digitalspace.com/ avatars/book/chtu/biblio.htm>. This also suggests that spectators have a "calling" and that their participation in the network is productive rather than a waste of time. However, the full ramifications of this new "light" or awareness remain unclear.

32. Stephenson, *Snow Crash*, 470.

33. Stephenson, *Snow Crash*, 470, and Free On-Line Dictionary of Computing (FOLDOC), "Habitat from FOLDOC," 7 Sept. 2004, <http://foldoc.doc.ic.ac.uk/foldoc/foldoc.cgi?Habitat>.

34. Poul Anderson, *The Avatar* (New York: Berkley-Putnam, 1978). Anderson uses the term "avatar" to describe constructed individuals that provide information about species to higher beings.

35. AV Creations provides a list of well over five hundred paint shops and other VP-related sites. AV Creations, "AV Creations Top 500," 28 July 2000, <http://seedesigns.com/avc/top100/ pages/topsites.html>.

36. See, for instance, VP Designer Choice Awards, 28 July 2000, <http://www.geocities.com/ SiliconValley/Drive/2472/>.

37. Hey Baby Grafx, "Hbgrafx Paintshop," 27 Sept. 2002, <http://h-b-grfx.net/>.

38. Image Reflections, "Mega Avatars & Painting by Image Reflections," 17 Apr. 2000, <http://www.geocities.com/SouthBeach/Lounge/4778/Image_Reflections/IRMain.htm>.

39. VP Essentials, "—[VP Essentials]—," 22 July 2004, <http://vpessentials.cjb.net/>.

40. Society of Gesture Makers, "Society of Gesture Makers—Member's Avatar Sites," 7 Sept. 2004, <http://www.geocities.com/SouthBeach/Palms/5456/avatars.html>.

41. Pollock, "Feminist Interventions," in *Vision and Difference*, 3. There are some differences in the ways that traditional art and VP are understood. Pollock notes that the artwork "goes from its private place of creation" into the public sphere. Avatar production is conceptualized as a more public arena.

42. Av Illusionz, 6 Mar. 2002, <http://avillusionz.cjb.net/>.

43. Linda Nochlin, "Women, Art, and Power," in *Women, Art, and Power and Other Essays* (New York: Harper & Row, 1984), 153.

44. Coombe, "Introduction," in *Cultural Life of Intellectual Properties*, 6.

45. Peter Jaszi, "On the Author Effect: Contemporary Copyright and Collective Creativity," in *The Construction of Authorship: Textual Appropriation in Law and Literature*, ed. Martha Woodmansee and Peter Jaszi (Durham, NC: Duke University Press, 1994), 40. Such music trading systems as Napster and Nutella are another example of property and copyright problems that have occurred because of the wide-scale availability of information through the Internet. However, musicians usually retain their individual authorship with MP3s. What has not remained under the artists' and labels' control is the ability to gain a profit from the sale of these works.

46. Ink, "Vivid Ink," 8 Mar. 2002, <http://www.vivid-ink.vze.com/>.

47. The Crackhouse," 13 Dec. 2000, <http://www.geocities.com/thecrackh0use/>, and The Crackhouse, 27 July 2004, <http://crackhouse.noparanoia.org/>.

48. _NNNuts_, "Excite Chat—[Excite Talk!: The Crackhouse]," 13 Dec. 2000, <http://www.geocities.com/thecrackh0use/>.

49. Bruce Ziff and Pratima V. Rao, "Introduction to Cultural Appropriation: A Framework," in *Borrowed Power: Essays on Cultural Appropriation*, ed. Bruce Ziff and Pratima V. Rao (New Brunswick, NJ: Rutgers University Press, 1997), 3.

50. Landow, "The Politics of Hypertext," in *Hypertext 2.0*, 300.

51. ...ThunderCat_22..., "VP Tattoo Paintshop and Avatars," 31 Jan. 2001, <http://www.geocities.com/tc_creations2000/VP>.

52. Vplaces, 20 June 2003, <www.vplaces.net/help/rules.htm>.

53. Silent Lucidity's Avatars, 28 July 2000, <http://www.geocities.com/slucidityavs/index.html>.

54. Eternal.Goku, "Excite Chat—[Excite Talk!: http://www.angelfire.com/yt2/sinn/index.html]," 2 Nov. 2000, <http://www.angelfire.com/yt2/sinn/index.html>.

55. Dramatic Expressions, "Dramatic Expressions (PaintShop Plus)," 3 Oct. 2000, <http://jodee01.tripod.com/DE-TOS.html>.

56. Callisto, "Realm of Virtual Dreams—Original Avatars & More," 30 June 2000, 3 Oct. 2002, <http://www.fortunecity.com/rivendell/rhydin/437/vp.htm>.

57. VPChat, "!VPChat: Avatar Shoppe: 2400 Avatars & Gestures!," 14 Apr. 2000, <http://www.vpchat.com/avatars/index.html>.

58. .::Erotic-BDsM::., 27 Sept. 2002, <http://www.erotic-bdsm.net/Avatars.html>, and VooDoo & Friends, 27 Sept. 2002, <http://www.angelfire.com/art2/lilvoodooavatars/index.html>.

59. "Xtreme Grafix Contest," Xtreme Grafix Paintshop, 1 Oct. 2002, <http://xtreme-grafix.net/contest.html>.

60. .::Erotic-BDsM::., 27 Sept. 2002, <http://www.erotic-bdsm.net/Avatars.html>.

61. Stanley Cavell, "Photograph and Screen," in *The World Viewed: Reflections on the Ontology of Film* (New York: The Viking Press, 1971), 24.

62. Society of Gesture Makers, "Society of Gesture Makers—Black List," 7 Sept. 2004, <http://www.geocities.com/SouthBeach/Palms/5456/banned.html>.

63. Wicked Creations, "Wicked Creations by _.MaNiC._ and _.WingZ.," 28 July 2000, <http://highintensitygraphics.com/wc/avlink.html>.

64. Silent Lucidity, "Silent Lucidity Avatars," 7 Sept. 2004, <http://www.geocities.com/slucidityavs/menu.html>.

65. Swooz, "Re:Re:An Avatar Thief? Why yes! I Am!," 26 July 2000, 3 Oct. 2000, <http://vpwire.vdirect.com/>.

66. .::Erotic-BDsM::., 27 Sept. 2002, <http://www.erotic-bdsm.net/Avatars.html>.

67. The Avatar Factory, "The Avatar Factory—VP Avatars—Megaheads—Gestures—Painters," 14 Apr. 2000, <http://www.theavatarfactory.com/>.

68. Shadow-Wolf, "Shadow-Wolfs Avatar Gallery," 31 Jan. 2001, <http://i_shadow_wolf_i.tripod.com/index.html>.

69. The Crackhouse, 9 Jan. 2001, <http://www.geocities.com/thecrackh0use/>.

70. Lil.voodoo, "Voodoo's Profile," Voodoo & Friends Paintshop, 3 Oct. 2002, <http://www.angelfire.com/art2/lilvoodooavatars/voodoosProfileGallery.html>.

71. Image Reflections, "Mega Avatars & Painting by Image Reflections," 30 Jan. 2001, <http://www.geocities.com/SouthBeach/Lounge/4778/Image_Reflections/IRMain.htm>, and Q's Avatar Shoppe, "VPChat: Avatar Shoppe: 2400 Avatars & Gestures!," 30 Jan. 2001, <http://www.vpchat.com/avatars/index.html>.

72. Xtreme Grafix Paintshop, "Xtreme Grafix Contest," 1 Oct. 2002, <http://xtreme -grafix.net/contest.html>.

73. Ibid.

74. poor.lady, "Excite Chat—[Excite Talk!: Ing's AV and Gesture Links—Over 2100 Links!!!]," 13 Mar. 2001, <members.aol.com/cowtowning/AVlinks.htm>.

75. Man, "Does An Avatar Define Someone?," VP on the Wire, 9 Nov. 2000, 27 Nov. 2000, <http://www.vpwire.com/>.

76. Blue Rhino Avatars, 8 Aug. 2002, 3 Oct. 2002, <http://avatars0plenty.tripod.com/>.

77. Sen, "Image," 27 Sept. 2002, <http://www.geocities.com/image_reflections/>.

78. Duncan, "The Modern Art Museum," in *Civilizing Rituals*, 108.

79. xX_Ms_Mike T.., "Excite Chat—[Excite Talk!: Doc's Av and Gesture Retreat]," 28 Nov. 2000, <http://members.aol.com/Docsexty9/Home/Home.html>.

80. XxX_Golden_XxX, "Excite Chat—[Excite Talk!: Doc's Av and Gesture Retreat]," 28 Nov. 2000, <http://members.aol.com/Docsexty9/Home/Home.html>.

81. Southern, "Excite Chat—[Excite Talk!: Doc's Av and Gesture Retreat]," 28 Nov. 2000, <http://members.aol.com/Docsexty9/Home/Home.html>.

82. UniQue Avatars, "UniQue Avatars: 2200+ Handcrafted Avatars," 30 Jan. 2001, <http://www .vpchat.com/unique/index.html>.

83. Pixelbox, 1 Oct. 2002, <http://pixelbox.interfaceconcepts.net/>.

84. Q's Avatar Shoppe, "VPChat: Avatar Shoppe: 2400 Avatars & Gestures!," 30 Jan. 2001, <http://www.vpchat.com/avatars/index.html>.

85. Landow, "Hypertext: An Introduction," in *Hypertext 2.0*, 22. Such celebratory announce-ments about the political possibilities of hypertext predate the availability of web-based hyper-texts. However, Landow and Bolter have more recently described the Internet and the web as active settings that also challenge originality and traditional ideas about authorship.

86. Bolter, "Preface," in *Writing Space*, x.

87. Bolter, "Introduction," in *Writing Space*, 3.

88. Landow indicates that "electronic text processing changes, to varying degrees, all aspects of the text that had made conceptions of authorial property practicable and even possible." Landow, "Politics of Hypertext," in *Hypertext 2.0*, 302.

89. Bacon-Smith, "Introduction," in *Science Fiction Culture*, 5.

90. Jenkins notes that many "significant science fiction writers emerged from fandom." Jenkins, "Interactive Audiences?," in *New Media Book*, ed. Harries, 159.

91. Jenkins, "In My Weekend-only World," in *Textual Poachers*, 278.

92. Jenkins, "Interactive Audiences?," in *New Media Book*, ed. Harries, 158.

93. Penley, "Brownian Motion," in *Technoculture*, ed. Penley and Ross, 139.

94. Charles Ess, "The Political Computer: Hypertext, Democracy, and Habermas," in *Hyper/Text/Theory*, ed. George P. Landow (Baltimore, MD: Johns Hopkins University Press, 1994), 225–267, and Martin E. Rosenberg, "Physics and Hypertext: Liberation and Complicity in Art and Pedagogy," in *Hyper/Text/Theory*, ed. Landow, 268–298.

95. Aarseth, "Introduction," in *Cybertext*, 14.

96. Andrea MacDonald, "Uncertain Utopia: Science Fiction Media Fandom & Computer Mediated Communication," in *Theorizing Fandom: Fans, Subculture, and Identity*, ed. Cheryl Harris (Cresskill, NJ: Hampton Press, 1998), 150.

97. Ibid.

98. George P. Landow, "Hypertext and Critical Theory," in *Hypertext*, 3.

99. "Let us first posit the image of a triumphant plural, unimpoverished by any constraint of representation (of imitation). In this ideal text, the networks are many and interact, without any one of them being able to surpass the rest; this text is a galaxy of signifiers, not a structure of signifieds; it has no beginning; it is reversible; we gain access to it by several entrances, none of which can be authoritatively declared to be the main one; the codes it mobilizes extend *as far as the eye can reach*, they are indeterminable (meaning here is never subject to a principle of determination, unless by throwing dice); the systems of meaning can take over this absolutely plural text." Barthes, *S/Z*, 5.

100. Stam, Burgoyne, and Flitterman-Lewis, *New Vocabularies in Film Semiotics*, 192.

101. Barthes, "On Reading," in *Rustle of Language*, trans. Richard Howard, 42.

102. Coombe, "Author(iz)ing the Celebrity," in *Cultural Life of Intellectual Properties*, 125.

103. Barthes, "Death of the Author," in *Image/Music/Text*, 142–148.

104. Broude and Garrard, "Introduction: The Expanding Discourse," in *Expanding Discourse*, ed. Broude and Garrard, 4.

105. Broude and Garrard also note that part of this effort came from early feminism, which was then absorbed into the postmodern project. Broude and Garrard, "Introduction," in *Expanding Discourse*, ed. Broude and Garrard, 17.

106. VP Headquarters, 3 Oct. 2002, <http://go.to/vpheadquarters>.

107. Griselda Pollock, *Avant-garde Gambits, 1883–1893: Gender and the Color of Art History* (London: Thames and Hudson, 1992), 8.

108. Broude and Garrard, "Introduction: Feminism and Art," in *Power of Feminist Art*, ed. Broude and Garrard, 16.

109. Guerilla Girls, "Does MOMA Really Know Best?," Postcard, 1997, 7 Sept. 2004, <http://www.guerrillagirls.com/posters/moma_card.html>.

110. Image Reflections, "Mega Avatars & Painting by Image Reflections," 4 July 2003, <http://www.geocities.com/SouthBeach/Lounge/4778/Image_Reflections/IRMain.htm>.

111. Krauss, "Originality of the Avant-garde," in *Originality of the Avant-garde and Other Modernist Myths*, 160.

112. Gonzalez, "Appended Subject," in *Race in Cyberspace*, ed. Kolko, Nakamura, and Rodman, 46.

113. A discussion of such binaries appears in Pollock, *Vision and Difference*.

114. Guerilla Girls, "Do Women Have to Be Naked to Get into the Met. Museum?," 1985–1989, 7 Sept. 2004, <http://www.guerrillagirls.com/posters/naked.html>.

115. There are some interesting exceptions to the limited depictions of bodies that appear on most sites. For instance, representations of erotic women are still a predominant feature, but Romany offers a range of "Full Bodied Avatars." The women appear to be of different sizes and ages. Romany, "AVATARS: Romany's Realm of Avatars for Virtual Places," 15 Apr. 2000, <http://www.fortunecity.com/westwood/blumarine/271/avatars/frames/specialtywear/bbw1.html>.

116. Nochlin "Women, Art, and Power," in *Women, Art, and Power and Other Essays*.

117. Kreations Unlimited, 27 Sept. 2002, <http://www.kreations-unlimited.com/>, and .::Erotic-BDsM::.., 27 Sept. 2002, <http://www.erotic-bdsm.net/Avatars.html>.

118. Todd Beaulieu, "Somatics Newest Delusion Paint Shop/1400+ Megas (Avatars, Gestures, Skins Are Available)," 17 Apr. 2000, <http://www.geocities.com/Hollywood/Boulevard/4759/index2.html>.

119. The reading of erotic male avatars as "gay" is an exception to this.

120. Anne Fausto-Sterling, *Sexing the Body: Gender Politics and the Construction of Sexuality* (New York: Basic Books, 2000).

121. For a discussion of this, see Suzanne J. Kessler and Wendy McKenna, *Gender: An Ethnomethodological Approach* (Chicago: University of Chicago Press, 1978).

122. The work of Fausto-Sterling and Butler suggests that embodied sex is also constructed through such things as scientific discourse. However, neither of them fully addresses the implications of this to the sex and gender system as it is currently theorized. Fausto-Sterling, *Sexing the Body*, and Butler, *Bodies that Matter*.

123. For a discussion of the ways women view these images, see Fuss, "Fashion and the Homospectorial Look," in *Identities*, ed. Appiah and Gates,

124. X_DAG_X , "Excite Chat—[Excite Talk!: East Coast (U.S.)]," 25 Oct. 2000, <http://talk.excite.com/chat/rooms/regional/eastcoast.html>, and Biggy71 "Excite Chat—[Excite Talk!: East Coast (U.S.)]," 25 Oct. 2000, <http://talk.excite.com/chat/rooms/regional/eastcoast.html>.

125. Punky, "So You Wanna Be a Cyberstud . . . ," The Black Hand, 18 Oct. 2000, <http://www.theblackhand.net/vp/>.

126. Slash is a term that derives from the "/" that is used to articulate the erotic pairings. There are an ever increasing number of slash pairings. Slash pairings include K/S (Kirk and Spock from *Star Trek*), Spike/Xander (from *Buffy the Vampire Slayer*), and Pacey/Jack (from *Dawson's Creek*).

127. LQQK_, "Excite Chat—[Excite Talk!: http://talk.excite.com/chat/rooms/regional/east coast.html 2]," 17 Oct. 2000, <http://talk.excite.com/chat/rooms/regional/eastcoast.html>.

128. Cyberfemme, "look ~Cyberfemme," LambdaMOO, 20 Sept. 2001, <telnet://lambda.moo.mud.org: 8888>.

129. _guest7827, "House & Garden Chat," 19 Apr. 2000, <http://talk.excite.com/channel/lifestyle/home_garden.html>.

130. Henry Jenkins discusses the different ways fans read texts. However, he does not provide a consideration of how such regulated meaning making and gate keeping might affect the collaborative authorial communities that he describes. Jenkins, "Layers of Meaning," in *Textual Poachers*, 238.

131. Wikipedia, "Leet—Wikipedia," 7 Sept. 2004, <http://www.wikipedia.org/wiki/Leet>.

132. Netlingo Dictionary of Internet Words," Netlingo, 7 Sept. 2004, <http://www.netlingo.com/lookup.cfm?term=newbie>.

133. Michel Foucault, "Two Lectures," in *Power/Knowledge: Selected Interviews and Other Writing*, ed. Colin Gordon (New York: Pantheon Books, 1980).

134. Said, *Orientalism*.

135. Hartsock, "Foucault on Power," in *Feminism/Postmodernism*, ed. Nicholson, 161.

136. Minh-ha, "No Master Territories," in *Post-colonial Studies Reader*, ed. Ashcroft, Griffiths, and Tiffin, 215.

137. Moyra, "The Golden Rule," 21 July 2000, <http://moyra.com/jewels/eleventh.html>.

138. Moyra, "Home," 29 July 2004, <http://moyra.com/jewels/eleventh.html>.

139. The Museum of Counter Art, "The Museum of Counter Art: Digits and Numbers," 5 Mar. 2004, 29 July 2004, <http://www.counterart.com/hiband/index.html>.

140. See, for instance, Maurine, "Friend's Call Me Silvercloud," 14 Mar. 2003, 7 Sept. 2004, <http://silvercloud30.tripod.com/main/index1.html>.

141. There is a web ring of these designers. "Designing Women: Jewels of the Web Webring Page," 22 July 2000, <http://homepages.go.com/~nsartring/index.html>. A number of these artists include a set of rules on their pages. See Writergirl, "CelticHeart Creations," 7 Sept. 2004, <http://www.writergirlscorner.com/CelticHeartCreations/index.html>, and Silver's Place, 30 July 2000, <http://www.cometosilver.com/please.html>.

142. Maurine, "Friend's Call Me Silvercloud," 14 Mar. 2003, 7 Sept. 2004, <http://silvercloud30 .tripod.com/main/index1.html>; Alison Beamon, "Terms of Use," 20 Nov. 2003, 29 July 2004, <http://www.alisonbeamon.com/terms.html>; Ann, "Ann's Whimsical Web Sets," 15 July 2004, 29 July 2004, <http://annswhim.topcities.com/>; and Backgrounds by Marie, "Terms of Use for Backgrounds by Marie," 29 July 2004, <http://www.artistic-designers.com/bkgds/tos.html>.

143. Silver's Place, 30 July 2000, <http://www.cometosilver.com>.

144. Vids are fan-produced works. The vidder selects and then edits a series of clips from a film or television show to accompany a song. The intent is to use the music, lyrics, and new editing in order to render a different narrative scenario, which sometimes includes creating new sexual relationships between same sex characters. Vids used to be and sometimes still are viewed on videotape. They are now also available through fan web sites.

145. Miz Jain, "ACCESSDENIED: MAIN HQ," 29 July 2003, <http://denied.mizjain.org/>. A statement about vidding theft is available at Fade to Black, "~* Mission *~," 7 Sept. 2004, <http:// www.dreamvision-entertainment.com/videoelite/fadetoblack.html>.

146. Miz Jain, "ACCESSDENIED: The MISSION—What Are We Doing?," 29 July 2003, <http:// denied.mizjain.org/mission.html>.

147. Some participants use sophisticated literature and concepts about cultural borrowing, which include a familiarity with Jenkins and other academic works, to justify their practices. For instance, elynross suggests that it is inappropriate to talk about edited works as theft because such practices have always been an aspect of art production. She indicates that the "little people who dismiss vidding" are unaware of the culture of "fannish vidding" and the "aspects of artistic creation involving montages and collages and pop art." elynross, "This is only tangentially about Gray Day," 6 May 2003, 24 May 2003, <http://www.livejournal.com/talkread.bml?journal=elynross&itemid=31632>.

148. sisabet, "Sisabet's Journal," LiveJournal, 30 Apr. 2003, 7 Sept. 2004, <http://www .livejournal.com/users/sisabet/2003/04/30/>.

149. taraljc, "My (ljc's) Other Little Corner," LiveJournal, 4 May 2003, 7 Sept. 2004, <http:// www.livejournal.com/users/taraljc/2003/05/04/>.

150. catscradle, "The Bratqueen: One Last Rant," LiveJournal, 1 Aug. 2002, 7 Sept. 2004, <http://www.livejournal.com/talkread.bml?journal=thebratqueen&itemid=92590>. There are exceptions to this fan culture scorning of money. Some fan artists sell their works at auctions and other events.

151. lunaris argues that there is "honor among thieves" because they "steal from the rich originators and give to the poor fen what the originators can't or won't." lunaris, "Vox Lunaris— Becky's Live Journal," LiveJournal, 1 May 2003, 7 Sept. 2004, <http://www.livejournal.com/users/ lunaris_/2003/05/01/>.

152. sockkpuppett, "Nothing but Blues and Elvis," LiveJournal, 29 Apr. 2003, 7 Sept. 2004, <http://www.livejournal.com/users/sockkpuppett/2003/04/29/>.

153. kita0610, "kita0610: Don't Fuck with the Headtilt, Man," LiveJournal, 29 Apr. 2003, 7 Sept. 2004, <http://www.livejournal.com/talkread.bml?journal=kita0610&itemid=62291>.

154. Shoshana Green, Cynthia Jenkins, and Henry Jenkins, "Normal Female Interest in Men Bonking: Selections from *The Terra Nostra Underground* and *Strange Bedfellows*," in *Theorizing Fandom*, ed. Harris, 9–40.

6 This Is Not Photography, This Is Not a Cohesive View: Computer-facilitated Imaging and Fragmented Spectatorship

1. The work of Carol Selter and Susan Silton is available at "UCR/CMP: Scanner as Camera," California Museum of Photography, 1998, 18 Aug. 2004, <http://www.cmp.ucr.edu/site/exhibitions/scanner2/>, and Ken Gonzales-Day at "Ken Gonzales-Day: On-line Portfolio," 18 Aug. 2004, <http://homepage.mac.com/kengonzalesday/Menu16.html>.

2. Photographers who underscore the constructed aspects of photographs include James Casabere, Cindy Sherman, and Laurie Simmons. There are also critical writings on this issue by such authors as Crimp, *On the Museum's Ruins*; Rosalind Krauss, *L'Amour Fou: Photography and Surrealism* (New York: Abbeville Press, 1985); Abigail Solomon-Godeau, "Representing Women: The Politics of Self-representation," in *Reframings: New American Feminist Photographies*, ed. Diane Neumaier (Philadelphia: Temple University Press, 1995), 296–310; Solomon-Godeau, *Photography at the Dock*; and Owens, "Discourse of Others," in *Anti-aesthetic*, ed. Foster, 57–82.

3. Anne-Marie Willis, "Digitisation and the Living Death of Photography," in *Culture, Technology, and Creativity in the Late Twentieth Century*, ed. Philip Hayward (London: John Libbey, 1990), 197–208, and William J. Mitchell, *The Reconfigured Eye: Visual Truth in the Post-photographic Era* (Cambridge, MA: MIT Press, 1992).

4. Of course, it is possible that the visibly constructed aspects of these works will be ignored. Spectators may continue to read Selter's images as access onto a hyperreal view of live and moving animal bodies and Gonzales-Day's works as diagrams of skin. One reason that there is not more writing about the ways that technologies produce spectators and representations, although certainly there has been a burgeoning of literature in "Internet studies" and "computer-mediated communication," is that spectators are encouraged to ignore the technologies.

5. Barthes, *Camera Lucida*; Barthes, *Roland Barthes by Roland Barthes*; and Sobchack, ed., *Metamorphing*.

6. Steinberg, "Other Criteria," in *Other Criteria*, 81.

7. Annette Kuhn, "Remembrance," in *Illuminations: Women Writing on Photography from the 1850s to the Present*, ed. Liz Heron and Val Williams (Durham: Duke University Press, 1996), 475.

8. Shawn Michelle Smith considers how photographic conventions, such as the baby portrait, produce very rigid conceptions of family. She indicates that at the turn of the century, such images followed a set of conventions and resonate "uncannily with the scientific fervor with which eugenicists stockpiled and studied child photographs." Shawn Michelle Smith, *American Archives: Gender, Race, and Class in Visual Culture* (Princeton, NJ: Princeton University Press, 1999), 9.

9. Baudry, "Ideological Effects," in *Narrative, Apparatus, Ideology*, ed. Rosen, 286–298. The camera obscura has been identified as a precursor to photography in varied histories of these optical technologies. See, for instance, Robert Hirsch, *Seizing the Light: A History of Photography* (Boston: McGraw Hill, 2000), 3–5; Beaumont Newhall, *The History of Photography: From 1839 to the Present Day*, 4th ed. (New York: Museum of Modern Art, 1981), 11; Naomi Rosenblum, *A World History of Photography*, 3rd ed. (New York: Abbeville Press, 1997), 15, 17; and Liz Wells, ed., *Photography: A Critical Introduction* (London: Routledge, 1997), 13.

10. André Bazin, *What Is Cinema?*, trans. Hugh Gray (Berkeley: University of California Press, 1967); Baudry, "Ideological Effects," in *Narrative, Apparatus, Ideology*, ed. Rosen, 286–298; and Siegfried Kracauer, "Basic Concepts," in *Theory of Film: The Redemption of Physical Reality* (London: Oxford University Press, 1976), 27.

11. Jacqueline Rose, "The Cinematic Apparatus: Problems in Current Theory," in *The Cinematic Apparatus*, ed. Teresa de Lauretis and Stephen Heath (New York: St. Martin's Press, 1985), 175, and Christian Metz, "Photography and Fetish," *October* 34 (Fall 1985): 82.

12. Laura Mulvey, "The 'Pensive Spectator' Revisited: Time and Its Passing in the Still and Moving Image," in *Where Is the Photograph?*, ed. David Green (Brighton: Photoforum and Photoworks, 2003), 113–122.

13. There are problems with the general apparatus model of spectatorship, which include the ahistoricity of the approach, the generalized links between vastly different experiences that are presumed by the psychoanalytic perspective, the resistance to imagining the ways that spectators move, and the denial of tactile engagements as part of the experience. Linda Williams suggests that there are "bodily-sensations produced by the image-machine" that are not addressed in apparatus theory. Linda Williams, "Corporealized Observers: Visual Pornographies and the 'Carnal Density of Vision,'" in *Fugitive Images: From Photography to Video*, ed. Patrice Petro (Bloomington: Indiana University Press, 1995), 14. I will address an erotic of viewing in the afterword to this book. Crary also proposes an alternative model of spectatorship than that proposed by apparatus theorists. He argues that these "developments have been presented as part of a continuous unfolding of a Renaissance-based mode of vision in which photography, and eventually cinema, are simply later instances of an ongoing deployment of perspectival space and perception." Jonathan Crary, "Modernity and the Problem of the Observer," in *Techniques of the Observer: On Vision and Modernity in the Nineteenth Century* (Cambridge, MA: MIT Press, 1991), 4. His concept that "nineteenth-century optical devices . . . involved arrangements of bodies in space, regulations of activity, and the deployment of individual bodies, which codified and normalized the observer within rigidly defined systems of visual consumption" relates to my reading of the photography spectator's culturally enforced engagement with the image. However, I disagree with his claim that the "guarantees of authority, identity, and universality supplied by the camera obscura are of another epoch." Crary, 18, 24. This position is still available to "appropriately" sexed, gendered, aged, and classed spectators who agree to the cultural production of certain categories and to address the image in specific ways.

14. Baudry, "Ideological Effects," in *Narrative, Apparatus, Ideology*, ed. Rosen, 289.

15. Metz, "Identification, Mirror," in *Imaginary Signifier*, 51.

16. Metz, "Identification with the Camera," in *Imaginary Signifier*, 49.

17. For a discussion of the identificatory positions offered by Hannah Höch's work, see Maud Lavin, "Androgyny and Spectatorship," in *Cut with the Kitchen Knife: The Weimar Photomontages of Hannah Höch* (New Haven: Yale University Press, 1993), 185–204.

18. Michael Fried, *Absorption and Theatricality: Painting and Beholder in the Age of Diderot* (Berkeley: University of California Press, 1980), and Michael Fried, *Courbet's Realism* (Chicago: University of Chicago Press, 1990). It is worth noting that Stanley Cavell employed Fried's theories in his work on film and art. Cavell, "Preface," in *World Viewed*, xv.

19. Teresa de Lauretis, "Through the Looking Glass," in *Narrative, Apparatus, Ideology*, ed. Rosen, 367.

20. Ken Gonzales-Day, "Analytical Photography: Portraiture, From the Index to the Epidermis," *Leonardo* 35, 1 (Feb. 2002), 9 Sept. 2004, <http://luna.wellesley.edu/search/tleonardo/tleonardo/1%2C133%2C183%2CB/l856&FF=tleonardo&9%2C%2C14%2C1%2C0>.

21. Allwords, "Allwords.com—Dictionary, Guide, Community and More," 18 Aug. 2004, <http://www.allwords.com/query.php?SearchType=3&goquery=Find+it%21&Language=ENG&Keyword=photography>.

22. Interestingly, there is a tendency to describe programming that eschews Dreamweaver and other software-produced HTML as "hand-coding." However, this discourse like that of photography changes the mediated experience with produced images into something that is material and experiential.

23. Barthes, *Camera Lucida*, 5.

24. Sontag, "Image World," in *On Photography*, 154.

25. Krauss, "Photographic Conditions of Surrealism," in *Originality of the Avant-garde and Other Modernist Myths*, 110.

26. Barthes, *Camera Lucida*, 6.

27. Krauss, "Photographic Conditions of Surrealism," in *Originality of the Avant-garde and Other Modernist Myths*, 110.

28. Bazin, "Ontology," in *What Is Cinema?*, 14.

29. Mary Ann Doane, "The Representability of Time," in *The Emergence of Cinematic Time: Modernity, Contingency, the Archive* (Cambridge, MA: Harvard University Press, 2002), 16, 10.

30. These narratives about lens-based photography also suggest aggressive acts of gaining power by owning the image, individual, space, and time.

31. This directive has also occurred with television and other Internet sites.

32. Alan Trachtenberg, "Walker Evans's Message, from the Interior: A Reading," *October* 11 (Winter 1979): 5.

33. Bolter and Grusin, "Digital Photography," in *Remediation*, 109.

34. John Tagg, "Introduction," in *The Burden of Representation: Essays on Photographies and Histories* (Minneapolis: University of Minnesota Press, 1993), 3.

35. Metz, "Photography and Fetish," *October*, 87.

36. Carol Armstrong, "Introduction," in *Scenes in a Library: Reading the Photograph in the Book, 1843–1875* (Cambridge, MA: MIT Press, 1998), 5, and John Tagg, "Introduction," in *Burden of Representation* (Minneapolis: University of Minnesota Press, 1993), 1. Barthes supported the referential aspects of photography by describing it as a "message without a code" in his earlier writings on photography. Roland Barthes, "The Photographic Message," in *Image/Music/Text*, 17.

37. Kuhn, "Remembrance," in *Illuminations*, ed. Heron and Williams, 475.

38. Barthes, *Camera Lucida*, 26.

39. This chapter may also reinscribe the link between photography and computer-facilitated images by discussing this problem.

40. Wikipedia, "Digital Photography—Wikipedia," 18 Aug. 2004, <http://www.wikipedia.org/wiki/Digital+photography>.

41. Michelle Pacansky, "UCR/CMP: Scanner as Camera," UCR California Museum of Photography, 1998, 18 Aug. 2004, <http://www.cmp.ucr.edu/site/exhibitions/scanner2/intro2.html>.

42. Mitchell, "Beginnings," in *Reconfigured Eye*, 5.

43. Ibid., 6.

44. Ibid.

45. Geoffrey Batchen, "Epitaph," in *Burning with Desire: The Conception of Photography* (Cambridge, MA: MIT Press, 1999), 211.

46. Timothy Druckrey, "L'Amour Faux," *Digital Photography: Captured Images, Volatile Memory, New Montage* (San Francisco: Camerawork, 1988), 4; Fred Ritchin, "Photojournalism in the Age of Computers," in *The Critical Image: Essays on Contemporary Photography*, ed. Carol Squiers (Seattle: Bay Press, 1990), 28; and Druckrey, "L'Amour Faux," in *Digital Photography*, 4. For a critique of Ritchin's position, see Sarah Kember, *Virtual Anxiety: Photography, New Technologies and Subjectivity* (Manchester: Manchester University Press, 1998).

47. Willis, "Digitisation," in *Culture, Technology, and Creativity*, ed. Hayward, 197, and Mitchell, *Reconfigured Eye*, 20.

48. Edward Said, "In the Shadow of the West: An Interview with Edward Said," in *Discourses: Conversations in Postmodern Art and Culture*, ed. R. Ferguson, William Olander, Marcia Tucker, and Karen Fiss (Cambridge, MA: MIT Press, 1990), 94.

49. This issue is discussed in Kuhn, "Remembrance," in *Illuminations*, ed. Heron and Williams, 472.

50. Richard Dyer, "Idol Thoughts: Orgasm and Self-reflexivity in Gay Pornography," in *The Visual Culture Reader*, ed. Nicholas Mirzoeff (London: Routledge, 1998), 504–515; Robert Stam, "The Politics of Reflexivity," in *Film Theory: An Introduction* (Malden, MA: Blackwell Publishers, 2000), 151–153; and Robert Stam, *Reflexivity in Film and Literature: From Don Quixote to Jean-Luc Goddard* (Ann Arbor: UMI Research Press, 1985).

51. "UCR/CMP: Scanner as Camera," UCR California Museum of Photography, 1998, 18 Aug. 2004, <http://www.cmp.ucr.edu/site/exhibitions/scanner2/>.

52. Michelle Pacansky, "UCR/CMP: Scanner as Camera," UCR California Museum of Photography, 1998, 18 Aug. 2004, <http://www.cmp.ucr.edu/site/exhibitions/scanner2/intro .html>.

53. William Gibson quoted in Larry McCaffery, "An Interview with William Gibson," *Mississippi Review* 16, 2/3 (1996), 1 Sept. 2004, <http://www.mississippireview.com/1996/9602gibs.html>.

54. Michelle Pacansky, "UCR/CMP: Scanner as Camera," UCR California Museum of Photography, 1998, 18 Aug. 2004, <http://www.cmp.ucr.edu/site/exhibitions/scanner2/intro2 .html>.

55. Michele White, "Where Is the Louvre?," *Space and Culture—The Journal* 4/5 (2000): 47–70.

56. Barthes, *Camera Lucida*, 27.

57. Ibid., 26–27.

58. Gallop, "The Pleasure of the Phototext," in *Illuminations*, ed. Heron and Williams, 396, and Roger Warren Beebe, "After Arnold: Narratives of the Posthuman Cinema," in *Meta-morphing*, ed. Sobchack, 163.

59. Barthes, *Camera Lucida*, 26.

60. Gallop, "Pleasure of the Phototext," in *Illuminations*, ed. Heron and Williams, 395.

61. Mikhail Bakhtin, "The Material Bodily Lower Stratum," in *Rabelais and His World*, trans. Hélène Iswolsky (Bloomington: Indiana University Press, 1984), 370.

62. Michelle Pacansky, "UCR/CMP: Scanner as Camera," UCR California Museum of Photography, 1998, 18 Aug. 2004, <http://www.cmp.ucr.edu/site/exhibitions/scanner2/intro3 .html>. An IRIS or giclée print is a recently developed printing process that uses advanced technologies and tiny spray jets to produce prints.

63. Susan Silton, *Susan Silton: Self Portraits (Cycle One, January–June 1995)* (Santa Monica: Delta Graphics, 1995). Published in conjunction with the exhibition Susan Silton: Self Portraits (Cycle One, January–June 1995), Craig Krull Gallery, Santa Monica, CA, 9 Sept.–14 Oct. 1995, n.p.

64. Susan Silton, "Images in a Post-photographic Age," 18 Aug. 2004, <http://cepa.buffnet.net/ exhibits/EXHIBIT.19992000/images/silton.html>.

65. Marks, "Video's Body," in *Touch*, 152, and Jeanette Winterson, *Written on the Body* (New York: Vintage Books, 1992), 89.

66. Elizabeth Grosz, "Sexual Difference and the Problem of Essentialism," in *Space, Time, and Perversion* (New York and London: Routledge, 1995), 35.

67. Barthes, *Camera Lucida*, 10.

68. Ibid.

69. Silton, *Susan Silton: Self Portraits*.

70. Barthes, *Camera Lucida*, 12.

71. Ibid.

72. Andrew Edgar and Peter Sedgwick, eds., "Other," in *Key Concepts in Cultural Theory* (New York: Routledge, 1999), 266.

73. Barthes, *Camera Lucida*, 13.

74. Silton references historical texts and asks, "Does she expect to have one vote or two? Has she the same opinion as herself on all subjects, or does she differ sometimes?," Susan Silton, "Anomaly," WomEnhouse, UCR California Museum of Photography, 18 Aug. 2004, <http://www.cmp.ucr.edu/womenhouse/html_s/silton9.html>.

75. Barthes, *Roland Barthes by Roland Barthes*, 36.

76. Susan Silton, "Cyborg," WomEnhouse, UCR California Museum of Photography, 18 Aug. 2004, <http://www.cmp.ucr.edu/womenhouse/html_s/silton3.html>.

77. Ken Gonzales-Day, "Next Monet—Fine Art for your Home and Office," 2 Jan. 2002, <http://www.nextmonet.com/art/artArtist.jhtml?sku=kgo01003>.

78. Ken Gonzales-Day, "Ken Gonzales-Day: On-line Portfolio," 18 Aug. 2004, <http://home page.mac.com/kengonzalesday/Menu16.html>.

79. Sweeney Art Gallery, "Sweeney Art Gallery | Exhibitions | Epidermal," 1999, 18 Aug. 2004, <http://sweeney.ucr.edu/exhibitions/projects1999/gonzalesday/gonzalesday.html>.

80. Ken Gonzales-Day, "Analytic Photography," 18 Aug. 2004, <http://homepage.mac.com/ken gonzalesday/PhotoAlbum9.html>.

81. Ken Gonzales-Day in Bill Kelley, Jr., "Interview Transcript," LatinArt.Com—The Definitive Online Source of Latin American Art, 20 Aug. 2002, 7 Sept. 2004, <http://www.latinart.com/faview.cfm>.

82. LatinArt.Com, "LatinArt.Com—The Definitive Online Source of Latin American Art," 7 Sept. 2004, <http://www.latinart.com/faview.cfm>. For considerations of this history, see the video by Coco Fusco and Paula Heredia, *The Couple in the Cage: A Guatinaui Odyssey*, 1993; Eleanor M. Hight and Gary D. Sampson, eds., *Colonialist Photography: Imag(in)ing Race and Place* (London: Routledge, 2002); Anne Maxwell, *Colonial Photography and Exhibitions: Representations of*

the 'Native' and the Making of European Identities (London: Leicester University Press, 1999); and Nicholas Mirzoeff, ed., *Diaspora and Visual Culture: Representing Africans and Jews* (London: Routledge, 2000).

83. Krauss, "Grids," in *Originality of the Avant-garde and Other Modernist Myths*, 9.

84. Cavell, "Photograph and Screen," in *World Viewed*, 24.

85. Metz, "Identification, Mirror," in *Imaginary Signifier*, 51.

86. Cinematic theories of suture identify shot/reverse shot and other features of the editing process as the ways that the spectator is connected to the text.

87. Silverman, "Suture," in *Subject of Semiotics*, 205.

88. Ibid., 221.

89. Fried, *Absorption and Theatricality*, and Fried, *Courbet's Realism*.

90. Spectators may also consolidate their positions by aligning with the power and privilege of the photographer, which is contrasted to the objectification of the person or object depicted.

91. Ken Gonzales-Day, "Sweeney Art Gallery | Exhibitions | Epidermal Interventions," 1999, 18 Aug. 2004, <http://sweeney.ucr.edu/exhibitions/projects1999/gonzalesday/gonzalesday.html>.

92. Lunenfeld employs overlapping grids as part of his critical strategy in Lunenfeld, *Snap to Grid*.

93. Keith Piper, *Relocating the Remains*, 8 June 2004, <http://www.iniva.org/piper/>. The complete version of this work was originally shown at the Gulbenkian Gallery of The Royal College of Art in 1997 and has toured internationally. Keith Piper, *Relocating the Remains/Excavating the Site* (London: Institute of International Visual Arts, 1997).

94. Keith Piper, "Exhumation of an Unmapped Body," from *Relocating the Remains/Excavating the Site*, 8 June 2004, <http://www.iniva.org/piper/UnMappedBody.html>.

95. Mark S. Frankel and Sanyin Siang, "Ethical and Legal Aspects of Human Subjects in Cyberspace," American Association for the Advancement of Science, 1999, 16 Aug. 2004, <http://www.aaas.org/spp/dspp/sfrl/projects/intres/main.htm>.

96. This part of the work, which is entitled "The Fictions of Science," is in the book and accompanying CD-ROM. Piper, *Relocating the Remains*, 16.

97. This tactic is similar to Fred Wilson's Mining the Museum and subsequent museum interventions where he reorganizes museum collections in order to foreground the pasts that have literally been hidden in warehouses and storage facilities. Lisa G. Corrin, ed., *Mining the Museum: An Installation by Fred Wilson* (Baltimore, MD: The Contemporary, in association with W. W. Norton, 1994). Published in conjunction with the exhibition Mining the Museum, The Contemporary and the Maryland Historical Society, 4 Apr. 1992–28 Feb. 1993.

98. Mongrel core members are Matsuko Yokokoji, Mervin Jarman, Richard Pierre-Davis, and Graham Harwood. Mongrel, "About Mongrel," 8 Apr. 2004, <http://www.mongrelx.org/About/>,

and Matthew Fuller, "Breach the Pieces," 2000, 8 Apr. 2004, <http://www.tate.org.uk/netart/mon grel/mat2.htm>.

99. Graham Harwood, "Mongrel | Tate St Ives | Index," 8 June 2004, <http://www.tate.org.uk/ netart/mongrel/stives/default.htm>.

100. Mongrel, "Natural-Selection," *Natural Selection*, 9 June 2004, <http://www.mongrel.org .uk/>.

101. Mongrel, "Company History," *Natural Selection*, 8 Apr. 2004, <http://www.mongrel.org.uk/ Natural/About/about.html>. This work is alternately attributed to Matthew Filofax and Graham Wang and to the more likely Matthew Fuller and Graham Harwood. Mongrel "Project," 9 June 2004, <http://www.mongrelx.org/Project/projects.html#natural>.

102. Sobchack, "Introduction," in *Meta-morphing*, xii.

103. Internet and Unix Dictionary, "Internet and Unix Dictionary:m.html," Dec. 2002, 6 Mar. 2003, <http://www.msg.net/kadow/answers/m.html#morph>, and *Oxford English Dictionary*, "OED Online—Morph v.," 6 Mar. 2003, <http://0-dictionary.oed.com.luna.wellesley.edu:80/cgi/ entry/00315909?query_type=word&queryword=morph&edition=3e&first=1&max_to_show=10 &sort_type=alpha&search_id=tlIB-EJdp00-6500&hilite=00315909>.

104. For a discussion of QuickTime, see Vivian Sobchack, "Nostalgia for a Digital Object: Regrets on the Quickening of QuickTime," *Millennium Film Journal* 34 (Fall 1999): 4–23.

105. For a discussion of this, see Druckrey, "L'Amour Faux," in *Digital Photography*, ed. Berger, 4.

106. Mark Dery, "Cyborging the Body Politic," *MONDO 2000* (1992): 102–103.

107. Bukatman, "Terminal Resistance/Cyborg Acceptance," in *Terminal Identity*, 304.

108. For a discussion of morphing as spectacle, see Beebe, "After Arnold," in *Meta-morphing*, ed. Sobchack, 159–182.

109. The ideal filmic spectatorial position, which is produced through appropriate distancing from the screen, is also disturbed by morphing. The intimacy of twisting objects and blurs, which persist in an in-between state, make the spectator seem too close to the screen. The spectator cannot obtain a satisfactory image and understanding of the object when morphing occurs.

110. Sobchack, "Introduction," in *Meta-morphing*, xi–xxiii, and *Oxford English Dictionary*, "OED Online—Morph n.5, Dec. 2002, 9 Sept. 2004, <http://0-dictionary.oed.com.luna.wellesley.edu :80/cgi/entry/00315908?query_type=word&queryword=morph&edition=3e&first=1&max_to _show=10&sort_type=alpha&search_id=tlIB-DVoKRy-6857>.

111. Amelia Jones, "Susan Silton's Mutations of Self/Image: The Portrait," in Silton, *Susan Silton: Self Portraits*, n.p.

112. Barthes, *Camera Lucida*, 78.

113. Sobchack, "Meta-morphing," in *Meta-morphing*, 134.

114. Metz, "Photography and Fetish," *October*.

115. Yvonne Spielmann, "Aesthetic Features in Digital Imaging: Collage and Morph," *Wide Angle* 21, 1 (Jan. 1999): 146, 9 Sept. 2004, <http://0muse.jhu.edu.luna.wellesley.edu/journals/wide_angle/v021/21.1spielmann.html>.

Afterword The Flat and the Fold: A Consideration of Embodied Spectatorship

1. quark2universe replied to a slashdot thread on "Walking Erect" by ironically noting, "I've been walking erect since I first saw that Farrah Fawcett poster in the '70s." quark2univers, "Walking Erect," Slashdot, 28 Feb. 2002, 26 Aug. 2004, <http://slashdot.org/comments.pl?cid=3088066&sid=28704>. A variety of similar comments in Internet settings continues to reinforce the relationship between masculinity and spectatorship.

2. A hierarchy of engagements with the Internet and computers is articulated in the hacker's dictionary as well as varied Internet forums. Eric S. Raymond, ed., *The New Hacker's Dictionary*, 3rd ed. (Cambridge, MA: MIT Press, 1996). Versions of this are also available as The Jargon Dictionary 4.4.7, 29 Dec. 2003, 14 Sept. 2004, <http://www.catb.org/~esr/jargon/html/index.html>. The term "programmer" has come to represent a variety of high-end Internet and computer technology jobs. It is not possible for me to articulate the different roles and power structures among hackers, programmers, script kiddies, web designers, system designers and administrators, IT workers, and other computer technology positions within the constraints of this study.

3. While Victor Vitanza employs the fold in considering MOOs, MUDs, and WOOs, he does not use it to consider the spectator's embodied position. Victor Vitanza, "Of MOOs, Folds, and Non-reactionary Virtual Communities," in *High Wired*, ed. Haynes and Holmevik, 286–310.

4. Elizabeth Grosz, "Architecture from the Outside," in *Architecture from the Outside: Essays on Virtual and Real Space* (Cambridge, MA: MIT Press, 2001), 73.

5. Sobchack, "Introduction," in *Meta-morphing*, xii.

6. Ken Gonzales-Day, "Analytic Photography," 26 Aug. 2004, <http://homepage.mac.com/kengonzalesday/PhotoAlbum9.html>.

7. Craig Owens, "Photography en Abyme," in *Beyond Recognition: Representation, Power, and Culture* (Berkeley: University of California Press, 1992), 17.

8. Gilles Deleuze, "Foldings, or the Inside of Thought," in *Foucault*, trans. Sean Hand (Minneapolis: University of Minnesota Press, 1988), 98.

9. Joan Key, "Unfold: Imprecations of Obscenity in the Fold," in *Other than Identity: The Subject, Politics and Art*, ed. Juliet Steyn (Manchester: Manchester University Press, 1997), 196.

10. Grosz, "Architecture from the Outside," in *Architecture from the Outside*, 64–65.

11. Jaron Lanier as quoted in Mike Featherstone and Roger Burrows, "Cultures of Technological Embodiment: An Introduction," in *Cyberspace/Cyberbodies/Cyberpunk: Cultures of Technological Embodiment*, ed. Mike Featherstone and Roger Burrows (London: Sage Publications, 1995), 13.

12. irongull, "The Ultimate Geek Food," Slashdot, 20 Feb. 2000, 26 Aug. 2004, <http://slashdot.org/comments.pl?sid=4041&threshold=1&commentsort=0&tid=144&mode=thread&cid=1257477>.

13. "Evolution of Mankind!!!," 26 Aug. 2004, <http://www.angelfire.com/ri/cardzzz/joke2.html>.

14. Gibson, *Neuromancer*, 6.

15. William Gibson, "Burning Chrome," in *Burning Chrome* (New York: Ace Books, 1986), 173.

16. Tom Maddox, "Snake-Eyes," in *Mirrorshades*, ed. Sterling, 16.

17. Stephenson, *Snow Crash*, 24.

18. Anne Balsamo, "Reading Cyborgs Writing Feminism," in *Cybersexualities: A Reader on Feminist Theory, Cyborgs and Cyberspace*, ed. Jenny Wolmark (Edinburgh: Edinburgh University Press, 1999), 145–156, and Anne Balsamo, "The Virtual Body in Cyberspace," in *The Cybercultures Reader*, ed. David Bell and Barbara M. Kennedy (London: Routledge, 2000), 489–503.

19. Kevin Robins, "Cyberspace and the World We Live In," in *Into the Image: Culture and Politics in the Field of Vision* (New York and London: Routledge, 1996), 89.

20. For a discussion of this issue, see Margrit Shildrick and Janet Price, "Openings on the Body: A Critical Introduction," in *Feminist Theory and the Body: A Reader*, ed. Janet Price and Margrit Shildrick (New York: Routledge, 1999), 1.

21. Ray Kurzweil, "Building New Brains . . . ," in *The Age of Spiritual Machines: When Computers Exceed Human Intelligence* (New York: Viking Penguin, 1999), 121.

22. Ray Kurzweil, "The Evolution of Mind in the Twenty-first Century," Are We Spiritual Machines, 2002, 26 Aug. 2004, <http://www.kurzweilai.net/articles/art0500.html?printable=1>, and Kurzweil, "Building New Brains . . . ," in *Age of Spiritual Machines*.

23. Kurzweil, "Building New Brains . . . ," in *Age of Spiritual Machines*, 125.

24. Hans Moravec, "Simulation, Consciousness, Existence," 1998, 26 Aug. 2004, <http://www.frc.ri.cmu.edu/~hpm/project.archive/general.articles/1998/SimConEx.98.html>.

25. Hans Moravec, "Grandfather Clause," in *Mind Children: The Future of Robot and Human Intelligence* (Cambridge, MA: Harvard University Press, 1988), 117.

26. Moravec, "Grandfather Clause," in *Mind Children*, 117, and Hans Moravec as quoted in Grant Fjermedal, *The Tomorrow Makers: A Brave New World of Living-brain Machines* (New York: Macmillan, 1986), 5.

27. Butler, *Bodies that Matter*, and Butler, *Gender Trouble*.

28. Ray Kurzweil, ". . . And Bodies," in *Age of Spiritual Machines*, 134, and Ray Kurzweil, "Live Forever—Uploading The Human Brain . . . Closer than You Think," *Psychology Today*, 2 Feb. 2000, 26 Aug. 2004,<http://www.kurzweilai.net/meme/frame.html?main=/articles/art0157.html>.

29. Kurzweil, "Prologue: An Inexorable Emergence," in *Age of Spiritual Machines*, 1.

30. Hans Moravec, "Simulation, Consciousness, Existence," 1998, 26 Aug. 2004, <http://www .frc.ri.cmu.edu/~hpm/project.archive/general.articles/1998/SimConEx.98.html>.

31. See, for instance, Dani Cavallaro, *Cyberpunk and Cyberculture: Science Fiction and the Work of William Gibson* (London: Athlone Press, 2000); Heidi J. Figueroa-Sarriera, "Children of the Mind with Disposable Bodies: Metaphors of Self in a Text on Artificial Intelligence and Robotics," in *The Cyborg Handbook*, ed. Chris Habels Gray (New York: Routledge, 1995), 127–138; and Hayles, *How We Became Posthuman*.

32. Hayles, "Toward Embodied Virtuality," in *How We Became Posthuman*, 4.

33. Ibid.

34. Margaret Morse, "Smarting Flesh: Pain and the Posthuman," in *When Pain Strikes*, ed. Bill Burns, Cathy Busby, and Kim Sawchuck (Minneapolis: University of Minnesota Press, 1999), 247.

35. For a discussion of this, see Margaret Morse, "What Do Cyborgs Eat? Oral Logic in an Information Society," in *Virtualities: Television, Media Art, and Cyberculture* (Bloomington: Indiana University Press, 1998).

36. Ibid., 125.

37. CaptCosmic, "Boredom Chasers?," Slashdot, 18 Nov. 2001, 26 Sept. 2004, <http://ask .slashdot.org/article.pl?sid=01/11/17/2040229&mode=thread&tid=127>; dmorin, "Boredom Chasers?," Slashdot, 19 Nov. 2001, 26 Sept. 2004, <http://ask.slashdot.org/article.pl?sid=01/11/ 17/2040229&mode=thread&tid=127>; and jchawk, "What to Do on the Nightshift Besides Work?," Slashdot, 20 May 2001, 26 Aug. 2004, <http://ask.slashdot.org/article.pl?sid=01/05/19/ 2330250&mode=thread&tid=95>.

38. Work or Spoon, "Work or Spoon . . . Which Will You Choose?," 19 Aug. 2004, <http://www .workorspoon.com/default.asp>.

39. "FuckedCompany.com defines itself as "the source for news about dot-com companies. Bad news, that is." FuckedCompany.com, 26 Aug. 2004, <http://www.fuckedcompany.com/whatis/>.

40. Morse, "Smarting Flesh," in *When Pain Strikes*, ed. Burns, Busby, and Sawchuck, 246.

41. shanga-langa-lang, "Comments: Northridge Betta Be Real Beautiful!," Fuck That Job!, 5 Aug. 2003, 26 Aug. 2004, <http://fuckthatjob.com/cgi-bin/mt/mt-comments.cgi?entry_id=249>.

42. nycdesigner, "Red Dot Special on Experts in Aisle 4," Fuck That Job!, 13 May 2003, 26 Aug. 2004, <http://fuckthatjob.com/archives/000220.html>.

43. Valence, "Dave Needs a Hug," Fuck That Job!, 11 June 2003, 26 Aug. 2004, <http:// fuckthatjob.com/cgi-bin/mt/mt-comments.cgi?entry_id=230>, and Edward, "Dave Needs a Hug," Fuck That Job!, 11 June 2003, 26 Aug. 2004, <http://fuckthatjob.com/cgi-bin/mt/mt -comments.cgi?entry_id=230>.

44. Name, "Must Book Hotels and Know TCP/IP Networking," Fuck That Job!, 27 Aug. 2003, 26 Aug. 2004, <http://fuckthatjob.com/archives/000259.html#more>, and SlappyJack, "Must Book Hotels and Know TCP/IP Networking," Fuck That Job!, 27 Aug. 2003, 26 Aug. 2004, <http://fuck thatjob.com/archives/000259.html#more>.

45. Reuters, "Cashiers Diapered to Avoid Breaks?," 1 Aug. 2003, 21 Aug. 2003, <http://story .news.yahoo.com/news?tmpl=story&u=/nm/20030801/od_nm/odd_diapers_dc>.

46. Tom, "Fuck That Job! Now That's a Crappy Job," Fuck That Job!, 5 Aug. 2003, 26 Aug. 2004, <http://fuckthatjob.com/cgi-bin/mt/mt-comments.cgi?entry_id=250>.

47. Marc Linder interviewed by Doug Henwood, "Radio Archive," 24 July 2003, 26 Aug. 2004, <http://www.leftbusinessobserver.com/Radio.html>. See also Marc Linder, *Void Where Prohibited Revisited: The Trickle-down Effect of OSHA's At-will Bathroom-break Regulation* (Iowa City: Fanpìhuà Press, 2003), and Marc Linder, *Void Where Prohibited: Rest Breaks and the Right to Urinate on Company Time* (Ithaca, NY: ILR Press, 1998).

48. Marc Linder interviewed by Doug Henwood, "Radio Archive," 24 July 2003, 26 Aug. 2004, <http://www.leftbusinessobserver.com/Radio.html>.

49. Jo Best, "Firm Bans E-mail to Boost Productivity," 19 Sept. 2003, 26 Aug. 2004, <http://zdnet .com.com/2100-1104-5079094.html?tag=sas_email>.

50. Cindy Brown as quoted in Selena Maranjian, "View from the Register," Fool.com, 4 Aug. 2003, 27 Aug. 2003, <http://story.news.yahoo.com/news?tmpl=story&u=/fool/20030804/bs_fool _fool/1060007700>.

51. Margaret Morse, "Body and Screen," *Wide Angle* 21, 1 (Jan. 1999): 73, 27 Feb. 2003, <http://0-muse.jhu.edu.luna.wellesley.edu/journals/wide_angle/v021/21.1morse.html>.

52. Melissa Scott, *Trouble and Her Friends* (New York: Tor Books, 1994), 115.

53. Pat Cadigan, *Dervish Is Digital* (New York: Tor Books, 2000), 31.

54. Ibid., 30.

55. PD, "Slashdot | Ergonomic Keyboards," Slashdot, 22 Feb. 2000, 26 Aug. 2004, <http://ask .slashdot.org/comments.pl?sid=4070&threshold=1&commentsort=0&tid=126&tid=4&mode =thread&cid=1253181>; twocoasttb, "Mouse Not Required," Slashdot, 19 Feb. 2003, 26 Aug. 2004, <http://ask.slashdot.org/article.pl?sid=03/02/19/0034216&mode=thread&tid=137>; and kma, "Geek Throne," Slashdot, 3 Nov. 2000, 26 Aug. 2004, <http://slashdot.org/comments.pl?sid =8657&threshold=1&commentsort=0&tid=159&mode=thread&cid=650245>.

56. Syncophant-16, "IMAK Smart Glove Review," Ars Technica, 11 Dec. 2002, 26 Aug. 2004, <http://episteme.arstechnica.com/eve/ubb.x?q=Y&a=tpc&s=50009562&f=174096756&m =9200903145&p=2>. Ars Technica is described as "the pc enthusiast's resource."

57. crystalmatrix, "IMAK Smart Glove Review," Ars Technica, 10 Dec. 2002, 26 Aug. 2004, <http://episteme.arstechnica.com/eve/ubb.x?a=tpc&s=50009562&f=174096756&m=9200903145 &r=9200903145#9200903145>.

58. ashtrashe, "IMAK Smart Glove Review," Ars Technica, 10 Dec. 2002, 26 Aug. 2004, <http://episteme.arstechnica.com/eve/ubb.x?a=tpc&s=50009562&f=174096756&m=9200903145&r=9200903145#9200903145>, and blasikov, "IMAK Smart Glove review," Ars Technica, 10 Dec. 2002, 26 Aug. 2004, <http://episteme.arstechnica.com/eve/ubb.x?a=tpc&s=50009562&f=174096756&m=9200903145&r=9200903145#9200903145>.

59. For a discussion of pain, bodily acknowledgment, and transcendence, see Susan Wendell, "Feminism, Disability, and the Transcendence of the Body," in *Feminist Theory and the Body*, ed. Price and Shildrick, 324–333.

60. Relgar, "IMAK Smart Glove Review," Ars Technica, 10 Dec. 2002, 26 Aug. 2004, <http://episteme.arstechnica.com/eve/ubb.x?a=tpc&s=50009562&f=174096756&m=9200903145&r=9200903145#9200903145>.

61. SaxMaster, "Follow Up on the Hacker's Diet?," Slashdot, 25 Apr. 2000, 26 Aug. 2004, <http://ask.slashdot.org/article.pl?sid=00/04/24/1047254&mode=thread>.

62. Adam "Stone Table" Israel, "IMAK Smart Glove," Ars Technica, 10 Dec. 2002, 26 Aug. 2004, <http://arstechnica.com/reviews/02q3/smartglove/smartglove-1.html>.

63. Ibid.

64. The position of female programmers remains disturbingly unaddressed in these narratives.

65. "Keyboards for One Hand?," Slashdot, 30 June 2003, 26 Aug. 2004, <http://ask.slashdot.org/article.pl?sid=03/06/30/1845234&mode=thread&tid=137>; Sigwich, "Keyboards for One Hand?," Slashdot, 30 June 2003, 26 Aug. 2004, <http://ask.slashdot.org/article.pl?sid=03/06/30/1845234&mode=thread&tid=137>; "Mouse Not Required?," Slashdot, 19 Feb. 2003, 26 Aug. 2004, <http://ask.slashdot.org/article.pl?sid=03/02/19/0034216&mode=thread&tid=137>; and Sigwich, "Keyboards for One Hand?," Slashdot, 30 June 2003, 26 Aug. 2004, <http://ask.slashdot.org/article.pl?sid=03/06/30/1845234&mode=thread&tid=137>.

66. Theweleit, "Male Bodies,'" in *Male Fantasies, Male Bodies*, 160.

67. Bordo, "Reading the Slender Body," in *Unbearable Weight*, 190.

68. Kim Sawchuck, Cathy Busby, and Bill Burns, "Introduction," in *When Pain Strikes*, ed. Burns, Busby, and Sawchuck, xxii.

69. Silverman, *Male Subjectivity at the Margins*, 2.

70. For a discussion of this, see David Glover and Cora Kaplan, "Introduction: Gendered Histories, Gendered Contexts," in *Genders* (London and New York: Routledge, 2000), 3.

71. Not surprisingly, most of these characters escape the "unhealthy" proximity to the screen in favor of "appropriate" heterosexuality by the end of the text.

72. Sir_Timothy, "Hacker's Diet," Slashdot, 12 July 1999, 27 Aug. 2004, <http://slashdot.org/comments.pl?sid=427&threshold=1&commentsort=0&tid=133&mode=thread&cid=1807758>.

73. Charles Arthur, "Hackers Code," *New Scientist* 22, Oct. 1994, 8 Feb. 2002, <http://archive.newscientist.com/archive.jsp?id=19483600>.

74. "Many Hackers Too Fat for the FBI," Slashdot, 3 Sept. 2002, 27 Aug. 2004, <http://slashdot
.org/comments.pl?sid=39233&threshold=1&commentsort=0&mode=thread&pid=4192002
#4192046>, and Rule, "Internet Chatroom Song," Geek-Ware.co.uk: Site of the Day, 18 June
2002, 21 Aug. 2002, <http://www.geek-ware.co.uk/SiteOfTheDay/>.

75. Ezatdz, "Ars Weight Loss Challenge," Ars Technica, 16 Aug. 2002, 27 Aug. 2004, <http://
episteme.arstechnica.com/eve/ubb.x?q=Y&a=tpc&s=50009562&f=34709834&m=9980947193
&p=24>; Sspy, "Eat a Horse and Be Like One Too?," Ars Technica, 13 Aug. 2002, 27 Aug. 2004,
<http://episteme.arstechnica.com/eve/ubb.x?q=Y&a=tpc&s=50009562&f=28609695&m=937091
2035&p=1>; and Cretion, "Eat a Horse and Be Like One Too?," Ars Technica, 13 Aug. 2002, 27
Aug. 2004, <http://episteme.arstechnica.com/eve/ubb.x?q=Y&a=tpc&s=50009562&f=28609695
&m=9370912035&p=1>.

76. For a discussion of this, see Myra Dinnerstein and Rose Weitz, "Jane Fonda, Barbara Bush,
and Other Aging Bodies," in *The Politics of Women's Bodies: Sexuality, Appearance, and Behavior*, ed.
Rose Weitz (New York: Oxford University Press, 1998), 189–206. Notkin suggests that women are
much more likely to be criticized for slight deviations from cultural conceptions of "correct"
body size. However, men also receive abuse when they are larger. Debbie Notkin, "Enlarging:
Politics and Society," in *Women En Large: Images of Fat Nudes*, ed. Laurie Toby Edison and Debbie
Notkin (San Francisco: Books in Focus, 1994), 93. Le'a Kent provides a critique of Notkin's essay
and her biological explanations of fat. Le'a Kent, "Fighting Abjection: Representing Fat Women,"
in *Bodies Out of Bounds: Fatness and Transgression*, ed. Jana Evans Braziel and Kathleen LeBesco
(Berkeley: University of California Press, 2001), 130–150.

77. TobyWong, "Aeron Chairs as Stupidity Barometers," Slashdot, 8 Aug. 2001, 27 Aug. 2004,
<http://slashdot.org/comments.pl?sid=20145&threshold=1&commentsort=0&tid=159&mode
=thread&cid=2148026>.

78. Tarrek, "Painless Chairs?," Slashdot, 16 July 2003, 27 Aug. 2004, <http://ask.slashdot.org/
article.pl?sid=02/07/15/2323238&tid=99&tid=4>, and mantid, "In Search of the Perfect Computer Chair," Slashdot, 26 Oct. 2000, 27 Aug. 2004, <http://ask.slashdot.org/article.pl?sid=00/10/
26/175245&tid=159>.

79. fuck dimension enter, "Hacker's Diet," Slashdot, 12 July 1999, 27 Aug. 2004, <http://slash
dot.org/comments.pl?sid=427&threshold=1&commentsort=0&tid=133&mode=thread&cid
=1807751>.

80. This narcissism, which is admittedly focused on an idealized image, is interesting because of
the societal aversion to the stereotyped male computer spectator's body.

81. Hairy_Potter, "The Ultimate Chair," Slashdot, 18 Oct. 2000, 27 Aug. 2004, <http://slashdot
.org/article.pl?sid=00/10/18/0213216&mode=thread>.

82. For instance, urbazewski believes that as "spring gets underway (in the northern hemisphere
anyway) it's a good time to start undoing the effects of a winter's worth of websurfing and game-
playing on your physical condition." urbazewski, "Lose Weight the Slow, Boring Way," Slashdot,
12 Apr. 2003, 27 Aug. 2004, <http://science.slashdot.org/article.pl?sid=03/04/12/2357234&mode
=thread&tid=134>.

83. Doom, "Hacker's Diet," Slashdot, 12 July 1999, 27 Aug. 2004, <http://slashdot.org/comments.pl?sid=427&threshold=1&commentsort=0&tid=133&mode=thread&cid=1807716>.

84. Susan Bordo, "Beauty (Re)discovers the Male Body," in *Beauty Matters*, ed. Peg Zeglin Brand (Bloomington: Indiana University Press, 2000), 143.

85. While I do not have space to consider it here, it would be useful to study why this material seems more real and thus makes research appear to be more intrusive than does analysis of other forums.

86. Diepilot, "Ars Weight Loss Challenge," Ars Technica, 29 July 2002, 27 Aug. 2004, <http://episteme.arstechnica.com/6/ubb.x?q=Y&a=tpc&s=50009562&f=34709834&m=9980947193&p=21>, and Benji, "Ars Weight Loss Challenge," Ars Technica, 4 Mar. 2002, 21 Aug. 2004, <http://episteme.arstechnica.com/eve/ubb.x?q=Y&a=tpc&s=50009562&f=34709834&m=9980947193&=2>.

87. "Hacker's Diet," Slashdot, 12 July 1999, 27 Aug. 2004, <http://slashdot.org/comments.pl?sid=427&threshold=-1&commentsort=0&tid=133&mode=thread&cid=1807732>.

88. Norrick, "Ars Weight Loss Challenge," Ars Technica, 9 Aug. 2002, 26 Aug. 2004, <http://episteme.arstechnica.com/6/ubb.x?q=Y&a=tpc&s=50009562&f=34709834&m=9980947193&p=23>.

89. Moira Gatens, "Power, Bodies and Difference," in *Feminist Theory and the Body*, ed. Price and Shildrick, 228.

90. MacMonkey, "Ars Weight Loss Challenge," Ars Technica, 9 Sept. 2002, 31 Aug. 2004, <http://episteme.arstechnica.com/6/ubb.x?q=Y&a=tpc&s=50009562&f=34709834&m=9980947193&p=26>, and Dave88, "Ars Weight Loss Challenge," Ars Technica, 9 Sept. 2002, 31 Aug. 2004, <http://episteme.arstechnica.com/6/ubb.x?q=Y&a=tpc&s=50009562&f=34709834&m=9980947193&p=26>.

91. Iris Marion Young, "Breasted Experience," in *Politics of Women's Bodies*, ed. Weitz, 126.

92. Susan Bordo, "Feminism, Foucault and the Politics of the Body," in *Feminist Theory and the Body*, ed. Price and Shildrick, 250.

93. Young, "Breasted Experience," in *Politics of Women's Bodies*, ed. Weitz, 129.

94. Dave88, "Ars Weight Loss Challenge," Ars Technica, 18 July 2002, 27 Aug. 2004, <http://episteme.arstechnica.com/6/ubb.x?q=Y&a=tpc&s=50009562&f=34709834&m=9980947193&p=18>, and Ferret, "Ars Weight Loss Challenge," Ars Technica, 12 Sept. 2002, 27 Aug. 2004, <http://episteme.arstechnica.com/6/ubb.x?q=Y&a=tpc&s=50009562&f=34709834&m=9980947193&p=26>.

95. MrDetermination, "Ars Weight Loss Challenge," Ars Technica, 7 May 2002, 27 Aug. 2004, <http://episteme.arstechnica.com/6/ubb.x?q=Y&a=tpc&s=50009562&f=34709834&m=9980947193&p=9>, and Norrick, "Ars Weight Loss Challenge," Ars Technica, 3 Apr. 2002, 27 Aug. 2004, <http://episteme.arstechnica.com/6/ubb.x?q=Y&a=tpc&s=50009562&f=34709834&m=9980947193&p=6>.

96. MrDetermination, "Ars Weight Loss Challenge," Ars Technica, 16 Aug. 2002, 27 Aug. 2004, <http://episteme.arstechnica.com/6/ubb.x?q=Y&a=tpc&s=50009562&f=34709834&m=99809471 93&p=24>.

97. Athos, "Ars Weight Loss Challenge," Ars Technica, 5 May 2002, 27 Aug. 2004, <http://epis teme.arstechnica.com/6/ubb.x?q=Y&a=tpc&s=50009562&f=34709834&m=9980947193&p=9>.

98. Kraicat, "Ars Weight Loss Challenge," Ars Technica, 10 Apr. 2002, 27 Aug. 2004, <http://epis teme.arstechnica.com/6/ubb.x?q=Y&a=tpc&s=50009562&f=34709834&m=9980947193&p=7>.

99. Carol Squires as quoted in Debbie Notkin, "Enlarging," in *Women En Large*, ed. Edison and Notkin, 100.

100. MrDetermination, "Ars Weight Loss Challege," Ars Technica, 16 Aug. 2004, 21 Aug. 2004, <http://episteme.arstechnica.com/eve/ubb.x?q=Y&a=tpc&s=50009562&f=34709834&m=998094 7193&p=92>.

101. Squires as quoted in Notkin, "Enlarging," in *Women En Large*, ed. Edison and Notkin, 100.

102. Theweleit, "Male Bodies," in *Male Fantasies, Male Bodies*, 206.

103. WideLoad, "Geeks and Weight-loss," Slashdot, 25 Dec. 2001, 27 Aug. 2004, <http://ask .slashdot.org/article.pl?sid=01/12/25/0552202&mode=thread&tid=146>.

104. Doane, "Desire to Desire," in *Desire to Desire*, 2.

105. Marks, *Touch*.

106. dhamsaic, "Aeron Chairs as Stupidity Barometers," Slashdot, 8 Aug. 2001, 27 Aug. 2004, <http://slashdot.org/comments.pl?sid=20145&cid=0&pid=0&startat=&threshold=5&mode =thread&commentsort=0&op=Change>.

107. Bordo, "Reading the Slender Body," in *Unbearable Weight*, 187.

108. Eve Kosofsky Sedgwick, "The Use of Being Fat," in *Fat Art, Thin Art* (Durham, NC: Duke University Press, 1994), 15.

109. Bernadette Bosky as quoted in Notkin, "Enlarging," in *Women En Large*, ed. Edison and Notkin, 98.

110. For a discussion of gay male web sites, see John Edward Campbell, *Getting It on Online: Cyberspace, Gay Male Sexuality, and Embodied Identity* (Binghamton, NY: Harrington Park Press, 2004).

111. Wraithlyn, "Walk Erect? How Leg-centric . . . ," Slashdot, 28 Feb. 2002, 27 Aug. 2004, <http://slashdot.org/comments.pl?cid=3088099&sid=28704>.

112. Nancy Mairs, "Body in Trouble," in *Waist-high in the World: A Life among the Nondisabled* (Boston: Beacon Press, 1996), 51.

113. Ibid., 54.

114. Mairs, "Home Truths," in *Waist-high in the World*, 16.

115. Feminist art historians have critiqued the ways women in paintings are often depicted as seated or reclining. See, for instance, Pollock, *Vision and Difference*.

116. Bordo, "Whose Body Is This?," in *Unbearable Weight*, 57.

117. Lily Kam summary of Toby Miller talk, "MIT3: Plenary 1," Television in Transition Conference, Massachusetts Institute of Technology, 2–4 May 2003, 27 Aug. 2004, <http://cms.mit.edu/mit3/subs/plenary1.html#summary>. This talk is also available on the site as an audio file.

118. United States Environmental Protection Agency, "Electronics: A New Use for Waste Prevention, Reuse, and Recycling," June 2001, 31 Aug. 2004, <http://www.epa.gov/epaoswer/osw/elec_fs.pdf>, and National Safety Council's Environmental Health Center, *Electronic Product Recovery and Recycling Baseline Report* (Washington, DC: National Safety Council, 1999), viii.

119. The City and County of Denver, "Give Your Old Computer a New Life," 23 May 2003, 31 Aug. 2004, <http://www.denvergov.org/newsarticle.asp?id=5863>. See also Environmental Protection Agency, "Municipal Solid Waste in the United States: 2000 Facts and Figures," June 2002, 27 Aug. 2004, <http://www.epa.gov/garbage/pubs/report-00.pdf>.

120. European Commission, "Commission Tackles Growing Problem of Electrical and Electronic Waste," 13 June 2000, 27 Aug. 2004, <http://europa.eu.int/rapid/start/cgi/guesten.ksh?p_action.gettxt=gt&doc=IP/00/602|0|RAPID&lg=EN>.

121. Computer Take Back Campaign, 27 Aug. 2004, <http://www.computertakeback.com/the_problem/index.cfm>.

122. Jim Fisher, "Poison PCs," Salon, 18 Sept. 2000, 27 Aug. 2004, <http://dir.salon.com/tech/feature/2000/09/18/toxic_pc/index.html?pn=1>; United States Environmental Protection Agency, "EPA: Resource Conservation Challenge," 14 Aug. 2003, 27 Aug. 2004, <http://www.epa.gov/epaoswer/osw/conserve/plugin/index.htm>; and Khalid Hasan, "Pakistan a Dump for High-tech Junk," *Daily Times*, 24 Feb. 2003, 27 Aug. 2004, <http://www.dailytimes.com.pk/default.asp?page=story_25-2-2003_pg7_1>.

123. The Basel Action Network and Silicon Valley Toxics Coalition, "Exporting Harm: The High-tech Trashing of Asia," Silicon Valley Toxics Coalition, 6, 25 Feb. 2003, 31 Aug. 2004, <http://svtc.igc.org/cleancc/pubs/harm.htm>.

124. Peter S. Goodman, "China Serves as Dump Site for Computers: Unsafe Recycling Practice Grows Despite Import Ban," *Washington Post*, A01, 24 Feb. 2003, 31 Aug. 2004, <http://www.washingtonpost.com/ac2/wp-dyn/A56653-2003Feb24?language=printer>.

125. The Basel Action Network and Silicon Valley Toxics Coalition, "Exporting Harm: The High-tech Trashing of Asia," Silicon Valley Toxics Coalition, 7, 25 Feb. 2003, 31 Aug. 2004, <http://svtc.igc.org/cleancc/pubs/harm.htm>.

126. Sheila Davis and Ted Smith, "Corporate Strategies for Electronic Recycling: A Tale of Two Systems," Silicon Valley Toxics Coalition and the Computer TakeBack Campaign!, 25 June 2003, 31 Aug. 2004, <http://svtc.igc.org/cleancc/pubs/prison_final.pdf>, and Peter S. Goodman,

"China Serves as Dump Site for Computers: Unsafe Recycling Practice Grows Despite Import Ban," *Washington Post*, A01, 24 Feb. 2003, 31 Aug. 2004, <http://www.washingtonpost.com/ac2/wp-dyn/A56653-2003Feb24?language=printer>.

127.   One inmate at the Atwater UNICOR facility, which is a trade name for the Federal Prison Industries, indicates, "Even when I wear the paper mask, I blow out black mucus from my nose everyday. . . . Cuts and abrasions happen all the time. Of these the open wounds are exposed to the dirt and dust and many do not heal as quickly as normal wounds." Quoted in Sheila Davis and Ted Smith, "Corporate Strategies for Electronic Recycling: A Tale of Two Systems," Silicon Valley Toxics Coalition and the Computer TakeBack Campaign!, 25 June 2003, 31 Aug. 2004, <http://svtc.igc.org/cleancc/pubs/prison_final.pdf>.

128.   There has also been a move in the United States and European Union to enact product stewardship, which would make companies take back and recycle their products. In some of these proposals, shipping such products to countries in more precarious social and economic positions would be stopped. According to NEPSI, *Product stewardship* means that all parties who have a role in producing, selling or using a product also have a role in managing it at the end of its useful life." See National Electronics Product Stewardship Initiative, "NEPSI—Homepage," 22 Aug. 2003, <http://eerc.ra.utk.edu/clean/nepsi/>; Product Stewardship Institute, 31 Mar. 2003, 31 Aug. 2004, <http://www.productstewardshipinstitute.org/>; and Northwest Product Stewardship Council, 21 July 2003, 31 Aug. 2004, <http://www.productstewardship.net/policies ElectronicsIntl.html>. The "European Commission has adopted a proposal for a Directive on Waste Electrical and Electronic Equipment (WEEE) and a proposal for a Directive on the restriction of the use of certain hazardous substances in electrical and electronic equipment. . . . Producers will be responsible for taking back and recycling electrical and electronic equipment" from consumers without charge. European Commission, "Commission Tackles Growing Problem of Electrical and Electronic Waste," 13 June 2000, 31 Aug. 2004, <http://europa.eu.int/rapid/start/cgi/guesten.ksh?p_action.gettxt=gt&doc=IP/00/602|0|RAPID&lg=EN>.

129.   David Koenig, "Dell Drops Recycling Company that Used Prison Labor," *San Jose Mercury News*, 3 July 2003, 1E. and Computer Take Back Campaign, "CTBC Releases 2004 Report Card," 19 Mar. 2004, 19 Aug. 2004, <http://www.computertakeback.com/news_and_resources/pr__2004 _report_card.cfm>.

130.   Michelle Kessler, "Office Depot Will Recycle Old PCs for Free in 'Fabulous' Offer," *USA Today*, 12 July 2004, 20 Aug. 2004, <http://www.usatoday.com/money/industries/technology/2004-07-12-recycle_x.htm?POE=MONISVA>.

131.   Jenn Shreve, "Strategy: Can Designers Save the World?," *eDesign* (Sept./Oct. 2002): 35–36, 31 Aug. 2004, <http://www.svtc.org/media/articles/2002/edesign.pdf>.

132.   Neal Stephenson, *Zodiac: The Eco-thriller* (New York: Bantam Books, 1995), 7.

133.   Bruce Sterling, *Heavy Weather* (New York: Bantam Books, 1994).

134.   Margaret Atwood, *Oryx and Crake* (New York: Anchor Books, 2004); Octavia Butler, *Parable of the Sower* (New York: Warner Books, 1993); and Sheri S. Tepper, *The Fresco* (New York: Eos, 2000).

135. Bruce Sterling, "The Dead Media Project: A Modest Proposal and Public Appeal," 24 Aug. 2004, <http://www.deadmedia.org/modest-proposal.html>, and Viridian, "The Viridian Design Movement," 6 Sept. 2004, <http://www.viridiandesign.org/>. Sterling also addresses the greenhouse effect in Bruce Sterling, *Tomorrow Now: Envisioning the Next Fifty Years* (New York: Random House, 2002).

136. Bruce Sterling, "Viridian Note 00422: The Spime," 24 Aug. 2004, <http://www.viridian design.org/notes/401-450/00422_the_spime.html>. Sterling argues that the "people who make Spimes want you to do as much of the work for them as possible. They can data-mine your uses of the spime, and use that to improve their Spime and gain market share. This would have been called 'customer relations management,' in an earlier era, but in a Spime world, it's more intimate. It's collaborative, and better understood as something like open-source manufacturing. It's all about excellence. Passion. Integrity. Cross-disciplinary action. And volunteerism. . . . So—as long as you could keep your eyes open—you would be able to swiftly understand: where it was, when you got it, how much it cost, who made it, what it was made of, where those resources came from, what a better model looked like, what a cheaper model looked like, who to thank for making it, who to complain to about its inadequacies, what previous kinds of Spime used to look like, why this Spime is better than earlier ones, what people think the Spime of Tomorrow might look like, what you could do to help that happen, the history of the Spime's ownership, what it had been used for, where and when it was used, what other people who own this kind of Spime think about it, how other people more or less like you have altered or fancied-up or modified their Spime, what most people use Spimes for, the entire range of unorthodox uses of Spimes by the world's most extreme Spime geek fandom, and how much your Spime is worth on an auction site. And especially—absolutely critically—where to get rid of it safely."

137. Bruce Sterling, "Viridian Note 00422: The Spime," 24 Aug. 2004, <http://www.viridian design.org/notes/401-450/00422_the_spime.html>.

138. Toby Miller, audio file, Television in Transition Conference, Massachusetts Institute of Technology, 2–4 May 2003, 31 Aug. 2004, <http://cms.mit.edu/mit3/subs/plenary1.html#sum mary>. It is worth noting that television studies and the related areas of cultural, communications, film, media, and Internet studies have addressed a variety of sites and questions that are not focused on subjectivity.

139. N. Katherine Hayles, "Flesh and Metal: Reconfiguring the Mindbody in Virtual Environments," in *Semiotic Flesh: Information and the Human Body*, ed. Phillip Thurtle and Robert Mitchell (Seattle: Walter Chapin Simpson Center for the Humanities, 2002), 53.

Acknowledgments

1. Hallmark, "Virtual Hug," Hallmark.com: Products, 11 Apr. 2005, <http://www.hallmark.com/ webapp/wcs/stores/servlet/ProductDisplay?catalogId=10051&storeId=10001&productId=526955 &CatIDsList=-2%3B-102001%3B11444%3B-102242&step=&tabOn=products&rank=P1R3SO>.

2. Butler, "Preface," in *Bodies that Matter*.

Selected Bibliography

Note: Most of the web sites that are discussed and quoted in this book are not listed in this selected bibliography. When a web site citation does appear, the date listed before the URL is the last time that the site was viewed in the format described. In instances where two dates are listed, the first date indicates when the current configuration of the site was first available, according to the site designers, or the date that the Internet "article" was offered. Formatting these diverse texts was difficult because evaluative implications accompanied each decision. The titles of Internet sites are not italicized because distinguishing between Internet journals and web sites created a hierarchy. Since titles are traditionally italicized in print literature, titles of articles that were available in print but accessed from a database or web site are italicized.

Aarseth, Espen. *Cybertext: Perspectives on Ergodic Literature*. Baltimore, MD: Johns Hopkins University Press, 1997.

Allen, Christina. *Virtual Identities: The Social Construction of Cybered Selves*. Ph.D. dissertation. Northwestern University, 1996.

Allen, Robert C., ed. *Channels of Discourse, Reassembled: Television and Contemporary Criticism*, 2nd ed. Chapel Hill: University of North Carolina Press, 1992.

Althusser, Louis. "Ideology and Ideological State Apparatuses (Notes toward an Investigation)." In *Lenin and Philosophy, and Other Essays*, trans. Ben Brewster, 85–126. New York: Monthly Review Press, 1972.

Amelunxen, Hubertus V., ed. *Photography after Photography: Memory and Representation in the Digital Age*. Amsterdam: G+B Arts, 1996.

Anderson, Poul. *The Avatar*. New York: Berkley-Putnam, 1978.

Armstrong, Carol. *Scenes in a Library: Reading the Photograph in the Book, 1843–1875*. Cambridge, MA: MIT Press, 1998.

Atwood, Margaret. *Oryx and Crake*. New York: Anchor Books, 2004.

Bacon-Smith, Camille. *Science Fiction Culture*. Philadelphia: University of Pennsylvania Press, 2000.

Bakhtin, Mikhail. *Rabelais and His World*, trans. Hélène Iswolsky. Bloomington: Indiana University Press, 1984.

Barbatsis, Gretchen, Michael Fegan, and Kenneth Hansen. "The Performance of Cyberspace: An Exploration into Computer-mediated Reality." Journal of Computer Mediated Communication 5, 1 (Sept. 1999). 1 Sept. 2004, <http://www.ascusc.org/jcmc/vol5/issue1/barbatsis.html>.

Barnes, Bingo. "I'll Show You Mine." *Las Vegas Weekly*, 9 Dec. 1999. 2 Sept. 2004, <http://www.lasvegasweekly.com/features/ill_show_you_mine.html>.

Barrios, Jorge R., and Deanna Wilkes-Gibbs. "How to MOO without Making a Sound: A Guide to the Virtual Communities Known as MOOs." In *High Wired: On the Design, Use, and Theory of Educational MOOs*, ed. Cynthia Haynes and Jan Rune Holmevik, 45–87. Ann Arbor: University of Michigan Press, 1998.

Barthes, Roland. *Camera Lucida: Reflections on Photography*, trans. Richard Howard. New York: Hill and Wang, 1981.

Barthes, Roland. *Image/Music/Text*, trans. Stephen Heath. New York: Hill and Wang, 1977.

Barthes, Roland. *The Pleasure of the Text*, trans. Richard Miller. New York: Hill and Wang, 1995.

Barthes, Roland. *Roland Barthes by Roland Barthes*, trans. Richard Howard. Berkeley: University of California Press, 1977.

Barthes, Roland. *The Rustle of Language*, trans. Richard Howard. New York: Hill and Wang, 1986.

Barthes, Roland. *S/Z: An Essay*, trans. Richard Miller. New York: Hill and Wang, 1974.

Bartle, Richard. "Interactive Multi-user Computer Games," Electronic Frontier Foundation, Dec. 1990. 2 Sept. 2004, <http://www.eff.org/Net_culture/MOO_MUD_IRC/>.

The Basel Action Network and Silicon Valley Toxics Coalition. "Exporting Harm: The High-tech Trashing of Asia," Silicon Valley Toxics Coalition, 25 Feb. 2003. 31 Aug. 2004, <http://svtc.igc.org/cleancc/pubs/harm.htm>.

Batchen, Geoffrey. *Burning with Desire: The Conception of Photography*. Cambridge, MA: MIT Press, 1999.

Baudrillard, Jean. *Simulacra and Simulation*, trans. Sheila Faria Glaser. Ann Arbor: The University of Michigan Press, 1994.

Baudry, Jean-Louis. "Ideological Effects of the Basic Cinematographic Apparatus." In *Narrative, Apparatus, Ideology: A Film Theory Reader*, ed. Philip Rosen, 286–298. New York: Columbia University Press, 1986.

Baumgärtel, Tilman. "Interview with Jodi." Telepolis, 10 June 1997. 7 Sept. 2004, <http://www.heise.de/tp/english/html/result.xhtml?url=/tp/english/special/ku/6187/1.html&words=Baumgaertel>.

Bazin, André. *What Is Cinema?*, trans. Hugh Gray. Berkeley: University of California Press, 1967.

Beebe, Roger Warren. "After Arnold: Narratives of the Posthuman Cinema." In *Meta-morphing: Visual Transformation and the Culture of Quick Change*, ed. Vivian Sobchack, 159–182. Minneapolis: University of Minnesota Press, 2000.

Bell, David, and Barbara M. Kennedy, eds. *The Cybercultures Reader*. New York: Routledge, 2000.

Bender, Gretchen, and Timothy Druckrey, eds. *Culture on the Brink: Ideologies of Technology*. Seattle: Bay Press, 1994.

Benedikt, Michael, ed. *Cyberspace: First Steps*. Cambridge, MA: MIT Press, 1992.

Benjamin, Walter. *Illuminations*, ed. Hannah Arendt, trans. Harry Zohn. New York: Schocken Books, 1969.

Bennett, Tony. *The Birth of the Museum: History, Theory, Politics*. New York: Routledge, 1995.

Berger, John. *Ways of Seeing*. London: Penguin Books, 1972.

Bersani, Leo. *The Freudian Body: Psychoanalysis and Art*. New York: Columbia University Press, 1986.

Berst, Jesse. "Around the World in Eight E-Links." ZDNeT, 24 Dec. 1998. 30 June 2002, <http://www.zdnet.com/anchordesk/story/story_2908.html>.

Birringer, Johannes. *Media and Performance along the Border*. Baltimore, MD: Johns Hopkins University Press, 1998.

Blair, Kristine and Pamela Takayoshi. "Navigating the Image of Woman Online: Whose Gaze Is It, Anyway?" Kairos 2, 2 (Fall 1997). 6 Sept. 2004, <http://english.ttu.edu/kairos/2.2/coverweb/invited/kb3.html>.

Bolter, Jay David. *Writing Space: The Computer, Hypertext, and the History of Writing*. Hillsdale, NJ: Lawrence Erlbaum Associates, 1991.

Bolter, Jay David, and Richard Grusin. *Remediation: Understanding New Media*. Cambridge, MA: MIT Press, 1999.

Bordo, Susan. *Unbearable Weight*. Berkeley: University of California Press, 1993.

Bosma, Josephine. "Text for Moscow: Between Moderation and Extremes. The Tensions between Net Art Theory and Popular Art Discourse." Switch 6, 1. 6 Sept. 2004, <http://switch.sjsu.edu/web/v6n1/article_b.htm>.

Brand, Peg Zeglin, ed. *Beauty Matters*. Bloomington: Indiana University Press, 2000.

Braziel, Jana Evans, and Kathleen LeBesco, eds. *Bodies Out of Bounds: Fatness and Transgression*. Berkeley: University of California Press, 2001.

Brooks, James, and Iain A. Boal, eds. *Resisting the Virtual Life: The Culture and Politics of Information*. San Francisco: City Lights, 1995.

Broude, Norma, and Mary D. Garrard, eds. *The Expanding Discourse: Feminism and Art History*. New York: HarperCollins, 1992.

Broude, Norma, and Mary D. Garrard, eds. *The Power of Feminist Art*. New York: Harry N. Abrams, 1994.

Brown, Janelle. "Life, Death and Everquest." Salon, 21 Nov. 2000. 6 June 2002, <http://www.salon.com/tech/feature/2000/11/21/virtual_suicide/index1.html>.

Bruckman, Amy. "Community Support for Constructionist Learning." *Computer Supported Cooperative Work* 7 (1998): 47–86. 2 Sept. 2004, <http://www.cc.gatech.edu/fac/Amy.Bruckman/papers/cscw.html>.

Bruckman, Amy. "Ethical Guidelines for Research Online." 4 Apr. 2002. 31 Aug. 2004, <http://www.cc.gatech.edu/~asb/ethics>.

Brundson, Charlotte, Julie D'Acci, and Lynn Spigel, eds. *Feminist Television Criticism: A Reader*. Oxford: Clarendon Press, 1997.

Bryson, Norman. "The Gaze in the Expanded Field." In *Vision and Visuality*, ed. Hal Foster, 87–114. Seattle: Bay Press, 1988.

Bukatman, Scott. *Terminal Identity: The Virtual Subject in Post-modern Science Fiction*. Durham, NC: Duke University Press, 1993.

Bul, Lee. "Beauty and Trauma." *Art Journal* 59, 3 (Fall 2000): 104–107.

Burch, Noël. *Theory of Film Practice*, trans. Helen R. Lane. New York: Praeger Publishers, 1973.

Burgin, Victor. "Jenni's Room: Exhibitionism and Solitude." *Critical Inquiry* 27, 1 (Autumn 2000): 77–89.

Burns, Bill, Cathy Busby, and Kim Sawchuck, eds. *When Pain Strikes*. Minneapolis: University of Minnesota Press, 1999.

Butler, Judith. *Bodies that Matter: On the Discursive Limits of "Sex."* New York: Routledge, 1993.

Butler, Judith. "The Force of Fantasy: Feminism, Mapplethorpe, and Discursive Excess." *Differences: A Journal of Feminist Cultural Studies* 2, 2 (Summer 1990): 105–125.

Butler, Judith. *Gender Trouble: Feminism and the Subversion of Identity*. New York: Routledge, 1989.

Butler, Octavia. *Parable of the Sower*. New York: Warner Books, 1993.

Cadigan, Pat. *Dervish Is Digital*. New York: Tor Books, 2000.

Cadigan, Pat. "Icy You . . . Juicy Me." *The Register*, 3 Sept. 2001. 15 July 2004, <http://www.theregister.co.uk/content/6/17497.html>.

Cadigan, Pat. *Synners*. New York: Bantam Books, 1991.

Campanella, Thomas J. "Be There Now." Salon, 7 Aug. 1997. 6 Sept. 2004, <http://www.salon.com/aug97/21st/cam970807.html>.

Campanella, Thomas J. "Who Says the Net Makes Cities Obsolete." Salon, 7 Aug. 1997. 6 Sept. 2004, <http://www.salon.com/aug97/21st/cities970807.html>.

Campbell, John Edward. *Getting It on Online: Cyberspace, Gay Male Sexuality, and Embodied Identity*. Binghamton, NY: Harrington Park Press, 2004.

Carr, Diane. "Play Dead: Genre and Affect in *Silent Hill* and *Planescape Torment*." Game Studies: The International Journal of Computer Game Research 3, 1 (May 2003). 31 Aug. 2004, <http://gamestudies.org/0301/carr/>.

Carson, Diane, Laura Dittmar, and Janice R. Welsch. *Multiple Voices in Feminist Film Criticism*. Minneapolis: University of Minnesota Press, 1994.

Cartwright, Lisa. *Screening the Body: Tracing Medicine's Visual Culture*. Minneapolis and London: University of Minnesota Press, 1995.

Cascone, Kim. "The Aesthetics of Failure: 'Post-Digital' Tendencies in Contemporary Computer Music." *Computer Music Journal* 24, 4 (Winter 2000): 12–18, 11 Sept. 2004, <http://0-lysander .ingentaselect.com.luna.wellesley.edu:80/vl=8538791/cl=14/nw=1/fm=docpdf/rpsv/cw/mitpress/ 01489267/v24n4/s4/p12>.

Cassell, Justine, and Henry Jenkins, eds. *From Barbie to Mortal Kombat*. Cambridge, MA: MIT Press, 1998.

Cavallaro, Dani. *Cyberpunk and Cyberculture: Science Fiction and the Work of William Gibson*. London: Athlone Press, 2000.

Cavell, Stanley. *The World Viewed: Reflections on the Ontology of Film*. New York: Viking Press, 1971.

Cha, Theresa Hak Kyung, ed. *Apparatus: Cinematographic Apparatus: Selected Writings*. New York: Tanam Press, 1980.

Cherny, Lynn. *Conversation and Community: Chat in a Virtual World*. Stanford, CA: CSLI Publications, 1999.

Cherny, Lynn, and Elizabeth Reba Weise, eds. *Wired Women: Gender and New Realities in Cyberspace*. Seattle: Seal Press, 1996.

Clover, Carol. *Men, Women, and Chain Saws: Gender in the Modern Horror Film*. Princeton: Princeton University Press, 1992.

Cohen, Alain J-J. "Virtual Hollywood and the Genealogy of Its Hyper-spectator." In *Hollywood Spectatorship: Changing Perceptions of Cinema Audiences*, ed. Melvyn Stokes and Richard Maltby, 152–163. London: British Film Institute, 2001.

Colomina, Beatriz, ed. *Sexuality and Space*. Princeton: Princeton University Press, 1992.

Cooke, Lynne, and Peter Wollen, eds. *Visual Display: Culture beyond Appearances*. Seattle: Bay Press, 1995.

Coombe, Rosemary J. *The Cultural Life of Intellectual Properties: Authorship, Appropriation, and the Law*. Durham, NC: Duke University Press, 1998.

Copjec, Joan. "The Anxiety of the Influencing Machine." *October* 23 (Winter 1982): 43–59.

Corrin, Lisa, ed. *Mining the Museum: An Installation by Fred Wilson.* Baltimore, MD: The Contemporary, in association with W. W. Norton, 1994. Published in conjunction with the exhibition Mining the Museum, The Contemporary and the Maryland Historical Society, 4 Apr. 1992–28 Feb. 1993.

Cosik, Vuk, and Alexei Shulgin, "Who Drew the Line?" Net Criticism, ZKP2 Proceedings, June 1996. 6 Sept. 2004, <http://www.nettime.org/desk-mirror/zkp2/theline.html>.

Crang, Mike, Phil Crang, and Jon May, eds. *Virtual Geographies: Bodies, Space and Relations.* New York: Routledge, 1999.

Crary, Jonathan. "Eclipse of the Spectacle." In *Art after Modernism: Rethinking Representation*, ed. Brian Wallis, 282–294. New York: New Museum of Contemporary Art, 1984.

Crary, Jonathan. *Techniques of the Observer: On Vision and Modernity in the Nineteenth Century.* Cambridge, MA: MIT Press, 1991.

Crimp, Douglas. *On the Museum's Ruins.* Cambridge, MA: MIT Press, 1993.

Curtis, Pavel. "Mudding Social Phenomena in Text-based Virtual Realities." Electronic Frontier Foundation MOO_MUD_IRC Archive. Paper presented at the conference on Directions and Implications of Advanced Computing, sponsored by Computer Professionals for Social Responsibility, Berkeley, CA, 1992. 2 Sept 2004, <http://www.eff.org/Net_culture/MOO_MUD _IRC/curtis_mudding.article>.

Curtis, Pavel. "Muds Grow Up: Social Virtual Reality in the Real World." Electronic Frontier Foundation MOO_MUD_IRC Archive, 5 May 1993. 2 Sept. 2004, <http://www.eff.org/ Net_culture/MOO_MUD_IRC/muds_grow_up.paper>.

Curtis, Pavel. "Not Just a Game: How LambdaMOO Came to Exist and What It Did to Get Back at Me." In *High Wired: On the Design, Use, and Theory of Educational MOOs*, ed. Cynthia Haynes and Jan Rune Holmevik, 25–44. Ann Arbor: University of Michigan Press, 1998.

Damer, Bruce. *Avatars! Exploring and Building Virtual Worlds on the Internet.* Berkeley, CA: Peach Pit Press, 1998.

Danet, Brenda. *Cyberpl@y: Communicating Online.* Oxford: Berg Publishers, 2001.

Darley, Andrew. *Visual Digital Culture: Surface Play and Spectacle in New Media Genres.* New York: Routledge, 2000.

Davis, Sheila, and Ted Smith. "Corporate Strategies for Electronic Recycling: A Tale of Two Systems." Silicon Valley Toxics Coalition and the Computer TakeBack Campaign! 25 June 2003. 31 Aug. 2004, <http://svtc.igc.org/cleancc/pubs/prison_final.pdf>.

de Lauretis, Teresa. *Alice Doesn't: Feminism, Semiotics, Cinema.* Bloomington: Indiana University Press, 1984.

de Lauretis, Teresa. *Technologies of Gender: Essays on Theory, Film, and Fiction.* Bloomington: Indiana University Press, 1987.

de Lauretis, Teresa. "Through the Looking Glass." In *Narrative, Apparatus, Ideology: A Film Theory Reader*, ed. Philip Rosen, 360–374. New York: Columbia University Press, 1986.

de Lauretis, Teresa, and Stephen Heath, eds. *The Cinematic Apparatus*. New York: St. Martin's Press, 1985.

Deleuze, Gilles. *Foucault*, trans. Sean Hand. Minneapolis: University of Minnesota Press, 1988.

Deleuze, Gilles, and Félix Guattari. *A Thousand Plateaus: Capitalism and Schizophrenia*, trans. Brian Massumi. Minneapolis: University of Minnesota Press, 1987.

Denzin, Norman K. "Cybertalk and the Method of Instances." In *Doing Internet Research: Critical Issues and Methods for Examining the Net*, ed. Steven G. Jones, 107–126. Thousand Oaks, CA: Sage Publications, 1999.

Dery, Mark. "Cyborging the Body Politic." *MONDO 2000* (1992): 101–105.

Dery, Mark. *Escape Velocity: Cyberculture at the End of the Century*. New York: Grove Press, 1996.

Dery, Mark. *Flame Wars: The Discourse of Cyberculture*. Durham, NC: Duke University Press, 1994.

Devereaux, Mary. "The Philosophical Status of Aesthetics." 6 Sept. 2004, <http://www.aesthetics-online.org/ideas/devereaux.html>.

Dibbell, Julian. *My Tiny Life: Crime and Passion in a Virtual World*. New York: Holt, 1998.

Dibbell, Julian. "A Rape in Cyberspace; or, How an Evil Clown, a Haitian Trickster Spirit, Two Wizards, and a Cast of Dozens Turned a Database into a Society." *The Village Voice*, 21 Dec. 1993, 36–42.

Dick, Philip K. *Do Androids Dream of Electric Sheep?* New York: New American Library, 1968.

Dietz, Steve. "Why Have There Been No Great Net Artists?" Webwalker 28, 23 Apr. 2000. 6 Sept. 2004, <http://www.walkerart.org/gallery9/webwalker/index.html>.

Dinnerstein, Myra, and Rose Weitz. "Jane Fonda, Barbara Bush, and Other Aging Bodies." In *The Politics of Women's Bodies: Sexuality, Appearance, and Behavior*, ed. Rose Weitz, 189–206. New York: Oxford University Press, 1998.

Doane, Mary Ann. *The Desire to Desire: The Woman's Film of the 1940s*. Bloomington: Indiana University Press, 1987.

Doane, Mary Ann. *The Emergence of Cinematic Time: Modernity, Contingency, the Archive*. Cambridge, MA: Harvard University Press, 2002.

Doane, Mary Ann. *Femmes Fatales: Feminism, Film Theory, Psychoanalysis*. New York: Routledge, 1991.

Doane, Mary Ann. "Misrecognition and Identity." *Cine-Tracts* 11 (Fall 1980): 25–32.

Doheny-Farina, Stephen. *The Wired Neighborhood*. New Haven, CT: Yale University Press, 1996.

Dolan, Jill. *The Feminist Spectator as Critic*. Ann Arbor: University of Michigan Press, 1991.

Dourish, Paul. "Where the Footprints Lead: Tracking Down Other Roles for Social Navigation." In *Social Navigation of Information Space*, ed. Alan J. Munro, Kristina Höök, and David Benyon, 15–34. London: Springer-Verlag, 1999.

Drucker, Susan J., and Gary Gumpert, eds. *Real Law@Virtual Space: Communication Regulation in Cyberspace*. Cresskill, NJ: Hampton Press, 1999.

Druckrey, Timothy, ed. *Electronic Culture: Technology and Visual Representation*. New York: Aperture, 1997.

Druckrey, Timothy. "L'Amour Faux." In *Digital Photography: Captured Images, Volatile Memory, New Montage*, ed. Marnie Gillett and Jim Pomeroy. San Francisco: Camerawork, 1988.

Duncan, Carol. *Civilizing Rituals: Inside Public Art Museums*. London: Routledge, 1995.

Dvorak, John. "Little Brother Is Watching." ZDNet, 20 Nov. 2000. 6 Sept. 2004, <http://zdnet.com.com/2100-1107-503080.html>.

Dyson, Esther. *Release 2.0: A Design for Living in the Digital Age*. New York: Broadway Books, 1997.

Ebert, Roger. "Rear Window Is Alive on the Web: Watching Is Weird, but So Is Being Watched." *Yahoo! Internet Life*, Nov. 2000. 30 Oct. 2000, <http://www.zdnet.com/yil/stories/features/0,9539,2644881,00.html>.

Eco, Umberto. *The Open Work*. Cambridge, MA: Harvard University Press, 1989.

Eco, Umberto. *Travels in Hyper Reality*. San Diego: Harcourt Brace Jovanovich, 1986.

Edgar, Andrew, and Peter Sedgwick, eds. *Key Concepts in Cultural Theory*. New York: Routledge, 1999.

Edison, Laurie Toby, and Debbie Notkin, eds. *Women En Large: Images of Fat Nudes*. San Francisco: Books in Focus, 1994.

Ess, Charles, ed. *Ethics and Information Technology* 4, 3 (2002).

Ess, Charles, and the AoIR Ethics Working Committee. "Ethical Decision-making and Internet Research: Recommendations from the AoIR Ethics Working Committee." Ethics Report/ Association of Internet Researchers, 27 Nov. 2002. 3 Oct. 2003, <http://www.aoir.org/reports/ethics.pdf>.

Ess, Charles, and Fay Sudweeks, eds. *Culture, Technology, Communication: Towards an Intercultural Global Village*. Albany: State University of New York Press, 2001.

Everett, Anna. "The Revolution Will Be Digitized: Afrocentricity and the Digital Public Sphere." Special Issue on Afrofuturism, ed. Alondra Nelson. *Social Text* 71, 20, 2 (Summer 2002): 125–146.

Everett, Anna, and John T. Caldwell, eds. *New Media: Theories and Practices of Digitextuality*. London: Routledge, 2003.

Fausto-Sterling, Anne. *Myths of Gender: Biological Theories about Women and Men*. New York: Basic Books, 1992.

Fausto-Sterling, Anne. *Sexing the Body: Gender Politics and the Construction of Sexuality*. New York: Basic Books, 2000.

Featherstone, Mike, and Roger Burrows. *Cyberspace/Cyberbodies/Cyberpunk: Cultures of Technological Embodiment*. London: Sage Publications, 1995.

Fernback, Jan. "There Is a There There: Notes toward a Definition of Cybercommunity." In *Doing Internet Research: Critical Issues and Methods for Examining the Net*, ed. Steven G. Jones, 203–220. Thousand Oaks, CA: Sage Publications, 1999.

Firth, Simon. "Live! From My Bedroom." Salon, 8 Jan. 1998. 6 Sept. 2004, <http://www.salon.com/21st/feature/1998/01/cov_08feature.html/>.

Fisher, Jim. "Poison PCs." Salon, 18 Sept. 2000. 27 Aug. 2004, <http://dir.salon.com/tech/feature/2000/09/18/toxic_pc/index.html?pn=1>.

Fjermedal, Grant. *The Tomorrow Makers: A Brave New World of Living-brain Machines*. New York: Macmillan, 1986.

Flanagan, Are. "Layers: Looking at Photography and Photoshop." *Afterimage* 30, 1 (July/Aug. 2002): 10–12.

Flanagan, Are. "Memory: Cleverly Disguised as a Database." *Afterimage* 29, 6 (May/June 2002): 12–13.

Foster, Hal, ed. *The Anti-aesthetic: Essays on Postmodern Culture*. Port Townsend, WA: Bay Press, 1983.

Foucault, Michel. *Discipline and Punish: The Birth of the Prison*. New York: Vintage Books, 1995.

Foucault, Michel. *Power/Knowledge: Selected Interviews and Other Writing*, ed. Colin Gordon. New York: Pantheon Books, 1980.

Foucault, Michel. "What Is an Author?" In *The Art of Art History: A Critical Anthology*, ed. Donald Preziosi, 299–314. Oxford: Oxford University Press, 1998.

Frankel, Mark S., and Sanyin Siang. "Ethical and Legal Aspects of Human Subjects in Cyberspace." American Association for the Advancement of Science, 1999. 14 Sept. 2004, <http://www.aaas.org/spp/dspp/sfrl/projects/intres/main.htm>.

Fried, Michael. *Absorption and Theatricality: Painting and Beholder in the Age of Diderot*. Berkeley: University of California Press, 1980.

Fried, Michael. *Courbet's Realism*. Chicago: University of Chicago Press, 1990.

Fried, Michael. *Three American Painters: Kenneth Noland, Jules Olitski, Frank Stella*. Cambridge, MA: Fogg Art Museum, 1965.

Friedberg, Anne. "The End of Cinema: Multi-media and Technological Change." In *Reinventing Film Studies*, ed. Christine Gledhill and Linda Williams, 438–452. London: Arnold, 2002.

Friedman, James, ed. *Reality Squared: Televisual Discourse on the Real*. New Brunswick, NJ: Rutgers University Press, 2002.

Fuss, Diana. *Essentially Speaking: Feminism, Nature, and Difference*. New York: Routledge, 1989.

Fuss, Diana. "Fashion and the Homospectorial Look." In *Identities*, ed. Kwame Anthony Appiah and Henry Louis Gates, Jr., 90–114. Chicago: The University of Chicago Press, 1995.

Gallop, Jane. "The Pleasure of the Phototext." In *Illuminations: Women Writing on Photography from the 1850s to the Present*, ed. Liz Heron and Val Williams, 394–402. Durham, NC: Duke University Press, 1996.

Gandy, Oscar H. *The Panoptic Sort: A Political Economy of Personal Information*. Boulder: Westview Press, 1993.

Garber, Marjorie. *Vested Interests: Cross-dressing and Cultural Anxiety*. New York: Routledge, 1992.

Gatens, Moira. "Power, Bodies and Difference." In *Feminist Theory and the Body: A Reader*, ed. Janet and Margrit Shildrick, 227–234. New York: Routledge, 1999.

Gauntlett, David, ed. *Web.studies: Rewiring Media Studies for the Digital Age*. London: Arnold, 2000.

Gibson, William. *Burning Chrome*. New York: Ace Books, 1986.

Gibson, William. *Neuromancer*. New York: Ace Books, 1984.

Glover, David, and Cora Kaplan. *Genders*. London and New York: Routledge, 2000.

Goldberg, Ken, ed. *The Robot in the Garden: Telerobotics and Telepistemology in the Age of the Internet*. Cambridge, MA: MIT Press, 2000.

Gomez-Peña, Guillermo. "The Virtual Barrio @ The Other Frontier (Or the Chicano Interneta)." ZoneZero: From Analog to Digital, Jan. 1997. 6 Sept. 2004, <http://www.zonezero.com/magazine/articles/gomezpena/gomezpena.html>.

Gonzales-Day, Ken. "Analytical Photography: Portraiture, from the Index to the Epidermis." *Leonardo* 35, 1 (Feb. 2002): 15–21.

Gonzalez, Jennifer. "The Appended Subject: Race and Identity as Digital Assemblage." In *Race in Cyberspace*, ed. Beth E. Kolko, Lisa Nakamura, and Gilbert B. Rodman, 27–50. New York: Routledge, 2000.

Goodman, Peter S. "China Serves as Dump Site for Computers: Unsafe Recycling Practice Grows Despite Import Ban." *Washington Post*, A01, 24 Feb. 2003. 31 Aug. 2004, <http://www.washingtonpost.com/ac2/wp-dyn/A56653-2003Feb24?language=printer>.

Grau, Oliver. *Virtual Art: From Illusion to Immersion*. Cambridge, MA: MIT Press, 2003.

Gray, Chris Habels, ed. *The Cyborg Handbook*. New York: Routledge, 1995.

Green, Eileen, and Alison Adam, eds. *Virtual Gender: Technology, Consumption and Identity*. New York: Routledge, 2001.

Greenberg, Clement. *Art and Culture: Critical Essays.* Boston: Beacon Press, 1961.

Grigar, Dene, and John F. Barber. "Defending Your Life in MOOspace: A Report from the Electronic Edge." In *High Wired: On the Design, Use, and Theory of Educational MOOs*, ed. Cynthia Haynes and Jan Rune Holmevik, 192–231. Ann Arbor: University of Michigan Press, 1998.

Grossman, Lev. "Salon 21st | Terrors of the Amazon." Salon, 2 Mar. 1999. 6 Sept. 2004, <http://archive.salon.com/21st/feature/1999/03/02feature2.html>.

Grosz, Elizabeth. *Architecture from the Outside: Essays on Virtual and Real Space.* Cambridge, MA: MIT Press, 2001.

Grosz, Elizabeth, ed. *Becomings: Explorations in Time, Memory, and Futures.* Ithaca, NY: Cornell University Press, 1999.

Grosz, Elizabeth. *Space, Time, and Perversion.* New York and London: Routledge, 1995.

Grosz, Elizabeth. *Volatile Bodies: Toward a Corporeal Feminism.* Bloomington: Indiana University Press, 1994.

Hafner, Katie. *Cyberpunk: Outlaws and Hackers on the Computer Frontier.* New York: Simon & Schuster, 1991.

Hafner, Katie. *Where Wizards Stay Up Late: The Origins of the Internet.* New York: Simon & Schuster, 1996.

Haraway, Donna. *Modest-Witness@Second-Millennium.FemaleMan-Meets-OncoMouse: Feminism and Technoscience.* New York: Routledge, 1997.

Haraway, Donna. *Simians, Cyborgs, and Women: The Reinvention of Nature.* New York: Routledge, 1991.

Harcourt, Wendy, ed. *Women@Internet: Creating New Cultures in Cyberspace.* London: Zed Books, 1999.

Harpold, Terry. "The Contingencies of the Hypertext Link," *The New Media Reader*, 2003. 7 Sept. 2004, <http://www.newmediareader.com/cd_samples/WOE/Harpold.html>.

Harries, Dan, ed. *The New Media Book.* London: BFI Publishing, 2002.

Harris, Cheryl, ed. *Theorizing Fandom: Fans, Subcultures and Identity.* Cresskill, NJ: Hampton Press, 1998.

Hartsock, Nancy. "Foucault on Power: A Theory for Women?" In *Feminism/Postmodernism*, ed. Linda J. Nicholson. New York: Routledge, 1990, 157–175.

Hasan, Khalid. "Pakistan a Dump for High-tech Junk." *Daily Times*, 24 Feb. 2003. 27 Aug. 2004, <http://www.dailytimes.com.pk/default.asp?page=story_25-2-2003_pg7_1>.

Haynes, Cynthia, and Jan Rune Holmevik, eds. *High Wired: On the Design, Use, and Theory of Educational MOOs.* Ann Arbor: University of Michigan Press, 1998.

Haynes, Cynthia, and Jan Rune Holmevik, eds. *High Wired: On the Design, Use, and Theory of Educational MOOs*, 2nd ed. Ann Arbor: University of Michigan Press, 2001.

Haynes, Cynthia, and Jan Rune Holmevik. "Lingua Unlimited: Enhancing Pedagogical Reality with MOOs." Kairos 1, 2 (1996). 6 Sept. 2004, <http://english.ttu.edu/kairos/1.2/binder2.html ?coverweb/HandH/start.html>.

Hayles, N. Katherine. *How We Became Posthuman: Virtual Bodies in Cybernetics, Literature, and Informatics*. Chicago: University of Chicago Press, 1999.

Hayles, N. Katherine. *Writing Machines*. Cambridge, MA: MIT Press, 2002.

Hebdige, Dick. *Subculture: The Meaning of Style*. London: Routledge, 1991.

Herman, Andrew, and Thomas Swiss, eds. *The World Wide Web and Contemporary Cultural Theory*. New York: Routledge, 2000.

Heron, Liz, and Val Williams, eds. *Illuminations: Women Writing on Photography from the 1850s to the Present*. Durham, NC: Duke University Press, 1996.

Herring, Susan. "Critical Analysis of Language Use in Computer-mediated Contexts: Some Ethical and Scholarly Considerations." *The Information Society* 12, 2 (1996). 12 Aug. 2004, <http://venus .soci.niu.edu/~jthomas/ethics/tis/go.susan>.

Herring, Susan. "Gender and Power in Online Communication." Center for Social Informatics, SLIS. Indiana University–Bloomington, Oct. 2001, 6 Sept. 2004, <http://www.slis.indiana.edu/ CSI/WP/WP01-05B.html>.

Hight, Eleanor M., and Gary D. Sampson, eds. *Colonialist Photography: Imag(in)ing Race and Place*. London: Routledge, 2002.

Higonnet, Anne. "Secluded Vision: Images of Feminine Experience in Nineteenth-century Europe." In *The Expanding Discourse: Feminism and Art History*, ed. Norma Broude and Mary D. Garrard, 171–186. New York: HarperCollins, 1992.

Hillis, Ken. *Digital Sensations: Space, Identity, and Embodiment in Virtual Reality*. Minneapolis: University of Minnesota Press, 1999.

Hine, Christine. *Virtual Ethnography*. London: Sage Publications, 2000.

Hirsch, Robert. *Seizing the Light: A History of Photography*. Boston: McGraw-Hill, 2000.

hooks, bell. *Black Looks: Race and Representation*. Boston: South End Press, 1992.

Humphreys. Christine. "Meet the Star of Jennicam." ABCNews.com, 4 Apr. 1998. 30 Oct. 2000, <http://abcnews.go.com/sections/tech/DailyNews/jennicam980422.html>.

Hutcheon, Linda. "Postmodernism and Feminisms." In *Postmodern Debates*, ed. Simon Malpas, 101–109. New York: Palgrave, 2001.

Irigaray, Luce. *This Sex which Is Not One*, trans. Catherine Porter. Ithaca, NY: Cornell University Press, 1985.

Jaggar, Alison M., and Susan R. Bordo, eds. *Gender/Body/Knowledge: Feminist Reconstructions of Being and Knowing*. New Brunswick, NJ: Rutgers University Press, 1989.

Jana, Reena. "David Ross: Director, San Francisco Museum of Modern Art." *Flash Art International* (Jan./Feb. 1999): 34–35.

The Jargon File 4.4.7, 29 Dec. 2003. 14 Sept. 2004, <http://www.catb.org/~esr/jargon/html/index.html>.

Jaszi, Peter. "On the Author Effect: Contemporary Copyright and Collective Creativity." In *The Construction of Authorship: Textual Appropriation in Law and Literature*, ed. Martha Woodmansee and Peter Jaszi, 29–56. Durham, NC: Duke University Press, 1994.

Jay, Martin. *Downcast Eyes: The Denigration of Vision in Twentieth-century French Thought*. Berkeley: University of California Press, 1994.

Jenkins, Henry. "Games, the New Lively Art." Forthcoming in *Handbook for Video Game Studies*, ed. Jeffrey Goldstein. Cambridge, MA: MIT Press. 1 Sept. 2004, <http://web.mit.edu/21fms/www/faculty/henry3/GamesNewLively.html>.

Jenkins, Henry. "Interactive Audiences? The 'Collective Intelligence' of Media Fans." In *The New Media Book*, ed. Dan Harries, 157–170. London: BFI Publishing, 2002.

Jenkins, Henry. *Textual Poachers: Television Fans and Participatory Culture*. New York: Routledge, 1992.

Johnson, Crockett. *Harold and the Purple Crayon*. New York: HarperCollins, 1955.

Johnson, Steve. *Interface Culture: How New Technology Transforms the Way We Create and Communicate*. San Francisco: HarperEdge, 1997.

Johnson, Victoria. "The Politics of Morphing: Michael Jackson as Science Fiction Border Text." *The Velvet Light Trap* 32 (Fall 1993): 58–65.

Jones, Amelia. *Body Art/Performing the Subject*. Minneapolis: University of Minnesota Press, 1998.

Jones, Caroline A. *Machine in the Studio: Constructing the Postwar American Artist*. Chicago: University of Chicago Press, 1996.

Jones, Steven G., ed. *CyberSociety: Computer-mediated Communication and Community*. Thousand Oaks, CA: Sage Publications, 1995.

Jones, Steven G., ed. *CyberSociety 2.0: Revisiting Computer-mediated Communication and Community*. Thousand Oaks, CA: Sage Publications, 1998.

Jones, Steven G., ed. *Doing Internet Research: Critical Issues and Methods for Examining the Net*. Thousand Oaks, CA: Sage Publications, 1999.

Kahin, Brian, and James Keller. *Public Access to the Internet*. Cambridge, MA: MIT Press, 1995.

Kant, Immanuel. *Critique of Judgment*, trans. J. H. Bernard. New York: Haffner Press, 1951.

Kaplan, E. Ann. *Women and Film: Both Sides of the Camera*. New York: Methuen, 1983.

Kember, Sarah. *Virtual Anxiety: Photography, New Technologies and Subjectivity*. Manchester: Manchester University Press, 1998.

Kent, Le'a. "Fighting Abjection: Representing Fat Women." In *Bodies Out of Bounds: Fatness and Transgression*, ed. Jana Evans Braziel and Kathleen LeBesco, 130–150. Berkeley: University of California Press, 2001.

Kessler, Suzanne J., and Wendy McKenna. *Gender: An Ethnomethodological Approach*. Chicago: The University of Chicago Press, 1978.

Key, Joan. "Unfold: Imprecations of Obscenity in the Fold." In *Other than Identity: The Subject, Politics and Art*, ed. Juliet Steyn, 185–197. Manchester: Manchester University Press, 1997.

Kirkham, Pat, ed. *The Gendered Object*. Manchester and New York: Manchester University Press, 1996.

Kirkup, Gill, Linda Janes, Katheryn Woodward, and Fiona Hovenden, eds. *The Gendered Cyborg: A Reader*. London: Routledge, 2000.

Knight, Brooke. A. "Watch Me! Webcams and the Public Exposure of Private Lives." *Art Journal* 59, 4 (Winter 2000): 21–25.

Kolko, Beth E. "Intellectual Property in Synchronous and Collaborative Virtual Space." In *Cyberethics: Social and Moral Issues in the Computer Age*, ed. Robert M. Baird, Reagan Ramsower, and Stuart E. Rosenbaum, 257–282. Amherst: Prometheus Books, 2000.

Kolko, Beth E., Lisa Nakamura, and Gilbert B. Rodman, eds. *Race in Cyberspace*. New York: Routledge, 2000.

Koppell, Jonathan G. S. "No 'There' There: Why Cyberspace Isn't Anyplace." *The Atlantic Monthly* 286, 2 (Aug. 2000): 16–18. 28 May 2002, <http://www.theatlantic.com/issues/2000/08/koppell.htm>.

Kotamraju, Nalini P. "Keeping Up: Web Design Skill and the Reinvented Worker." *Information, Communication, and Society* 5, 1 (2002): 1–26.

Kotz, Liz, and Judith Butler. "The Body You Want." *Artforum* (Nov. 1992): 82–89.

Kracauer, Siegfried. *Theory of Film: The Redemption of Physical Reality*. London: Oxford University Press, 1976.

Krauss, Rosalind. *L'Amour Fou: Photography and Surrealism*. New York: Abbeville Press, 1985.

Krauss, Rosalind. "Originality as Repetition: Introduction." *October* 37 (Summer 1986): 35–40.

Krauss, Rosalind. *The Originality of the Avant-garde and Other Modernist Myths*. Cambridge, MA: MIT Press, 1994.

Kuhn, Annette, ed. *Alien Zone: Cultural Theory and Contemporary Science Fiction*. London: Verso, 1990.

Kuhn, Annette. "Remembrance." In *Illuminations: Women Writing on Photography from the 1850s to the Present*, ed. Liz Heron and Val Williams, 471–478. Durham, NC: Duke University Press, 1996.

Kurzweil, Ray. *The Age of Intelligent Machines*. Cambridge, MA: MIT Press, 1990.

Kurzweil, Ray. *The Age of Spiritual Machines: When Computers Exceed Human Intelligence*. New York: Viking Penguin, 1999.

Kurzweil, Ray. "Live Forever—Uploading The Human Brain . . . Closer than You Think." *Psychology Today*. 2 Feb. 2000. 26 Aug. 2004, <http://www.kurzweilai.net/meme/frame.html ?main=/articles/art0157.html>.

Lacan, Jacques. *Écrits: A Selection*, trans. A. Sheridan. New York: W. W. Norton, 1977.

Lacan, Jacques. *The Four Fundamental Concepts of Psycho-analysis*, trans. A. Sheridan. New York: W. W. Norton, 1981.

Landman, Howard A. "Sonnets to JenniCam," I, 7, Poetry and Song Lyrics, 25 Jan. 1999. 30 June 2002, <http://www.polyamory.org/~howard/Poetry/jennicamI07.html>.

Landow, George P., ed. *Hyper/Text/Theory*. Baltimore, MD: Johns Hopkins University Press, 1994.

Landow, George P. *Hypertext: The Convergence of Contemporary Critical Theory and Technology*. Baltimore, MD: Johns Hopkins University Press, 1992.

Landow, George P. *Hypertext 2.0: The Convergence of Contemporary Critical Theory and Technology*. Baltimore, MD: Johns Hopkins University Press, 1997.

Laurel, Brenda. *Computers as Theatre*. Reading, MA: Addison-Wesley, 1993.

Lavin, Maud. "Androgyny and Spectatorship." In *Cut with the Kitchen Knife: The Weimar Photomontages of Hannah Höch*, 185–204. New Haven, CT: Yale University Press, 1993.

Linder, Marc. *Void Where Prohibited: Rest Breaks and the Right to Urinate on Company Time*. Ithaca, NY: ILR Press, 1998.

Linder, Marc. *Void Where Prohibited Revisited: The Trickle-down Effect of OSHA's At-will Bathroom-break Regulation*. Iowa City: Fanpìhuà Press, 2003.

Lister, Martin, ed. *The Photographic Image in Digital Culture*. New York: Routledge, 1995.

Long, Elizabeth. "Textual Interpretation as Collective Action." In *Viewing, Reading, Listening: Audiences and Cultural Reception*, ed. Jon Cruz and Justin Lewis, 181–212. Boulder: Westview Press, 1994.

Ludlow, Peter, ed. *High Noon on the Electronic Frontier: Conceptual Issues in Cyberspace*. Cambridge, MA: MIT Press, 1996.

Lunenfeld, Peter, ed. *The Digital Dialectic: New Essays on New Media*. Cambridge, MA: MIT Press, 1999.

Lunenfeld, Peter. *Snap to Grid: A User's Guide to Digital Arts, Media, and Cultures*. Cambridge, MA: MIT Press, 2000.

Lyon, David. *The Electronic Eye: The Rise of Surveillance Society*. Minneapolis: University of Minnesota Press, 1994.

Lyon, David, ed. *Surveillance as Social Sorting: Privacy, Risk, and Digital Discrimination*. London and New York: Routledge, 2003.

Lyon, David. *Surveillance Society: Monitoring Everyday Life*. Buckingham, UK: Open University, 2001.

Mairs, Nancy. *Waist-high in the World: A Life among the Nondisabled*. Boston: Beacon Press, 1996.

Malraux, André. "Museum without Walls." In *The Voices of Silence: Man and His Art*, trans. Stuart Gilbert, 13–130. Garden City, NY: Doubleday, 1953.

Mandelbrojt, Jacques. "The Aesthetic Status of Technological Art." *Leonardo* 32, 3 (1999): 211–215.

Manovich, Lev. *The Language of New Media*. Cambridge, MA: MIT Press, 2000.

Marks, Laura U. *Touch: Sensuous Theory and Multisensory Media*. Minneapolis: University of Minnesota Press, 2002.

Mast, Gerald, Marshall Cohen, and Leo Braudy, eds. *Film Theory and Criticism: Introductory Readings*. New York and Oxford: Oxford University Press, 1992.

Maxwell, Anne. *Colonial Photography and Exhibitions: Representations of the 'Native' and the Making of European Identities*. London: Leicester University Press, 1999.

Mayne, Judith. *Cinema and Spectatorship*. London: Routledge, 1993.

Mayne, Judith. "Feminist Film Theory and Criticism." In *Multiple Voices in Feminist Film Criticism*, ed. Diane Carson, Linda Dittmar, and Janice. R. Welsch, 48–64. Minneapolis: University of Minnesota Press, 1994.

Mayne, Judith. *Framed: Lesbians, Feminists, and Media Culture*. Minneapolis: University of Minnesota Press, 2000.

McCaffery, Larry. "An Interview with William Gibson." *Mississippi Review* 16, 2/3 (1996). 1 Sept. 2004, <http://www.mississippireview.com/1996/9602gibs.html>.

Mellencamp, Patricia, ed. *Logics of Television: Essays in Cultural Criticism*. Bloomington: Indiana University Press, 1990.

Melville, Stephen, and Bill Readings, eds. *Vision and Textuality*. Durham, NC: Duke University Press, 1995.

Metz, Christian. *The Imaginary Signifier: Psychoanalysis and the Cinema*, trans. Celia Britton, Annwyl Williams, Ben Brewster, and Alfred Guzzetti. Bloomington: Indiana University Press, 1982.

Metz, Christian. "Photography and Fetish." *October* 34 (Fall 1985): 81–90.

Minh-ha, Trinh T. "No Master Territories." In *The Post-colonial Studies Reader*, ed. Bill Ashcroft, Gareth Griffiths, and Helen Tiffin, 215–218. London: Routledge, 1995.

Mirzoeff, Nicholas, ed. *Diaspora and Visual Culture: Representing Africans and Jews*. London: Routledge, 2000.

Mirzoeff, Nicholas, ed. *The Visual Culture Reader*. London: Routledge, 1998.

Mitchell, William J. *City of Bits: Space, Place, and the Infobahn*. Cambridge, MA: MIT Press, 1995.

Mitchell, William J. *The Reconfigured Eye: Visual Truth in the Post-photographic Era*. Cambridge, MA: MIT Press, 1992.

Moravec, Hans. *Mind Children: The Future of Robot and Human Intelligence*. Cambridge, MA: Harvard University Press, 1988.

Moravec, Hans. "Simulation, Consciousness, Existence." The Field Robotics Center at Carnegie Mellon University's Robotics Institute, 1998. 26 Aug. 2004, <http://www.frc.ri.cmu.edu/~hpm/project.archive/general.articles/1998/SimConEx.98.html>.

Morse, Margaret. "Body and Screen." *Wide Angle* 21, 1 (Jan. 1999): 63–75.

Morse, Margaret. "Smarting Flesh: Pain and the Posthuman." In *When Pain Strikes*, eds Bill Burns, Cathy Busby, and Kim Sawchuck, 247–254. Minneapolis: University of Minnesota Press, 1999.

Morse, Margaret. *Virtualities: Television, Media Art, and Cyberculture*. Bloomington: Indiana University Press, 1998.

Moser, Mary Anne, and Douglas MacLeod. *Immersed in Technology: Art and Virtual Environments*. Cambridge, MA: MIT Press, 1996.

Moulthrop, Stuart. "Error 404: Doubting the Web." In *The World Wide Web and Contemporary Cultural Theory*, ed. Andrew Herman and Thomas Swiss, 259–276. New York: Routledge, 2000.

Moulthrop, Stuart. "Traveling in the Breakdown Lane: A Principle of Resistance for Hypertext." *Mosaic* 28, 4 (1995): 55–77.

Moulthrop, Stuart. "Traveling in the Breakdown Lane: A Principle of Resistance for Hypertext," 1995. 3 July 2004, <http://iat.ubalt.edu/moulthrop/essays/breakdown.html>.

Mulvey, Laura. "Afterthoughts on 'Visual Pleasure and Narrative Cinema' Inspired by *Duel in the Sun*." *Framework* 15–17 (1981): 12–15.

Mulvey, Laura. "The 'Pensive Spectator' Revisited: Time and Its Passing in the Still and Moving Image." In *Where Is the Photograph?*, ed. David Green, 113–122. Brighton, UK: Photoforum and Photoworks, 2003.

Mulvey, Laura. *Visual and Other Pleasures*. Bloomington: Indiana University Press, 1989.

Mulvey, Laura. "Visual Pleasure and Narrative Cinema." *Screen* 16, 3 (Autumn 1975): 6–18.

Munro, Alan J., Kristina Höök, and David Benyon, eds. *Social Navigation of Information Space*. London: Springer-Verlag, 1999.

Munt, Sally R., ed. *Technospaces: Inside the New Media*. New York: Continuum, 2001.

Murray, James A. H., Henry Bradley, W. A. Craigie, and C. T. Onions, eds. *Oxford English Dictionary*, vol. 1. Oxford: Clarendon Press, 1961.

Nakamura, Lisa. *Cybertypes: Race, Ethnicity, and Identity on the Internet*. New York: Routledge, 2002.

National Safety Council's Environmental Health Center. *Electronic Product Recovery and Recycling Baseline Report*. Washington, DC: National Safety Council, 1999.

Nelson, Alondra, ed. *Technicolor: Race, Technology, and Everyday Life*. New York: New York University Press, 2001.

Newhall, Beaumont. *The History of Photography: From 1839 to the Present Day*, 4th ed. New York: Museum of Modern Art, 1981.

Nichols, Bill. "The Work of Culture in the Age of Cybernetic Systems." *Screen* 29, 1 (Winter 1988): 22–45.

Nochlin, Linda. *Women, Art, and Power and Other Essays*. New York: Harper & Row, 1984.

Notkin, Debbie. "Enlarging: Politics and Society." In *Women En Large: Images of Fat Nudes*, ed. Laurie Toby Edison and Debbie Notkin, 91–107. San Francisco: Books in Focus, 1994.

Nye, David E. *Narratives and Spaces: Technology and the Construction of American Culture*. New York: Columbia University Press, 1997.

Odasz, Frank. "Issues in the Development of Cooperative Networks." In *Public Access to the Internet*, ed. Brian Kahin and James Keller, 115–136. Cambridge, MA: MIT Press, 1995.

Olson, Marisa S. "Weighing In on Net Art's Worth." Wired News, 15 May 2000. 7 Sept. 2004, <http://www.wired.com/news/culture/0,1284,36320,00.html>.

Owens, Craig. *Beyond Recognition: Representation, Power, and Culture*. Berkeley: University of California Press, 1992.

Owens, Craig. "The Discourse of Others: Feminists and Postmodernism." *The Expanding Discourse: Feminism and Art History*, ed. Norma Broude and Mary D. Garrard, 487–502. New York: HarperCollins, 1992.

Paccagnella, Luciano. "Getting the Seats of Your Pants Dirty: Strategies for Ethnographic Research on Virtual Communities." Journal of Computer Mediated Communication 3, 1 (June 1997). 1 Sept. 2004, <http://www.ascusc.org/jcmc/vol3/issue1/paccagnella.html>.

Penley, Constance. "Brownian Motion: Women, Tactics, and Technology." In *Technoculture*, ed. Constance Penley and Andrew Ross, 135–162. Minneapolis: University of Minnesota Press, 1991.

Penley, Constance. *The Future of an Illusion: Film, Feminism, and Psychoanalysis*. Minneapolis: University of Minnesota Press, 1989.

Penley, Constance, Elisabeth Lyon, Lynn Spiegel, and Janet Bergstrom, eds. *Close Encounters: Film, Feminism, and Science Fiction.* Minneapolis: University of Minnesota Press, 1991.

Penley, Constance, and Andrew Ross, eds. *Technoculture.* Minneapolis: University of Minnesota Press, 1991.

Penny, Simon. *Critical Issues in Electronic Media.* Albany: State University of New York Press, 1995.

Petro, Patrice, ed. *Fugitive Images: From Photography to Video.* Bloomington: Indiana University Press, 1995.

Piper, Keith. *Relocating the Remains.* London: Institute of International Visual Arts, 1997.

Plant, Sadie. *Zeros + Ones: Digital Women + The New Technoculture.* New York: Doubleday, 1997.

Pollock, Griselda. *Avant-garde Gambits, 1883–1893: Gender and the Color of Art History.* London: Thames and Hudson, 1992.

Pollock, Griselda. "Beholding Art History: Vision, Place, and Power." In *Vision and Textuality*, ed. Stephen Melville and Bill Readings, 38–66. Durham, NC: Duke University Press, 1995.

Pollock, Griselda. *Vision and Difference: Femininity, Feminism and the Histories of Art.* London: Routledge, 1988.

Poster, Mark. *What's the Matter with the Internet?* Minneapolis: University of Minnesota Press, 2001.

Price, Janet, and Margrit Shildrick, eds. *Feminist Theory and the Body: A Reader.* New York: Routledge, 1999.

Radner, Hillary. *Shopping Around: Feminine Culture and the Pursuit of Pleasure.* New York: Routledge, 1995.

Raymond, Eric S., ed. *The New Hacker's Dictionary*, 3rd ed. Cambridge, MA: MIT Press, 1996.

Rheingold, Howard. *The Virtual Community: Homesteading on the Electronic Frontier.* Reading, MA: Addison-Wesley, 1993.

Richter, Gerhard, ed. *Benjamin's Ghosts: Interventions in Contemporary Literature and Culture.* Stanford, CA: Stanford University Press, 2002.

Rickert, Anne, and Anya Sacharow. "It's a Woman's World Wide Web." Media Metrix and Jupiter Communications, 2000. 15 Nov. 2003, <http://www.beachbrowser.com/Archives/News-and-Human-Interest/August-2000/web-la-feminine.pdf>.

Ringley, Jennifer. "Reallifemacs: Jennifer Ringley." MacAddict.com, 1 Nov. 2000. 2 Nov. 2000, <http://www.macaddict.com/community/reallifemac/jenni3.shtml>.

Robins, Kevin. *Into the Image: Culture and Politics in the Field of Vision.* New York and London: Routledge, 1996.

Robins, Kevin, and Frank Webster. *Times of the Technoculture: From the Information Society to the Virtual Life.* New York: Routledge, 1999.

Rosen, Philip, ed. *Narrative, Apparatus, Ideology: A Film Theory Reader*. New York: Columbia University Press, 1986.

Rosenblum, Naomi. *A World History of Photography*, 3rd ed. New York: Abbeville Press, 1997.

Ross, Christine. "The Insufficiency of the Performative: Video Art at the Turn of the Millennium." *Art Journal* 60, 1 (Spring 2001): 28–33.

Said, Edward. "In the Shadow of the West: An Interview with Edward Said," *Discourses: Conversations in Postmodern Art and Culture*, ed. Russell Ferguson, William Olander, Marcia Tucker, and Karen Fiss, 93–103. Cambridge, MA: MIT Press, 1990.

Said, Edward. *Orientalism*. New York: Random House, 1979.

Salecl, Renata, and Slavoj Žižek, eds. *Gaze and Voice as Love Objects*. Durham, NC: Duke University Press, 1996.

Schivelbusch, Wolfgang. *The Railway Journey: Trains and Travel in the 19th Century*. New York: Urizen Books, 1979.

Scott, Melissa. *Dreamships*. Alexandria, VA: Tor Books, 1993.

Scott, Melissa. *Trouble and Her Friends*. New York: Tor Books, 1994.

Sedgwick, Eve Kosofsky. *Between Men: English Literature and Male Homosocial Desire*. New York: Columbia University Press, 1985.

Sedgwick, Eve Kosofsky. *Epistemology of the Closet*. Berkeley: University of California Press, 1990.

Sedgwick, Eve Kosofsky. *Fat Art, Thin Art*. Durham, NC: Duke University Press, 1994.

Seiter, Ellen. *Television and New Media Audiences*. Oxford: Clarendon Press, 1999.

Shade, Leslie Regan. *Gender and Community in the Social Construction of the Internet*. New York: Peter Lang Publishing, 2002.

Shea, Virginia. *Netiquette*. San Francisco: Albion Books, 1994.

Shea, Virginia. "Rule 5: Make Yourself Look Good Online." The Core Rules of Netiquette. 7 June 2004, <http://www.albion .com/netiquette/rule5.html>.

Shreve, Jenn. "Strategy: Can Designers Save the World?" *eDesign* (Sept./Oct. 2002). 26 Aug. 2003, <http://www.svtc.org/media/articles/2002/edesign.pdf>.

Silton, Susan. *Susan Silton: Aviate*. City of Industry, CA: Pace Lithographers, 2000. Published in conjunction with the exhibition Aviate, Angles Gallery, Santa Monica, CA, 17 Nov. 2000–6 Jan. 2001.

Silton, Susan. *Susan Silton: Self Portraits (Cycle One, January–June 1995)*. Santa Monica: Delta Graphics, 1995. Published in conjunction with the exhibition Susan Silton: Self Portraits (Cycle One, January–June 1995), Craig Krull Gallery, Santa Monica, CA, 9 Sept.–14 Oct. 1995.

Silver, David. "Looking Backward, Looking Forward: Cyberculture Studies, 1990–2000." In *Web.studies: Rewiring Media Studies for the Digital Age*, ed. David Gauntlett, 19–30. New York: Oxford University Press, 2000. 20 Mar. 2002, <http://www.com.washington.edu/rccs/>.

Silverman, Kaja. *Male Subjectivity at the Margins*. New York: Routledge, 1992.

Silverman, Kaja. *The Subject of Semiotics*. New York: Oxford University Press, 1983.

Simons, Patricia. "Women in Frames: The Gaze, the Eye, the Profile in Renaissance Portraiture." In *The Expanding Discourse: Feminism and Art History*, ed. Norma Broude and Mary D. Garrard, 39–58. New York: HarperCollins, 1992.

Smith, Greg M. *On a Silver Platter: CD-ROMs and the Promises of New Technology*. New York: New York University Press, 1999.

Smith, Shawn Michelle. *American Archives: Gender, Race, and Class in Visual Culture*. Princeton: Princeton University Press, 1999.

Sobchack, Vivian, ed. *Meta-morphing: Visual Transformation and the Culture of Quick Change*. Minneapolis: University of Minnesota Press, 2000.

Sobchack, Vivian. "Nostalgia for a Digital Object: Regrets on the Quickening of QuickTime." *Millennium Film Journal* 34 (Fall 1999): 4–23.

Sobchack, Vivian. *Screening Space: The American Science Fiction Film*. New York: Ungar Press, 1987.

Solomon-Godeau, Abigail. *Photography at the Dock: Essays on Photographic History, Institutions, and Practices*. Minneapolis: University of Minnesota Press, 1991.

Solomon-Godeau, Abigail. "Representing Women: The Politics of Self-representation." In *Reframings: New American Feminist Photographies*, ed. Diane Neumaier, 296–310. Philadelphia: Temple University Press, 1995.

Sontag, Susan. *On Photography*. New York: Penguin Books, 1977.

Spielmann, Yvonne. "Aesthetic Features in Digital Imaging: Collage and Morph." *Wide Angle* 21, 1 (Jan. 1999): 131–148.

Squiers, Carol, ed. *The Critical Image: Essays on Contemporary Photography*. Seattle: Bay Press, 1990.

Stam, Robert. *Film Theory: An Introduction*. Malden, MA: Blackwell Publishers, 2000.

Stam, Robert. *Reflexivity in Film and Literature: From Don Quixote to Jean-Luc Godard*. Ann Arbor: UMI Research Press, 1985.

Stam, Robert, Robert Burgoyne, and Sandy Flitterman-Lewis. *New Vocabularies in Film Semiotics: Structuralism, Post-structuralism, and Beyond*. New York: Routledge, 1992.

Steinberg, Leo. *Other Criteria: Confrontations with Twentieth-century Art*. London: Oxford University Press, 1972.

Stephenson, Neal. *Snow Crash*. New York: Bantam Books, 1993.

Stephenson, Neal. *Zodiac: The Eco-thriller*. New York: Bantam Books, 1995.

Sterling, Bruce. *Heavy Weather*. New York: Bantam Books, 1994.

Sterling, Bruce. *Holy Fire: A Novel*. New York: Bantam Books, 1996.

Sterling, Bruce, ed. *Mirrorshades: The Cyberpunk Anthology*. New York: Ace Books, 1988.

Sterling, Bruce. *Tomorrow Now: Envisioning the Next Fifty Years*. New York: Random House, 2002.

Stone, Allucquère Rosanne. "Virtual Systems." In *Incorporations*, ed. Jonathan Crary and Sanford Kwinter, 608–621. New York: Zone Books, 1992.

Stone, Allucquère Rosanne. *The War of Desire and Technology at the Close of the Mechanical Age*. Cambridge, MA: MIT Press, 1995.

Suler, John. Psychology of Cyberspace, July 1999. 12 Sept. 2004, <http://www.rider.edu/users /suler/psycyber/partobs.html>.

Swiss, Thomas, ed. *Unspun: Key Concepts for Understanding the World Wide Web*. New York: New York University Press, 2000.

Tagg, John. *The Burden of Representation: Essays on Photographies and Histories*. Minneapolis: University of Minnesota Press, 1993.

Tambini, Damian. "New Media and Democracy: The Civic Networking Movement." *New Media & Society* 1, 3 (1999): 305–329. 2 Apr. 2002, <http://www.sagepub.co.uk/frame.html?http://www .sagepub.co.uk/journals/details/j0182.html>.

Taylor, Chris. "Jenni and the Bishops." Time Daily, 27 Mar. 1998. 14 July 2004, <http://www.time .com/time/search/article/0,8599,10769,00.html>.

Tepper, Sheri S. *The Fresco*. New York: Eos, 2000.

Theweleit, Klaus. *Male Fantasies, Male Bodies: Psychoanalyzing the White Terror*, vol. 2. Minneapolis: University of Minnesota Press, 1989.

Thurtle, Phillip, and Robert Mitchell, eds. *Semiotic Flesh: Information and the Human Body*. Seattle: Walter Chapin Simpson Center for the Humanities, 2002.

Trachtenberg, Alan. "Walker Evans's Message, from the Interior: A Reading." *October* 11 (Winter 1979): 5–29.

Treichler, Paula, Lisa Cartwright, and Constance Penley, eds. *The Visible Woman: Imaging Technologies, Gender, and Science*. New York and London: New York University Press, 1998.

Tsagarousianou, Roza, Damian Tambini, and Cathy Bryan, eds. *Cyberdemocracy: Technology, Cities and Civic Networks*. London and New York: Routledge, 1998.

Turkle, Sherry. *Life on the Screen: Identity in the Age of the Internet*. New York: Simon & Schuster, 1995.

Turkle, Sherry. "Who Am We?" *Wired Magazine* 4.01 (Jan. 1996). 1 Sept. 2004, <http://www.wired.com/wired/archive/4.01/turkle.html?pg=1&topic=&topic_set=>.

United States Environmental Protection Agency. "Electronics: A New Use for Waste Prevention, Reuse, and Recycling," EPA: Wastes, June 2001. 31 Aug. 2004, <http://www.epa.gov/epaoswer/osw/elec_fs.pdf>.

United States Environmental Protection Agency. "Municipal Solid Waste in the United States: 2000 Facts and Figures," Municipal Solid Waste, June 2002. 27 Aug. 2004, <http://www.epa.gov/garbage/pubs/report-00.pdf>.

Vidler, Anthony. *Warped Space: Art, Architecture, and Anxiety in Modern Culture*. Cambridge, MA: MIT Press, 2000.

Virilio, Paul. *The Lost Dimension*, trans. Daniel Moshenberg. New York: Semiotext(e), 1991.

Virilio, Paul. *Open Sky*, trans. Julie Rose. London: Verso, 1997.

Vitanza, Victor. "Of MOOs, Folds, and Non-reactionary Virtual Communities." In *High Wired: On the Design, Use, and Theory of Educational MOOs*, ed. Cynthia Haynes and Jan Rune Holmevik, 286–310. Ann Arbor: University of Michigan Press, 1998.

Walker, John, and Sarah Chaplin. *Visual Culture: An Introduction*. Manchester: Manchester University Press, 1997.

Wallis, Brian, ed. *Art after Modernism: Rethinking Representation*. New York: New Museum of Contemporary Art, 1984.

Ward, Mark. "Coming Soon, The Musclebound Nerd." *New Scientist Magazine* 152, 2061 (21 Dec. 1996). 8 Feb. 2002, <http://archive.newscientist.com/ archive.jsp?id=20613700>.

Wardrip-Fruin, Noah, and Nick Montfort, eds. *The New Media Reader*. Cambridge, MA: MIT Press, 2003.

Warnick, Barbara. *Critical Literacy in a Digital Era: Technology, Rhetoric, and the Public Interest*. Mahwah, NJ: Lawrence Erlbaum Associates, 2002.

Weibel, Peter, and Timothy Druckrey, eds. *Net_Condition: Art and Global Media*. Cambridge, MA: MIT Press, 2001.

Weil, Benjamin. "Untitled (äda'web)." Walker Art Center: Gallery 9. 6 Sept. 2004, <http://www.walkerart.org/gallery9/dasc/adaweb/weil.html>.

Weitz, Rose, ed. *The Politics of Women's Bodies: Sexuality, Appearance, and Behavior*. New York: Oxford University Press, 1998.

Wells, Liz, ed. *Photography: A Critical Introduction*. London: Routledge, 1997.

White, Michele. "The Aesthetic of Failure: Net Art Gone Wrong." *Angelaki: Journal of Theoretical Humanities* 7, 1 (Apr. 2002): 173–193.

White, Michele. "Cabinet of Curiosity: Finding the Viewer in a Virtual Museum." *Convergence: The International Journal of Research into New Media Technologies* 3, 3 (Autumn 1997): 28–70.

White, Michele. "Regulating Research: The Problem of Theorizing Community on LambdaMOO." *Ethics and Information Technology* 4, 1 (2002): 55–70.

White, Michele. "Representations or People?" *Ethics and Information Technology* 4, 3 (2002): 249–266.

White, Michele. "Too Close to See: Men, Women, and Webcams." *New Media and Society* 5, 1 (2003): 7–28.

White, Michele. "Where Is the Louvre?" *Space and Culture—The Journal* 4/5 (2000): 47–70.

Williams, Linda. "Corporealized Observers: Visual Pornographies and the 'Carnal Density of Vision.'" In *Fugitive Images: From Photography to Video*, ed. Patrice Petro, 3–41. Bloomington: Indiana University Press, 1995.

Williams, Linda, ed. *Viewing Positions: Ways of Seeing Film*. New Brunswick, NJ: Rutgers University Press, 1995.

Willis, Anne-Marie. "Digitisation and the Living Death of Photography." In *Culture, Technology, and Creativity in the Late Twentieth Century*, ed. Philip Hayward, 197–208. London: John Libbey, 1990.

Wilson, Stephen. *Information Arts: Intersections of Art, Science, and Technology*. Cambridge, MA: MIT Press, 2003.

Winokur, Mark. "The Ambiguous Panopticon: Foucault and the Codes of Cyberspace." CTheory, 13 Mar. 2003. 16 July 2004, <http://www.ctheory.net/text_file.asp?pick=371>.

Winterson, Jeanette. *Written on the Body*. New York: Vintage Books, 1992.

Wollstonecraft, Mary. *A Vindication of the Rights of Woman: With Strictures on Political and Moral Subjects*. London: J. Johnson, 1792.

Wolmark, Jenny, ed. *Cybersexualities: A Reader on Feminist Theory, Cyborgs and Cyberspace*. Edinburgh: Edinburgh University Press, 1999.

Worth, Sarah. "Feminist Aesthetics." In *The Routledge Companion to Aesthetics*, ed. Berys Gaut and Dominic McIver Lopes, 437–446. New York: Routledge, 2001.

Young, Iris Marion. "Breasted Experience." In *The Politics of Women's Bodies: Sexuality, Appearance, and Behavior*, ed. Rose Weitz, 125–136. New York: Oxford University Press, 1998.

Ziff, Bruce, and Pratima V. Rao, eds. *Borrowed Power: Essays on Cultural Appropriation*. New Brunswick, NJ: Rutgers University Press, 1997.

Index